RESISTING DIALOGUE

Resisting Dialogue

MODERN FICTION AND THE FUTURE OF DISSENT

Juan Meneses

University of Minnesota Press
Minneapolis
London

The University of Minnesota Press gratefully acknowledges the financial assistance provided for the publication of this book by the College of Liberal Arts and Sciences at the University of North Carolina, Charlotte.

An earlier version of chapter 2 was published as "Historical Restoration, Narrative Agency, and Silence in Graham Swift's *Waterland*," *Journal of Modern Literature* 40, no. 3 (2017): 135–52; doi:10.2979/jmodelite.40.3.10.

Copyright 2019 by the Regents of the University of Minnesota

All rights reserved. No part of this publication may be reproduced, stored in a retrieval system, or transmitted, in any form or by any means, electronic, mechanical, photocopying, recording, or otherwise, without the prior written permission of the publisher.

Published by the University of Minnesota Press
111 Third Avenue South, Suite 290
Minneapolis, MN 55401-2520
http://www.upress.umn.edu

The University of Minnesota is an equal-opportunity educator and employer.

Library of Congress Cataloging-in-Publication Data
Names: Meneses, Juan, author.
Title: Resisting dialogue : modern fiction and the future of dissent / Juan Meneses.
Description: Minneapolis : University of Minnesota Press, 2019. | Includes bibliographical references and index. |
Identifiers: LCCN 2019009072 (print) | ISBN 978-1-5179-0675-7 (hc) |
  ISBN 978-1-5179-0676-4 (pb)
Subjects: LCSH: Literature and society. | Dialogue in literature. | Politics and literature. |
  Fiction—Social aspects. | Fiction—History and criticism. |
  BISAC: Political Science / History and Theory. | Philosophy / Political.
Classification: LCC PN51 .M467 2019 (print) | DDC 809.3—dc23
LC record available at https://lccn.loc.gov/2019009072

CONTENTS

	Prologue: Reading Dangerously	vii
	Introduction: Resisting Dialogue	1
1	Impasse: Cosmopolitanism at the End of Empire	31
2	Contra I: A History of Silence	79
3	Deflection: Neoliberalism and the Affective Regulation of Citizenship	99
4	Contra II: Terrorist Counters	149
5	Reframing: Visualizing Environmental Violence in the Anthropocene	171
	Epilogue: Arguing On	219
	Acknowledgments	225
	Notes	227
	Index	255

PROLOGUE

Reading Dangerously

This book explores how certain novels written in the past hundred years provide us with strategies to combat the erasure of political agency in the contemporary moment. The critical center of the work lies in the notion of "postpolitics." Developed rather unsystematically by a group of theorists including Jacques Rancière, Chantal Mouffe, and Slavoj Žižek, postpolitics describes the idea that politics—generally understood as the actions undertaken by individuals and collectives to examine, question, challenge, and redefine for the better the fundamental assumptions that govern civic life—is constantly under the threat of being neutralized. This does not mean that acts like participating in grassroots activism, becoming involved in the electoral process, engaging in debate, or protesting in the streets have disappeared. This means, instead, that whereas such acts may have been able to cause change in the past, they are gradually being evacuated of their capacity to do so. To voice one's dissent, one of the most common manifestations of the idea of acting politically, is not only compatible with the notion of postpolitics; it is in fact, as I will try to show in this book, a central part of it.

Postpolitical theory takes its cue from and directly confronts discourses such as Francis Fukuyama's much-contested thesis concerning the "end of history," according to which ideology ceased to be the motor of history during the last stages of the twentieth century. The suggestion is that we have reached "the end point of mankind's ideological evolution" and must now, as a result, accept "the universalization of Western liberal democracy as the final form of human government."[1] This reduces the meaning of politics to mere forms of management, policy making, and policing. In the face of this new order, the line that separates the traditional right and left camps, as well as attendant alignments, has become harder and harder to distinguish (a phenomenon that is sometimes associated with the development of an additional position, often referred to as the "third way" or "middle way"). Free from the tensions caused by ideological confrontation, then, postpolitics is the framework in which what is described as "pragmatic" governance emerges to operate as a "realistic" administration of public life that is not bogged down by a constant war of positions.

Of course, the neutral sheen of postpolitics is only a cover that conceals something else. The postpolitical is the context in which governments, institutions, and certain individuals pass interested and ideologically charged plans as unaligned agendas that appear to be aimed at collective betterment but seek, instead, to perpetuate a specific state of affairs that benefits the powerful few. At its core, postpolitics enables such actors to impose a preestablished division of what is right and wrong, good and evil, appropriate and inappropriate, necessary and unnecessary, and so forth that cannot be disputed on ideological, emancipatory, or ethical grounds. In other words, it describes their attempt to bring political action to an end.[2] One of the most important components of any effective political movement in the current moment, thus, must involve the establishment of strategies that prevent the postpolitical from becoming the dominant mode for the administration of public matters.

The effectiveness of postpolitics to thwart the emergence of an alternative political landscape is contingent on its command over the notion of consensus. Consensus is fixed by two opposed though complementary operations. On the one hand, it is the collective agreement of the members of a community according to which public life is organized through a variety of codes, such as the law, civic rules, ethical precepts, and professional procedures, as well as the result of the collaborative effort that is necessary when these have to be updated. Consensus, then, is an essential cohesive element that provides individuals with a sense of belonging and agency as they exercise the rights and responsibilities that their community bestows upon them. This understanding of consensus is consubstantial with the notion of democracy insofar as both are concerned with the conscientious participation of the members of the community. On the other hand, as a principle that rests on the power of a majority to decide the parameters of life in common, consensus is also an important mechanism that regulates the functioning of a community. In this sense, it is the agreement of all its members that determines what behaviors and actions are inside or outside the boundaries of the acceptable. The elimination of political agency, thus, can be attained by passing as the first sense (i.e., collaboration) this understanding of consensus. Antonio Gramsci offers a particularly useful critique to understand this maneuver.

At the center of Gramsci's radical theory of emancipation is the argument that consensus must be understood as intimately connected to common sense—to which it is in fact etymologically linked—and, therefore, to the normalization of the codes that govern public affairs. The consensus established by the members of a community to declare certain codes acceptable depends largely on the perception that they are right because they are customary or traditional. This has what Gramsci calls "hegemonic" consequences. Consensus secures the prevalence of the "'spontaneous' consent given by the great masses of the population to the general direction imposed on social life by the dominant fundamental group," rendering unnecessary the employment of a "coercive power which 'legally' enforces discipline" when individuals or collectives "do not 'consent' either actively or passively."[3] Despite its collaborative appeal, thus, we need to understand consensus as protecting and encouraging certain social behaviors while censoring others on the arbitrary grounds of their commonality. As a result, consensus enables the more powerful members of a community to impose a *pensée unique*—a set of unilateral views that admit no alternative—onto the rest of the community. Common sense, then, ceases to be simply a form of individual judgment and becomes the dominant logic that governs the social and political rules that the collective must accept.

Resisting Dialogue investigates the central role that dialogue plays in the regulatory operation of consensus. Specifically, it explores what it means to "reach a consensus" (perhaps one of the defining phrases of our era), which requires at least two parties to engage in some sort of debate in order to agree on a given outcome. Yet what is the use of dialogue if what we have left is pragmatic or "commonsensical" decision-making processes that supersede the ideological positioning of interlocutors? This is a question of particular importance given that dialogue is today branded culturally and politically as one of the preeminent platforms for democracy to remain healthy and robust. A paradox seems to emerge: while it is common sense and not ideology that should motivate decisions about the governing of communal life, we are nonetheless encouraged to cultivate and practice dialogue as a way to bring together any and all differing political views. How, then, can we reconcile the idea that disagreement is the basis of a healthy democratic system with the fact that a consensus determined by a powerful minority dictates the governance of a community? As I demonstrate in the following chapters, dialogue is the perfect instrument to secure and administer the disciplinary function of consensus, as it involves the participation—and not the exclusion—of those who devote themselves to resist it.

As Gramsci points out, the hegemonic valences of consensus make coercion unnecessary. It is not surprising, therefore, to see that the current moment is characterized by the multiplication of political agents (especially those aiming to cause change) that seek to become visible, in dialogic fashion, by speaking up. Most activist organizations and radical movements perform their strategic interventions by, first of all, articulating, disseminating, and amplifying their messages with the purpose of raising awareness of and responding to specific forms of injustice. Yet the visibility and self-representation necessary for such dialogic engagements to be effective must be pursued carefully and diligently. As I show below, to speak up is precisely the first step toward the depoliticization of dialogue as I examine it here. A dialogue is never a neutral event and, as such, it needs to be approached critically as a (post)political problem and not simply as a solution. This book, however, is not only concerned with putting forward a critique of this phenomenon. In the spirit of Gramsci's own work,[4] it is as much about recognizing the dispossession of individuals and collectives in certain dialogic events as it is about how they can mount strategies to articulate an effective disagreement that intervenes in the consensus that governs them.

While exploring the postpolitical from a dialogic point of view, I also seek to expand here its historical horizon. Adopting a genealogical approach, I provide readings of a series of modernist, postmodernist, and contemporary Anglophone novels in order to investigate this phenomenon in the larger frame of the last hundred years. According to most accounts, the notion of postpolitics is relatively recent, originating during the last phase of the Cold War as the regime of governance propping up the new financial doctrine of neoliberalism sometime between the 1970s and 1980s. Yet I want to investigate how the elimination of dissent produced by the disciplinary administration of consensus via the deployment of dialogue has a longer and more variegated history. Further, and as I explain in more detail in the introduction, I have chosen to work with novels written in English to demonstrate how this question can be traced as a phenomenon that has concerned writers from across the world. My intention is to reveal how the narratives I have selected foster the articulation of what Rancière calls a "dissensus," that is, "not a conflict of interests, opinions or values . . . [but] a division inserted in 'common sense': a dispute over what is given and about the frame within which we see something as given."[5] These novels, I will argue, redraw the parameters of dialogic political activity so that the act of speaking up is not absorbed, and therefore annulled, by the consensual operation of "politics as usual." At the same time, I will seek to expose the wider range of influence of postpolitics. Neoliberalism and participatory democracy—around which most debates revolve—are indeed the subjects of one of the chapters below (chapter 3). The rest, though, will be concerned with exploring the role of dialogue in other thematizations of the postpolitical in contexts as diverse as the end of the British Empire (chapter 1), memory and the work of historians (chapter 2), modern terrorism (chapter 4), and the representation of ecological disasters in the global South (chapter 5).

At the level of analysis, the main goal of *Resisting Dialogue* is to demonstrate that literary critique has potential to intervene successfully in the operations of postpolitics. In the ambit of critical theory, authors such as Jacques Rancière, Giorgio Agamben, or Michael Hardt and Antonio Negri, to name a few, sometimes resort to literary examples to illustrate their points, proving that literature can indeed be of help in the discussion of issues of political import; literature is very useful to translate, explain, and typify them. Some of them have even produced examinations with a literary focus. These tend to be, however, either arguments that find common points between their larger agendas and certain works, or investigations of specific examples directed toward demonstrating a specific theoretical argument. What I am proposing here is to broaden the relationship between political and literary theory in order to reveal not only how the study of literature can help us better understand postpolitics but also how certain literary texts have an intrinsic radical power that works in concrete ways to dismantle its governing consensual precepts.

Literature has on occasion influenced political activism. Certain works have historically had an important impact on citizens while others might be read and circulated widely, inspiring and consolidating a sense of commitment to particular causes. These are, however, rather anecdotal examples. Well-established approaches—some of which I engage with in this book, such as postcolonial studies and ecocriticism—have provided solid critical agendas that bring to the fore the power of literature to affect public discourses and attitudes about pressing political problems. Yet it is my sense that the discipline of literary studies as a whole needs to develop a more programmatic critique that addresses current challenges specifically from a postpolitical perspective. As far as I am aware, there is no formulation of the contours of this kind of critique and the analytical processes that it might necessitate.

Some efforts, especially those attempting to discern the radical political charge of literary aesthetics from a philosophical perspective,[6] are important pillars upon which this critique rests. However, the threat that postpolitics poses to the possibility for emancipatory discourses and practices to correct some of the most egregious forms of depoliticization warrants that we look more systematically at specific aspects of the practice of literary analysis, such as craft, literary history, critical reception, genre, authorship, translation, adaptation, and rhetorical mode; engage in cultural, comparative, phenomenological, and many of the other analytical strategies one could adopt; and even address questions concerning publishing, dissemination, and book history. Most important, we need to bring this form of critique to engage in current disciplinary debates so that it can benefit from the developments emerging in other modes of critical interpretation. With these notions in mind, thus, I would like to sketch here—in an admittedly schematic fashion—the methodological precepts of a critical discourse that explicitly targets the postpolitical, at least as far as this book is concerned.

I propose to think of this critique as an intellectual exercise that is nonetheless grounded in practice. What political theory and politics can do with literature is clear, but what can literature do with politics? Or perhaps an even better question might be, What can literature do *to* politics? We can take our cue from the theorists. In his book *The Year of Dreaming Dangerously*, Žižek argues that the intense political activity that occurred between 2008 and 2011, from the anti-austerity protests that took place after the 2008 global financial crisis and the so-called Arab Spring to the Occupy movement and the student demonstrations in cities around the world, were "signs from the future."[7] That series of loosely connected movements (if only because of their near simultaneity and relatively parallel agendas) generated a rupture in the global consensus that allowed for a new politics to be conceived; those movements showed that it was possible to imagine *a political otherwise*. To dream dangerously was to conceive the inconceivable, to begin thinking about how politics could be practiced differently. Adapting Žižek's title phrase, then, I want to propose that readers engage here in what can be called the act of "reading dangerously," that is, the pursuit of forms of nonconsensually sanctioned political agency through the exercise of the literary imagination. This is the basis of the type of critique I seek to formulate here.

As an emancipatory hermeneutics, a critique that hinges on the act of reading dangerously aims to grapple with questions of power, discourse, historicity, race, class, gender, narrative, subjectivity, social justice, representation, dissent, sovereignty, and resistance. Furthermore, ideas that either define or require urgent scrutiny of our historical moment, such as precarity, environmental destruction, bare life, dignity, knowledge, information, work, wealth, and death, will be as important. In terms of how it might constellate all of these key notions, this critique can adopt infinite shapes. However, as I deploy it this book, reading dangerously is first and foremost a kind of analysis that, in probing the regulation of discourses and practices that give shape to our political lives, sheds crucial light on alternative, dissensual modes of thinking that can be mobilized to debunk directly and decisively the idea of the end of politics.

To put in practice this act of reading dangerously in order to confront the hegemonic prevalence of postpolitics, then, is not to relinquish what is called simply political critique.[8] The neutralization, absorption, and co-optation of many emancipatory practices—dialogue being one of the most salient—requires, in my view, a new agenda that articulates effective ways to describe political action when the very notion has been vacated by the dominant consensus that administers public life. The current moment warrants a critical apparatus that stands up to the totalizing purview of postpolitics, and the expertise of literary critics can be extremely helpful to resist its attempts at erasing ideology (an otherwise impossible task). One of the most deleterious aspects of postpolitics is that it acts preemptively by incorporating the language of resistance into its own. As a preclusive regime, it "no longer merely 'represses' the political . . . but much more effectively forecloses it."[9] Through its grip on language, the postpolitical is a hegemonic mode that celebrates democracy, free speech, and multiculturalism and defends tolerance, mutual understanding, and collaboration. At the same time, however, it spuriously impedes the emergence of dissenting responses in the name of the very principles it extols by labeling them disruptions of the "normal" functioning of politics. This makes it necessary to seek a form of critique that looks underneath, past, and through the edges of language to investigate the ways in which literature can contribute to the dismantling of this hostile, interested assault on representation and meaning-making. At a time when critics have been asking what, after all, we gain when we read literature,[10] a critical discourse that targets the workings of postpolitics might be useful to constitute what Alain Badiou calls "a *change of world*," which "is real when an inexistent of the world," that is, a political break that is not yet materialized, "starts to exist in this same world with maximum intensity."[11] Literature can definitely help us begin imagining such a change of world.

Reading dangerously is, thus, a form of engaged inquiry that highlights the radical intervention of literature in postpolitics' regulation of public (and private) life. In order to take on this challenge, we need to understand literature, following Rancière, "as a historical mode of visibility of writing, a specific link between a system of meaning of words and a system of visibility of things,"[12] so that we can dig out possible strategies that allow us to recuperate the terrain of discourse and ideas that consensus has taken away. In other words, the grip of postpolitics on representation is also a grip on the imagination, and this mode of critique must, therefore, aim at underscoring how the "visibility of writing" can make us imagine the necessary "changes of world." Critics who seek to tackle the postpolitical might consequently concern themselves with highlighting the power of literary expression to propose, through its aesthetic appeal to readers, accounts that identify and separate consensual modes of thinking from the discourses that they have arrogated. If the thrust of postpolitics is contingent on the pervasive dissemination of consensus as *pensée unique*, an effective critical apparatus should be concerned with the constitution of analytical approaches that dissensually counter it. In doing so, we will be able to understand the political crisis that results from the uncritical acceptance of consensus as the ultimate goal in our negotiation, every day, of the terms that organize life in common, from the extremely localized to the utterly global. This is why an interdisciplinary methodology will certainly be appropriate to undertake such a task — one that builds bridges between literary studies and other disciplines, from economics to history and from political philosophy to visual studies, as I do below.

In its critical assessment of the deployment of dialogue as a depoliticizing tool to perpetuate consensus, *Resisting Dialogue: Modern Fiction and the Future of Dissent* puts in practice the act of reading dangerously that I have attempted to outline here. The point of departure of the book, as I explain in the introduction that follows, is the fact that, contrary to what ordinary political practices seem to suggest, to engage in certain dialogues is in fact to succumb to a very insidious act of dispossession. This will take me to consider questions concerning recognition, voice, and silence, among many others, so as to investigate in numerous historical and geopolitical contexts a phenomenon that is as pervasive as it seems to be inconspicuous. In the three main chapters following the introduction, I will make the case that certain works of prose fiction have the power to both render this employment of dialogue manifest and provide us with solutions to combat it, while in the two intervening ones I will explore problems that emerge precisely in dialogic encounters intended to be emancipatory. Historically grounded, one by one the chapters of *Resisting Dialogue* perform a series of engaged close readings that, anchored in specific examples, seek to understand, contextualize, and challenge dialogue as a problem. If we intend to live in a world governed by the principles of democracy, dialogue is one of the crucial ways in which our political relationships are and, without a doubt, will be configured in the future. The deterioration of the capacities of dialogue to uphold an egalitarian politics, then, requires that we conceive of its role in new, creative, and counterintuitive ways.

INTRODUCTION

Resisting Dialogue

> Violence can sometimes accomplish less than humane actions.
> —Niccolò Machiavelli, *The Discourses*

> We have to accept that every consensus exists as a temporary result of a provisional hegemony, as a stabilization of power, and that it always entails some form of exclusion.
> —Chantal Mouffe, *The Democratic Paradox*

> Words are never "only words"; they matter because they define the contours of what we can do.
> —Slavoj Žižek, *First as Tragedy, Then as Farce*

In 1998, the United Nations General Assembly declared 2001 the Year of Dialogue among Civilizations. The choice of the year 2001 could not have been more significant. As former UNESCO director-general Kōichirō Matsuura stated at a prefatory roundtable that inaugurated the 2000 Millennium Summit and brought together more countries than any other United Nations meeting to the date, "It is . . . particularly fitting that the first meeting of the dialogue is held at such a symbolic time, on the eve of the world Millennium Summit, not only to explore one another's past legacies but to reflect on what future may lie in store for the diverse civilizations, values and creeds which form the fabric of humanity."[1] In selecting this historical threshold, the United Nations could draw attention to the importance of dialogue as a universal instrument for the peaceful cohabitation of all the members of the international community as they transitioned from one millennium to the next. Appropriately preparing for the challenges of the future, Matsuura's speech underscored, would only be possible with the necessary historical perspective, an extremely productive attitude especially at the end of a century punctuated, among others, by the rise and fall of several fascist regimes, two world wars, the dismantling of the European empires and the complicated process of decolonization, the emergence of new regimes of despotic rule, the advent of globalization as world order, the widening gap between the world's richest and poorest, and the proliferation of violence and military confrontations in the form of civil wars and terrorist attacks.

The celebration of the Year of Dialogue among Civilizations, though, was not a spontaneous project that simply took advantage of the historical symbolism of the year 2001. It was part of a larger effort to renew the paradigm of international relations, and it took some time to materialize. The first iteration of the notion of "dialogue amongst civilizations" was the 1974 "Cultural Self-Comprehension of Nations" movement led by Austrian philosopher Hans Köchler, former Austrian president Rudolf Kirchschläger, and first president of postcolonial Senegal, co-founder of the Négritude movement, and poet Léopold Sédar Senghor. The initiative immediately took root, and several conferences and events were organized as sites for the practice and advocacy of international dialogue. After an enthusiastic start, however, the promising campaign unfortunately fell out of favor, although it regained appeal a few decades later. In 1998, then Iranian president Mohammad Khatami proposed that the United Nations embrace dialogue as a response to Samuel Huntington's contentious "clash of civilizations" theory, which characterized global relations as the confrontation "between peoples belonging to different cultural identities" in a state of permanent conflict and conceived of the world as ineluctably divided into a "Western" and a "non-Western" camp.[2] Aimed at defeating such an essentialist discourse, dialogue was to be upheld as a crucial component of an agenda to recuperate in the new millennium a sense of global collaboration that was not dictated by the entrenchment of difference but, instead, by the cultivation of connections between the members of the international community.

As the significant historical moment in which the Year of Dialogue among Civilizations was celebrated suggests, dialogue is one of the foremost political instruments to facilitate amicable international relations in the contemporary occasion. While it has been key to resolve international discord in many episodes of our recent past, such as the so-called Troubles in Northern Ireland and the disarmament of terrorist groups in the Basque Country and Colombia, dialogue is currently an important mechanism to maintain peace, assuage tensions, and prevent attendant violent conflicts. It is indisputably essential for the functioning of diplomacy, too. Beyond easing international relations and managing global hostilities, dialogue is also essential to navigate other questions. It plays a crucial role in coordinating the common interests and strengthening the positions of coalitions formed around trade agreements, migration accords, and security treaties. Dialogue also facilitates humanitarian operations targeted, for instance, to secure human rights, foster education, and eradicate hunger under the tutelage of institutions like the United Nations and nongovernmental organizations. Very importantly, the policies that determine how we face the consequences of climate change and the mass extinction of species are being established by the dialogue that is currently taking place at the planetary level.

Dialogue also has a prominent place in state matters and people's political lives. It allows millions to be involved in democratic systems at the regional, national, and even supranational levels (in the case, e.g., of the European Union). Democratic participation in the form of suffrage can, from this perspective, be considered a form of dialogue, and it can be found embedded in other mechanisms of representation. For instance, the Brexit referendum (a dialogue itself between the United Kingdom's government and its citizens) was followed by initiatives like the "All-Island Civic Dialogue," a debate proposed by the Irish government "to seek broad based views on all-island implications" of the UK's decision to withdraw from the European Union.[3] Other forms of political activity can also be conceived in dialogic terms, such as demonstrations, rallies, and grassroots activism, as citizens demand reforms from their governing bodies. Dialogue is, too, an instrument to resolve ethnic and racial strains, and it is bound to remain essential as transnational migration increasingly diversifies national populations around the world. In countries with historically unresolved tensions, such as South Africa, "expressions of racial distrust emphasise the need for greater social dialogue on the issue of race."[4] Dialogue, further, brings cultures closer together by promoting inclusivity, pluralism, and tolerance. Ultimately, understanding and coping with difference will only be possible if certain channels of communication are permanently open and an atmosphere of curiosity and solidarity is secured for individuals, communities, and institutions to engage with one another.

Lastly, dialogue is equally prevalent in the world of cultural, creative, and intellectual activity. It has helped cement the particularly conciliatory spirit I have begun outlining here. A Sundance Institute film program, for instance, recently aimed to explore original ways "to enhance greater cultural understanding, collaboration and dialogue around the globe."[5] Sondre Bratland and Javed Bashir pursued a similar goal when they sought to connect the musical cultures of their home countries, Norway and Pakistan, in their 2006 album *Dialogue*.[6] A few years later, The New Museum in New York featured an exhibition titled *Talking Back: The Audience in Dialogue*, which reflected on the contribution that visitors had in the making of previous exhibitions in the tradition of "participatory aesthetics."[7] We have also seen in the later decades a proliferation of work in cultural criticism and commentary that finds, by way of comparative analysis, links between religions, nations, and artistic traditions in the key of dialogue. The language of dialogue, more broadly speaking, is often employed, too, as a trope to articulate the process in which knowledge and epistemological paradigms are created and modified, as scientists and scholars "enter" and "shift" conversations in their respective fields. This trope is similarly pervasive in the public sphere, where civil society engages in debates about certain topical issues related to the current state of affairs. Finally, we have witnessed the emergence of the language of dialogue to describe the kind of networked, "real-time" exchange on which internet-based social media communication hinges. In short, its undeniable ubiquity and versatility makes it reasonable to claim that ours is, indeed, the Age of Dialogue.

Despite what its title might seem to imply, *Resisting Dialogue* is far from a polemic, an apology for anarchy, or a defense of intolerance and authoritarianism. A volume concerned with literary analysis, neither is it an exercise in speculative criticism. Why a book, then, proposing to resist the idea of dialogue? There are multiple types of dialogue, and many are indeed tremendously productive for the preservation of cultural, social, historical, and political relations. Yet it is also true that anything that can be called a dialogue (and the term has become extremely loose) is today automatically accepted as a positive and productive event. This is a problem, because it promotes an uncritical understanding of dialogue that has important political ramifications. Thus, I seek to rethink here our general assumptions about dialogue. While complicating what Jean-François Lyotard once called "the traditional alternative between manipulatory speech and the unilateral transmission of messages on the one hand, and free expression and dialogue on the other,"[8] I want to consider its aptness as a mechanism for the practice of a truly collaborative and just politics.

In particular, I aim to develop a method of inquiry that identifies the insidious and depoliticizing employment of dialogue that, I argue, is symptomatic of the current postpolitical threat against the emergence of emancipatory discourses and practices. I will call this phenomenon *illusory dialogue*. As we will see in more detail later, in an illusory dialogue what I call a "minor voice" is offered the chance to speak up and express disagreement with a "dominant" one in order to provoke the necessary political change. This type of interaction, however, is merely a spectacle of tolerance controlled by the dominant voice and is designed precisely to prevent any meaningful change from occurring when authoritarian, antidialogic, or simply oppressive practices are either unfeasible or no longer tolerated. My task, then, will be to expose how, disguised as the "humane action" (to employ Machiavelli's phrase) of letting the disenfranchised have a voice,[9] illusory dialogue is deployed as a dispossessing communicative engagement that, cementing a hegemonic consensus, renders the terms of the status quo incontestable. This form of dispossession is in part possible because dialogue has lost its capacity to operate as a radical political instrument in certain contexts. Its ubiquity as well as the positive aura that envelops any reference to dialogue have certainly contributed to its debilitation. Yet such debilitation is not merely a consequence of its incorporation into virtually all aspects of modern life. To concentrate on what is the result of a process of normalization would be simply to examine the circumstances that precisely allow for the deployment of illusory dialogue. It is crucial that we move beyond ascribing circumstantial value to this phenomenon; only then will we be able to explore how dialogue can be intentionally employed to eliminate dissent.

In both echoing and engaging critically with Kōichirō Matsuura's speech at the 2000 UN Millennium Summit, *Resisting Dialogue* maps out how it is possible to revitalize the politically productive valences of dialogue. Yet not all five of its chapters have the same objective. If illusory dialogue is a disciplinary instrument based on the fictional empowerment of disenfranchised voices, I will turn to another kind of fiction for ways to neutralize it. Bearing in each of their titles a general strategy against this employment of dialogue ("Impasse," "Deflection," and "Reframing"), the three main chapters investigate how a series of Anglophone novels from the last hundred years offer potential scenarios of resistance. Interspersed between them, two shorter chapters ("A History of Silence" and "Terrorist Counters") propose a counterargumentative approach that explores, against the grain, the obverse of the book's general thesis. Each of these two chapters—or *contras*—analyzes a novel for its capacity to reveal that, rather than resolve an issue, engaging in dialogue to right a wrong sometimes opens up further questions about silence and the limits of discursive agency. All of the chapters, then, demonstrate the importance, as "unreasonable" as it might seem, of considering dialogue a defining problem of our modern era.

Rethinking Dialogue: Writing after Bakhtin

To characterize dialogue as a problem, as I am suggesting here, is to question a long theoretical tradition that conceives of it as an essentially productive discursive, epistemological, and political tool. While largely employed in the premodern period as a rhetorical trope, dialogue has been the object of unprecedented critical analysis in the modern era, mostly due to the versatility of dialectical thinking as a theoretical framework.[10] The sheer number of pioneering investigations of dialogue that have appeared in the last century demonstrate its unwavering importance, from Edmund Husserl's study of the phenomenology of intersubjectivity to Emmanuel Levinas's ethics of the Other and Jürgen Habermas's theory of public discourse, and from Hans-Georg Gadamer's dialogic hermeneutics and Martin Buber's existentialist theology to Paulo Freire's application of dialogue in critical pedagogical theory, all of which continue to animate long and deep-rooted debates.[11]

Particularly for scholars of literature, however, the most important figure in this modern surge of critical theorizations of dialogue is no doubt the Russian critic Mikhail Bakhtin, of whom I must make separate mention here for several reasons. As Peter Womack has boldly put it, Bakhtin's "influence is such that, today, any theoretical book about dialogue is bound in part to be about Bakhtinian 'dialogism.'"[12] Bakhtin's general theory has arguably influenced more and wider-ranging critical work than any other, and has especially attracted the attention of critics concerned with explaining the resisting spirit that can be found in certain forms of discursive action. Notions such as "heteroglossia," "polyphony," and "the carnivalesque" are employed by scholars in a phenomenal variety of areas, while studies about Bakhtin continue to be published, demonstrating the currency of his work. Always present in anthologies of criticism and theory and a curricular requirement in many academic programs, Bakhtin's texts have achieved a canonical status in the university classroom and remain attractive to students. More importantly, Bakhtinian dialogism reflects many of the underlying assumptions in most definitions of the work of dialogue in the current moment.

Thus, an appropriate way to begin rethinking dialogue is by revisiting some of the main tenets of Bakhtin's thesis. His preoccupation with bringing to the fore the discursive character of political structures and hierarchies, exploring the capacity of voices to dismantle them, and demonstrating the crucial role of the novel in such processes is vital for the present study. However, in order to produce a theory of dialogue that responds to both the postpolitical erosion of its radical force and the consequent emergence of illusory dialogue, it is imperative that we acknowledge the shortcomings of dialogism and, ultimately, move beyond it. To point out its limitations, though, is to do nothing new; many arguments have been produced with that goal. Nonetheless, it seems to me that, because Bakhtin has reached canonical status and some of the key precepts of his theory have been incorporated into the general lexicon of literary and cultural commentary, it is worth briefly returning to his work—not to corroborate the insufficiencies of dialogism but to renew the political basis on which it rests. Yet I must warn readers that I do not intend to provide a full commentary of Bakhtin's corpus. Neither do I want to launch a critique that throws Bakhtin off his proverbial pedestal. This is not a book about Bakhtin, and the broad points that follow will not satisfy readers in search of a full discussion.

There is a simple reason why Bakhtin's work is not satisfactory to think through the kind of dialogic dispossession with which I am concerned here. Bakhtin did not really write about dialogue. In his texts "there is hardly any analysis of two-sided conversation, or everyday dialogue," but instead "a case for 'the novel' or 'artistic prose' *in the name of* dialogue."[13] What eventually turned into a bold general theory of dialogism indeed stems from Bakhtin's original goal to defend the novel as a prosaic genre capable of making up for the political and discursive limitations of the classic literary genres preceding it. For example, in *Problems of Dostoevsky's Poetics*, Bakhtin describes the Russian novelist as an exceptional author who, far from subordinating his plots to the authority of an all-powerful narrator, constructed his novels as textual platforms for his characters to remain in constant interaction with one another while firmly maintaining their individuality. He calls this phenomenon "polyphony": "What unfolds in [Dostoevsky's] works is not a multitude of characters and fates in a single objective world, illuminated by a single authorial consciousness; rather a *plurality of consciousnesses, with equal rights and each with its own world*, combine but are not merged in the unity of the event" as "*subjects of their own directly signifying discourse.*"[14] From the point of view of literary craft, the innovative nature of this narrative mode lies in the novelist's refusal to position his narrators as all-knowing, puppeteer-like figures whose presence dominates not only the plot but, more importantly, also the very portraits that the characters provide of themselves as they speak. Thus, Bakhtin argues, Dostoevsky's work is unique in that it is dialogically governed by an authorial orchestration of individualities that places characters and narrators at the same level, emphasizing the function of voice as the vehicle of singularity.

Bakhtin expands his theorization of the politics of dialogism in later work. In *Rabelais and His World,* he examines the counterhegemonic qualities of laughter and impropriety in the early modern period. In tracing the provocative nature of Rabelais's writing, Bakhtin sheds important light onto the ideas of folklore, high and low culture, and public space by excavating the power of collective anonymity and the disruption of established social orders. These notions are key for his investigation of the "carnivalesque" (which appears sketched out in previous work),[15] material aspects of the body (conception, childbirth, death, wounds), and "grotesque realism," to mention only a few of the radical components he highlights. The crucial point is that, by placing the study of specific social and historical contexts front and center in his literary explorations, Bakhtin adds a new political layer to his general theory of dialogism. This is evident, most notably, in his argument that Rabelais's writing must be explored beyond the limits of the imaginative worlds it creates. While avoiding its construction as "a means for attaining a goal outside the sphere of his writings," he insists a text like *Gargantua and Pantagruel* runs against the grain of certain historical, cultural, and social tenets of the Renaissance and, ultimately, reveals the political work of "folk humor" in "its general ideological, philosophical, and aesthetic essence."[16]

It is, however, in his best-known collection of essays, *The Dialogic Imagination*, and in particular the essay "Discourse in the Novel," that Bakhtin produces the most succinct and lucid articulation of dialogism. Without losing sight of the radical aesthetics of the novelistic genre, Bakhtin proposes an investigation of dialogism conceived as linguistically concrete and, therefore, closer to the idea of dialogue. The central argument in "Discourse in the Novel" is that to view language as an abstract system of signification is to conceal the ideological charge that lies at the core of important questions concerning hierarchy, individuation, and Otherness. Bakhtin, then, offers a systematic account of dialogism that considers language in its actual materialization, focusing on the utterance as the conduit for individuals—who are always politically positioned within a linguistic system—to express their singularity. This situates the dialogic properties of voice at the intersection of two complementary forces.

On the one hand, as the formulation of "a world-view, even as a concrete opinion," every linguistic iteration is for Bakhtin "ideologically saturated."[17] Therefore, it is through the manifestations of discourse that a speaker's voice is reflected as the most intimate expression of their singularity. He labels this a "centrifugal" force, which denotes the dissociation of the utterance from the abstract rules of a given linguistic system in which it is inscribed, motivating what he calls "heteroglossia," or the internal variety and coexistence of differing points of view within that system (*DI* 271). On the other hand, Bakhtin identifies an opposite, simultaneous "centripetal" force that constitutes "the theoretical expression of the historical processes of linguistic unification and centralization" and determines the linguistic system's basic rules, which speakers both abide by and legitimize in speaking to each other. This centripetal movement contributes to the stability of the system and the cohesion of communities by "guaranteeing a certain maximum of mutual understanding" among their members that "crystalliz[es] into a real . . . unity," without which communication would be extremely difficult to attain (270–71). One negative consequence of the presence of this centripetal tendency, however, is that, if it is not appropriately counterbalanced by the disaggregating power of heteroglossia, it can become a dangerous force that encroaches upon the singularity of speakers, that is, a "monoglossic" linguistic regime ruled by the primacy of a dominant official code that causes the restriction—sometimes even the outright suppression—of divergent points of view.[18]

Culminating his theoretical investigation, Bakhtin conceives of "dialogic heteroglossia" as the radical communicative mode capable of responding to different manifestations of monoglossia. With this term, Bakhtin articulates the complementary relationship of difference and unity among speakers (the centrifugal and centripetal forces I have just discussed), adding a historical dimension that "represents the co-existence of socio-ideological contradictions between the present and the past, between differing epochs of the past, between different socio-ideological groups in the present, between tendencies, schools, circles and so forth" (*DI* 291). As a consequence, "forming itself in an atmosphere of the already spoken" and "determined by that which has not yet been said" (291, 280), the exercise of speech is also an orientation toward the Other, as it "passes freely and easily into the private property of the speaker's intentions [while] it is populated . . . with the intentions of others" (292). As an "anonymous and social . . . but simultaneously concrete, filled with specific content and accented" phenomenon, then, dialogic heteroglossia represents a discursive opening for the unrestricted interaction of voices and the encounter of opposing worldviews (272).

Without a doubt an important model for the analysis of discursive politics and the resisting values of the utterance, the theoretical framework of dialogism is nevertheless constrained by certain limitations. In particular, and despite Bakhtin's insistence on theorizing language always as it actually materializes, questions concerning the conditions of dialogic exchange remain unanswered. These questions are key to understanding how illusory dialogue works.

Beyond Dialogism

As rich blend of philosophical, political, and literary commentary, Bakhtinian dialogism is remarkably versatile. Its adaptability and relative simplicity have made it an extremely productive theory, particularly because it accurately reflects widespread ideas of what a politically healthy society should look like. In underscoring the inclusion of all voices as the basis for a cooperative political arrangement where "different points of view, conceptual horizons, systems for providing expressive accents, [and] various social 'languages' come to interact with one another," dialogism can be identified with some of the central tenets of the liberal tradition on which modern democracy rests (*DI* 282). Although its actual manifestations differ considerably from its theoretical formulation, democracy as it is currently understood pivots on the dialogic articulation of social relations insofar as it organizes the voices of the members of a community and enables them to contribute to the decisions that will shape it. This identification has contributed to the entrance of Bakhtinian theory into a variety of scholarly fields, especially among those practicing what has come to be known as "political criticism."

Since it was first adopted by Anglo-American critics in the 1980s, Bakhtinian dialogism has been a fruitful trope in analyses seeking to combat the disenfranchisement of underrepresented, marginalized, or underprivileged minorities subjected to the policing of monoglossic regimes of dominance and exclusion. According to such analyses, the invisibility caused by those minorities' inability to speak up, which amounts to their very ontological negation, can be neutralized if their voices are dug out and reinscribed in the social, historical, and cultural contexts from which they have been erased. As Bakhtin would put it, "*To be* means *to communicate*. Absolute death (non-being) is the state of being unheard, unrecognized, unremembered" (*PDP* 287; emphasis original). The opposite, thus, must be true: being heard, recognized, and remembered authenticates the experiences of the disenfranchised and, therefore, should prompt a readjustment in the distribution of political roles and relationships that remedies their adversity. In conceiving of resistance as an active rhetorical exercise, therefore, Bakhtinian dialogism offers a link between speech and politics that enables a triangulation between the expression of disagreement, the performance of acts of dissent, and the establishment of egalitarian participation.

The universality of this paradigm, however, presents a multiplicity of analytical challenges. Among them, three play an essential role that render dialogism an inadequate theoretical tool to investigate the realities of dialogue as an emancipatory tool. The first one is the institutionalization of Bakhtin and dialogism, which, in certain ways, has also resulted in the institutionalization of dialogue itself.[19] A remark that Edward Said once made in conversation with Raymond Williams might illustrate the problem that this poses. In talking about the appearance of an "inherent dominative mode" in cultural studies, Said suggests that

> we must find a rather more critical, engaged, interactive, even—though one hates to use the word dialogical because of the recent cult of Bakhtin—a dialogical approach, in which alternatives are presented as real forces and not simply to provide a kind of balance leaving, of course, the holder of the balance invisible behind the screen—the person who really has the power. . . . The great horror I think we should all feel is towards systematic or dogmatic orthodoxies of one sort of another that are paraded as the last word of high Theory. . . . I mentioned for instance the interest in Bakhtin, but it could equally have been the interest in many varieties of theory in the past two or three decades; you become a convert to them and see the world entirely through those eyes.[20]

Dialogism is not the target of Said's criticism. In fact, he advocates for the kind of open-ended, destabilizing power with which Bakhtin originally instilled it. The problem, he observes, lies in embracing it as a supreme analytical lens without recognizing its limitations. Effective criticism is an unfinished practice that needs constant reshaping in step with the political changes it addresses. This means that dialogism, like any other theoretical apparatus, is susceptible of becoming a "dogmatic orthodoxy" unless its premises are continually rethought.

My claim is that it is simply not rigorous to characterize indiscriminately any form of discursive exchange or responsive action as a manifestation of the radical politics with which dialogism is largely associated. Speaking up and participating alongside other voices in debate does not always result in a change in the status quo, but may instead constitute what Alain Badiou has called the principle of "communicability." Simply put, communicability is a depoliticizing phenomenon that "undoes the radicality of the multiple," as it "suggests that the plurality of opinions is sufficiently wide-ranging to accommodate difference." As a result, this principle of discursive activity gives rise to the "subjective unity of this plurality," that is, a restrictive and restricted version of plurality that negates its indeterminacy (thus annulling its egalitarian potential) and "opens the way for a doctrine of *consensus*."[21] Unless we identify and contextualize them very precisely, celebrating the coming together of voices because they represent a collection of various points of view, the voicing of disagreement because it expresses difference, or the encounter of divergent opinions because it stages what we expect of a democratically governed community is, in my mind, to sacrifice the critical diligence that is necessary to comprehend the problems that those moments address. This is of especial consequence if the disenfranchisement that certain voices seek to combat becomes intensified precisely when they speak up.

The second challenge is related to the indeterminate ways in which dialogism manifests in an actual exchange between interlocutors. As I have already suggested, Bakhtin emphasizes the concreteness of the speech act. In fact, he acknowledges the importance of "*who* speaks and under what conditions he speaks" (*DI* 401; emphasis original). Yet he limits this to individual expression while deemphasizing the circumstances in which the utterance takes place, conceiving of dialogic relationships almost as if they occurred in a vacuum.[22] The oscillation between an indistinct understanding of the emancipatory properties of dialogism and the notion that it works against a generalized sense of depoliticization, thus, limits the analytical scope of his theory. The radical power of dialogue can only be discernible in the specificity of its manifestations; what is more, not all dialogues are the same. In looking to examine the role of dialogue at the intersection of discursive agency and political emancipation, then, we will need to pay close attention to the ways particular iterations originate and evolve so that we do not make the universalizing claim that any dialogic interaction is always productive and liberatory.

To do so, we must take into account several aspects. I want to highlight, however, a constellation of three—power relations, subjectivity, and context—that I think provide a solid initial platform to consider the particularities of a dialogue. Power is the most important of the three. Not least, examining it brings to the fore the discursive nature (in the Foucauldian sense) of dialogue, yet Bakhtinian theory fails to do so. Dialogic heteroglossia, as mentioned, brings together a collection of singular voices that can act against the imposition of the disciplinary regime of monoglossia. In zeroing in on the collective effort and accomplishments of those voices, though, Bakhtin neglects to analyze how a dialogue is an "interplay of forces affecting and transforming one another" that "can be seen as aiming to order, to give form to or interpret other forces."[23] Crucial factors need to be identified that go beyond the purely linguistic, such as who can speak up and who cannot, what is said and what remains unsaid, what can be said and in what circumstances, who can remain silent and what their silence means, the tone that can and cannot be employed, the (explicitly or implicitly) preestablished rules of an interaction and how they are negotiated (if they are), the position from which participants speak, or what or who they represent. As we will see in a moment, the question of power is crucial to understand dialogue in the context of radical discursive politics, especially because, as Foucault incisively observes, "discourse transmits and produces power; it reinforces it, but also undermines and exposes it, renders it fragile and makes it possible to thwart it."[24] Power is inherently neither positive nor negative. In the context of dialogue, therefore, it is the force that enables interlocutors to exert pressure onto the interaction that brings them together.

Intimately related to the question of power is the role of the interlocutors themselves, for whom Bakhtin does not offer a full account either. As one of his commentators has recently suggested, Bakhtin's work is "uneasily suspended between a critique of the transcendental subject, a position founded on the singularity, concreteness, and embodiment of all human experience, and an equally compelling recognition of metaphysics as a constitutive vector of subjectivity."[25] This leaves an important gap if one is interested in understanding the sociopolitical character of those who speak up to address a wrong and, in doing so, generate a solution for it. In placing "the living voice of an integral person" at the center of dialogism, Bakhtin imagines individuals as immutable, self-constituted subjectivities (*PDP* 10). This is because he privileges the synchronic nature of the utterance over the asynchronic dimensions that make the dialogic engagement possible in the first place, which he regards as structural aspects that frame the utterance but not as factors that determine it. Who the participants are, were, and will be crucially determines the significance and scope of a dialogue.[26] Precisely because "individuation is impossible to avoid" and participants "must be able to defend each act they commit and each judgment they pass,"[27] it is necessary to complicate the link between dialogue and subjectivity to reveal the entangled relationship of mutual influence and interference that a dialogic exchange really is.

Finally, in triangulation with the inherent power relations among participants and the constitution of subjectivities in and through dialogue, contextual questions open up that require urgent attention. What happens before and after is as essential as what occurs during a dialogue. Bakhtin does instill his theory with historical depth, but this only accounts for the linguistic genealogies to which an encounter and its participants are intimately tied, the literary tradition in which the novel as the ultimate dialogic genre rises, or the future projection inherent in the dialogic act to which he refers in his theorization of open-endedness. When it comes to a dialogue proper, however, dialogism remains blinded by its own attention to the "coexistence and interaction" of "all available meaningful material, all material of reality, [organized] in one time-frame, in the form of a dramatic juxtaposition" (*PDP* 28). If a dialogue is first and foremost a relationship of power between subjectivities in the making, it is necessary to pay attention to the aspects that participants can and cannot influence, such as the larger historical backdrops against which they interact, unplanned events that modify the course of the encounter, the material conditions that define the environment of a dialogue, interpersonal registers that determine the rules of engagement on affective and ethical planes, aspects pertaining to time and temporality, and questions about distance and proximity.

In addition to its institutionalization and its failure to account for the specificities of an interaction, the third analytical challenge is about a central question to which I have already alluded. Dialogism is rooted in an individual's voluntary impulse to express his or her singularity. As Bakhtin puts it, "In a human being there is always something that only he himself can reveal, in a free act of self-consciousness and discourse, something that does not submit to an externalizing secondhand definition" (*PDP* 58). This reveals an internal problem. Externally, the political implications of dialogism are clear: it operates in direct opposition to the pressures of certain monologic forces that seek to foreclose the decentering capacities of heteroglossia. Internally, however, it fails to grapple with the fact that the erosion of an individual's freedom of self-expression can indeed occur in a dialogue.[28] It is necessary, then, to interrogate the ways in which participation in dialogue is not always a self-motivated endeavor, a fact for which dialogism does not satisfactorily account: How do we articulate disagreement when dialogue is compromised, in the best of cases, and forced against its own principles in the worst? Is a linguistic exchange a political event when one of the interlocutors has no control over it? Must we discriminate between types of visibility? How is a response politically relevant when only those already in agreement with it will listen to it or when it is the only admissible option?

These three major challenges mandate that we reassess the politics of dialogic agency in what I have called the Age of Dialogue. Overtly optimistic or abstract views are insufficient—even risky—if we want dialogue to stand for something more than the *potential* of linguistic expression to rectify a wrong. Even when we consider the utterance as a concrete manifestation, Bakhtinian dialogism fails to observe, theorize, and offer solutions to the fact that a given interaction might indeed be subjected to preemptive measures that directly encroach upon individuals' political capacities. Disagreement and its transformation into efficacious dissent, therefore, cannot be conceived only as mere forms of opposition. Instead, they need to be thought of in terms of an engagement that can achieve what Arundhati Roy, one of the most important voices of dissent of our time, eloquently calls the "magnificent, shining thing" that is "a new kind of politics. Not the politics of governance, but the politics of resistance."[29] A new vocabulary is necessary that accounts for the rhetorically, historically, and narratively specific questions that define such politics dialogically. One key idiom in that vocabulary is *illusory dialogue*.

Illusory Dialogue

A dialogue is never a neutral exchange in which at least two interlocutors address each other as equals.[30] This rather simple notion points to this book's central concern, namely, that a dialogic engagement does not always result in an act of political emancipation. On many occasions, it is the ineluctable power imbalance between participants that prevents the re-enfranchisement of those who speak up. What is more, this imbalance can be exploited so that a dialogue is intentionally deployed with the purpose of evacuating its political function. This is what I call illusory dialogue, a disciplinary instrument that pursues the repression of dissent under the veneer of democratic collaboration. If censorship and the curtailment of freedom of speech are perhaps the clearest pillars on which a monologic regime (to employ Bakhtin's vocabulary) rests, an even more dangerous eradication of dissent can be attained when the very act of speaking up is promoted in order to undermine further the political agency of those already disenfranchised. I consider it more dangerous because, in motivating the manifestation of resistance instead of forbidding it, illusory dialogue eliminates dissent as a means to expose an injustice and redraw the political relations that sustain it.

To understand how this depoliticizing tool operates one must first consider the power arrangement that is constituted as two voices engage with each other. As I have already suggested, a dialogue is informed by pre-existing conditions that dictate, for instance, the acceptable registers that can be employed, whether those registers can be (re)negotiated, and what it means if an interlocutor breaks with them. With a few circumstantial exceptions, such parameters are established by the interlocutors' positions with respect to one another, which will have a determining impact on the outcome of the dialogue. This is clear in the hypothetical scenario where a country's responsibilities toward an indigenous community and its land rights are finally discussed by representatives of both sides. An initial encounter will not likely result in a final agreement that resolves the issue but will be used to define the shape of future encounters. In particular, state spokespersons will seek to safeguard the state's power by placing themselves in a dominant position over their counterpart. Anywhere between avoiding making a commitment and proposing to compensate for the hardships endured by the indigenous community, the state officials' goal will be to establish a position of sufficient autonomy and authority with respect to the terms of action that the two parties will eventually agree to follow—in other words, to the consensus that they seek to reach.

As it is fundamentally the state's discretion whether to tackle the historical violation of the indigenous group's rights, the state spokespersons' power over the dialogue will be sanctioned from the beginning. This means that any indigenous representative will not be an equal participant (there cannot be more than one dominant party) but a minor voice, one whose power to negotiate the rules of engagement is considerably lesser. Because they must devote a great deal of their efforts to maintaining their already weak position as well as meeting the requirements to participate before the encounter even takes place, minor voices are at a clear disadvantage from the start. Thus, the representative of the indigenous group will struggle to exert her community's right to have a voice in the matter, which she might have unsuccessfully tried to do in the past but is a possibility only now *because* the state has decided that it is an issue to be debated. The encounter, therefore, is governed by an asymmetrical distribution of voices. What is more, this distribution will effectively decimate the indigenous representative's capacity to reach a consensus dictating that, say, her community's right to the land must be observed on the basis of its presence prior to the colonial occupation that legitimates the country's national sovereignty. The power for the indigenous voices to exert fully their political agency, consequently, will be determined by their representative's success in becoming an equal participant, a notion that is rendered utterly impossible by the very historical specificities of this new dialogue between them and the state.

In thinking through the particularities of this asymmetry, one might be forced to adopt a cynical or, rather, realistic attitude and consider this an inevitable condition for an encounter to take place. After all, a perfectly symmetrical relationship between interlocutors is no less utopian than the (postpolitical) "common ground" on which many argue that all dialogues take place.[31] This asymmetry, therefore, can be critically addressed by contemplating ways to increase the visibility of minor voices and activating vocabularies that can be used to strengthen their political capacities and combat oppression, injustice, discrimination, and marginalization. However, as long as we focus on issues of acknowledgment, participation, and equality within the confines of dialogue without questioning whether dialogue itself is the appropriate means for resistance, discussions about how minor voices are subjected to mechanisms that compound their disenfranchisement will always be severely limited. The term "illusory dialogue" is helpful to mount a more nuanced critique that upholds the political possibilities of minor voices from a different angle.

The radical potential of dialogue resides in the fact that the matrix of power relations underlying it is not permanently fixed but is, instead, susceptible to the impact of its participants' rhetorical activity. This activity can shift, destabilize, or redistribute dominant and minor positions, and it is part and parcel of the circumstances that give shape to a dialogue and its outcome. An illusory dialogue, by contrast, works exclusively toward perpetuating the hierarchy that determines the dominant/minor distribution. Speaking from a dominant position, an interlocutor can direct an interaction toward securing the consensus that precedes it, turning it into a dialogic trap that neutralizes the efforts of minor voices to challenge it. This means that, while it needs to be put in place by a dominant voice to curtail a minor voice's political agency, illusory dialogue is at the same time a self-disciplining discursive apparatus. In their participation ("one must strive to be heard" is today's mantra), minor voices are condemned to a form of exclusion as they are led to believe that, when aimed to changing the mind of their counterparts, their disagreement will have an impact on any subsequent measures following the end of the exchange. This is, of course, simply a pretense, since the dominant voice is the only one who has the power to modify the conditions that initially placed the interlocutors in their respective positions. As a result, consensus prevails and the status quo is unaltered. Once things are discussed, nothing remains but the illusion of a political moment. To modify Carl von Clausewitz's dictum that war is a continuation of politics by other means, illusory dialogue is *a continuation of coercion by other means.*

This form of postpolitical coercion is hidden under the positive sheen of tolerance and inclusion that dominates the Age of Dialogue. Critics have cataloged certain negative registers that characterize the regime of postpolitics.[32] It is, indeed, easy to identify hostile tactics in illusory dialogue, such as restrictive terms of participation dictated by dominant counterparts, limited time for minor voices to speak, or non-argumentative gestures (ad hominem attacks, fearmongering, slippery-slope assertions, false accusations, etc.) that motivate a negative tenor to social relations at all levels. However, these are compensated for by the general productive charge with which dialogue is invested, and which illusory dialogue exploits. On the surface, it is a reaffirming kind of relationship. As I suggested earlier, one of the defining aspects of dialogue is that it constitutes the subjectivities of the interlocutors via their self-representation vis-à-vis one another. A dominant voice deploying an illusory dialogue, then, takes advantage of this constituting relationship by recognizing its minor counterpart's subjectivity and celebrating its expression.[33] This means that, unlike traditional systems of oppression, which demonize their Others by casting them as passive objects, illusory dialogue encourages minor voices to behave as active subjects who will only accomplish their political goals when their voices are heard.

Illusory dialogue is, thus, a political and discursive spectacle. In fact, it bears a number of connections with Guy Debord's theorization in his visionary *Society of the Spectacle*. Debord indeed discusses the spectacle in opposition to a critical understanding of dialogue that, unfortunately, he does not fully articulate.[34] Yet, if the spectacular nature of illusory dialogue as a self-referential and consensual disciplinary instrument is undeniable, this is preceded by the spectacularization of dialogue at large. Not all instantiations of dialogue are spectacles; dialogue *as a gesture*, however, is increasingly prioritized over its argumentative dimension, which should commit all parties involved to a fair form of discursive engagement that eliminates, or at least mitigates, the inequalities that separate them. The outcome of a dialogue, instead, is very frequently less important than the performance of dialogue itself. Consider, for instance, the endless repetition of deadlocks in which the international climate change talks have ended over the years. Each time, agreements are signed that require later ratification and the celebration of further talks, cynically postponing the already-late measures that states must urgently implement. Overshadowed by the spectacle of the talks, the calls for prompt action as well as the disagreement with the unsatisfactory results of the meetings expressed by activists and small countries already suffering the consequences of climate change become, in turn, absorbed by the process. Instead of a means, the idea of dialogue has become an end in itself. This is precisely what allows illusory dialogue to thrive.

Protected by the spectacular veneer with which dialogue has been overlaid, in addition, illusory dialogue emerges as a neutral event in which interlocutors appear to act as if in a vacuum. Minor voices are, as a result, presumed to be capable of justly representing themselves and their struggles. This enables illusory dialogue to operate as an "ideal speech situation," which, as Jürgen Habermas maintains, "allows assertions to be methodically verified . . . and decisions about practical issues to be rationally motivated," the result of which is "a rational consensus."[35] As I have been arguing, this ideal discursive encounter is at odds with the realities of dialogue. Hidden underneath it are unanswered key questions, such as who decides what qualifies as a "rational motivation" for the "decisions about practical issues" to be taken (in other words, who will stipulate the ground rules that precede and follow an engagement by which all interlocutors must consent to abide) and whether it is possible for a minor voice to make a "rational" (i.e., commonsensical) case about its adverse situation if the dominant voice has the power to determine what is rational and what is not. Resistance, therefore, cannot be understood as the capacity of dissenting participants to break with a given consensus, which "exists as a temporary result of a provisional hegemony, as a stabilization of power, and . . . always entails some form of exclusion."[36] In an illusory dialogue, consensus is not a temporary and provisional hegemony but, in pure postpolitical fashion, the permanent exclusion of minor voices.

Illusory dialogue, then, transcends in crucial ways the mere discursive realm in which it is initially inscribed. As Slavoj Žižek has asserted, "Words are never 'only words'; they matter because they define the contours of what we can do."[37] Beyond simply delaying any decision that might modify the current state of affairs, illusory dialogue eliminates the agency of the minor voices invited to participate. It preempts the emergence of dissent (a political endeavor) by neutralizing the radical attributes of disagreement (a discursive action). This is based on a reciprocal operation: a dominant voice succeeds in maintaining its position of power by deploying an illusory dialogue only because its minor interlocutor has tried but is incapable of challenging it. To put it differently, dominant voices *require* their minor counterparts to participate so that the status quo that sustains their position remains unaltered. Illusory dialogue, therefore, is an aggressive disenfranchising instrument because it transforms inclusion into a form of obligatory participation. On the one hand, in accepting to participate, minor voices become complicit in their own dispossession. On the other, if they refuse to engage they will at best be written off as subjects rejecting the opportunity to address their disenfranchisement (an opportunity that is, furthermore, granted to them rather than generated by them), and at worst they will be denied the possibility to establish that such disenfranchisement exists at all. This is why, as far as this dialogic relationship is concerned, minor voices are not required to muster the necessary willpower to be heard; instead, they are cordially invited to take part in this deceitful collaborative effort, which concludes with a "mutual" agreement that nothing related to their status will change. We are, then, not simply considering the manufacture of consent but the active—though surreptitious—destruction of dissent. This is one of the most dangerous aspects of illusory dialogue: while exclusionary, the disenfranchisement it causes is never visibly violent, abusive, or belittling, but the product of a "common intention to hear each other out."

I want to make a final point about the political ramifications of an illusory dialogue once it has taken place. The aim of illusory dialogue is to maintain the premise that there is ultimately no room for an alternative to the current status quo, that "all points of view have been considered" and "this is as far as we can reasonably get," whereas its conclusion is frequently portrayed as the "middle ground" on which intervening parties "agree to meet." Yet it also acts as a future deterrent, foreclosing the possibility for a minor voice to revisit the issue that brought it and the dominant voice together. After the conclusion of an illusory dialogue, the problem is no longer on the dominant participant's agenda. It is, in other words, reintroduced unaltered into the state of affairs. This implies a further dispossessing gesture. Under the pretext that those matters have already been dealt with, dominant voices can simply refuse to engage again in a discussion while imposing (authorized precisely by their position) that minor interlocutors abide by the resulting consensus they were once "given the chance" to change. This projection toward the future, as we will see in the chapters below, will be crucial in my argument about how modern literature can help us isolate and resist the destructive workings of illusory dialogue.

Having identified the contours of illusory dialogue and begun, by contrast, outlining what a truly critical dialogue looks like (i.e., one that allows minor voices to cause changes in the existing consensus with the purpose of pursuing a better life), I would like to offer an account of how minor voices can recuperate their political agency in the face of this scheme. Given that they are forced by their dominant counterparts into an obligatory participation, this will require a strategic response that combines their acceptance that the encounter is designed to undermine their political capacities with the appropriate tactics that impede their intended disenfranchisement. By tapping into the semantic versatility of this introduction's subtitle, I now want to formulate how minor voices can upend the principles of illusory dialogue and turn it into a critical dialogic exchange that allows them to resist—that is, how they can engage in *a resisting* dialogue in order *to resist* (illusory) dialogue.

Resisting Dialogue

The essential postpolitical quality of illusory dialogue lies in the fact that, in a play of smoke and mirrors, it constitutes the subjects it engages while it dictates the rules of a *malpractice* of politics that disempowers them. Interpellated by dominant voices as such, minor voices are simply incapable of representing themselves without having to employ the discursive tools previously authorized by their interlocutors. And if dominant speakers allow them a certain degree of freedom, it is only because the consensus that secures the status of the former is not at risk. Thus, the work of an illusory dialogue is not merely concerned with disciplining but, more fundamentally, with producing the political agency of minor voices, which is regulated by the registers, conditions, and scope of the interaction. Minor voices, then, have no part in giving shape to the consensual regime in which they are inscribed.

This is the language used by Jacques Rancière in his important *Disagreement: Politics and Philosophy*. In the book, Rancière offers a critique that powerfully dissects how political agency is distributed and authorized. According to him, it is imperative to establish a distinction between politics proper and what he calls "the police." The various sanctioned forms of what is usually labeled as politics are practiced by the police, which designates not the institution in charge of maintaining public order but "an order of bodies that defines the allocation of ways of doing, ways of being, and ways of saying, and sees that those bodies are assigned by name to a particular place and task; it is an order of the visible and the sayable that sees that a particular activity is visible and another is not, that this speech is understood as discourse and another as noise."[38] The police are the constitutive regime that generates, distributes, and arbitrates consensus. Within the framework of illusory dialogue, it should be clear by now, the dominant voices are the voices of the police, regulating the discursive practices of minor voices, deciding what can be discussed and what cannot and, as a result, rendering the alteration of the existing consensus impossible. On the other hand, minor voices are constituted and forced to exert, as they speak up, what can be described as a "void empowerment"—that is, the futile articulation of their resistance given that they are only allowed to refer to their dispossession in the language prescribed by the police, which determines what is visible, sayable, and doable. Absorbed by this totalizing regime, they play no role in the constitution of the consensus that governs the rules and rhythms of public life. The question, thus, is how minor voices can interrupt the process of disenfranchisement to which they are subjugated. To put it another way, how can they restore disagreement as an efficacious political instrument?

An arduous task in the Age of Dialogue, this must entail a reactivation of radical forms of resistance. It is important that we understand this explicitly as a reactivation, for illusory dialogue, as we have seen, is not intended to eliminate disagreement; that is the goal of direct repression. On the contrary, it constantly opens up ground for it, encouraging those who try to challenge the hegemonic state of affairs to express themselves. Their voices are actively and conscientiously listened to, only to be engulfed in a farcical encounter that maintains them occupied and divests them of any political transcendence. It is dissent, or the construction of a politically meaningful position that can challenge the status quo, that becomes neutralized. At the same time, I am calling for this reactivation because refusal to participate is not sufficient to revert the obsolescence of disagreement caused by illusory dialogue.

Refusal is an important and necessary response to many forms of violence and dispossession. In certain circumstances, it is crucial that saying no remains an option. Yet it does not offer much of an alternative to articulate resistance. First, as I have already pointed out, a refusal can (and will) be interpreted as a capitulation by dominant voices. In the words of Michael Hardt and Antonio Negri, "refusal certainly is the beginning of a liberatory politics, but it is only the beginning. The refusal in itself is empty. . . . [It] leads only to a kind of social suicide."[39] Second, in their refusal, minor voices discard the best opportunity to hold dominant voices accountable for their abjection. Thus, if the restitution of disagreement cannot be carried out by simply answering in the negative, what must be sought is not the articulation of antidialogic strategies so much as *counterdialogic* strategies that redefine the terms in which the issue at stake can be discussed. In Rancière's words, "Disagreement is not concerned with issues such as the heterogeneity of regimes of sentences and the presence or absence of a rule for assessing different types of heterogeneous discourse. It is less concerned with arguing than what can be argued, the presence or absence of a common object between X and Y. It concerns the tangible presentation of [a] common object, the very capacity of the interlocutors to present it."[40] Therefore, I want suggest that, because dominant voices necessitate the participation of their counterparts so that they do not retain their hegemonic position by force, minor voices can indeed legitimize their disagreement by presenting their disenfranchisement in the very terms imposed on them.

An effective counterdialogic resistance against illusory dialogue materializes not as an antagonistic position but as an agonistic one, that is, "less of a face-to-face confrontation that paralyzes both sides than a permanent provocation."[41] A provocation is an act that, if carried out correctly, elicits a response from one's adversary; in discursively provoking its dominant interlocutor, therefore, a minor voice can gain a certain degree of power to redirect the interaction and reformulate its goals. This allows the minor voice to intervene in the regulatory mechanisms against which it speaks, causing the transformation of disagreement into dissent. This transformation amounts to what Rancière calls simply the practice of "politics": "Politics exists when the natural order of domination is interrupted by the institution of a part of those who have no part. This institution is the whole of politics as a specific form of connection. It defines the common of the community as a political community, in other words, as divided, as based on a wrong that escapes the arithmetic of exchange and reparation."[42] As a result, the substance of politics manifests not in the transformation of minor voices into dominant ones but in their naming of a wrong that "institutes a singular universal, a polemical universal, by tying the presentation of equality . . . to the conflict between parts of society" and, ultimately, gives the lie to "the presupposition of inclusion of all parties and their problems that prohibits the political subjectification of a part of those who have no part."[43]

In an illusory dialogue, the exercise of politics by minor voices results in the production of new, self-legitimizing enunciations of their struggle and is, thus, contingent on their capacity to interpret and take advantage of the context as well as the qualities of the power relationship in which they are involved. The battle to activate the political potential of disagreement, therefore, lies in disputing the police's monopoly on referentiality. The moment minor voices create a shift in the regulation of representation, they will be able to address their political dispossession without setting in motion the destructive mechanisms of its predetermined language, thus breaking up the exclusionary consensus to which they were bound. This inaugurates a process of emancipation as they articulate their disagreement autonomously while addressing it directly to the dominant voices. In repurposing the momentary discursive power that illusory dialogue authorizes, then, minor voices open a rift in the (false) symmetry that the interaction simulates. This process does not simply enable them to tackle the particular issue that is presented for argument; it also introduces a resisting gesture that destabilizes the encounter altogether.[44] Consequently, the emancipation of minor voices through self-representation, which Rancière calls "subjectification" (the process that "decomposes and recomposes the relationships between the ways of *doing*, of *being*, and of *saying* that define the perceptible organization of the community"),[45] results in the unmediated exercise of their discursive power to substantiate difference in nonconsensual terms and configure themselves as the actors of their own struggles.

Putting in practice this act of self-empowerment demands a doubled endurance on the part of minor voices, since they must uncover with compelling arguments the coercive purposes of illusory dialogue while making themselves vulnerable to it. The success of this enterprise, thus, will depend on their capacity to formulate creative solutions. In search of guidance for the exercise of such counterdialogic politics, we may look at how the creative work of literature can help us imagine ways to perform this double endurance. The novel in particular, with its investment in character construction (i.e., specific forms of subjectivity) and human relations, as well as its emphasis on context (historical or otherwise), is an ideal genre to imagine new ways to generate effective positions of dissent.

The Futures of the Modern Anglophone Novel

In the prologue I made the case that literature can influence in crucial ways the politics that we practice. More concretely, I suggested that what I called the act of "reading dangerously" reveals how literature offers us ways to imagine our political horizons otherwise. Jeanette Winterson, the author of one of the novels I examine here, expressed a version of this idea in a speech she gave at the 2006 PEN Festival. In that speech, Winterson relayed how literature helped her overcome the difficulties of growing up as a lesbian, autonomous young girl in an extremely conservative household dominated by her mother's religious dogmatism:

> "Happy" . . . "normal." "Normal" . . . "happy." Were such words always in tension? Were they in perpetual fight? Or, could there be some harmony, some sympathy between them? And beginning to weigh those words, I started to weigh other words too. Words like "good" and "evil," "black" and "white," "right" and "wrong," "faith" [and] "reason." Were these things always going to be oppositions, dichotomies? Was there a way of healing up these spaces? . . . And I began to realize that what we must not do is accept false choices . . . imposed on us by other people. And for me, one of the things that books have done—literature's done, art has done—is refuse those false choices, but rather to offer a world where mind and body can be healed, where the heart can be healed, where it is possible to imagine a world constructed differently, a world that we could invent differently, a world that we could live in differently.[46]

Literature provided Winterson with a language that gave concrete shape to an alternative, dissensual worldview. New relationships between words and meaning—between the realms of reality and the imagination—emerged from their pages, giving rise to an "egalitarian imaginary"[47] that resisted the imposed binaries governing her home. This imaginary enabled her identity no longer to be the aberration of a sanctioned mode of being in the world but rather a positive affirmation of her subjectivity. Ultimately, Winterson's compelling remarks illustrate how, in our intimate relationship with certain texts, we are pushed to both reconsider the limits of our political imagination and test our self-awareness as political subjects. It is this relationship that I seek to explore in the chapters below.

Certain aesthetic and formal qualities of the novel make it an ideal genre to imagine counterdialogic strategies against the threat of illusory dialogue. As Bakhtin realized, one of the most important attributes of the novel is that it brings together the voices of narrators and characters, who reflect varying sensibilities and express different views. Investigating how those voices interact with one another, then, I will be able to shed light onto the possibilities for certain individuals to recuperate their capacity for self-representation and conceptualize alternative political landscapes that are invulnerable to the regulative discursive regime of illusory dialogue. The novels I read in the following chapters are, in some sense or another, about people demanding to talk, talking to and at each other, sometimes speaking to imaginary interlocutors, interpellated as well as interpellating, speaking to the wrong person, refusing to talk, and even speaking to the reader. The tension between dominant and minor voices will certainly be central to my discussion. Yet, in order to reveal fully the counterdialogic qualities of these works of fiction, I will pay special attention to two temporal orientations, one internal and the other external.

One of the very few defining features of the novel on which critics tend to agree is that it is a "long" kind of text (how long remains up for debate). This is important for our study of illusory dialogue. As works of narrative prose, novels are made of systems of plots and subplots that are developed carefully and have distinct chronologies, allowing readers to contemplate the factors that shape the dialogic interactions at their core. In the face of the increasing domination of the fast and literal over the slow and nuanced in the current moment, there is something of value in the prolonged acts of imaginative engagement into which novelists invite their readers.[48] This is the first, internal temporal orientation that will drive my analysis. Long narratives let us dwell on the relationships among voices, allowing us to appreciate slow and progressive developments as well as sudden changes, concrete political pressures, and the subtle implications, nuances, and details of the employment of language for both coercive and emancipatory purposes. This is not to say that all the novels I have selected to examine are "good" examples to discuss the counterdialogic politics I am formulating here. As we will see, some of the works I read are in fact "negative examples"—narrative rehearsals of failure, oversight, misapprehension, deadlock, and infringement.

Close reading, therefore, will be the most appropriate evaluative method to pursue this task. In analyzing key components of dialogic exchange, such as tone, context, silence (voluntary or imposed), specific rhetorical tactics, or intent, I will be able to dissect that which, from the distance or on the surface, might look like a critical dialogue that incorporates voices on the basis of their difference but in reality is not. Yet as I have already suggested, the purpose of this book is to go beyond the study of literature as an end in itself. Consequently, close reading cannot merely be taken as a technique for literary assessment. At a time when postpolitics relentlessly threatens to invalidate resistance and emancipation while the complexities of the most urgent political issues are reduced to selected, unchallengeable, and consensual forms of representation, close reading must be understood as an activity that promotes political literacy and, therefore, as a legitimate tool for fashioning one's civic duties and commitments. Reading texts carefully helps us read the world in the same way. For if literature can create imaginative spaces for the reader to inhabit, these do not always have to be alternate universes to which one can mentally escape in search for solace or respite. Following Said's argument about "the coexistence of and interrelationship between the literary and the social, which is where representation . . . plays an extraordinarily important role,"[49] I will show how in meticulously exploring these novels we gain a better understanding of the operations of illusory dialogue and the ways in which it determines our political options in the "real" world. Crucially, this exploration will require that we expose ourselves to the uncertainty of the new political landscapes that the novels conjure up for us.

This last point about the uncertainty of imagining an alternative politics leads me to the other, external temporal orientation and major preoccupation of this book, namely, the future of dissent. As I suggested in the opening pages of this introduction, in declaring 2001 the Year of Dialogue among Civilizations the United Nations wished to look to the past to shed light onto the challenges that the new millennium would bring about. Likewise, I want to look back to the past in order to consider the contours of the future counterdialogic politics to which the novels point. Thus, I will approach my task from a historical point of view by pairing my reading of modernist, postmodernist, and contemporary novels with key moments in which illusory dialogue has emerged as an apparatus deployed to maintain a hegemonic consensus. Yet, in looking at the past to face the future, I do not simply want to fasten those literary works to "their" periods but to understand their political value for us today. The progressive chronology of the book, which starts with the early decades of the twentieth century and ends almost a hundred years later, is intended to create an arc that considers illusory dialogue a modern problem. I will frame my critique as an investigation of what Amir Eshel calls a sense of "futurity," which "marks the potential of literature to widen the language and to expand the pool of idioms we employ in making sense of what has occurred while imagining whom we may become."[50] In different ways, the novels I read look both at their present—that is, as narratives intimately connected to their historical moment—as well as their future. This allows me to cast the strategies against illusory dialogue that I identify below as varieties of a counterdialogic resistance to come. The projection toward the future of these counterdialogic strategies, then, reveals the historical roots of illusory dialogue while allowing readers to consider their value and function in their own political junctures.

A final point about the novels I investigate here. To offer an expansive rather than reductive critique of illusory dialogue, I have chosen to work with a number of texts that I will call here *Anglophone* for a specific reason. Genealogically connected to other descriptors such as "postcolonial" or the now outdated "Commonwealth" literature (both too complex and underpinned by too many disciplinary debates to be dealt with here in any substantial or fair way), the history of the term *Anglophone* is rooted in the efforts of literary critics concerned with the literature originating or bearing historical, cultural, or socioeconomic links with the territories that once belonged to the British Empire as opposed to what is still commonly known as "British" (and sometimes "English") literature. Placing front and center the impact and consequences of imperialism, critics sought to emphasize the political implications that derived from the colonies' urgent act of "writing back,"[51] the reassessment of the metropolis's representation of the occupied lands and their peoples, the connections engendered by the circulation of capital, bodies, and knowledge across the imperial map, the decolonization process, and the colonial and neocolonial foundations of globalization. As a result, the discipline of literary studies in English has undergone in the last decades an important shift. The transition from the narrow national focus of British literature to the comprehensive global scope of Anglophone literature has reconfigured in extremely productive ways the study of what must ineluctably be considered a world system of representation and imagination.

Despite the emancipatory rationale underlying them, such scholarly efforts have their own drawbacks. Indeed, they have prompted adverse responses about the cultural, linguistic, and geographical homogenization that this approach might perpetuate in capturing the immensely variegated English-speaking world under one signifier. These is a valid criticism. However, I employ the term *Anglophone* here with the explicit purpose of overcoming these limitations, seeking to reveal the important global egalitarian thrust it denotes. As Susie O'Brien and Imre Szeman have argued, despite the reservations that the term might elicit, *Anglophone* "is—and perhaps always has been—globalized," not only because of its connections with the history of empire and the attendant dissemination of English across the world, but also because it "forces us to consider the relationship of the literatures and culture of the United Kingdom and the United States to globalization, and not just those literatures and cultures that could be imagined as emerging out of minority, immigrant, or diasporic groups within these countries."[52] The label, then, is useful to uncover a multiplicity of connections among works that unsettle the stability of the literary canon.

In deemphasizing (though never effacing) the postcolonial impulses that gave rise to it, I want to employ the term *Anglophone* to open up a space that allows for the consideration of how the regulatory apparatus of illusory dialogue and the possible articulation of dissent against it pertain to the history of imperialism but also transcend that history. At the same time, in constellating British and U.S. literatures alongside other literatures within the English-speaking world, that is, in "worlding" these categories, the term *Anglophone* allows me to retain the original decentering drive of postcolonial criticism while integrating those literatures into a larger corpus that they do not dominate. In this sense, my understanding of the worlding of Anglophone literature is anchored in what Pheng Cheah has called literature's "power or efficacy to change the world according to a normative ethicopolitical horizon."[53] Consequently, my goal is not to put the literatures that the designator "Anglophone" encompasses "in dialogue with each other" (that would mean to undertake a consensual operation similar to the one I am critiquing here). In reflecting on how differently they are grounded culturally and geopolitically, I seek instead to produce an assemblage of perspectives on the varying shapes that illusory dialogue takes and how it forges the ways in which we understand the world.

Anglophone literature, I want to suggest, operates as one strand of world literature that emphasizes the global nature of English (both as a language and as literary production) without contributing to the creation of new literary "ghettos."[54] It defines the contours of English, to echo Pascale Casanova, as a "world literary space," that is, a space that is "not an abstract and theoretical construction, but an actual—albeit unseen—world made up by the lands of literature; a world in which what is judged worthy of being considered literary is brought into existence; a world in which the ways and means of literary art are argued over and decided."[55] While Casanova's main concern is with a web of literary "boundaries . . . capitals . . . highways, and . . . forms of communication" that "do not completely coincide with those of the political and economic world,"[56] her formulation of the worldliness of literature is akin to the kind of aesthetic imagination I seek to excavate here, which is not conjectural or fantastical (dismissing literature on such grounds is a typical postpolitical gesture) but is, instead, a concrete intellectual space for the cultivation of dissensual political thought. My intention, like Casanova's, is to "overcome the supposedly insurmountable antinomy between internal criticism, which looks no further than texts themselves in searching for their meaning, and external criticism, which describes the historical conditions under which the texts are produced, without, however, accounting for their literary quality and singularity."[57] Additionally, as a world literature, Anglophone literature signals the linguistic character of a body of literature alongside other world literary systems or, in Emily Apter's words, "world literatures" or "world forms of literature."[58] This classificatory move, ultimately, reframes national literatures as iterations of a global corpus that admits no totalizing closure and provides the sufficient room for appropriately framing historically and geographically the sites in which political tensions materialize.

The category of "Anglophone literature" allows me to consider the local, national, and global entanglements in which illusory dialogue operates. Thus, I will be able to encapsulate the detached cosmopolitanism that impedes friendship between members of the British colonial class and the Indian elites in E. M. Forster's *A Passage to India* and the resistance against a certain form of colonial recognition of the white Anglo-Caribbean protagonist in Jean Rhys's *Voyage in the Dark*, both of which I discuss in chapter 1. It is also a productive label to categorize a novel that deals with rural England, such as Graham Swift's *Waterland* (chapter 2), given the continuities between the imperial practices of the protagonist's distant relatives and the alternative history he produces of his native village. Similarly, at the level of state politics, it seems suitable to consider the translation of aggressive Thatcherite neoliberalism into an affective disciplinary order in the United Kingdom, which I examine in chapter 3 with readings of Ian McEwan's *The Child in Time* and Jeanette Winterson's *The Passion*, as a factor in the shaping of contemporary democracy and the resulting disaffection with electoral representation we are currently witnessing across the world. "Anglophone literature" is also the appropriate term to categorize the writing of Mohsin Hamid, whose novel *The Reluctant Fundamentalist* (which I explore in chapter 4) takes place between Pakistan and the United States before, during, and after the 9/11 attacks. Lastly, it seems most apt to designate the efforts of Indra Sinha's *Animal's People* and Helon Habila's *Oil on Water* to challenge the general narrative of the Anthropocene as it is currently being constructed with alternative representations of environmental violence in Nigeria and India, which I discuss in chapter 5.

In evoking Anglophone literature as simultaneously comprehensive and differential, *Resisting Dialogue: Modern Fiction and the Future of Dissent* reveals the historical and literary continuities between particular struggles, shedding light onto the possibilities of recuperating the radical power of dialogue while drawing attention to some of the negative ramifications of engaging in specific forms of dialogic resistance. My ultimate goal, to emphasize this point one more time, is to demonstrate the power of certain novels to speak to the political environments of their readers—near and far—as they seek to formulate forms of dissent that escape the "false choices" that sustain the hegemonic orders they oppose. I turn now to the modernist fiction of E. M. Forster and Jean Rhys to explore a first strategy to resist illusory dialogue.

CHAPTER ONE

Impasse

Cosmopolitanism at the End of Empire

The colonist and the colonized are old acquaintances. And consequently, the colonist is right when he says he "knows" them. It is the colonist who *fabricated* and *continues to fabricate* the colonized subject.
— Frantz Fanon, *The Wretched of the Earth*

Hegemony is achieved not by force or coercion alone, but also by creating subjects who "willingly" submit to being ruled.
— Ania Loomba, *Colonialism/Postcolonialism*

The labour of producing a counter-discourse displacing the system of knowledge installed by colonialism and imperialism rests with those engaged in developing a critique from outside its control, and in furthering a contest begun by anti-colonial movements, theorists of colonial discourse will need to pursue the connections between "epistemic violence" and material aggression, and disclose the relationships between its ideological address to the colonial and metropolitan worlds.
— Benita Parry, *Postcolonial Studies: A Materialist Critique*

I begin with the end of empire because, as a chronologically loose yet decisive historical event, it plays an essential role in the erasure of politics that characterizes the current postpolitical moment. I will consider empire as a geopolitically and historically situated institution: the object of this chapter will be the British Empire rather than simply empire as a theoretical notion. By "the end of empire," furthermore, I mean the moment, sometime in the mid-twentieth century, in which imperialism finally became a historical and political incongruence, inaugurating the current postcolonial epoch.

This transition, of course, was neither a neutral affair nor the origin of a new egalitarian global politics. First, its formal end by no means meant the dissolution of imperialism and colonialism. One of the earliest voices to express this idea was Kwame Nkrumah, who denounced the new relationships of exploitation engendered by the end of empire as "neocolonial" only a few years after leading Ghana to its independence in 1957.[1] Second, notions like independence, freedom, and sovereignty have proved to be extremely inaccurate to describe the foundations of the alleged liberatory politics laid out by the postcolonial epoch, especially when co-opted by Western powers to argue that their hegemonic global status is the result of savvy management and not the plundering of overseas territories and the subjection of their peoples.[2] I will, thus, employ the term *postcolonial* to signal not the end of colonialism but the inauguration of the new world order that emerged out of the process of decolonization in which relationships of domination and dependence between Britain and its former colonies were maintained by means other than "force or coercion."[3]

In order to address the complicated transition into the postcolonial era, I will begin by exploring an example of how imperialism was adapted so that the British government could substitute the regime of exploitation and subjugation that sustained its relationship with the colonies with a new "collaborative" paradigm intended to retain its power over them. This paradigm, I argue, was made possible by the employment of an illusory dialogue that established a new consensus in which Britain remained in its dominant position under the aegis of a new cosmopolitan politics. Then, aiming to critique cosmopolitanism as a principle that "partakes of the negation of 'the political,'"[4] I will offer readings of two novels from the modernist period—E. M. Forster's *A Passage to India* (1924) and Jean Rhys's *Voyage in the Dark* (1934)—that respond to this new postcolonial consensus. My goal will be to show the ways in which the protagonists of these novels employ counterdialogic strategies to constitute a form of radical cosmopolitanism that reactivates their political agency.

My argument responds to a major concern among critics about the capacity of postcolonial studies to dissect and provide effective answers to the political challenges of the twenty-first century. Whereas the tropes of empire and imperialism have been prolifically employed in analyses of globalization, this has often been so with the express intention to move beyond the colonial/postcolonial sequence.[5] Debates in the discipline, at the same time, have been forming around the question of whether global studies should or will substitute the discourses of colonial domination, imperialism, decolonization, and postcoloniality as a more suitable framework to tackle those challenges.[6] What I hope to show here is that, at a point at which the thrust of postpolitics is gaining increasing presence in questions concerning democracy and citizenship across the world—for example,

West's passivity toward disastrous migration crises caused by civil war, expulsion, natural disasters, or poverty; the renovation of hypernationalist agendas in the realm of parliamentary representation in many countries; or the resurgence of historically unresolved racism and violence—postcolonial studies offers us a rich archive and a versatile set of analytical tools to understand its global impact.

Adopting a cosmopolitan approach is no longer simply useful but necessary to navigate the system of international networks that configure globalization and the kind of world they construct. Yet certain assumptions about its political substance need to be reconsidered. In particular, as Pheng Cheah has put it, cosmopolitanism must be much more than "an abstract universal normative view of the ideal unity of the world."[7] Following Cheah, I want to examine how a postcolonial methodology can help us overcome the limitations of such a received view. In considering cosmopolitanism from the perspective of the history of the British Empire and its aftermath, I will seek to emphasize the radical potential of postcolonialism to renovate its political and theoretical fundamentals. To put it another way, I will show how cosmopolitanism reveals that the "post" in postcolonial is, in many ways, the "post" in postpolitics.[8]

The emergence of a postcolonial cosmopolitan politics during the period of decolonization established a thread that links imperial history and the postpolitical in very tangible ways. This is why I will tackle my analyses of Forster's and Rhys's novels from a materialist point of view. As postcolonial studies have become institutionalized in past decades, certain critics have argued that a materialist approach is a necessary counterweight to the textual and culturalist emphases in much work in the discipline. One of the leading proponents of this approach, Benita Parry, has advocated for examinations in which "actually existing political, economic and cultural conditions, past and present, are no longer separated from metacritical speculations, or culture and discourse from histories that have happened or are still in the making." As a result, those examinations will not be "ensnared in an increasingly repetitive preoccupation with sign systems and the exegetics of representation."[9] From a similar angle, Neil Lazarus has proposed reconsidering the main tenets of postcolonial studies, critiquing among others "an undifferentiating disavowal of all forms of nationalism and a corresponding exaltation of migrancy, liminality, hybridity, and multiculturality," as well as "an aversion to dialectics" and "a refusal of an antagonistic or struggle-based model of politics," which he sees currently informing much of the field.[10]

Exploring the role of dialogue not as a mere discursive phenomenon but as a depoliticizing instrument intended to produce very tangible regulatory outcomes, as I do here, sheds light onto the formation of the consensual cosmopolitan order with which I am concerned. Perhaps due to the dovetailing of Bakhtinian theory and postcolonial studies (their emergence in the Anglo-American academy was almost simultaneous), dialogue has played an important role in mystifying otherwise concrete (post)colonial conflicts, often reducing them to questions of representation with little or no grounding in either the material conditions that produced them or the political tensions emerging from them. To counter such mystification, then, I will center my readings of Forster's and Rhys's novels on crucial aspects such as racial relations, national identity, and geographical affiliation. This will allow me to explore their protagonists as embodiments of the "differend"[11] that appears when the colonizer/colonized binary is substituted by a dominant/minor distribution of voices under the new consensual regime of postcolonial cosmopolitanism.

Postcolonial Modernism and Cosmopolitan Politics

My decision to examine the work of two modernist authors stems from the fact that they offer, in their aesthetic choices, important reflections on the politics of decolonization. Modernist literature, which "represents perhaps the most intense and unprecedented site of encounter between institutions of European cultural production and the cultural practices of colonized peoples,"[12] provides us with some of the richest explorations of the collision of two worlds, the metropolis and the colony, and the resulting confronted politics that the dissolution of empire would eventually reveal. While its reification is contingent on a number of factors that determined the arrangement of new postcolonial relations, the *idea* of decolonization represented a general rift that demanded a refashioning of the modern political imagination, in which modernist writers played a crucial role. Indeed, the implication of literary modernism in this process has been the subject of incisive analysis ever since the movement's relationship to empire became of interest to figures such as Fredric Jameson and Edward Said.[13] This relationship, furthermore, has been one of the central points in the more recent reevaluation of the discipline of modernist studies, as evinced in Douglas Mao and Rebecca L. Walkowitz's argument about why we can talk, as we have for a while now, about a "New Modernist Studies."[14] Aiming to test the stretches of modernism by exploring its possible postpolitical registers, my examination of cosmopolitanism at the end of empire contributes to this well-established agenda.

In the last decade, several studies have investigated cosmopolitanism as a political question in modernist literature, often from a postcolonial angle.[15] For the most part, however, these accounts conceive of cosmopolitanism as a constitutive process of subjectivation, a positive relational politics at the transnational level, or the vehicle for the rejection of certain oppressive aspects of metropolitan life. Here I want to consider cosmopolitanism instead as the complicated engagement of a dissensual ontology with a relational politics that threatens to foreclose it. In response to this threat of foreclosure, as we will see, the colonial subject resists by destabilizing the consensual regime that regulates relations across the colonial divide. As a result, the colonial subject's defiance of the new, hegemonic consensus replacing imperial rule opens up a postcolonial futurity that serves as the basis for the fashioning of a new and autonomous cosmopolitan subjectivity.

My analysis of this kind of emancipatory cosmopolitanism in Forster's and Rhys's novels is structured according to three related parameters. First, whereas I will concentrate on decolonization as the moment for this radical cosmopolitanism to flourish, I will tackle it from an oblique angle, projecting the modernist qualities of the novels into a later time. Because I am interested in the proleptic properties of fiction against the preemptive operation of illusory dialogue, I will explore how the novels imagine a future postcolonial politics based on the counterdialogic strategies employed by their protagonists. Thus, instead of producing accounts of the specific decolonization of the locales with which the novels are concerned, I examine how those narratives anticipate the drawbacks of addressing decolonization in dialogic terms while considering how they can be read, ultimately, as attempts to counter a preestablished consensus that co-opts the voices of postcolonial subjects. At a time when new debates are considering the historical reach and boundaries of modernism,[16] I see these two novels as prime examples of how the movement can offer responses to a later postpolitical moment. If it can be said that a common concern among modernist authors was to offer an alternative to realism's representational stringency, it can also be said that a parallel aspiration for some of them was to propose an alternative politics that challenged the consensual regime governing imperialism and its reincarnation in the postcolonial epoch.

This leads me to the second factor, namely, the dialectical nature of the opposition that gives rise to the anti-imperial resistance of the novels' protagonists. A dialectical approach in a discussion framed within postcolonial studies might elicit criticism due to its reliance on a binary system of opposed pairs. Many of the central debates in the discipline in fact derive from a direct rejection of the binaries on which imperial and colonial thinking rest. However, this is inevitable for the study of an intrinsically dialectical phenomenon such as dialogue. Furthermore, an effective resistance to illusory dialogue, as I suggested in the introduction, must be articulated agonistically rather than antagonistically. I propose the term *impasse* to describe this agonistic resistance. At face value, to bring an illusory dialogue to an impasse might appear to be an antagonistic act. However, this is more than simply saying no. I envision impasse here as a way to provoke an indefinite suspension without resolution of the consensus that it imposes. This indefinite suspension, therefore, produces the necessary vacuum for the articulation of a new postcolonial politics. Thus, my readings of the novels will reveal an alternative way to conceive of an anti-imperial politics that operates dialectically but does not formulate opposition in a reductive binaristic fashion. In fact, this approach will be crucial to offer a point of entry to the fractal relationships that the protagonists of *A Passage to India* and *Voyage in the Dark* develop as focal points of the tension generated by the colonial divide.

Finally, in locating my analysis of the dispossession caused by illusory dialogue in the context of postcolonial modernism, I adopt a "planetary" approach that, as Susan Stanford Friedman has put it, "encompass[es] multitudes on a global grid of relational networks. And that means encompassing contradictions, tensions, oppositions, asymmetries."[17] The political efforts of the novels' protagonists situate the metropolis and its colonies on a planetary plane where the imperialist and anticolonial worldviews clash, thus deterritorializing the cosmopolitan consensus intended to seam together the empire and its postcolonial afterlife. As we will see, though, this planetary grounding does not presuppose an open-ended global system, a neutral "middle ground" in which they challenge the consensus as free agents. On the contrary, the power asymmetries engendered by imperialism remain. In generating their own emancipatory cosmopolitan politics, therefore, the protagonists of Forster's and Rhys's novels cause a rift in the consensual continuum intended to perpetuate their political dispossession and, in turn, empower themselves to become fully autonomous agents of their postcolonial sovereignty.

Before providing close readings of the novels, I want to offer a brief account of the formation of the postcolonial consensus that they confront. To do so, I will chart the historical trajectory between speeches given by two British prime ministers: Arthur Balfour and Harold Macmillan. These two speeches illustrate the transformation of the hegemonic relationship between Britain and its colonies as it moves from a direct form of colonial subordination to the kind of cosmopolitan consensus I will examine later in my readings of Forster's and Rhys's fiction.

Imperialism, Decolonization, Consensus

To begin thinking about the emergence of a new, postcolonial consensus following the decolonization period we can turn to Edward Said's book *Orientalism*. A landmark in the discipline of postcolonial studies, *Orientalism* offers an invaluable critique of the discursive operation underpinning imperial ideology. In it, Said examines the titular notion of "Orientalism," which, he argues, "can be discussed and analyzed as the corporate institution for dealing with the Orient—dealing with it by making statements about it, authorizing views of it, describing it, by teaching it, settling it, ruling over it: in short . . . as a Western style for dominating, restructuring, and having authority over the Orient."[18] After a thorough introduction, Said begins to excavate in a series of examples the kinds of imperialist attitudes that this discourse enables. The first example he brings up is a speech given to the House of Commons in 1910 by Arthur Balfour—British prime minister between 1902 and 1905 and leader of the opposition at the time—about Britain's colonial role in Egypt.

The presence of Britain in Egypt, which began with its occupation in 1882, became a controversial issue in the earlier part of the twentieth century both because it was by now a growing burden on the British economy and because of mounting tensions that resulted in clashes between a loosely organized resistance movement and the colonial authorities, such as the one in Denshawai in 1906. Trying to placate skeptics and opponents, Balfour justifies in his speech the continuation of Britain's occupation by claiming that "through the whole history of the Orientals . . . you never find traces of self-government. . . . Conqueror has succeeded conqueror; one domination has followed another; but never in all the revolutions of fate and fortune have you seen one of those nations of its own motion establish what we, from a Western point of view, call self-government. This is the fact." As a result, Britain's control of Egypt is "good . . . not merely for the sake of the Egyptians, though we are there for their sake; we are there also for the sake of Europe at large" (32–33).

Said then proceeds to dissect Balfour's Orientalism, which the politician paradoxically employs to exhort his audience *not* to think of the Egyptian question in binary terms: "Do let us put this question of superiority and inferiority out of our minds."[19] As Said demonstrates, however, Balfour's appeal is but a "rhetorical performance" (34) that conceals his intention to present the question otherwise. The politician's words are self-defeating: "There are Westerners, and there are Orientals. The former dominate; the latter must be dominated" (36). The unsophisticated Orient's inability to establish its own forms of government, Balfour's argument goes, must be tackled by the enlightened European powers for the good of both sides of the colonial divide, with Britain at the head. Thus, his claim against considering this issue from a binaristic angle is immediately contradicted by such a line of argument. Yet something else arises that tells us about the imperial ideology in which the speech is drenched, namely, a preestablished consensus with which Balfour turns Britain's presence in Egypt—and, by extension, in all the other territories overseas—into an indisputable question.

In order to gain the favor of his audience, the former prime minister vehemently argues that the Egyptian question can only be solved with realistic and pragmatic solutions, given the "fact" that the Orient is a retrograde region where people do not comprehend the value of the democratic values that Britain's leadership is meant to preserve: "Every person, with an intimate knowledge of Egypt, to whom I have spoken . . . [has] *agreed with one voice* that the position in Egypt is now eminently unsatisfactory. They also agree that it is eminently unsatisfactory because the authority of what they frankly say is *the dominant race*—and as I think ought to remain the dominant race—has been undermined."[20] The consensus, thus, is that Egypt needs to be retained as a colonial territory on the simple grounds that Britain's "race" is the dominant one, a status that must now be ratified given the Egyptians' audacious attempt to challenge it. This circular argumentation, which was at the core of many discourses of imperialism, worked to preempt an open discussion about the legitimacy of the British presence in Egypt, which lasted several decades more after Balfour spoke to the House of Commons. The sort of thinking exhibited in his speech ensured that there was no room for alternative views on Britain's imperial agenda, even in the face of increasing tensions in the region and despite the critical voices that arose from within Britain's borders—few as they might have been. Significantly, Britain's occupation of Egypt would only be interrupted by the historic 1956 Suez crisis, which many consider "the precipitant that brought colonial empire to an end."[21]

In the interval between Balfour's speech and the Suez crisis, a succession of events signaled that the empire was indeed on its last legs, with historians now dating the decolonization process approximately between the 1920s and the 1960s. Most notably, the two world wars and multiple anticolonial, nationalist movements that came to fruition after long battles against the empire radically changed the map of global relations. During this period, the former colonies rose to the international platform as independent nations in the new postcolonial global order that had begun to take shape thanks, in part, to the creation of the United Nations and its precursor, the League of Nations. Perhaps the most important event, though, was the 1955 Bandung Conference, in Indonesia, which hosted representatives of twenty-nine newly independent countries from Africa and Asia. The objective of the gathering was to establish an international coalition against imperialism, which the twenty-nine nations had fought and to which other territories were still subjected; to defend those nations' right to be equal participants in international affairs; to promote alliances for the modernization of what started to be known as the Third World; and to declare themselves "non-aligned" in the incipient Cold War.

Yet the transitional period from the colonial to the postcolonial epochs did not establish the egalitarian politics that the end of empire was meant to inaugurate. The efforts of the newly independent nations to have a part in the rapidly changing postcolonial world were not only hindered by numerous setbacks at home in the form of corrupt governments, military coups, and the formation of new elites that replaced the colonial authorities. More importantly, the new nations' development of a meaningful role in the international arena was thwarted by the West's institution of a new hegemonic order that replicated some of the precepts of the imperial era and in which Britain played an essential role. Resolved to impose such a new order, the British government had to produce a version of the unilateral consensus that was previously employed to justify imperialism, as we have seen in Balfour's speech. In doing so, Britain could remain a dominant global power while inviting the former colonies to have an unthreatening part in the international community and share the responsibility of upholding the new democratic spirit that the times demanded. This could be done by means of an illusory dialogue.

We can find perhaps the clearest illustration of this strategy in the words of another British prime minister, Harold Macmillan (1957–63), a "pragmatist" statesman and the author of *The Middle Way,* arguably one of the first postpolitical treatises.[22] In 1960, Macmillan toured Africa in an attempt to gauge the seriousness of the proliferation of nationalist movements, appease worried settlers, and assess the state of imperial relations in the continent. This was not a trivial item in Macmillan's agenda, though. The tour was a response to the accelerating decline of British rule overseas. In addition to the independence of a number of colonies (India and Pakistan in 1947, Sri Lanka and Myanmar in 1948, Sudan in 1956, and Nigeria in 1960, among others), resistance movements and colonial crises (Suez in 1956, but also the 1948–60 Malayan Emergency or the 1952–60 Mau Mau Uprising in Kenya) rocked the foundations of the already damaged imperial rule. Additionally, the condition of the domestic economy—which was in dire straits despite its recovery thanks to Beveridge's welfare state program following World War II—and the increasing pressure to contribute to the efforts of the capitalist bloc against Soviet communism from the United States (whose financial and military support was essential for Britain to retain its status as a global power) further contributed to the imposition of a new consensus as a solution to the imperial crisis.

Because Macmillan "tended to become involved directly in colonial policy only when it impacted upon wider international relations or the government's standing in the country,"[23] his tour must be understood as something more than a diplomatic gesture. Beyond mollifying settlers and redressing colonial relations with a few concessions, Macmillan was ready to shift Britain's rhetoric to acknowledge the remaining colonial territories' right to join the international community as free nations. Decolonization was inevitable now, and Macmillan sought to safeguard whatever power Britain had left over those territories. This was dramatically exhibited in the last stop of his tour in Cape Town, where he gave the speech famously titled "Wind of Change," a speech that was crucial for the refashioning of Britain's relationships with the colonies. In it, Macmillan acknowledges "the awakening of national consciousness in peoples who have for centuries lived in dependence upon some other power." "In different places it takes different forms," he said, but "the wind of change is blowing through this continent . . . [this] is a political fact. . . . We must accept it . . . and our national policies must take account of it."[24] The novelty, of course, is Macmillan's casting of decolonization as an explicitly positive process—and not as the disintegration of Britain's already feeble grip on its last colonies—while emphasizing his government's intention to work with them once they attained independence. This is the first symptom that betrays the illusory dialogue with which he intended to shift Britain's colonial relations. His message had a different, underlying purpose: to spread the capitalist economic system championed by the Anglo-American coalition to foil the Soviet communist threat. As the authors of an important study on the "imperialism of decolonization" have argued, Britain's new strategy was to unite forces with the United States and support "independence [in order] to prolong imperial sway and secure British economic and strategic assets" so as to "exchange colonial control for informal empire."[25] As a result, the "post-war empire . . . survived . . . [more like] a multinational company that, after taking over other people's countries, was hiving them off again, one by one, as associated concerns."[26]

Thus, Macmillan proposed in his speech an international alliance that cohered around the idea that capitalism was the only viable global economic system under which decolonization could occur:

> The world today is divided into three main groups. First there are what we call the Western Powers. You in South Africa and we in Britain belong to this group, together with our friends and allies in other parts of the Commonwealth. In the United States of America and in Europe we call it the Free World. Secondly there are the Communists—Russia and her satellites in Europe and China. . . . Thirdly, there are those parts of the world whose people are at present uncommitted either to Communism or to our Western ideas. (357)

The bias in Macmillan's language is hard to overlook, from the unsubtle contrast between the "free" countries and those others rendered non-free by communism to the implied invitation for South Africa (addressed intimately in the second person) to be an ally in the midst of the yet "uncommitted" African world. A new postcolonial consensus is in the making, Macmillan's speech announces, and the colonies' endeavors to attain independence vitally depend on it:

> As I see it the great issue in this second half of the twentieth century is whether the uncommitted peoples of Asia and Africa will swing to the East or to the West. Will they be drawn into the Communist camp? Or will *the great experiments in self-government* that are now being made in Asia and Africa, especially within the Commonwealth, prove *so successful*, and by their example *so compelling*, that the balance will come down *in favour of freedom and order and justice*? . . . What can we show them to help them to *choose right*? (357; emphasis added)

Making no mention of Britain's responsibility in depriving them for centuries of their sovereignty while blatantly presenting the future of colonial emancipation as an oversimplified matter of right and wrong choices, Macmillan links here the prospect of independence to an epic understanding of history. A new political universe is opening up, and it is up to the colonies to decide if they want to take part in this historic process or, on the contrary, sink in the darkness of disorder and injustice. Simply put, Macmillan's message was a coercive offer (a covert form of blackmail) for the former and remaining colonies to enter the global stage by embracing capitalism. The smooth and prosperous process of independence would only be possible if they agreed to a new world order explicitly governed in economic terms by Britain and the United States. A condition with enormous ramifications, their acceptance of this prerequisite would secure Britain's leading position along with the United States as a dominant global force. A quick look to the second half of the twentieth century demonstrates the success of such a strategy.

The history of decolonization is obviously much more complex and nuanced than what Balfour's and Macmillan's speeches reflect in juxtaposition. The independence of each colony responded to specific circumstances and led to largely varying results. Yet the speeches signal a clear trajectory in the transition from the imperial order to a postcolonial consensual regime that maintained the status quo in a "more subtle, less bloody" way, as Frantz Fanon would put it,[27] propped up by an overwhelmingly imbalanced set of power relations rooted in the history of colonialism. New relations of dependence emerged as the postcolonial nations contemplated their economic future: whereas "most of the new states would have to cooperate with one side or the other in the cold war if they were to fulfill their national aspirations . . . prospects of development generally depended on the superior capacity of the West."[28] The end of the imperial era, furthermore, was marked by the perpetuation of hierarchical relationships at many more levels than the economic. Independence also meant a chance at modernization, social development, and participation in matters of global policy. As Macmillan himself put it, joining Britain and the West would be the gateway to "self-government," "freedom," "order," and "justice," notions that can easily be translated into the governmental, military, diplomatic, legal, and even cultural support necessary for those nations to be part of the international community. This would be, of course, at the expense of agreeing to play a minor part, since, as the prime minister's invitation implies, it was the power to recognize the colonial territories as independent that allowed Britain and the rest of the West to prescribe the terms of the new framework for global relations.

Ultimately, this transition into a new postcolonial consensus complicates what Dipesh Chakrabarty has called "the dialogical side of decolonization," or "the question of whether or how a global conversation of humanity could genuinely acknowledge cultural diversity without distributing such diversity over a hierarchical scale of civilization—that is to say, an urge toward cross-cultural dialogue without the baggage of imperialism."[29] A reflection on this "global conversation," I think, must urgently center on whether the conditions to participate in it penalize minor voices and whether it is possible for such voices to be able to cause change in the status quo. As I have already argued, dialogue cannot be taken as a neutral engagement. Therefore, rather than conjecture that it may be possible for a postcolonial dialogue to occur "without the baggage of imperialism," we might produce a better critical assessment of its political possibilities by first acknowledging such baggage. It is simply impossible to understand global relations as articulated through a dialogue in which all participants intervene as equals on some sort of idealized cosmopolitan world stage. In other words, we cannot reduce this question to "the simple idea that . . . we need to develop habits of coexistence: conversation in its older meaning, of living together, association."[30] This is precisely how an illusory dialogue such as the one deployed by Macmillan conceals its power to neutralize the constitution of emancipating forms of political agency. Concentrating exclusively on the appeal of notions such as collaboration, reliance, friendship, mutual recognition, and fellowship will obscure the fact that they can be, as we have seen in the "Wind of Change" speech, invoked with the purpose of strengthening the hegemonic character of consensus.

It is at the level of interpersonal relationships that *A Passage to India* and *Voyage in the Dark* show how the imbalance between dominant and minor participants must be addressed as the fulcrum of the consensual cosmopolitan system of relations that emerged following the decline of the colonial order. Thus, I want to turn now to the novels to explore how their protagonists resort to an agonistic resistance that emerges as an effective response to the entrapments of imperial ideology. This resistance is based on a radical cosmopolitanism that disputes the terms of engagement laid out by the illusory dialogue in which they are pressured to participate. As a result, an impasse is provoked that first dislocates the imposition of the postcolonial consensus I have just described and then gives rise to an autonomous subject position that is not forced to align with it. I begin with Forster's novel.

E. M. Forster's *A Passage to India*, Friendship, and Detached Liberalism

Published in 1924, merely twenty-three years before the independence of India, *A Passage to India* can be described as a fictional portrayal of the strained relations between the metropolis and the colony during the last stages of the Raj. It is, in fact, historically grounded as a reimagination of a missionary woman's rape during the turmoil following the 1919 Amritsar massacre, in which 379 peaceful protesters were killed and twelve hundred more were wounded by the British army.[31] In the narrative, an Indian subaltern, Dr. Aziz, is accused of attacking a young British woman, Adela Quested, in the mysterious Marabar Caves. The novel, however, is also about the inadequacy of imperial ideology to conceive of a suitable cosmopolitan politics that sustains the relations between colonizer and colonized. This inadequacy is not only its subject but is, first and foremost, its own limitation. Many have read *A Passage to India* as an example of Orientalist literature, particularly, as Said notes, because it fails to characterize India, its natural and material world, and its peoples other than "as subordinate and dominated."[32] More pointed critiques condemn Forster for his ideological bias, making the novel, as Sara Suleri has claimed, "an undiminished embarrassment to postcolonial discourse" given the text's continual attempts to "address the latent infantilism within the possibility of cross-cultural friendship."[33]

These critiques gesture toward important problems concerning political and literary representation that cannot be brushed aside. Yet the novel's very shortcomings show us crucial aspects about the relationship between Britain and India, particularly as they foreshadow an imminent post-independence future. Reading it as a progressive anti-imperial narrative, we will incur a number of serious debts difficult to pay. Reading it for its capacity to reveal the limitations of the imperial representational codes that it employs, though, we will be able to discern the novel's self-indicting conclusion that, while resulting from a crisis in literary representation, modernism must also face its own crisis with regard to the representation of the relations that will result from the end of imperial rule. To explore this issue, I want to put into question the conciliatory spirit of Forster's famous axiom "only connect."[34] I will examine the failed attempt of Dr. Aziz, a westernized Muslim Indian doctor working at a British hospital, to establish a cosmopolitan friendship with two British individuals that might engender a strong intimacy capable of piercing through the cultural and political barriers established by colonialism. I will argue that these friendships, whose failure is rooted in the aftermath of the Marabar Caves incident, expose the impossibility for dialogue to overcome the division that separates colonizer and colonized. From this reading I will conclude that, no matter its liberal-humanistic aspirations, a cosmopolitan relationship that presumes all participants to be equal political actors is based on an illusory dialogue that eliminates the possibility for an equitable postcolonial politics to emerge.

Colonial Framing

Before I begin teasing out the qualities of those friendships, I want to tackle the way the novel frames the impossibility for a dialogue free from the dogmatic conscriptions of imperialism to take place. Doing so is important because it reveals Forster's preoccupation with the possibilities of a future postcolonial era. Importantly, it also demonstrates the limitations of the novel's ideological coordinates, which are clearly articulated at the beginning. The narrative opens with a general view on the colony:

> Except for the Marabar Caves—and they are twenty miles off—the city of Chandrapore presents nothing extraordinary. . . . The streets are mean, the temples ineffective. . . . In the bazaar there is no painting and scarcely any carving. The very wood seems made of mud. . . . Houses do fall, people are drowned and left rotting, but the general outline of the town persists, swelling here, shrinking there, like some low but indestructible form of life.[35]

The prejudice in the description of the city as a filthy, undistinguishable space that lacks both spiritual depth and political organization is evident. The very idea of a life worth living (indeed a livable life) is negated. This is contrasted by its positive counterpart. Opposed to this impenetrable, muddy lower section of the city, the narrator registers the colonial settlement, which lies above the latter in a geographical articulation of the superiority of the colonial authorities: "Inland, the prospect alters. There is an oval maidan, and a long sallow hospital. Houses belonging to Eurasians stand on the high ground by the railway station" (5). This middle point is where the practical matters of the colony are carried out and where we find the subaltern population. Beyond this, "a second rise" emerges where "the little Civil Station" sits, "and viewed hence Chandrapore appears to be a totally different place. It is a city of gardens. It is no city, but a forest sparsely scattered with huts. It is a tropical pleasance, washed by a noble river" (5–6). Here, the colony is seen as neatly arranged, almost exotic, yet tempered by the rationality that fills the imperial mind with pride. The Civil Station "provokes no emotion . . . charms not, neither does it repel . . . [it] is sensibly planned . . . [and] shares nothing with the city" (6). From this third point, the British supervise colonial activities.

A passage that recalls Mary Louise Pratt's critical notion of the "monarch-of-all-I-survey," this opening description replicates the overseeing of the colony by a higher representational power. The narrator's elevated position, from which the fictional city is captured whole, might suggest a neutral distance, but as Pratt points out, this is intended to transform "local knowledges" such as life in Chandrapore "into European national and continental knowledges associated with European forms and relations of power."[36] This initial framing, thus, performs a clear epistemological maneuver that forces the reader to adopt the point of view of the colonizer. As if trying to offset it, however, Forster introduces a natural element that is literally and figuratively above the political realities of the colony. Toward the end of the short introductory chapter, the narrator states that these three contrasting spaces are nonetheless connected by "the overarching sky," which barely changes and, even when it does, its "core of blue persists" (6). The sky, which is referenced on numerous occasions throughout the novel, acts as an all-encompassing dome under which relationships between the colonial authorities and Chandrapore's inhabitants take place. In binding the city's spaces by means of an inversion of the "common ground" metaphor, appearing now as a "common sky," the novel arguably gestures at the possibility of a cross-cultural dialogue among the three locales. Yet this is only a way of naturalizing the causes of the colony's internal divisions, which are, of course, the result of the presence of the British in Chandrapore. By placing the three sections of the colony under the equalizing sky, Forster deploys a certain universality that obscures the fact that dialogue can never be a neutral affair as long as it is inscribed within the frame of colonial relations.

The novel's thinly veiled attempt to do away with the ideological bias of its framing is, nevertheless, soon fully disclosed. As the plot advances, the tripartite arrangement of the city quickly dissolves, giving rise to a distribution that oversimplifies the political landscape of Chandrapore. In terms of the actors involved, relations across the colonial divide are limited to the two "superior" sections of the city, with only marginal appearances of characters from the filthy, lower Chandrapore, which is in turn reduced to a mere undetermined and unromantic backdrop for a number of scenes. This betrays an important limitation in Forster's portrait of the native population, the processes of imperial subjectification, and the articulation of a possible postcolonial Indian politics of which, as we will see later, the novel nevertheless seems to be aware. In imagining the dialogic politics of the colony, the novel restricts its explorations to the Eurasian population of the city's first elevation (descendants of mixed-race marriages, Indian members of the elite educated in Europe, colonial officials, etc.) and the British denizens of the Station. Any and all dialogues, therefore, must be understood as selective encounters governed by the ideological, historical, and discursive conditions that subtend the relationships between the colonists and their subalterns.

Cosmopolitan Friendship across the Colonial Divide

Immediately after this initial portrait of Chandrapore, the narrative dives into a discussion between Mahmoud Ali, a barrister, and Hamidullah, a Cambridge-educated man of undetermined occupation, that sets the stage for the novel's exploration of the possibility of a dialogic relationship between British and (subaltern) Indians. In the presence of a quiet Dr. Aziz, the two men argue about whether or not one could truly become friends with the English. After a few exchanges, the discussion turns to the legacy of empire: after centuries of colonial rule, can the English engage with India and its peoples in a nonreductive way, recognizing the particularities that define them, or, on the contrary, will the English always maintain the imperative that all colonial subjects belong to a second class? Sanctioned by their unacknowledged position as members of the subaltern class who indeed have a voice in such matters,[37] the debate is immediately interrupted by Aziz's reaction. Standing in between the two, Aziz refuses to take a side: "Why talk about the English? Brrrr . . . ! Why be either friends with the fellows or not friends? Let us shut them out and be jolly!" (10). Aziz's agitated response is not a simple negative. It reveals a more radical mindset, one that discards the idea that colonial subjects should entertain the question of a possible friendship with the British in the first place. Yet, as a subaltern, Aziz will have to accept the limitations of such a view until he is capable of forging a more effective opposition against the British, which he is only capable of doing at the end of the novel, as we will see later.

Following the interaction, the novel reformulates the question from the other side of the colonial divide as a declaration of intentions by representatives of the ruling class. Mr. Turton, the city's tax collector, throws a "bridge party" to which he uncharacteristically invites a few members of the Indian elite, including Dr. Aziz. The party, of course, is not meant for attendees to play the popular card game but "to bridge the gulf between East and West; the expression was [Turton's] own invention, and amused all who heard it" (24). However, the function predictably fails to fulfill its purpose. English and Indians literally remain on each side of the lawn where it takes place, and the event has no positive impact on relations in the colony. On the contrary, it contributes to widening the gap that separates them. As we will see, the party's failure to act as a social bridge prompts Dr. Aziz to host Adela Quested and Mrs. Moore on a trip to the fascinating Marabar Caves, where Adela is allegedly assaulted, causing the crisis on which the novel's plot hinges.

Having established this negative precedent, Forster then presents an alternative way of conceiving a possible dialogue between both sides of the colonial divide. This materializes as two friendships. The first one involves Dr. Aziz and Mrs. Moore, a devout Christian visiting India to plan the marriage between Adela Quested and her son, the city's strict magistrate and ultimate embodiment of colonial authority. The second friendship is between Dr. Aziz and Cyril Fielding, a liberal schoolmaster known for disavowing the exalted nationalism displayed by British officials and civilians alike. Forster's choice of characters to participate in such relationships reveals an intention to explore the viability of a dialogic exchange away from the cultural, social, and historical pressures of imperialism. On the one hand, Aziz is, as we see when he is introduced, a disgruntled subaltern whose resentment toward the colonial occupation is stronger than his initial refusal to entertain the possibility of a friendship with the British. His interest in these two individuals, thus, seems motivated by something else: both Mrs. Moore and Fielding live at the margins of the colony's operations and sometimes even express their aversion toward them. On the other hand, the two British characters seem to pursue their friendships with Dr. Aziz as an attempt to establish an alternative kind of relationship guided by their distinct cosmopolitan impulses, which aim to transcend the fact that colonialism is the reason they are in Chandrapore.

Mrs. Moore seeks a connection with Aziz as a representative of the Indian Other on the basis of what could be called a "theistic cosmopolitanism," since her attachment to him derives from a spiritualism that impels her to identify with his vestigial Muslim values. This is evident, for instance, in their first encounter at a mosque, where Aziz is surprised that Mrs. Moore knows and respects Islam's traditions and has entered the temple unshod. Yet Aziz shows no real interest in religion. His self-identification as a Muslim seeks to establish a cultural identity that becomes reinforced when confronted by the capriciousness of his colonial superiors, thus rendering this friendship a rather moot attempt at dialogue based on spiritual affinities.[38] Indeed, Aziz conflates on several occasions his understanding of the Indian principles on which a nation will eventually have to be built with those of Islam, an attitude that is underscored by his frequent dismissive remarks about Hindus. Later, while hearing a poem by the Urdu poet Ghalib, which resonates with him not as "a call to battle, but as a calm assurance . . . that India was one; Moslem," the narrator notes how Aziz "liked to hear his religion praised" (96). Still, despite Aziz's culturalist articulation of his Muslim identity, Mrs. Moore will show great respect for what she perceives as India's mysticism in her friendship with him and other Indians, at least until she is overcome by a personal crisis following her visit to the Marabar Caves, which makes her withdraw from the colony's social life altogether.

Cyril Fielding's friendship with Aziz, on the other hand, seems to be more promising. A "hard-bitten, good-tempered, intelligent" man, Fielding is introduced as a seasoned liberal cosmopolitan. While he admits that he was "caught by India late" in his life, he states that his past travels "conditioned" his "new impressions" upon arriving; India's peninsula and its peoples bear for him a certain resemblance to the "smaller and more exquisitely shaped" Italian one: "To regard an Indian as if he were an Italian is not, for instance, a common error, nor perhaps a fatal one, and Fielding often attempted analogies between this peninsula and that other"

(56). Fielding's cosmopolitanism is, in addition, significantly secular, as he bluntly expresses in a later visit to Aziz ("I don't believe in God" [101]), grounded in an understanding of the world as "a globe of men who are trying to reach one another and can best do so by the help of goodwill plus culture and intelligence" (57). Fielding is further described as having "no racial feeling—not because he was superior to his brother civilians, but because he had matured in a different atmosphere, where the herd-instinct does not flourish" (57). Yet the schoolmaster's cosmopolitanism is of far more interest to Aziz for another reason.

To complete his portrait, Fielding stands in stark contrast to the colonial officials by pointing out his high regard for logical argumentation and his tendency to be critical while accepting reasoned criticism. This attitude automatically places him outside of the imperial discourse that separates colonizer and colonized as metaphysical and incorruptible categories:

> He was not unpatriotic, he always got on with Englishmen in England, all his best friends were English, so why was it not the same out here? Outwardly of the large shaggy type, with sprawling limbs and blue eyes, he appeared to inspire confidence until he spoke. Then something in his manner puzzled people and failed to allay the distrust which his profession naturally inspired. . . . The feeling grew that Mr Fielding was a disruptive force, and rightly, for ideas are fatal to caste, and he used ideas by that most potent method—interchange. (56–57)

Fielding's liberal brand of cosmopolitanism, which Forster celebrates with this ironic passage, is sustained by his intellectual autonomy, what we could call today a "multicultural" approach to difference, and the rejection of imposed social and cultural categories. Due to the freedom that his status as a British citizen and as schoolmaster in the colony bestow on him, however, Fielding's is also what Peter Kalliney calls an "elective" cosmopolitanism, one that rests on "a form of political and ethical detachment, enabled by elitist attitudes and relative affluence."[39] Unlike Mrs. Moore—who, despite her reluctance, begrudgingly accepts her role within the frame of colonial rule by overseeing the preparations of her son's marriage—Fielding rises above the colonial structures not only to engage with the difference of the Indian Other but also to dissociate himself from national, religious, or other types of allegiances imposed by the rigid social codes of the colony.

Fielding's detached cosmopolitanism extricates him from the rampant imperial prejudice that pervades the colony while revealing an ideological position that he characterizes as apolitical. For Fielding, connections across the colonial divide are subordinated to his own autonomy. As he admits to Aziz and several members of the Indian elite, for instance, "I am out here personally because I needed a job" (102), while he justifies his own profession in terms of this autonomy: "I believe in teaching people to be individuals, and to understand other individuals" (111). More significantly, as his "zeal for honesty" prevents him from replicating the imperial precept that "England holds India for her good," Fielding explains his presence in Chandrapore by underscoring this individualistic cosmopolitanism: "I'm delighted to be here—that's my answer, there's my only excuse. I can't tell you anything about fairness. It mayn't have been fair I should have been born. I take up some other fellow's air, don't I, whenever I breathe? . . . [I]f one's happy in consequence, that's some justification" (102). This attitude is extremely appealing to Aziz, as he might be able to adopt it to establish his increasingly dissenting position against the colonial administration, which is not based on his role as a subaltern but on the Indian identity that he forges for himself.[40] The prospects of Dr. Aziz's friendships with Mrs. Moore and Fielding, however, are altered by an unexpected turn of events.

Difference and Unintelligibility

Following the failed bridge party, Aziz, Mrs. Moore, and Adela visit the Marabar Caves. This visit, which Aziz plans so that Adela can see "the real India" (21), is the novel's point of inflection. Its central episode involves Adela's alleged assault in the dark of one of the caves, which is imputed to Aziz after a series of disingenuous misunderstandings and fraudulent presumptions, triggering a colonial crisis that the authorities, led by Ronny Heaslop in a doubled prosecuting role as city magistrate and Adela's future husband, employ to shore up imperial authority. Famously left unresolved, the incident has been interpreted as linked to the symbolic meaning of the caves, whose portrayal suggests an exploration of the limitations of imperial epistemology. When introduced by the narrator, the caves are described as impossible to represent: "Nothing, nothing attaches to them, and their reputation—for they have one—does not depend upon human speech. . . . They are dark caves. Even when they open toward the sun, very little light penetrates down the entrance tunnel into the circular chamber. There is little to see, and no eye to see it, until the visitor arrives for his five minutes, and strikes a match" (116). Accordingly, what happens in the caves between Aziz and Adela is irretrievable, and Forster's exploration of their enclosed space as the incomprehensible locus of nothingness, as a result, poses important questions about the novel's self-acknowledged representational limits.

The narrator's employment of the lexicon of nothingness may be read as an attempt to obliterate India, its people, and their history. However, as

Parry has argued, the "valencies of the 'Nothing'" in Forster's characterization are in fact "a symptom of what the novel is unable to comprehend intellectually, accommodate within its preferred sensibility or possess in its available language," which ultimately "challenges the west with its irreducible and insubordinate difference."[41] If the ideological leanings of *A Passage to India* are unequivocally complicit with the discursive underpinnings of the imperial doctrine, as I showed in my commentary of its opening, such complicitness also presents us with an opportunity to consider what this nothingness does for the historical vacuums that it gestures toward but fails to account for in affirmative terms.

The caves arguably play an important role in signaling the impossibility for a radical cosmopolitan politics to emerge. Whereas for the narrator nothing happens in the caves, this nothingness is nevertheless registered aurally. The presence of human bodies—outsiders, like the British in India— invariably provokes a response that rejects any interpretation other than as the caves' cacophony, which the narrator is unable to decipher: "The echo in a Marabar cave . . . is entirely devoid of distinction. Whatever is said, the same monotonous noise replies, and quivers up and down the walls until it is absorbed into the roof. 'Boum' is the sound as far as the human alphabet can express it, or 'ou-boum'—utterly dull. Hope, politeness, the blowing of a nose, the squeak of a boot, all produce 'boum'" (137). The inside of the caves, thus, is not just unrepresentable. Given Forster's emphatic adherence to the imperial codes of signification, the caves' interior substantiates the novel's self-acknowledged representational limitations. Furthermore, while the narrator cannot provide a visual description of the caves, we are nonetheless given a very specific sonic depiction of what occurs inside them, which points to their dialogic significance.

Understood symbolically, the booming emerging from the caves can be read as the articulation of a political discourse coming from the otherwise unknown heart of India that the imperial ear, while able to register it, is incapable of understanding. The "boum" emitted in response to their visitors is not mere senseless noise. Indeed, it is a noise full of meaning, which resides not in its mysterious unintelligibility but in the incapacity of the narrator to identify it otherwise. As R. Radhakrishnan puts it, in the novel "the sovereignty of meaning has to be understood as a mode of vulnerability to the echo rather than as a masterful self-evidence that preempts the 'dangerous' alterity of the echo."[42] The "boum" coming out of the caves confirms the empire's inability to communicate with colonial India in a non-imperial idiom, a representational inadequacy that equally assails the narrator. The description of the echoes, thus, enacts a powerful disruption of the colonial order in which the novel is entrenched and that, more importantly, foreshadows the unviability of Aziz's friendships with Mrs. Moore and Fielding and, consequently, the impossibility for him to argue with his interlocutors honestly and critically.

Whereas Adela's sexual assault in the caves has received a great deal of critical attention, Mrs. Moore's incident in the caves is perhaps more illuminating to understand the novel's message about the possibility of a cosmopolitan dialogue across the colonial divide. Initially, Mrs. Moore's experience of the caves is marked by the anxiety that assails her in one of them: "the circular chamber began to smell. She lost Aziz and Adela in the dark, didn't know who touched her, couldn't breathe, and some vile naked thing struck her face and settled on her mouth like a pad" (137). While stressful and construed at first as an appalling offense, this event is nonetheless explained as a run-in with a mother and her baby. However, the caves' echoes, which remain in her head after she returns to Chandrapore, have a disturbing impact on Mrs. Moore: "For an instant she went mad, hitting and gasping like a fanatic. For not only did the crush and stench alarm her; there was also a terrifying echo" (137). The overwhelming booming takes a ruthless grip on Mrs. Moore, who is never the same after hearing it. This has important consequences for the character. If her cosmopolitan impulses are at first driven by her wish to connect with Indians through a mutual religious commitment, the damage that this sound does to her spirituality betrays an incompatibility that ultimately proves insurmountable.

Following the visit to the caves, Mrs. Moore removes herself from all social and public engagements. She gives up on a budding friendship with Professor Godbole, the Brahmin with whom she has found the theistic connection she could never attain with Aziz, and refuses to take a part in Aziz's trial, not in protest against his clear demonization by the colonial authorities as the trial proceeds without evidence of his attack, but out of sheer existential exhaustion. The caves' "boum," thus, causes irreparable damage to Mrs. Moore's spirituality, subsuming her into a stupefied state that tellingly makes her develop an aversion to verbal expression. The prospects of a possible dialogue, therefore, vanish with Mrs. Moore's silence. While writing a letter to her children, for instance, "suddenly, at the edge of her mind, Religion appeared, poor little talkative Christianity, and she knew that all its divine words from 'Let there be light' to 'It is finished' only amounted to 'boum.' Then she was terrified by an area larger than usual; the universe, never comprehensible to her intellect, offered no repose to her soul . . . and she realized that she . . . didn't want to communicate with anyone, not even with God" (139). In another scene, Mrs. Moore is unable to describe to Adela the echoes, which have also assailed the young woman: "'Say, say, say,' said the old lady bitterly. As if anything can be said! I have spent my life in saying or in listening to sayings; I have listened too much. It is time I was left in peace" (188). Eventually, she leaves for England and dies at sea, making a last, spectral appearance when the Indian audience chants "Esmiss Esmoor" in protest against Aziz's farcical trial (212). Mrs. Moore's fate could, thus, be interpreted as Forster's liberal-humanist indictment of the ways she seeks to form connections with the colonial Other. Literally negating her ability to communicate, her depleted spiritualism evidences the unsuitability of a theistic kind of cosmopolitanism as an adequate frame for the kind of supracolonial dialogue that the novel explores.

Whereas the end of Aziz's friendship with Mrs. Moore has no further consequences, the strain on his relationship with Fielding is much more significant because it brings to the surface Aziz's deep anticolonial sentiments. The eventual failure of their friendship is caused not by the events that take place in the caves but by the expectations they have about each other in the aftermath of Aziz's botched trial. At the height of the proceedings, Adela withdraws her accusation, which unleashes a crisis that sweeps through the colony. Initially, Fielding is supportive of his friend during the trial. Yet once the crisis is over the apolitical nature of his detached cosmopolitanism becomes apparent to Aziz, who realizes that his friend's support was not motivated by an anticolonial stance but by his liberal individualism. Tellingly, Fielding strikes a friendship with Adela after she is repudiated by Heaslop and the rest of the colonial class for frustrating their opportunity to reaffirm the strength of the imperial law. This new friendship leads him to defend Adela against the resentment harbored by Aziz for her silence during the trial, which is presented as the product of the pressures of the colony's British elites to make an example of the Indian doctor, though the latter can only see it as an enabling form of complicity. Fielding, thus, urges Aziz to "treat her considerately," arguing that "she mustn't get the worst of both worlds" (237).

At the same time, Fielding's national and ancestral affiliations resurface as a result of the crisis. He confesses to Aziz, for instance, that he now feels as if "something racial [had] intruded" and that he could not, as Aziz once asked him, "give in to the East" (246), wondering later if he would "defy all his own people for the sake of a stray Indian" (303). His ethical and political detachment is now exposed: living a cosmopolitan life was precisely a way not to have to deal with the question of Britain's colonial presence in India, and his friendship with Aziz had concealed all along his participation in the asymmetrical relationship between colonizers and colonized. While Fielding had been a free agent in the colony who could afford to criticize the imperial rule and support the cause of his wrongly accused friend, Aziz had been forced to defend his innocence against the entire colonial establishment and later face its unfounded hostility before being betrayed by the only British individual he trusted.

As a result, Fielding and Aziz grow distant, especially after the doctor is led to believe that the schoolmaster is returning to England to marry Adela. Aziz considers their friendship terminated and is left with no other option but to feel resentful toward an entire colonial class (Fielding included) to which he had dutifully deferred as a subaltern. It is the failure of this friendship, ultimately, that enables Aziz to begin formulating a radical anticolonial politics that nullifies the possibilities of a dialogue with the British and displays clear nationalistic attributes. While running the risk of replicating some of the nationalist principles upon which imperialism operates, Frantz Fanon once noted, a national identity can be an appropriate vehicle for "the collective thought process of a [colonized] people to describe, justify, and extol the actions whereby they have joined forces and remained strong" in order to "counter colonialism's endeavors to distort and depreciate" while "shap[ing] the future and prepar[ing] the ground where vigorous shoots are already sprouting."[43] Thus, Aziz's anger toward Fielding leads him to declare himself openly "anti-British" (236), and he begins to write progressive poems about India's future national identity ("The song of the future must transcend creed" [259]) and the rights of women ("the purdah must go . . . otherwise we must never be free" [279]). Yet a last chance appears for Aziz and Fielding to recuperate their friendship, only to be finally quashed by the doctor's argument that the liberal cosmopolitan politics that once united them is in fact compromised by the imperial frame in which it is inscribed.

An Impossible Friendship

Two years after the trial, Fielding returns to India as a school overseer and meets Aziz in Mau, where the latter is now the Rajah's personal doctor. After avoiding him several times convinced that he has indeed married Adela, Aziz finally runs into Fielding at a Hindu festival in celebration of Krishna and they seem to rekindle their friendship. However, Aziz ultimately refuses to restore his bond with the former schoolmaster, a decision that reveals the political tenor of the novel. By reuniting them, Forster dramatizes in a final clash how a cosmopolitan relationship will be futile to bridge the colonial gap, even when the distance between them is somewhat shortened. In its stead, the novel considers the contours of a postcolonial politics to come, which the narrator is capable of articulating at least in its basic, incipient configuration.

As it draws to a close, the narrative dramatizes the illusory dialogue on which Aziz and Fielding's friendship has been based, and which Aziz must stall as a way to preserve his newly formulated anticolonial stance. This final encounter takes on a symbolic charge because, in fending off the detached cosmopolitanism that once let him down, Aziz clearly signals that this kind of cosmopolitan politics will be the very insurmountable obstacle for Fielding to understand the urgency of a free India, which Aziz now pursues without hesitation. It is precisely Aziz and Fielding's parting of ways that underscores the inevitability of such an obstacle. From Aziz's point of view, it is simply impossible for them to have a critical dialogue about the presence of the British in India. As Fielding's realization of his own national allegiances following the trial demonstrates, it is a mistake to assume that their relationship could ever be founded on neutral ground, unaffected by the power structures governing imperialism. The ending, thus, illustrates the unresolved nature of the colonial question. This is not to say that the novel closes in an open-ended fashion, suggestive of multiple interpretations. Instead, it reaches the conclusion that the premise upon which Forster explores a possible dialogue across colonial lines forestalls the sort of radical cosmopolitanism that the postcolonial era will necessitate. The final confrontation between Aziz and Fielding could be read as the novel's self-reflective interruption (i.e., a necessary cul-de-sac) that colonial relations must reach before a postcolonial horizon can open up.

In the closing scene the two men appear riding side by side toward the city of Mau while they animatedly "wrangled about politics. Each had hardened since Chandrapore, and a good knock-about proved enjoyable. They trusted each other, although they were going to part, perhaps because they were going to part. Fielding had 'no further use for politeness,' he said, meaning that the British Empire really can't be abolished because it's rude. Aziz retorted, 'Very well, and we have no use for you,' and glared at him with abstract hate" (305). Their commonalities are dispelled by the inevitable recontextualization of their relationship. Their differences, however, disorderly and passionately erupt in this last interaction. Diplomacy, recoded here as "politeness," is now for Aziz insufficient to sustain the relationship between both sides of the colonial divide that their friendship symbolizes. In response, Fielding mockingly belittles him: "Away from us, Indians go to seed at once. Look at the King-Emperor High School! Look at you, forgetting your medicine and going back to charms. Look at your poems," to which Aziz responds: "Jolly good poems, I'm getting published Bombay side." Fielding presses on: "Yes, and what do they say? Free our women and India will be free. Try it, my lad. Free your own lady in the first place, and see who'll wash [your children's] faces. A nice situation!"

(305). Fielding's detached cosmopolitanism, which leads him to condemn cynically certain conservative attitudes he has seen in India, in fact brings him closer to the imperial ideology that he has criticized for years. In clumsily counterposing those problematic attitudes to Britain's colonial presence, he is incapable of recognizing that the forms of justice that India might need can only be attainable from a resisting position like Aziz's.

In response to this attack, Aziz argues that the agency of the Indians cannot be granted to them by the Empire but must be the result of a collective will to render India independent from Britain. The seeds of this popular will are visible in Aziz's attitude: "He rose in his stirrups and pulled at his horse's head in the hope it would rear. Then he should feel in a battle. He cried: 'Clear out, all you Turtons and Burtons. We wanted to know you ten years back—now it's too late. If we see you and sit on your committees it's for political reasons, don't you make any mistake'" (305). Aziz's outburst suggests that his refusal to take part in the illusory dialogue that Fielding proposes has its roots in an anti-imperial agenda with an already firm historical footing. By strategically participating in the committees in which they have nonetheless played secondary roles, the members of the elite have been able to generate a certain amount of power that will be crucial to attain India's independence. Once the idea of a sovereign nation becomes a certainty, the elites (not the population at large, as the narrator has reminded us all along) will be able to articulate their political agency on their own postcolonial terms.

Aziz continues expressing his opposition against the imperial apparatus: "His horse did rear. 'Clear out, clear out I say. Why are we put to so much suffering? We used to blame you, now we blame ourselves, we grow wiser. Until England is in difficulties we keep silent, but in the next European war,—aha, aha! Then is our time!'" (305). Aziz's words present a political program in its own right, which will be further benefited, as the novel rightly predicts, by the weakening of Britain's empire by the imminent World War II. In facing this rebuff, Fielding asks what possible alternative can there be to British imperialism: "'Who do you want instead of the English? The Japanese?' Fielding jeered, drawing rein" (305). Paying no heed to his taunt, Aziz deems that the political and ideological differences among the peoples of a post-imperial India will be subordinated to the constitution of an independent nation (as he declares earlier, a "Hindu-Moslem entente" [251]) that frees its inhabitants from the British, their common enemy: "It will be arranged—a conference of oriental statesmen" (306). Still, Fielding condescendingly questions the suggestion that a truly critical forum for Indian national matters may be conceivable, which is met with anger. Recalling Fielding's earlier generalization about certain traditional values he sees as endemic to India, Aziz accusingly retorts that the colonial administration will disseminate the "Old story that 'We will rob every man and rape every woman from Peshawar to Calcutta,' I suppose, which you get some nobody to repeat and then quote every week in [the colonial newspaper] in order to frighten us into retaining you! We know!" (306).

This rejoinder is, however, undercut by Aziz's momentary realization of the possible complications of a postcolonial, independent India: "Still he couldn't quite fit in Afghans at Mau, and, finding he was in a corner, made his horse rear again until he remembered that he had, or ought to have, a mother-land. Then he shouted: 'India shall be a nation! No foreigners of any sort! Hindu and Moslem and Sikh and all shall be one! Hurrah! Hurrah for India!'" (306). National cohesion, as the history of post-independence India would confirm, might cause the proponents of an Indian nation to impose the homogenization of its culturally, religiously, and linguistically distinct peoples. Yet, Aziz seems to reason, this cannot be a hindrance to the larger goal of expelling the British. He is set in defending as the only solution to the colonial question the formation of a strategic nationalism, which is, as Partha Chatterjee has argued, "posited not on an identity but rather on a *difference* with the . . . forms of the national society propagated by the modern West."[44] Thus, "in an awful rage," Aziz responds to Fielding's derisive comments: "Down with the English anyhow. That's certain. Clear out, you fellows, double quick I say. We may hate one another, but we hate you most" (306). Finally, Aziz expresses the political thrust of a postcolonial discourse as he acknowledges the agency of the dissenting peoples of India joining forces against the British rule.

As the novel reaches its closure, Aziz proclaims that the reestablishment of their friendship is contingent on a dialogue that, while recognizing imperial history as its undeniable background, is not determined by a perpetuation of the colonial relationships that it challenges: "'We shall get rid of you,'" Aziz dramatically affirms, "'yes, we shall drive every blasted Englishman into the sea, and then'—he rode against him furiously—'and then,' he concluded, half kissing him, 'you and I shall be friends'" (306). Only after the imperial hierarchy that has shaped their relationship is overturned and their roles as members of the colonial class and the Indian elite are dismantled will they be friends again. This assurance of a friendship to follow the emancipatory revolution that Aziz announces, however, is not a restoration of Fielding's detached cosmopolitanism or even a regenerative brief respite. It is, instead, the affirmation that an unconditional friendship as the foundation for a cordial and mutually acknowledging relationship must be reimagined in the new historical context that Aziz's position inaugurates. Sensing the seriousness of Aziz's assertion, Fielding finally asks what seems to him a simple question: "'Why can't we be friends now?' said the other. 'It's what I want, it's what you want'" (306). Fielding is incapable of seeing the limitations of his own cosmopolitanism, which makes him disregard the historical basis determining the difference of the colonized Other.

By way of conclusion, Forster animates the landscape against which this argument occurs to respond symbolically to the political and historical dilemma that Fielding's question represents: "But the horses did not want it—they swerved apart; the earth didn't want it, sending up rocks through which riders must pass single-file; the temples, the tank, the jail, the palace, the birds, the carrion, the Guest House, that came into view as they issued from the gap and saw Mau beneath: they didn't want it, they said in their hundred voices: 'No, not yet,' and the sky said 'No, not there'" (306). As he does in the opening, Forster employs a geographical metaphor that reveals the extent to which the novel must be read as inscribed in the imperial ideology whose limits it explores, perhaps admitting his inability to free his own writing from it. Aziz and Fielding become the center figures immortalized in the textual equivalent of a landscape, "a particular historical" painting genre "associated with European imperialism."[45] The temples, the birds, the two men, and the horses they ride all become objects we now look at against the background of a soon-to-be-postcolonial India. This static landscape, one might conclude, offers a historical reflection by casting the reader as a spectator observing the scene from a distance, taking in all the details in the picture as well as the abnegation ("not there" and "not yet") that separates the two characters.

If it does not imagine a clear path for future relations, in framing this historical moment the narrative at least anticipates the sort of counter-dialogic strategies that will be necessary for a future postcolonial politics. As Forster himself would put it in a 1960 note warning against the adaptation of his novel into a play, "I tried to indicate the human predicament in a universe which is not, so far, comprehensible to our minds. This aspect of the novel is displayed in its final chapters."[46] Rather than simply curbing the critical power of his novel, Forster's avowed inability to imagine a future postcolonial world underscores its capacity to exhort readers to consider the mechanisms that imperialism employed to prevent it from materializing, such as the dialogic kind of cosmopolitan relationship I have explored here. The modernism of *A Passage to India*, thus, is not only characterized by its imperial complicity. Perhaps as important are its efforts to consider its own limitations while valorizing the need for a new language that, unlike the unintelligible "boum" that emerges from inside of the Marabar Caves, it can begin formulating. The end of this friendship, then, symbolizes the counterdialogic impasse that Aziz provokes in response to Fielding's detached cosmopolitanism. As we have seen, a friendship based on a mutual cosmopolitan recognition can only begin to occur provided Aziz—and by extension all Indians—constitutes a new, postcolonial Indian subject position. Only from this position, which is the product of his own autonomy and not granted to him, can he participate in the imminent international plane of relations that, as the novel intuits, will unavoidably replace the increasingly untenable imperial order.

I want to tackle now a different iteration of this impasse with a reading of Jean Rhys's 1934 *Voyage in the Dark*. While it heralds the new, postcolonial horizon that results from the imminent obsolescence of the political structures of empire[47] in similar ways to Forster's, Rhys's novel offers a different perspective. It explores the struggles of the colonial migrant in Britain instead of the ramifications of the presence of the British in the colony. At the same time, it focuses more heavily on the personal cost of articulating a resisting cosmopolitanism that forestalls a form of recognition aimed at negating the autonomy of the (post)colonial subject.

Divided and Doubled: Colonial Misrecognition in Jean Rhys's *Voyage in the Dark*

There is a moment in Jean Rhys's *Voyage in the Dark* where its narrator and protagonist, Anna Morgan, looks at herself in a mirror and is troubled by what she sees. Put off by the disconnection between her appearance and her sense of self, she narrates: "It was as if I were looking at somebody else. . . . I felt as if I had gone out of myself, as if I were in a dream."[48] This feeling of irreconcilability, though, is not isolated. On numerous occasions, Anna grows anxious at her own reflected image. While on the surface this points to the character's self-conscious reticence and discomfort in certain social situations, the tensions between Anna's selfhood and its appearance are also deeply rooted in the conflict caused by her colonial ancestry and her intention to modulate her identity in opposition to it. A narrative whose arc is described by Anna's arrival in Britain from the Caribbean and a subsequent existential attrition that culminates in her near undoing, the novel dwells on the kinds of pressures she must endure—one internal and the other external—that threaten her self-constitution as a cosmopolitan postcolonial subject.

First, as a West Indian migrant of Welsh descent in Britain, Anna is subjected to the disciplining of her racial and geographical affiliations, which stand in direct opposition to the colonial precepts of kinship that mandate her alignment with the colonial class. Second, because she is white, Anna is recognized as an English woman; this evidences the extent to which the white race rests firmly as a normative register that dictates the terms of the consensus regulating imperial politics, a precept that also has a particular command over her womanhood. The combination of these two pressures, as we will see, will result in the illusory dialogue that she is forced to enter into with several individuals in England while she tries to rise as a chorus girl and, later, as a kept woman. In response to it, Anna constructs an identity based on the counterdialogic destabilization of what Paul Gilroy calls the "*principles* of solidarity and collectivity that produces 'races' as totalities,"[49] which allows her to constitute her own radical subjectivity. As an individual whose sense of self violently emerges at the fault line between her colonial ancestry and her affiliative impulses, Anna ultimately embodies a complex and resilient cosmopolitanism that is as deeply rooted in the history of imperialism as it is intended to work toward its occlusion. This, as I will conclude, sheds important light on the novel's bildungsroman qualities.

In prefiguring "the artistic domain of post-coloniality, in which the priorities of high modernism acquire a radically different political charge,"[50] *Voyage in the Dark* maps out Anna's cosmopolitanism as it challenges the imperial order that regulates the distribution of colonial and metropolitan identities. It constructs a character that embodies a dissensual ontology that results from her incongruous geographical and racial affiliations, causing her sense of self to be simultaneously divided and doubled. To explore this, I will begin by arguing, against the grain of hybridity theory, that Anna's straddling of the colonial divide as a white West Indian does not lead up to the formation of a complete, amalgamated self. Following it, I will explore how her divided subjectivity resists the pressures accompanying her constant exclusion from the social and sexual circles of London. Finally, I will conclude by describing the kind of resilience that is necessary to fashion a radical cosmopolitanism like Anna's.

An Irreconcilable Division

Narrated in the first person and featuring many of the experimental gestures typical of modernism, such as free indirect speech and stream of consciousness, Anna's story is constantly haunted by often-nostalgic memories of Dominica[51] that stand in contrast with passages about the difficulties of her life in Britain, creating a fragmented narrative texture that parallels the psychological impact of her migrating experience. One might be tempted to consider this clash dialogically in the Bakhtinian sense (i.e., as the integration of two differing worldviews that derives into a combinative outcome), with the "home" (Dominica) and "away" (Britain) portions of the novel engaging in an ongoing give-and-take that gives rise to a new subjectivity. Anna's identity, according to this reading, would undergo the sort of self-formation theorized by Homi Bhabha in his work on hybridity, the third space, and the in-between.[52] For Bhabha, one inevitable historical outcome of the contact between colonizer and colonized is the production of subjectivities that emerge from their dialectical negotiation with the cultural spaces and discourses that, once declared at odds by imperial decree, they now experience and live by. As he puts it, "If the effect of colonial power is seen to be the production of hybridization rather than the noisy command of colonialist authority or the silent repression of native traditions, then an important change of perspective occurs. The ambivalence at the source of traditional discourses on authority enables a form of subversion, founded on the undecidability that turns the discursive conditions of dominance into the grounds of intervention."[53] This generates an irresolute subjectivity that negates the national, ideological, and cultural fixity sustaining imperialism while offering a solution to the impossibility of a nativist return to precolonial times.

However, to conceive of Anna's migrating self exclusively through the lens of hybridity theory is to overlook key material aspects that constitute her radical cosmopolitan politics and, particularly, her effort to embed herself in the economic and racial nexuses of which she ultimately becomes a victim. Understanding her as a hybrid in a metaphorical third space implies a consensual gesture that solves—instead of straining—the clashing bipartite distribution of home versus away, black versus white, West Indies versus Britain, and metropolis versus colony that defines her identity. To conceive of Anna's subjectivity as a product of such a dialogically assimilative process,[54] which aggregates the tensions between the cultures of colonizer and colonized, is to obscure the dissensual self-formation of an individual whose struggle is precisely defined by the colonial relations that shape her troubled migratory experience. Furthermore, while Anna's white Creole identity might be considered the result of the historical incorporation (largely through appropriation) of certain Caribbean cultural and ethnic attributes by the European settlers, her identity is in fact translated from that of a member of the colonial class in the Caribbean to that, as we will see, of a white English woman in Britain. An alternative reading, then, would conceive of Rhys's protagonist not as defined by the syncretism of a transnational identity often ascribed to migrants but as radically divided between those two irreconcilable poles.

We get a sense of Anna's divided self very early in the novel: "It was as if a curtain had fallen, hiding everything I had ever known. It was almost like being born again. The colours were different, the smells different. The feeling things gave you right down inside yourself was different" (7). Anna is confronted with two disparate worlds: a familiar one left behind that returns in flashing memories and haunting dreams, and a foreign one where a better future might await her. This division, however, is not between two extremes on a continuum that cast her as a cosmopolitan agent bridging the now obsolete West Indian plantation economy and London's metropolitan path to socioeconomic mobility. To adapt Said's terminology in his important essay "Secular Criticism," instead, it complicates her need to replace her "filiative" connections to the metropole (by way of her European ancestry) with an "affiliative" bond that articulates a sense of belonging in the West Indies.[55] Thus, Anna cannot be considered simply a cosmopolitan, but a *dissensual* cosmopolitan. Instead of expanded, as "traditional" cosmopolitanism entails, her sense of affiliation is directed to a colonial elsewhere, contradicting the imperial rationale of kinship and exposing the historical vacuum in which she seeks to ground her sense of self.

Dominica and England are, in Anna's imagination, mutually exclusive: "Sometimes it was as if I were back there and as if England were a dream. At other times England was the real thing and out there was the dream, but I could never fit them together" (8). This opposition is the expression of an identity at odds with either side of the colonial divide. On the one hand, Anna's fruitless struggle to find her place in England is initially accompanied with descriptions of the drab towns she begins to tour as a chorus girl after arriving from Dominica: "There was always the little grey street . . . and rows of houses with chimneys like funnels of dummy steamers and smoke the same colour as the sky; and a grey stone promenade running hard, naked and straight by the side of the grey-brown or grey-green sea" (8). Later, those uninviting, grey towns where at times she "would shut my eyes and pretend that the heat of the fire . . . was sun-heat" (7) are replaced by the much harsher London environment, bringing about profound anxieties due to her inability to belong: "hundreds thousands of white people white people [*sic*] rushing along and the dark houses all alike frowning down one after the other all alike all stuck together . . . oh I am not going to like this place I'm not going to like this place I'm not going to like this place" (17). Separating her from the indistinguishable mass of white bodies marching the streets, Anna's alienation in the metropolis is replicated in the spaces she inhabits afterward, such as "ghastly" hostels and intimidating restaurants (18), when she quits the theater company and seeks to live as a kept woman.

On the other hand, Anna's home island appears equally hostile. In her memories of the Caribbean, Anna often casts herself as the personification of the imperial anachronism that is provoked by the inevitable dissolution of the colonial class, which has forced her to flee given that there is no economic future in her family's estate. In one early scene, for instance, she notes the collision of English manners with the hot tropical climates when she remembers how "carefully putting on your gloves" as "you begin to perspire and you feel . . . a wet patch" running "underneath your arms" is "a disgusting and a disgraceful thing to happen to a lady" (42). A quick look at the British fashion trends of the first decades of the twentieth century, when Rhys began work on the novel, makes it easy to imagine how injudicious it is to observe such social practices in the tropics. This incompatibility, furthermore, signals Anna's anxiety about her future, which is emphasized a moment later when she complains about the lack of class mobility on the island: "The poor do this and the rich do that, the world so-and-so and nothing can change it" (43). It is precisely this stagnancy that causes her eventual migration to Britain and, subsequently, the reconfiguration that her sense of self undergoes as a misrecognized subject in London.

As a member of a once-prosperous, plantation-owning family clutching at such impracticable European class conventions, Anna feels that there is no place for her in Dominica. This sentiment is most visibly encapsulated by her refusal to meet the demands of her dour stepmother, Hester ("the text's most glaring mouthpiece of imperial prejudice"),[56] to act like an "English gentlewoman" (57). Even when Anna is highly nostalgic about the island, her memories can only modulate this rejection. We see this, for example, in her reflection on the Orientalist exoticism displayed on such a mundane object as a box of biscuits: "Biscuits Like Mother Makes, as Fresh in the Tropics as in the Motherland. . . . There was a tidy green and a shiny pale-blue sky, so close that if the little girl had stretched her arm up she could have touched it" (149). The escapist mood of this thought, which is anchored in the foregone comfort of her childhood, is nonetheless undercut immediately by her realization that there is "a high, dark wall behind the little girl." This wall, furthermore, is recoded in her imagination, representing what "my idea of what England was," a stifling environment that leaves no space for her to thrive: "it was the wall that mattered" (149).

The alienation that Anna experiences in both locales is intensified by the negation of her affiliative impulses. In Dominica she expresses an affinity with the Afro-Caribbean population that, as a critic has put it, "is

Designs by Lucile for *Good Housekeeping* (1912). Courtesy of Home Economics Archive: Research, Tradition and History, Albert R. Mann Library, Cornell University.

at best naïve and at worst neo-imperialist."[57] Anna's oblivious efforts to identify herself with the black West Indians of her childhood reveal an incongruous affiliation that, while askew and largely unsuccessful, is aimed at disavowing her position as a member of the colonial plantocracy. Thus, she admits in reminiscing about home that "I wanted to be black, I always wanted to be black. . . . Being black is warm and gay, being white is cold and sad" (31). The unviability of this affiliation is underscored later by her lament that Francine, her childhood nurse and one of the West Indians to whom she feels closest, "of course . . . disliked me too because I was white," a sentiment further emphasized by her realization that no solidarity can emerge between them on account of their racial difference: "I would never be able to explain to her that I hated being white" (72). Despite its unviability, nevertheless, this affiliation is all she has to embody a subjectivity that is not confined to the protocols of the colonial system of relations.

Anna also turns to this incongruous affiliation to undo her filiative connections with the colonial caste while in London, an effort that is equally unsuccessful. For instance, in an intimate moment with Walter Jeffries, with whom she realizes that being a lover to married men might be the avenue for the mobility she cannot access either in Dominica or working in the theater in England, Anna struggles to assert her Caribbean identity. As she insists that "I am a real West Indian" (55) in an attempt to establish a personal connection with the man by "mak[ing] him see what it was like" (53) on the island, Walter first responds with lukewarm interest ("I'm sure it's beautiful . . . but I don't like hot places much" [54]) and then teases her in order to placate her, farcically playing the role of the prostitute's client: "Well, let's go upstairs, you rum child, you rum little devil" (55). Walter's dismissal of her claims to a West Indian identity acquires colonial undertones, as his playful choice of the epithets "rum" (i.e., a peculiar or odd person) and "devil" unfold as clichéd references to unmistakable tropes such as the plantations from which the sugar used to produce rum is extracted or the devil-worshipping rituals wrongly attributed to certain Caribbean religious practices.

Anna's migration to the metropolis, thus, throws significant light onto her Caribbean affiliation and is key to understanding her process of self-formation. As I have argued, in Dominica it has the purpose of articulating her detachment from the colonial class. In Britain, however, Anna's affiliation is reframed as an outsider status that is based as much on the disavowal of her connections with her ancestry as it is on her attempt to ground her selfhood in a certain idea of home. Anna's journey, therefore, activates in important ways the radical valences of her identity, which emerges as a result of the collision of the colonial and metropolitan spaces between which her subjectivity oscillates. This is what I earlier referred to as the first, internal kind of pressure she must withstand. Since there is "no common ground . . . between Western Europe and the West Indies" in the novel,[58] no cohesive (i.e., hybrid) cosmopolitan worldview can reconcile her affiliative impulses to identify herself as a Caribbean with the system of colonial filiative relations that she seeks to repudiate. It is in Britain, furthermore, that Anna's identity-shaping choices become the foundation of her resistance to the illusory dialogue that governs several of her personal and sexual relationships. We turn now to the second, external pressure that she endures, which threatens her to deprive her of the possibility to express her subjectivity dissensually.

White Doubling and the Spectacle of Womanhood

If Anna struggles to perform her dissensual cosmopolitanism by trying to establish affiliative bonds, she is also exposed to another kind of pressure that results from the way her whiteness is decoded in England. This causes her to become, apart from irreconcilably divided, doubled in the eyes of others. The racial complexities of the novel have been discussed at length by critics, particularly in relation to Anna's affinities with the West Indies' black population that I have just considered. While historically and racially incongruent, this self-identification has nonetheless a resisting thrust. Peter Kalliney, for instance, has argued that Anna's "fantasizing about being black" highlights "the forms of sexual oppression and violence to which women are subjected."[59] This is clear in a scene that takes place moments after she and Walter have sex for the first time. In yet another highly reflective passage, Anna reminisces about Maillotte Boyd, the "mulatto, house servant" whose name she once saw on a "slave-list" in the family's home (52–53), a memory that enmeshes the sexual exploitation of her migrating body with her family's complicity in the history of slavery.

The resisting force of moments like this, however, is negated throughout the novel as Anna's West Indian identity is systematically erased by her recognition as a white woman and, according to the colonial codes regulating race and kinship, therefore English. This is of particular importance given that her sense of self progressively becomes consumed by the commodification of her body as both a chorus girl and a kept woman. In identifying her as white and English, the people with whom she interacts betray a variation of what Michael Hardt and Antonio Negri call the "negative dialectic of recognition" that subtends imperial ideology, which establishes that "the colonizer does produce the colonized as negation, but, through a dialectical twist, that negative colonized identity is negated in turn to found the positive colonizer Self."[60] Anna can certainly not be considered a colonized subject. Yet the way her identity is decoded by the colonizing mentality permeating Britain situates her in a parallel position to the colonized vis-à-vis the metropolitan class. Thus, if this dialectic of recognition establishes that the colonizer's self is constructed as a response to his fashioning of the colonized as a negative ontology, with Anna we witness a further twist.

Anna undergoes a twofold negation given that her subjectivity is regulated by both stages of this dialectical operation. Whereas her affiliative efforts to identify herself with the colonized are negated both in the Caribbean and England, her identity is disciplined in England on the basis of her skin color, making her stand as a double. Her recognition as a white English woman is never an acknowledgment of Anna as a sovereign subject in her own right but only the result of a process of imposed assimilation that threatens to close the rift opened by her migrant presence in London. This literally superficial understanding of Anna causes her to embody a perverse version of what Ross Chambers has called "the unexamined," that is, the unchallengeable, blank status of the white race against which all other racial categories are measured up.[61] In Anna's case, this manifests particularly as a reversal of Chambers's critique of whiteness because it effects the erasure of her difference, recognizing her as part of the dominant racial and colonial caste that she relinquishes. To put it differently, her dissenting position is preemptively neutralized by the illusory dialogue in which she is forced to engage with several British individuals, as I will show in a moment. This determines beforehand that she is an "equal" among her interlocutors and, therefore, that she simply cannot harbor the anticolonial (and thus anti-British) sentiments that motivate her cosmopolitanism.

Anna is extremely aware of the pressures of her misrecognition. This is clear in the myriad passages in which she remarks on her image as reflected in surfaces like mirrors, shop windows, and, most importantly, the eyes of others. These moments become more dramatic as the plot advances, reinforcing the anxiety produced by the conflict between her filiative and affiliative relationships as well as the assimilative negation of her dissensual identity as a West Indian. An acute observer of her surroundings, Anna records the metropolitan framework of appraisal in which the full expression of her radical cosmopolitan self is occluded. We see this in her frequent use of the comparative formula "as if," which she employs in a variety of contexts, always betraying her distrust of appearances and her resistance against a neat correlation between the look of things and what they really are. Anna provides an account of her own looks, for instance, the moment she "walked up to the looking-glass and . . . stared at myself" after rejecting an initial approach by Walter Jeffries: "It was as if I were looking at somebody else. . . . I felt as if I had gone out of myself, as if I were in a dream" (23). There are also passages in which the narrative reveals the importance of her appearance in the eyes of others, as when she reports how Mrs. Dawes, one of her landladies, "was always like that—placid and speaking softly, but a bit as if she were watching me sideways" (91). Toward the end of the novel, appearances acquire a more somber tone. Anna comments: "Everything was perfectly still, as if it were dead"

(169). At times manifested as a distrust and at times as a way to make sense of the circumstances, these moments reveal how the instability of appearances marks for Anna the terrain for her struggle to fashion a subjectivity of her own.

A great number of Anna's relationships, then, are determined by the illusory dialogue that recodes the color of her skin as undeniably English and, thus, threatens to dissolve the political power of her dissensual cosmopolitanism. This is crucial considering that the success of Anna's migratory experience depends on her ability to commodify her womanhood via the spectacularization of her white body. This is obvious during her time as a chorus girl whose body is purposely placed on stage for audiences to look at it. Yet the spectacularization of her body *as white body* acts in more insidious ways as Anna exploits her sexuality for financial purposes. As a kept woman, she must perform, in the words of her friend Maudie, as "swank" and "ladylike" as possible (45). It is true that, as the narrator reveals very early, the girls in her company call her "the Hottentot," which links her to Saartjie Baartman, the Khoikhoi woman brought to London in 1810 to be exhibited under the name "Hottentot Venus" and later turned into a mythical representation of the African woman in Europe. This connection, however, seems to be motivated by Anna's self-identification as a West Indian rather than by the girls' actual perception of her. As Maudie herself claims, Anna "was born . . . in the West Indies *or somewhere*" (13; emphasis added). Such a remark emphasizes her status as born in one of the imperial territories (a fact that has historically been no deterrent for many, especially white members of the colonial classes, to self-describe as English citizens) over her own identification with the Afro-Caribbeans of Dominica. This is further underscored by the fact that Anna's is not particularly reminiscent of the Hottentot Venus's hypersexualized black body present in the racist European imagination. As she admits, "my collarbones stick out in my first-act dress," which makes her consider using "Venus Carnis," a product for breast augmentation (17).

Her interactions with lovers are also governed by this detrimental spectacularization of her white body. Walter's insistence on the economic and sexual aspects of their complicated affair reduces Anna's identity to the use he can make of her unexoticized body, which is emphasized by her recurrent remarks about how he "*looked* at me *as if* he was trying to size me up" and "*as if* he didn't believe what I was saying" (21; emphasis added). Walter talks of "your predecessor" (who "was certainly born knowing her way about," i.e., who peddled her sexualized body according to Walter's expectations) as a way of reaffirming Anna's role in the transaction and, therefore, of limiting their interactions to a superficial interpretation of her body and its function as a commodity (51). This is also the case after Anna is traumatically abandoned by Walter, after which she takes on a number of lovers and clients. One of them, an American nicknamed Joe, also insists on the transactional nature of their relationship, emphasizing by omission her whiteness in an equally assimilative identification of her body. At a restaurant with her friend Laurie, Laurie's lover Carl, and Joe, the latter remarks that "I don't like the way English girls dress" after being asked if he is interested in Anna, thus revealing his understanding of her as English (118). Later, Joe admits to Laurie that he likes Anna but prefers a "dark" girl named Renée (124), confirming that he perceives Anna as distinctly white. Furthermore, as they engage afterward in small conversation in a hotel room where Anna begins to feel ill, Joe teases her by saying that he knows where she comes from ("Trinidad, Cuba, Jamaica—why, I've spent years there") and that "I knew your father—a great pal of mine." When Anna realizes that Joe is taunting her and that his knowledge of the Caribbean is insufficient to make him seriously conceive of her as a white *and* West Indian, she settles the argument by saying that she "was born in Manchester." Continuing with his farcical provocations, Joe seems unfazed by her comment, thus reiterating his construction of her whiteness as English (124–25).

While not based on the demand that she exploit her body sexually, relationships with other white women nonetheless replicate this assimilative recognition, forcing Anna to perform her womanhood as explicitly white. Anna's stepmother, Hester, is the person who most clearly pressures her into embodying what Judith Butler has called "the appearance of an abiding substance or gendered self . . . produced by the regulation of attributes along culturally established lines of coherence."[62] If her interactions with Hester intensely fuel Anna's rejection of her filiative relationship with the colonial class, this is so precisely because of Hester's insistence that she act the role assigned to her as a white English woman. In trying to make her disavow her West Indian affiliations, Hester first suggests that Anna might be of mixed-race descent. While thinking about Maillotte Boyd, Anna remembers that "the sins of the fathers Hester said are visited upon the children unto the third and fourth generation" (53). Since her memories of the mulatto girl on the slave list connect her in traumatic ways with Dominica's black West Indians, as we have seen, it is understandable that, initially, Anna does not respond negatively to Hester's provocations. Later, however, Hester resorts to a more aggressive strategy by "insinuat[ing] that my mother was coloured," which Anna roundly denies, indirectly admitting the white English identity she keeps disavowing: "You always did try to make that out. And she wasn't" (65). Ultimately, though, Hester's concern is with Anna's performance as a "proper" (i.e., white) English woman, which she opposes to acting as a black person. Hester says as much in Anna's account of their conversation: "I tried to teach you to talk like a lady and behave like a lady and not like a nigger and of course you couldn't do it. Impossible to get you away from the servants" (65). This reveals Hester's awareness of the dissensual character of Anna's early identity performance as she delinks her English ancestry from the cultural and social behaviors that are, to Hester's racist mind, inherently white.

The other woman who assimilates Anna by means of her misrecognition as a white individual is Ethel Matthews, with whom Anna moves in to work as a manicurist at her massage business after her chances to live as a kept woman become slimmer and slimmer. This is a difficult relationship from the beginning. While Ethel seems to have no friends, causing her to be jealous of Anna's busy but slowly declining social life, she constantly reiterates that hers is a moral business, clearly insinuating her disapproving suspicion that Anna is a prostitute. Yet for all their differences, Ethel desperately hangs onto Anna's friendship. If their relationship is punctuated with constant arguments about Anna's poor manicuring skills, her weak commitment to their enterprise, and her nights out with men, it is also determined by Ethel's desperate identification of Anna as a fellow English woman. After they watch a movie in the cinema theater the day they first meet, Ethel (whose "eyes were cleverer than the rest of her") reproduces the very indicting gaze that stifles Anna throughout the novel (107). While judgmentally commenting on the film's protagonist, Ethel searches for Anna's validation: "'Did you see that girl? I mean, did you notice the curls she had on at the back? . . . Well' she said, 'that girl who did [the movie] was a foreigner. . . . Couldn't they have got an English girl to do it? It was because she had this soft, dirty way that foreign girls have'" (109). A foreigner herself and assailed by the undermining sense of being constantly observed and misrecognized, Anna does not respond. A few moments later, in defending the propriety of her occupation, Ethel reiterates her sentiment, to which Anna replies with further silence: "Mind you, when I say I'm a masseuse I don't mean like some of these dirty foreigners. Don't you hate foreigners?" (110). Meant to incite in Anna a sense of fellowship with her, Ethel's xenophobic comments clearly denote her assumption that Anna is not a foreigner. The deep prejudice of her words, moreover, dispels the notion that Ethel might consider citizens from the colonies as "domestic"; as far as Ethel is concerned, therefore, Anna is English because she is white.

Cosmopolitan Resilience

It is at the end of the novel that Anna's cosmopolitan resistance to the illusory dialogue that undergirds her relationships in sexual, familial, and social circles reaches its culmination. As her chances to find a lover who provides for her dissipate, Anna seems to understand that becoming a prostitute will be the only way to survive in London. This projects a grim future that, after she is thrown out of Ethel's apartment, is nevertheless put on hold by her unexpected pregnancy. The anxiety produced by her helplessness increases, and Anna's distrust of appearances takes on added significance. Anticipating the social consequences of her pregnancy, Anna employs the trope of the mask (which appears a few other times earlier in the novel)[63] to describe the hypocritical reactions of detractors of her life choices such as Ethel: "They watch you, their faces like masks, set in the eternal grimace of disapproval. I always knew that girl was no good" (164). These masks, further, bear a connection with the masks that Anna sees in the final episode of the novel, which signal the evident damage caused by her efforts to exert her dissensual identity. Immersed in a troubling dream provoked by the complications of the abortion she decides to undergo, Anna revisits a childhood memory of a masquerade that, in a last manifestation of her resistance against the illusory dialogue that threatens to foreclose her dissensual cosmopolitanism, impugns celebratory accounts of the carnivalesque as a productive political performance.

Critics have read this scene as a wistful, final act of identification with the black West Indians of her home island.[64] Yet I want to argue that Anna also seems to reflect on the conflict that her identification provokes in her sense of self. The masks in Anna's dream can be read as a partial replication of the metaphor of white masks on black skins that Frantz Fanon used to describe the psychological strain of the black individual living in a white world, "a direct consequence of the colonial enterprise."[65] The text presents Anna watching a procession *"from between the slats of the jalousies"* of her white family's Dominica home (an architectonic mask of sorts) and, thus, removed from the celebrations (185; emphasis original). In her delirious state, Anna hears her father's indicting voice, angrily remarking on the racial tensions that the masquerade explicitly brings to the surface: *"a pretty useful mask that white one watch it and the slobbering tongue of an idiot will stick out . . . it ought to be stopped somebody said it's not a respectable way to go on"* (184). In Fanonian terms, this could be interpreted as a colonial rebuke directed at the carnivalesque rendition of whiteness by the West Indians. The passage, however, can also be understood as the symbolization of the heavy toll that trading with the spectacularization of her white body has taken on Anna, especially given her impossibility to perform her whiteness as the racial marker of her West Indian affiliation. Anna realizes the impossibility of her position: "*I was looking out of the window and I knew why the masks were laughing*" (186). Arguably, the West Indians' laughter simultaneously signals a disdain for her father's racism as much as a denial of her cosmopolitan resolve. The dream, then, mixes with Anna's account of her abortion, which she experiences semiconsciously. The dream's conclusion, however, seems to adjudicate on her dissensual self-fashioning aspirations. Anna looks at "*a cold moon looking down on a place where nobody is a place full of stones where nobody is . . . I thought I'm going to fall nothing can save me now but still I clung desperately*" (187). She then admits to Laurie, who has been with her during the procedure: "'I fell,' I said. 'I fell for a hell of a long time then'" (187). If falling is often taken to symbolize a loss or a failure, here it can be understood to epitomize a traumatic emancipation caused by the negation of her sense of self (as a "nobody" who "nothing" can save) by the colonial regime of (self-)representation against which she has been fighting.

Following the dream, then, Anna's radical subjectivity is fully realized, which is illustrated by both the original and the official versions of the novel's ending. As it is well known, Rhys produced an initial ending in which Anna dies as a consequence of her abortion, but her editor rejected it, suggesting that she write a more optimistic one.[66] In its revised, official version, Anna's life is absorbed into a new cycle: "I lay and watched it and thought about starting all over again. And about being new and fresh. And about mornings, and misty days, when anything might happen. And about starting all over again, all over again" (188). While their resolutions could not be more different, the message about Anna's cosmopolitanism remains. The abortion can be read as Anna's symbolic rejection of her filiative links with England, which would be otherwise restored through the birth of a child in all probability fathered by a white man, therefore pointing to a latent resistance that exceeds a consensual conciliation with the colonial order that she seeks to upend.

Whether leading Anna to her own death—and thus ending her journey in the dark—or making her persevere in her precarious state as a divided and doubled individual while preparing to start "all over again," her radical position derives from the willfulness she has shown throughout the novel not to relinquish her dissensual cosmopolitanism. As Sara Ahmed has argued, "To be unwilling to obey the will of the sovereign is to accept the charge of willfulness. An acceptance can be a ruin. The history of disobedience is a history of those who are willing to be ruined by standing against what is instituted as right by law."[67] Both endings mark Anna's acceptance of the charge of willfulness, which becomes the core principle of her strenuous resistance against the illusory dialogue that the negation of her affiliative impulses and her misrecognition as a white English woman force her to confront. As she tells Hester, who warns her that people will not like her in England if she speaks her mind, "I don't care," after which she begins "to repeat the multiplication-table because I was afraid I was going to cry" (71). Her response is, as in the rest of the novel, an effective—though no less painful—impasse that suspends the colonial regulation of her affiliative bonds to the Caribbean.

Anna's willfulness, ultimately, is the main cause of her development into an individual with full political agency. Her determination not to give in to the pressures of her social environment in London reveals that *Voyage in the Dark* is, to borrow Joseph R. Slaughter's term, a "dissensual *Bildungsroman*."[68] Traditionally, a bildungsroman ends in a resolution (usually a lesson learned, a moment of self-realization, a major accomplishment, etc.) that changes the course of the protagonist's life. Anna's abortion and its ramifications in either version of the ending can hardly be deemed constructive along such lines. To consider her formative process a failure, however, would be to force it into a normative understanding of the registers of the bildungsroman, instead of construing it as a modernist intervention of such registers. Anna, I argue, embodies a dissensual form of development that is only visible in the face of the impossibility of her affiliative impulses and her misrecognition as a white member of the colonial class in England. She counterdialogically resists the assaults on her sense of self by either learning from her few allies to "swank" her body or staunchly enduring the hostility of her adversaries. Anna observes, criticizes, corrects, and trades in appearances. More importantly, in the willfulness of her resistance she also generates a new horizon of possibility. In refusing to perform according to the identity that is constantly assigned to her while underscoring the tenacious anticolonial coordinates of her incongruous affiliations, Anna grows in her persistence to become a model for a new subject formation that escapes the imperial order of identification and can, therefore, be called postcolonial.

Modernist Futures

Modernism, especially in its treatment of the history of imperialism and its aftermath, can teach us a valuable lesson about the threat of postpolitics in the contemporary moment. The engagement of novels such as *A Passage to India* and *Voyage in the Dark* with the planetary politics that the postcolonial world inaugurates sheds important light on the power imbalances and forms of dispossession that emerged during the process of decolonization and, on many levels, remain operative. In my analysis, I have shown how Forster's and Rhys's novels lay bare the work of dialogue to secure a consensus aimed to quash the political agency constituted by certain cosmopolitan subjects who refuse to align with it. I have explored, additionally, how these two novels point to an alternative political landscape for the development of a relationship between Britain and the former colonies. In response to the threat that a new undemocratic consensus might replace the old imperial order, the minor voices in Forster's and Rhys's novels provide us with examples of an effective resistance that combats cosmopolitanism, the latter understood as "a form of consensual governance transcending the political, conflict and negativity."[69] In rethinking the limitations of a world determined by the ideological and material structures of empire and their attendant codes of representation, they reveal irreconcilable tensions between the colonies and the metropolis. The impasse that Dr. Aziz and Anna Morgan put into effect as they refuse to be participants in their respective depoliticizing relationships with the British, then, is a successful counterdialogic strategy that prevents the prescription of a consensual cosmopolitan politics of the kind Harold Macmillan sought to impose in his "Wind of Change" speech. More than a mere interruption, then, this impasse stops the inegalitarian and deceptive illusory dialogue sustaining the relationships in which they are pressured to participate while, at the same time, also making way for something else to emerge.

In effecting an impasse, Aziz and Anna put in practice their own versions of a radical cosmopolitan politics that gives shape to a new postcolonial horizon. In this sense, these novels suggest that, in some regards, the "post" in postcolonial is indeed the "post" in postpolitics. As I argued at the beginning of this chapter, the term *postcolonial* signals not the end of empire itself but the need for a truly democratic politics that tackles the relations of domination that define both the colonial moment and the new epoch following the process of decolonization. However, in their projections of an emancipatory future, the novels do not offer idealistic solutions. Rather, they reject in very realistic ways the continuation of the consensual regime governing empire, which comes at a high personal cost in the form of the severance of certain intimate personal ties, in one case, and one's very ruination, in the other. The attrition that the protagonists experience is nonetheless necessary and productive, as it gives way to new processes of subjectification that substantiate the postcolonial politics that the novels envisage. Such impasses, then, are not retreats from aggression but important gestures for the legitimation of radical global ontologies that are rooted in the history of imperialism yet evolve into something autonomous from it.

While trying to stall a consensual kind of cosmopolitanism that depoliticizes the efforts of their protagonists, each novel conceives of impasse as a strategy differently. In *A Passage to India*, as we have seen, Aziz's resistance is contingent on the construction of an Indian nation that legitimates his position before his friendship with Fielding (and the international relations that this friendship symbolizes) can be reinstated. The national identity that Aziz seeks to constitute so as to disrupt the consensus perpetuated by the schoolmaster's detached cosmopolitanism is, of course, not exempt from its own problems. One could argue that to embrace nation building as a solution betrays an agreement with a decidedly Western form of economic, legislative, and administrative governance and is, therefore, perhaps too great a political concession. In addition, the continuities between nationalism and the state might motivate conflicts caused by exclusivist claims to the national identity, which are hinted at in Aziz's wishes for a Muslim India and have unfortunately had a central role in the history of India ever since the partition of the subcontinent. While these and other questions may seem to compromise its emancipatory capacities, a dissensual postcolonial politics based on national identity is nevertheless an effective antidote to the operation of illusory dialogue at the global level, as it requires the composition of an international arena that, while not impervious to the development of new exploitative relationships, cannot be governed as an extension of the colonial order.

Voyage in the Dark, on the other hand, presents a much more intimate portrait of this radical cosmopolitanism. Anna's dissensual sense of self, especially in the face of the relentless hostility that she is forced to endure, manifests in the tenacity with which she resists performing an identity that is imposed on her. While racially and historically incongruent, her affiliative impulses operate in Dominica as a rejection of her connections to the obsolete imperial order, a response that becomes reified not only by the useless European social conventions enforced by her stepmother but also by the lack of economic prospects that her family's defunct plantation powerfully exemplifies. After migrating to the metropolis, Anna is pushed to renegotiate her filiative ties with the colonial class from which she descends while her identification with the Afro-Caribbeans is refashioned as a radical response to her misrecognition as a peer by a number of British individuals. As a result, her white female body becomes the site in which a dissensual future erupts, both as it progressively turns into a failed spectacularized commodity that thwarts her chances to aspire to a better life and as it negates, via her traumatic abortion, the continuation of her ancestral links with the colonial class. Yet, in enduring the social pressures that the misrecognition of her white body brings onto her, Anna does not become a sacrificial figure. On the contrary, her resistance reveals the nature of the commitment that her cosmopolitanism demands while unveiling the risks that it entails for the integrity of the postcolonial subjectivity she embodies.

The kind of postcolonial politics to come that both novels promote, to conclude, transforms an initial antagonistic response into an agonistic relationship. In other words, while the resistance of their protagonists takes the shape of a confrontation that rejects the terms of engagement dictated by the imperial order, they nonetheless challenge the colonial dialectic against which they mount their counterdialogic strategies with a negation that requires a new foundation. In the words of Gayatri Chakravorty Spivak, "the name 'post-colonial' [is] specifically useful" as an "impossible 'no' to a structure, which one critiques, yet inhabits intimately."[70] It is this "impossible no," the utopic affirmation of an emancipatory politics, that forces us to rethink our understanding of dialogue as an intrinsic aspect of cosmopolitanism not only in the past but also in the present. Forster's and Rhys's postcolonial modernism, thus, provides us with crucial clues to navigate important global issues of our time, such as migrancy, cultural exchange and negotiation, and neocolonial relations, casting the complexities of a postcolonial politics to come as a model for a positive form of intervention. *A Passage to India* and *Voyage in the Dark* demonstrate the value of the thrust toward the future of certain forms of radical cosmopolitanism. This thrust, as we have seen, is crucial to destabilize and reformulate relationships between the agents involved in the construction of a global politics that, while still influenced by the inequities of imperialism, is susceptible of being recalibrated so that a regulatory consensus is not installed with the purpose of resolving cultural incompatibilities and frictions.

Fictional explorations of the depoliticizing mechanisms of dialogue and consensus are not exclusive of modernism. In the next two chapters, I continue to rethink this question in a number of postmodern novels. Specifically, in the next chapter I offer my first *contra*, an investigation of the setbacks of speaking back to dominant voices with the intention of performing a political act of resistance (in this case, of a historiographic nature) and the repercussions of that act upon others. To do so, I will discuss the politics of historical representation as connected to issues of lineage, silence, and narrative authority in Graham Swift's novel *Waterland*. After that short chapter, I will pursue in the next one the same goal I have done here by revealing the counterdialogic potential of another two novels, Ian McEwan's *The Child in Time* and Jeanette Winterson's

The Passion. In that chapter, however, I will consider questions of democracy, citizenship, and affective attachment as important anchors in the relationship between citizens and figures of governance to investigate how those novels oppose the establishment of another consensual order, neoliberalism, via the deployment of illusory dialogue. The strategy for resistance that they offer is different too; if in this chapter I showed how Forster's and Rhys's fictions resort to an impasse, I will show in chapter 3 how the protagonists of McEwan's and Winterson's novels resort to deflection as a way to neutralize the dispossessing capacities of the illusory dialogues they confront.

CHAPTER TWO

Contra I
A History of Silence

> Silence itself—the thing one declines to say, or is forbidden to name, the discretion that is required between different speakers—is less the absolute limit of discourse, the other side from which it is separated by a strict boundary, than an element that functions alongside the things said, with them and in relation to them within over-all strategies. There is no binary division to be made between what one says and what one does not say; we must try to determine the different ways of not saying such things, how those who can and those who cannot speak of them are distributed, which type of discourse is authorized, or which form of discretion is required in either case.
>
> —Michel Foucault, *The History of Sexuality, Vol. 1: An Introduction*

Our first stop along the way. This chapter offers a first attempt to consider the obverse of the argument I have been making so far. It investigates the dispossessing effects of dialogue when it is aimed at righting a wrong by demonstrating how the discursive articulation of resistance by a silenced minor voice can have harmful consequences for other minor voices. The questions of whether, how, and in what capacity the silenced can speak up are crucial in our historical moment. Yet these are not questions that are easily resolved. As Gayatri Chakravorty Spivak has famously showed,[1] at the center of this issue is the fact that the silenced cannot be given a voice or simply be expected to constitute one freely and autonomously in order to overcome the negation of their speech (if, of course, this is their goal and not an expectation imposed on them). Their silence is, as the passage by Michel Foucault in my epigraph suggests, embedded instead in a complicated entanglement of agential relations, social dynamics, and disciplinary pressures. The same goes for the silenced voices of history.

As much theoretical writing from and about the postmodern period has shown, history is not the past but a reconstruction of events that we can only access via their representation—that is, the ways we choose to narrate them.[2] This means, consequently, that the fundamentally textual nature of history makes the latter susceptible to being challenged by alternative narratives. The work of Jean-François Lyotard has been indispensable to understanding this question. For Lyotard, postmodernism is characterized by an "incredulity" toward what he calls "metanarratives" or "grand narratives": narratives that legitimize the acceptance of particular principles as normal and normative.[3] In the face of this incredulity, Lyotard invokes what he calls "small narratives," which he describes as "quintessential form[s] of imaginative invention" that, while defying its totalizing nature, render "the principle of consensus . . . inadequate."[4] Following Lyotard's model of epistemological contestation, a narrative approach to history is politically productive insofar as it exposes the construction of dominant (or grand) narratives that purport to tell "the whole story." This approach can prompt important questions about the principles that determine what is worth being chronicled (and therefore remembered) and what is not, whose voices take part in the making of history and whose are silenced, or what representational modes are appropriate to do so. In short, it can shed crucial light onto the ways consensus is built to regulate how we know the past as well as to shape the political horizon of our present. Putting these questions at the center of its argument, this chapter deals with the ways in which a "small narrative" addresses certain silences in the historical record.

The constitution of "small" historical accounts is vital to challenge consensual narratives of the past (usually referred to as the emphatically capitalized "History"). The operation of emancipatory interventions of this kind is rooted, to follow Ernesto Laclau, in the fact that they are always both "constitutive" and "contingent."[5] To rephrase this in a vocabulary of dialogic dissent, this means that the formation of a minor voice hinges on the prior identification of a consensual grand narrative to and against which to speak. Yet crucial corollaries result from the generation of such moments of emancipation. While a minor voice proposes to mend or substitute a narrative with another, the legitimization to do so is, too, the legitimization to impose a new hegemonic consensus. Because of the contingency of their status, voices that were minor in the face of a dominant narrative might in time become dominant with respect to others, whose historical presence is now determined by the new corrective narrative. Graham Swift's 1983 *Waterland*, a quintessential postmodern novel concerned with challenging the official history of a small town in the English region of East Anglia, offers an illustrative exploration of this issue, probing the role of narrative agency in the transformation of what once was a dissensual narrative into a consensual one. This is why I will tackle *Waterland* here not for its capacity to respond to the grand narrative against which its narrator composes his story—as a great deal of critics have done—but for the shortfalls it reveals when he does so.

In Response to History: Graham Swift's *Waterland*

Waterland is a novel with a double purpose. The moment it sets off, its protagonist and narrator makes it clear that he intends to produce a story in order to come to terms with his past. Tom Crick, a London-based history teacher and native of the rural, marshy Fens, is prompted by an incident involving his wife, Mary, to recount a series of events from his youth. At the center of the account are teenaged Mary's botched abortion, Crick's troubled relationship with his half brother, Dick, and the strange death of a local boy, Freddie Parr. As he begins to tell of his recollections, however, Crick also strives to restore the silenced historical relevance of his paternal ancestors, who have lived for centuries under the heel of his mother's side of the family, the capitalist Atkinsons. After an early chapter aptly titled "About the End of History," the first of many moments in which he challenges the immutability of history, Crick proceeds to lay out his alternative chronicle of the Fens: "And the Cricks come to work for Atkinson. . . . It was Atkinson who put Francis Crick in charge of the new steam-pump on Stott's Drain. . . . Yet why, you may ask, did the Cricks rise no further?"[6]

The enmeshing of these two narrative modes causes Tom Crick's autobiographical aspirations to become contiguous with larger concerns about history and storytelling, rendering *Waterland* a prime example of Linda Hutcheon's landmark notion of "historiographic metafiction."[7] Hutcheon, who includes a reflection on Swift's novel in *The Politics of Postmodernism*,[8] sheds important light on how this postmodern literary subgenre "foregrounds and thus contests the conventionality and unacknowledged ideology" of what she calls "the seamless quality of the history/fiction" that is "implied by realist narrative," while exposing the ways in which "representation legitimizes and privileges certain kinds of knowledge."[9] Consequently, historiographic metafiction requires us to consider narrative representation, historical or fictional, "as a mode of knowledge and explanation, as unavoidably ideological, as a localizable code."[10] This emphasis on representation, then, makes works like *Waterland* extremely productive novels, first because they highlight the capacity of fiction writing to reveal the processes by which historical narratives are made, and second because they open up a space to reflect on the political implications underlying the construction of narratives at large.

This means that *Waterland* cannot be exempt from the very critical scrutiny it performs. In fact, the novel motivates an investigation of the ideological and discursive entanglements of its narrator's intervention by placing him in a dialogic relationship with history. Crick's account is a response that addresses an adversary version of past events and seeks to challenge the consensus it establishes. The dialogic nature of this relationship is, furthermore, emphasized by the fact that the narration is grounded in a speech situation involving him and his students, and in particular a boy named Price, who occasionally tests the history teacher.[11] Thus, I want to explore here how, in responding to the official history of the Fens via his conversation with his students, Crick reveals the contradictory and deleterious implications of his account. In what follows, I will address how Crick positions himself as an exclusionary voice in a chronicle that establishes a continuity between, on the one hand, his impulse to question the prevalence of the Atkinsons in order to redeem the Cricks, and on the other, his need to narrate the events surrounding Freddie Parr's death. More concretely, I aim to show the impact of his story on his father, Henry, and his half brother, Dick, who are helplessly subordinated to his narrative power. While emphatically deriding Henry and Dick for being unable to tell their stories, Crick imposes a new account that privileges narrative agency and rules out silence as an alternative way of dealing with the past, thus reproducing the historical order he aims to counter.

Yet, whereas "narrative itself is the representation of power," as Edward Said has suggested,[12] silence is not always the representation of powerlessness. To explore this idea, I will reflect on how one event at the center of the narrative, Dick's suicide, interrupts Crick's retelling of Freddie's death and eventually brings it to a halt. Dick's self-inflicted death, which I read as a silence that the account cannot penetrate, not only articulates a certain "postmodern suspicion of closure."[13] More importantly, it exposes the limitations of Crick's intervention by undermining his prioritization of narrative agency and his authority to speak in the name of others. This dynamic, I will conclude, provides an unambiguous indictment of the narrator's inability to break away from the very philosophy of history that he challenges. *Waterland*, ultimately, offers an important political reflection by complicating the narrative entanglement of individual and collective pasts and uncovering the shortfalls of certain dialogic emancipatory discourses aimed to counteract an injustice on behalf of others.

"The Waters Will Return"

Tom Crick's run-in with history is provoked by his wife's attempt to kidnap a baby during a period of estrangement: "the Here and Now, gripping me by the arm, slapping my face and telling me to take a good look at the mess I was in, informed me that history was no invention but indeed existed—and I had become a part of it" (53). As he mulls over the genealogy of this incident, which has gained the urgency intrinsic to the present, Crick turns to explore Mary's abortion during her teenage years (which causes her to be infertile and later leads her to the pitiful kidnapping), as well as Freddie Parr's death, and Dick and Crick's involvement in it. However, now that his job as a history teacher is about to be terminated as a result of the kidnapping incident, he takes an alternative angle to revisit the past that eliminates the strict boundary separating fact from fable. The narrator "begins by questioning the purpose, truthfulness, and limitations of stories while at the same time making clear that he believes history to be a form of storytelling."[14] From the very beginning, then, the chronicle is replete with circular threads, cycles, repetition, myths, false starts, and inconclusive subplots. Indeed, the novel sets off with a reference to the "fairy tale world" where Tom Crick, his father, and his half brother lived, in a "lock-keeper's cottage, by a river, in the middle of the Fens" (1).

This is not simply an ironic gesture by the narrator to distance himself from the official history, a move otherwise rather frequent in a great deal of postmodern writing. As Daniel Lea puts it, "Swift is a problematic figure amongst post-modernist writers largely because he questions the cynical or detached irony of many of its proponents. Instead, he reminds us that writing and reading are fundamentally ethical pursuits that cannot stand outside history, aloof and indifferent."[15] By undoing the chronological sequence of key events and deliberately undermining the veracity of his own story, Crick can compose a dissensual history of what returns as "the Here and Now" against the linear, historical grand narrative of the Fens. Telling the story in such a fashion allows him to respond to its totalizing power in order to gain full control over the events he narrates: "History is that impossible thing: the attempt to give an account, with incomplete knowledge, of actions themselves undertaken with incomplete knowledge" (94). If history is inconclusive, flawed, and unsatisfactory, the only thing we have left is "yarns," as he constantly refers to his project, equally unsatisfactory tales that force us to relinquish the hope that, in revisiting the past, we will recover a sense of reassuring stability (6). Furthermore, Crick legitimizes his dissenting account by emphasizing his role as teacher-turned-narrator: "But listen, listen. Your history teacher wishes to give you the complete and final version" (7–8). By exhorting his students to listen, Crick can replace history's official narrative with another narrative that I will call *his-story*.[16]

Crick's self-appointment as the new chronicler of the Fens materializes most distinctly the moment the school principal tells him that the episode involving Mary will cost him his job and that the school will minimize the presence of history in its general curriculum out of financial necessity. Crick responds: "Cutting back History? Cutting *History*? If you're going to sack me, then *sack* me, don't dismiss what I stand for. Don't banish my history" (21; emphasis original). Entwined with his protestation against the school's trivialization of such an important subject is Crick's dialogic vindication of his right to challenge history's grand narrative. This challenge seems to be his strongest motivation to spend the last days on the job: "If you're tired of school and lessons, if you want to be out there, in the real world of today, let me tell you" (142). Liberated from professional protocols and the constrictions of the once-protective institution that now repudiates him, Crick takes on this new role to construct a *his-story* that privileges his subjective point of view ("my history") over the facts that he narrates.[17] The storyteller can now stand his ground against any pressure that may censure or undervalue his historiographic enterprise: "You should know how inadequate was that phrase, so cruel in its cursoriness, 'for personal reasons,' that our worthy headmaster, Lewis Scott, used in his morning assembly announcement. And you should know how beside the point, by the time they were applied, were those pressures brought to bear by this same Lewis in the name of a so-called educational rationale. . . . You should know, because it was you who were witness to the fact that old Cricky, your history teacher, had already in one sense, and of his own accord, ceased to teach history" (5). The freedom that Crick acquires through his dismissal is, above all, his legitimization as narrator. "Old Cricky" is now the voice of authority in an alternative *his-story* that his students (and readers) are bound to accept as what really happened, intertwining Freddie's death—to which I will return later—with the presence of the Atkinsons and the Cricks in the Fens.

Exploiting the symbolic potential of the antithetical relationship between land and water, the narrator sets up a chronicle of the Fens that is grounded in the ancestral confrontation between the Cricks and the capitalist Atkinsons, who are "heavily implicated in the linear narrative of progress" that dominates the official history.[18] Crick first offers an extensive lineage of the well-established Atkinsons, to whom he significantly refers as "the land folk," starting with their arrival in the Fens several centuries ago and emphasizing their immediate impact on the landscape: "The keys of the river? [William Atkinson] sees no river; only a series of meres, marshes and floodlands through which perhaps a watery artery is vaguely traceable. . . . 'Drainage'" (68). Under the Atkinsons' exclusive control, the Fens quickly become territorialized and transformed into both the site and product of a multigenerational capitalistic activity: "Because in five or six years' time

[Thomas Atkinson] can sell the same land with the water squeezed out of it, at a tenfold profit" (68).

By tracing the Atkinsons' impact on the land, Crick can orient his efforts toward formulating *his-story* as a dissenting narrative that denounces their drive to tame, contain, and exploit the Fens and its native inhabitants, the Cricks. The more the account reinforces the imperialistic activities of the Atkinsons, the more it operates as an urgent effort to redeem the Cricks: "How many times does the Union Jack flutter above the arched and motto-inscribed entrance to the New Brewery to mark some occasion of patriotic pride? How many times do George and Alfred and Arthur [Atkinson] pause in their boardroom addresses, hands in lapels, to allude to some new instance of imperial prowess?" (93). Literally standing under the sign of the British Empire, the Atkinsons are portrayed as endorsed by and contributing to what is undoubtedly one the most important and lasting historical lineages, Britain's national and imperial narrative. History, the family's business enterprise, and the Fens' geography are merged into a single narrative charted out by landmarks, topographic elements, and buildings bearing the family's name such as the Atkinson Lock, the Atkinson Water Transport Company, and the Atkinson Brewery.

Crick's rendition of the Atkinson clan, however, reveals how he cannot avoid reproducing the same pervasive representational force that once relegated him and his paternal ancestors to the margins of history. The portrait of the entrepreneurial Atkinsons is complemented with the inclusion of individuals who are ill-equipped to establish or maintain the family's imperialistic grip on the Fens in what seems to be an effort to continue providing the "complete and final version." This is nonetheless quickly undermined by the way he describes those who, like the Cricks, are of little relevance for the grand narrative. The Atkinson women are a case in point. They do make it into the account, but only as peripheral semi-sacred mother figures or the carriers of a strain of insanity that runs through the family. The relevance of the Atkinson mothers, wives, and daughters as well as their material impact on the Fens is simply erased, betraying a blinkered understanding not only of this part of the family's ancestry but also of women's historical invisibility at large. Furthermore, as Katrina Powell has argued, "Swift's representations of [their] bodies" contribute to his "privileging of the (male) act of story-telling as means to control reality."[19] In my view it is primarily Crick who must be taken to task for this. Yet I agree with Powell that the choice to include the women (and how this is done) implies their explicit subjection to Crick's narrative power and reinforces the idea that *his-story* will pervade over the past like the Atkinsons did over the Fens, thus revealing the political pitfalls of the account.

Opposed to the Atkinsons' is the story of the Cricks or, as the narrator suitably refers to them, "the water people," a descriptor that secures the binary structure upon which *his-story* rests (13). This part, however, is not constructed with a parallel, centuries-long lineage of the Cricks, but is mapped out instead by means of a shift in the scope of the narrative. At the end of the Atkinson genealogy is Ernest, Crick's maternal grandfather and the "only Atkinson who is vocally and politically anti-imperialist."[20] Suspected to have caused the fire that destroys the Atkinson Brewery and, with it, the family's empire, Ernest commits suicide months before his son Dick's birth and a few years before the narrator's (216). This marks the point where Crick's larger historical concerns inevitably seep into his own personal experiences. When he refers to the "water people," Crick provides little information about his distant ancestors, whose lives are rather cursorily (yet appropriately) chronicled as those of the men employed by the Atkinsons to keep the Fens drained.

Instead, the account is mainly concerned with Tom, Dick, and Henry Crick and the most important event in their lives as a family, Freddie Parr's mysterious death. Thus, after revisiting their early lives, we find the two teenage boys and Henry waiting for Freddie's inert body to float down the Leem River toward them, as if awkwardly posing for a family portrait. The three are "grouped silently on the concrete towpath," from which one can see "a stone inset bearing the date 1875, and, above the date, in relief, the motif of two crossed ears of corn which, on close inspection, can be seen to be not any old ears of corn but the whiskered ears of barley," the emblem of the Atkinson Brewery (32). Framed by the Atkinsons' towering presence in the Fens, the scene quickly turns from dreary to ominous as the Crick men, speechless witnesses rather than memorable figures, try to find a rational explanation: "We got Freddie Parr out of the water. . . . [W]hen a body floats into a lock kept by a lock-keeper of my father's disposition, it is not an accident but a curse" (30–31). The historical presence of these Cricks, like that of their ancestors, is accessory and devoid of intent, dictated by the watery curse to which the narrator will return several times in an attempt to make sense of it.

If it is a convenient tool to inscribe the Cricks into his chronicle, the language of water is also extremely useful for the narrator to articulate the impact and arrangement of his project, thus linking the historical abandonment of the Cricks to the emancipatory spirit of his narrative. As a critic has noted, water "configures nature's cyclical and devolutionary processes."[21] In identifying his narrative with the Fens' waters, Crick puts historical reparation on a level with the laborious restoration of the "natural" order of things:

> And the Cricks come to work for Atkinson. . . . It was Atkinson who put Francis Crick in charge of the new steam-pump on Stott's Drain. . . . And it was another Atkinson, Thomas's grandson, who, in 1874, after a violent flooding had destroyed lock, sluice and lock-keeper's cottage, rebuilt the lock and named it the New Atkinson. A Crick did not then become lock-keeper—but a Crick would.
>
> Yet why, you may ask, did the Cricks rise no further? . . . Because they did not forget, in their muddy labours, their swampy origins; that, however much you resist them, the waters will return; that the land sinks; silt collects; that something in nature wants to go back. (16–17)

"The waters will return," says Crick, heralding the flood at the novel's end that inundates the marshlands of the Fens, gushing past the Atkinson sluice gates that contain them and, finally, restoring historical justice: "No Napoleon can go carving up the map of Europe without getting his come-uppance. . . . However much you coax it, this way and that, [water] will return, at the slightest opportunity, to its former equilibrium" (72).

In appealing to water's pervasive nature and relentless propensity to return, however, the narrative reveals once again Crick's reproduction of the very principles against which it is meant to work. His appropriation of the indomitable essence of water to characterize the markedly consensual rise of the Cricks and his battle against the colonization of the Fens betrays Crick's teleological understanding of the workings of *his-story* as an equally consensual regime. A gravity-driven element, water inevitably invades the territory and erodes its solidity, turning it into "silt," an element "which shapes and undermines continents; which demolishes as it builds; which is simultaneously accretion and erosion; neither progress nor decay . . . [it] obstructs as it builds; unmakes as it makes" (8–11). Thus, *his-story* is meant to run uncontrollably, filling up the gaps of the past, submerging the land and its inhabitants—Atkinsons and Cricks alike—under a new, totalizing narrative order that discredits its purported dialogic intent.

Silence at the Margins

The blending of Crick's autobiographical attempt to come to terms with the past and his inundation of it with *his-story* has insidious representational consequences for Henry and Dick Crick. His deployment of water to characterize both his family and the workings of his account allows Crick to invest himself with the power of speaking for his father and brother, who are emphatically described as incapacitated—albeit in different ways—by their own silence. In choosing storytelling as a way to challenge the official history of the Fens while appointing himself as the surrogate voice of those whose autobiographies are written for them,[22] Crick implicitly rules out the possibility that his relatives might quietly bear their historical precariousness otherwise. His narrative intervention suggests that by not speaking up, they renounce their historical agency altogether.

Thus, after first positioning himself as the authoritative voice, and then establishing a neat binary to articulate the dispute between the two families, Crick reveals the third and most salient way in which *his-story* replicates the exclusionary historical order that has governed the Fens. The narrator is not only incapable of understanding the silence of his relatives. With the clear mission of flooding the Fens' past with (his) discourse, he must also characterize silence as an aberration of the natural impulse to narrate. Otherwise he would have to admit it as an alternative to his model of historical reparation, which would render his attempt to respond to the official chronicle with a counternarrative completely pointless.

Crick does not hesitate to abuse Henry's shell-shock-induced amnesia about his experiences during World War I, brushing it off as a rebuff to the act of remembering: "Henry Crick forgets. He says: I remember nothing. But that's just a trick of the brain. That's like saying: I don't care to remember, and I don't care" (222). Yet, following a period immediately after the war of only recalling "bizarre anecdotes of those immemorial trenches and mudscapes" (149), Henry is finally capable of facing his traumatic memories of the battlefield with the help of a nurse, Helen Atkinson, his future wife and later mother of Dick and Tom. Helen shows him the very therapeutic power of narrative that Crick will inherit: "So Henry Crick, who is learning about love, learns, also, to tell those stories of old Flanders which he will tell again, more embellished, more refined . . . and which will lead on to other stories, till the pain, save for sporadic twinges in the knee, is almost gone" (225). Storytelling seems to be a way for Crick's father, too, to cope with the past.

Despite this initial breakthrough, another experience becomes the major obstacle for Henry to transform traumatic memories into a historically coherent narrative. Before Henry and Helen meet at the hospital where he is recovering, she becomes pregnant with Dick as a result of "lov[ing] her father, both in the way a daughter should and in the way a daughter shouldn't" (228). Yet Helen knows that this relationship, which Crick qualifies as unnatural with the help of the language of water, is not viable: "when fathers love daughters and daughters love fathers it's like . . . a stream wanting to flow backwards" (228). She then meets Henry, falls in love with him, and decides to leave her father's side to marry him "so that when the child is born it will seem like his child and will be brought up by him and [Helen] as if it were the true child of [their] marriage" (229). Henry, however, is incapable of embracing narrative as a remedy against the historical burden that this situation becomes, for which Crick reproaches him later: "Does the father fill in the gaps (gaps! Chasms!) in the narrative with a tale of his own? How he and Helen Atkinson—? How he and the brewer's daughter—? No. He seems to have lost his storytelling knack. He seems to remember nothing" (325). It is with the bitter resentment provoked by this failure that Crick assumes the historical responsibility of telling the story of Ernest and Helen, Ernest's suicide, and the true identity of Dick's father, of which he has learned after reading a letter that Ernest leaves for Dick.

Dick's place in *his-story*, on the other hand, is much more complex. Dick is a "figure of stoppage, interruption, and obscure visitation."[23] The product of an incestuous relationship between an Atkinson and his own daughter, Dick embodies an inadmissible loop in the logic of ancestry and is therefore an individual difficult to categorize. Aware of the genealogical inconsistency that this provokes, the narrator resorts to a metaphorical solution to inscribe Dick in his account by identifying him with the eel, an animal at home both on the land and swimming the waters of the Fens. The disruptive presence of Dick nonetheless prevails, as Crick relates that "eels are adept at extricating themselves even from the most unlikely predicaments" (193), while emphasizing the disturbing, murky nature of "this snake-like, fish-like, highly edible, not to say phallically suggestive creature" whose "life cycle [is] still obscure" to natural historians (196). Presented at the very opening of the novel as a creature belonging to "the mystery of darkness" (1), the eel symbolizes on one level Dick's sexuality (his extraordinary genitals, which are remarked upon on several occasions, clearly intimidate the narrator) while on another it represents the impossibility for Crick to inscribe him in his land/water binary arrangement.

Yet it is Dick's silence that proves to be the most inconvenient aspect, since Crick cannot simply dismiss it, as he does with Henry's muting amnesia. Crick's portrayal of Dick and his silence can be explained in terms of Giorgio Agamben's characterization of *homo sacer*, a form of human life typified by Roman law that is "included in the juridical order . . . solely in the form of its exclusion (that is, of its capacity to be killed)."[24] This is a paradoxical subjectivity since, as "the person whom anyone could kill with impunity," *homo sacer* "was nevertheless not to be put to death according to ritual practices" (77). An individual at once included and excluded, *homo sacer* is condemned to live a "bare life," a marginal existence subordinated to a political order in which he has no agency (2–6). Additionally, Agamben notes, the status of this depoliticized subject is rooted in the employment of language as the basis for a sovereign order to constitute *homo sacer* as such: "There is politics because man is the living being who, in language, separates and opposes himself to his own bare life and, at the same time, maintains himself in relation to that bare life in an inclusive exclusion" (8). Thus, Dick functions as the exceptional subjectivity in Crick's new sovereign order, *his-story*. Subordinated to his alternative account, Dick is cast as the victim of a historical abandonment caused by the grand narrative and, simultaneously, as a figure whose communicative incompetence poses a threat to Crick's designation of narrative agency as the exclusive vehicle for his project of historical reparation.

Crick describes his brother very early in the novel as significantly unable to tell his own story: "Dick lacks, indeed, certain accomplishments which even the mechanically minded find useful. Dick cannot read or write. He is not even good at putting a spoken sentence together" (37). This incapacity is vital for Crick, who describes himself as "the brainy one" in the family while labeling Dick the "brainless one" (39). Attributing Dick's silence to an innate intellectual disability allows Crick to legitimize his self-assigned responsibility to speak for his half brother too. Yet Dick's silence is punctuated by his own defective and futile attempts to use language in a number of unproductive narrative moments. For, although Crick characterizes him as an individual "not even good at putting a sentence together," Dick does make use of language: "he talks, for solace, to his motor-bike, more than he talks to any living thing" (38). This ineffective linguistic ability might appear to be an anecdote or even an inconsistency in the account, but it in fact reinforces Crick's strategy. That Dick is relegated to speaking only with objects is a clear manifestation of an isolated subjectivity with no means to communicate properly with others. In the narrator's eyes, Dick is technically capable of speaking up, yet his narrative skills are too unsophisticated to respond to the way the Fens and its people have been historically represented. Thus, by unapologetically emphasizing Dick's "natural" incapacity to narrate himself, Crick can frame his own account as an altruistic and valiant effort to counter the historical invisibility of his family. Furthermore, he can present his effort as a moral exercise of solidarity, portraying Dick as the victim of his own inarticulacy, that is, as an individual who would seek to attain historical relevance had he the linguistic means to do so.

While included in the narrative as a victim of both the Atkinsons' historical rule and his own incapacity to narrate properly, Dick is also excluded by the new *his-storical* order that contains him. Dick's silence is not simply the cause of his own historical poverty; Crick also seems to understand it as a withdrawal from speech and, as a result, a potential obstacle to the success of *his-story*. Dick might speak "half in baby-prattle, if he speaks at all," but more important to Crick is the fact that he "never asks questions, doesn't want to know" (242). Dick's indifference to inquiry prompts Crick to counter the threat that his silence might pose to the new, explicitly enunciative historical order. Because, if Crick sees that it is his responsibility "to accept the burden of our need to ask why," his brother's silence is a reminder that one might choose not to shoulder that burden (108).

The narrator, therefore, does everything in his power to maintain Dick's visibility in the narrative while disqualifying him due to his intellectual disability. One instance of this strategy is his description of Dick in mechanical terms: "It could be said that Dick's love of machines, if love it is, springs from the fact that Dick himself is a sort of machine—in so far as a machine is something which has no mind of its own" (32). His dismissal of Dick's lack of discernment is followed by another rendition, one that crucially hints at the narrator's fear of his brother's "*deceptive* air of ineptitude": Dick "can give the impression that he looks down from his lofty and lucid mindlessness, half in contempt and half in pity at a world blinded by its own glut of imagination" (38; emphasis added). The possibility that he might indeed be intellectually capable is constantly undermined by the harshness of his diction, which pervades the entire novel until the end: "A potato-head. Not a hope for the future. A numb-skull with the dull stare of a fish" (242). Unable to either write Dick into the neat category of the "land folk" and dismiss him as a historical adversary or cast him as a member of the helpless "water people," Crick must employ his narrative dexterity to malign his half brother relentlessly so that he can characterize him as an individual to be redeemed in spite of his ungrateful ignorance.

Thus, in order to safeguard the restorative capacity of his project, Crick deploys a preemptive narrative containment of his brother that integrates his double status as included/excluded. If "entities are defined [in *Waterland*] not only by their presence, but also by their absence,"[25] Dick's *his-storical* existence is no exception. In maintaining him in the account's periphery, Crick assigns Dick a presence-in-absence with which to emphasize, and then exploit, a historical abandonment that justifies the chronicle. Yet, this representational arrangement, clearly much more than a mere plot embellishment, becomes upended at the end of the novel. When it reaches the point where Dick commits suicide following Freddie's death, the account collapses upon itself, neutralizing the power of *his-story* to inundate the Fens.

The End of Narrative

From the beginning, Freddie's death is presented as a suspicious event. As the corpse is hauled out of the water, Crick registers a certain complicity among the Cricks:

> And Dad does not see, in his agitation, something to make this scene even more endless and indelible. For under and around the gash on Freddie Parr's temple [that Henry had caused with a hook in fishing him out] is a dark, oval bruise. Or perhaps Dad does see it, which is why he goes on levering Freddie's arms, not wanting more Trouble [*sic*]. And perhaps Dick sees it, which is why he turns away and spits in the lock-pen. Perhaps we all see it; but I am the only one to consider . . . that the bruise on Freddie's right temple, which is a dull yellow at the edges, was not made by the boat-hook. (34)

In the face of this realization, Crick remains silent, but the girl who will become his wife years later cannot. Mary is quick to accept that, by telling Dick that she is pregnant with Freddie's child and not Tom's (even though Tom is the real father), she has incited him to kill Freddie, admitting immediately afterward that "we're to blame too" (35). Despite Mary's willingness to assume her responsibility then and there, Crick refuses to acknowledge his involvement in what emerges as a crime of passion. Later in the novel, Crick expresses his elation in hearing that Freddie's death has been declared accidental some time after the body is found: "That neat phrase — it was official — meant that no one was guilty. If death was accidental then it couldn't have been murder, could it, and if it couldn't have been murder then my brother couldn't have been — And if my brother wasn't, then Mary and I weren't — " (131). In contrast with his father's inability to shield himself from the affair between Helen and her father with a narrative, Crick embraces the official forensic explanation. He corroborates: "Accidental death. So it's all right. All right. Nothing's changed" (131).

This fleeting reassurance is nonetheless inevitably undercut by Crick's inability to finish his sentences — which Swift signals with conspicuous long dashes — as he tries to reconstruct the sequence of events, opening up an important gap in his unwavering determination to give us, decades later, the "complete and final version." This gap is initially pointed out by young Mary, who boldly claims that embracing the official version is a futile attempt to replace reality with self-serving stories aimed to expiate his guilt. While suggesting that they are both directly involved in Freddie's death, Mary criticizes Crick's selective engagement with the event: "It's not all right. Because it wasn't an accident. Everything's changed" (131). Mary's intention to reject the official version, however, remains dormant up until the moment she tries to abduct the baby. As Powell observes, the attempted kidnapping is as much an effort to overcome the trauma provoked by her botched abortion as it is a refusal "to passively tell stories to reclaim the past." The threat that this poses to Crick's narrative, Powell continues, is quickly thwarted as Mary is brushed aside when she is admitted to a mental institution to become yet another silence in the story.[26]

Crick's account, thus, begins to unravel. By uncoupling a sense of closure and a sense of an ending, Swift unveils how Crick finally loses control over the past; he becomes incapable of containing it narratively. In a flashback that brings us to the moment of Dick's suicide after Freddie's death, *his-story* is finally superseded by an event that no narrative can explain, bringing the novel to its end. Fulfilling Crick's prophecy that "the waters will return" to the land once drained by the Atkinsons, "one of the most calamitous floods on record" invades the Fens that restores the "natural" state of things and prefigures the completion of Crick's invasive project of historical reparation (340). The flood, however, acquires ominous significance in light of a previous scene. After reading Ernest's letter to Dick, Crick discloses to his brother that his father is not Henry Crick but Ernest Atkinson, and that Mary is pregnant with Crick's child and not Freddie's (322). The novel then rushes on; the revelation of his true father's identity and the muddled crime of passion that he commits drive Dick to throw himself into the Ouse River headfirst before the rising waters swallow him: "[He] punctures the water, with scarcely a splash. And is gone.... There'll come no answering, no gurgling, rescue-me cry. He's on his way. Obeying instinct" (357). Dick is nowhere to be found. Crick, his father, and a few other men "scan and scour the water.... [They] row back against the current, tie up the Rosa and climb aboard. No wet and shivering Dick (our last, thin hope), who has tricked [them] all and, swimming in a circle, clambered back on deck" (358). The novel finally drifts inconsequentially toward its unresolved end: "Someone best explain," demands one of the men, for which there are no possible words. There is nothing left for Crick to tell: "We trip over empty bottles. Peer from the rails. Ribbons of mist. Obscurity. On the bank in the thickening dusk, in the will-o'-the-wisp dusk, abandoned but vigilant, a motor-cycle" (358). The novel closes.

Dick's suicide, which the narrator cannot help describing as animalistic and irrational, is not a desperate, meaningless act of self-destruction. Dick escapes the guilt of having killed an innocent person. However, his suicide also frees him from the historic flood that, as announced, will regain the Fens land ruled for centuries by the Atkinsons. He no longer embodies the convenient presence-in-absence that Crick has fashioned for him in his narrative, thus proleptically transcending *his-story* by inscribing himself outside of it. Neither speaking up—of which Crick has suggested he is capable—nor deliberately remaining silent about Freddie's death, in taking his own life Dick incarnates an absolute historical absence, which has crucial implications for the dialogic thrust of *his-story*. As it ripples through to the present, Dick's self-inflicted death exposes the incapability for the new representational order to take a full grip on the past. In this sense, the exclusionary motivations of Crick's project, which mirror the imperialistic presence of the Atkinsons in the Fens, surface one more time. As Balachandra Rajan has argued, "Narrative itself . . . can be singled out as the agent of imperialism, with the natural movement of narrative to closure signifying the advance of imperial power to its ordained objectives."[27] In preventing the account from reaching closure, the main reason that Crick constructs his narrative in the first place, Dick then impedes *his-story*'s grasp on the Fens and its past. His disappearance, furthermore, ineluctably spares Crick the difficulty of having to face the fact that his wife was once sexually involved with his half brother, and that the hands of the individual he has saved from historical oblivion were indeed stained with the blood of a Fens boy. These conclusions run undoubtedly against the grain of *his-story*, a reparatory story, and must therefore sink into the waters along with Dick. The latter's suicide, then, provokes the ultimate occlusion of the narrative as much as it provides a safe conduct for its narrator.

In arresting *his-story*, Dick's final move also proves to be a radical event that successfully renders visible Crick's crucial dependence on his half brother as *homo sacer*, a figure with no representational power who legitimizes the new chronicle of the Fens. More importantly, Dick's suicide turns Crick's battle against silence on its head. In stark contrast with Mary's attempt to deal with the past with something other than a story, for which she is locked away, Dick's final move reverts the meaning of the Cricks' silence. Against Tom Crick's need for narrative agency, Dick's death can be read as a silence that bears what Maurice Blanchot once called "the signification of a difference obstinately maintained."[28] His self-erasure redescribes his own silence as an antinarrative gesture instead of the historical abandonment that Crick has so far intended it to be.

The silence of *his-story*'s *homo sacer*, then, is no longer a linguistic deficiency or a refusal to speak up, but the event that neutralizes the representational power that Crick wields to construct his response to the official history of the Fens. To recall Foucault's words in the epigraph above, "Silence . . . is less the absolute limit of discourse, the other side from which it is separated by a strict boundary, than an element that functions alongside the things said, with them and in relation to them within overall strategies."[29] Here Foucault addresses in particular the silence of those who, excluded by authorized discourses, would speak up if they could — the very premise that Crick exploits to legitimize his account. Yet his thematization of silence also sheds light onto the silence of those who do not challenge their own exclusion through the use of language. Seen as the articulation of an absence, Dick's silence points to the "over-all strategy" deployed by Crick to saturate the past with what he now designates to be the new, ultimate authorized discourse. In featuring a narrator who so insistently asks to be listened to, *Waterland* is therefore also signaling its readers to listen to the silences that appear not in spite of, but as alternatives to what he says.

This alternative silence, furthermore, teaches us something about the construction of historical subjectivities as absences. Dick's death intervenes radically in a historico-narrative order that prioritizes one's subjective self-determination as markedly enunciative, yet his silence does not allow us to reach any easy conclusions as regards (his) historical representation. As Spivak has noted, "we cannot put [the question of representation] under the carpet with demands for authentic voices; we have to remind ourselves that, as we do this, we might be compounding the problem even as we are trying to solve it."[30] We only have access to Dick as constructed by Crick. In thinking of Dick's place in the narrative, then, we cannot assume that he breaks free of its grip with the clear objective of preventing its closure. Instead, we are pressed to consider his plunge into the Ouse as an ahistorical event that takes place in the very fault line between speaking up and remaining deliberately (or traumatically) silent. Dick's suicide is not a challenge of his role as a presence-in-absence dictated by Crick that corrects *his-story*, but the categorical negation that it has to be interpreted as such. What we encounter, therefore, is an alternative form of agency that exposes from within the representational arrangement rooted in Crick's privileging of narrative agency.

An Unfinished Business

The disjuncture of closure and ending provoked by Dick's suicide demonstrates that Crick's account cannot be the restorative dialogic narrative equipped to redress his family's historical status in the Fens he intends it to be. As *his-story* becomes indefinitely interrupted, Crick is stripped of any authority to speak for his father and brother, the last Cricks, and becomes incapable of accounting for their silences as something other than absences that he must redeem. Thus, Crick's historiographic project reveals itself to be nothing but the replication of the representational regime to which the Atkinsons have subjected him and his family.

A section significantly titled "About Empire-building" that appears in the last pages elucidates the particular philosophy of history underlying the account. The explanation that Crick offers is extremely suggestive, particularly as it comes near the novel's abrupt end, rendering the account's inconclusiveness even more dramatic. Crick observes: "There's this thing called progress. But it doesn't progress, it doesn't go anywhere. Because as progress progresses the world can slip away. . . . My humble model for progress is the reclamation of land. Which is repeatedly, never-endingly retrieving what is lost. A dogged, vigilant business. A dull yet valuable business. A hard, inglorious business. But you shouldn't go mistaking the reclamation of land for the building of empires" (336). Despite the fact that *his-story* is a direct response to the Atkinson family's domination of the official historical record, Crick chooses to explain his task as an economy of the past, much like the Atkinsons had established their presence in the history of the Fens in terms of an economy of the land. For both Tom Crick and the Atkinsons, history is a "business" that yields gains and generates losses, and Dick's final move demonstrates that, if the loss in the official history against which Crick narrates is the dismissal of the non-entrepreneurial Cricks, the loss in *his-story* is constituted by those who are buried under his exclusionist establishment of narrative agency. In this light, then, it is difficult *not* to mistake the narrative "reclamation of land" for "the building of empires." In imposing the kind of narrative agency that he practices, Crick presents a contradictory historiographic model that hinges on his authority to recount his version of the Fens' past as witness and protagonist while preemptively negating possible contestations to it, especially if they are formulated as silences.

In other words, no dialogue is admitted that questions *his-story* in the same way it has sought to challenge official history. As a result, Crick's legitimacy to speak as a representative of a collective minor voice is denied by the fact that he has sought, no matter how unsuccessfully, to become the dominant voice narrating the Fens. What might be initially read as a political effort takes on clear postpolitical attributes due to its foreclosing of emancipatory responses that might seek to challenge his own. As a failed model of historical reparation, *Waterland* warns us that ostensibly benign attempts to overcome the limitations of grand narratives via the establishment of alternative accounts might in fact replicate the very destructive methods they originally seek to counter. The figure of Tom Crick—witness, protagonist, and narrator—provides us with the opportunity to consider how, in appealing to familial, regional, and even national affiliations that justify their counternarratives, certain individual voices determined to correct dialogically the historical record can slip into dogmatic positions that negate their authority to speak for others, regardless of how ironically they approach their task.

The historiographic gestures of Swift's novel are complex and at times contradictory. *Waterland* is as much about the presence of the Cricks in the historical record as it is about Tom's power to address it. Yet an important lesson on the politics of history writing emerges when we pay close attention to the ways in which he carries out his task. As I have shown, the novel tests the limits of narrative agency and its legitimacy to articulate dissent while posing important questions about the constitutive and contingent nature of resistance. It illustrates how challenging the established historical record can result in the imposition of a new representative order that dictates, against their consent, not only the terms in which other individuals must express their dissent but, more importantly, also the very fact that they must do so. Tom Crick's failure to rectify the history of the Fens evidences how the pervasive nature of certain consensual regimes of representation requires the coordination of collective efforts seeking to dismantle depoliticizing grand narratives in such a way that they do not become prescriptive by claiming the exclusive right to speak up in the name of others. Otherwise, such efforts are bound to articulate, despite themselves, new consensual orders that preclude further critical engagements and encroach upon the political capacities of other minor voices, especially, as the novel shows, when they choose to remain silent.

After considering the failure of the narrator and protagonist of *Waterland* to formulate an equitable corrective response that disputes, dialogically, the prevalence of the Fens' official history, I turn now to two other postmodern novels with a different goal. In the next chapter, I return to the analytical approach that I adopted in chapter 1 in order to explore further the counterdialogic power of certain works of narrative fiction. To do so, I will consider how Ian McEwan's *The Child in Time* and Jeanette Winterson's *The Passion*, which were written in direct response to UK prime minister Margaret Thatcher's neoliberal agenda in the 1980s, can also be read as warning narratives that work against the employment of illusory dialogue to maintain neoliberalism as the dominant form of social and economic organization in the post-2008 moment. I will, therefore, place at the core of my argument questions of citizenship and democracy. Additionally, as I did with the modernist narratives I analyzed in the previous chapter, I will pay special heed to the proleptic orientation of the novels, which denotes both a discursive motivation to anticipate the preemptive operation of illusory dialogue and a historical concern with the imposition of neoliberalism in their future—our present. Ultimately, my discussion of how these fictional reactions to Margaret Thatcher can indicate ways to resist current forms of disciplinary governance will reveal the protean nature of neoliberalism, an unchallengeable doctrine that has relentlessly admitted no alternative ever since its inception.

CHAPTER THREE

Deflection

Neoliberalism and the
Affective Regulation of Citizenship

This first stage of the Cameron project has been like a sorbet between courses, intended to cleanse the electorate's palate of late Thatcherism. Now that the bitter taste is gone, tougher policies on welfare, immigration and public services can be pursued without being dismissed as typical products from the "nasty party."

—Richard Reeves, "This Is David Cameron"

We've lost a great leader, a great Prime Minister and a great Briton. She was a titan in British politics. I believe she saved our country.

—David Cameron, former UK prime minister, on Margaret Thatcher's death

While neoliberal policy was often imposed through fiat and force in the 1970s and 1980s, neoliberalization in the Euro-Atlantic world today is more often enacted through . . . "soft power" drawing on consensus and buy-in, than through violence, dictatorial command, or even overt political platforms. Neoliberalism governs as sophisticated common sense, a reality principle remaking institutions and human beings everywhere it settles, nestles, and gains affirmation.

—Wendy Brown, *Undoing the Demos: Neoliberalism's Stealth Revolution*

For many, to think of postpolitics is first and foremost to think of the work of neoliberalism to dismantle individual and collective political agency in the last few decades. The more common genealogies of the idea of postpolitics certainly point in that direction. Emerging at the tail end of the Cold War—which concluded with the consolidation of capitalism as the world's dominant financial system—and helped by triumphalist narratives about the end of history that celebrate Western democracy as the ultimate form of political organization, the irruption of neoliberalism into all aspects of private and public life is one of the mainstays of the regulatory operation of postpolitics.

Writing about its "totalizing" logic, Fredric Jameson argued in his famous analysis of postmodernism that one of the most important attributes of neoliberalism (or "late capitalism," as he called it) was the installation of the notion of the market at the center of a "cultural logic" that, presented as "a simple, 'natural' fact of life," has come to be "so omnipresent as to be invisible."[1] Indeed, ever since the neoliberal turn in the late 1970s, financial administration has been the primary engine of national and international governance as well as a basic principle at the core of political life. This hegemonic cultural logic, therefore, must be approached as more than a mere form of policy making. Yet I begin with Jameson not because he offers a more insightful critique of the consensual nature of neoliberalism than others. In fact, most critics of neoliberalism center their ideas on this very aspect, be it as a form of "governmentality," as Michel Foucault and Wendy Brown following him have argued; as a market-driven ideology with devastating social implications in Pierre Bourdieu's account; or as a regulatory project aimed at maintaining the elites in power, as David Harvey has contended.[2] My reference to Jameson, instead, is meant to characterize the postpolitical entrenchment of neoliberalism as a specifically postmodern problem.

For the purpose of my argument, my working definition of *neoliberalism* (a famously slippery term) will be the fundamental ideology inaugurated, in the UK, by Conservative prime minister Margaret Thatcher, according to which the management of collective life (i.e., politics in the administrative sense) is determined by the rules of the market; the well-being of the citizenry is considered one more aspect within the purview of private capitalist enterprise; and the state, as directed by its government, will only intervene to safeguard the financial system, agents of capital, and conditions that allow institutions and corporate bodies to engage in profit-making activities. From among the many negative consequences of this regime of governance, I will concentrate here on how illusory dialogue plays a role in weakening the sovereignty of citizens to the point of causing all but no impact on the actual decision-making processes that affect their polities. This manifests in two interrelated ways. On the one hand, the traditional channels for citizen participation in parliamentary politics have become impoverished to such an extent that, to many, it has become ineffective, symbolic, and sometimes even a mere simulacrum.[3] On the other, this has also resulted in the more diffuse but not less dramatic disciplining of citizens' lives by "procedures of governmentality"[4] that determine the increasingly low threshold of what constitutes a dignified life as well as the ever dwindling responsibilities of the state to guarantee and protect the welfare of the social body.

In order to investigate such political disempowerment, I read here two postmodern novels that were written in response to Thatcher's neoliberal government.[5] Yet my objective will not be to show how Thatcher employed illusory dialogue as a tactic to eliminate dissent during her premiership between 1979 and 1990; if anything, Thatcher will be remembered precisely for her hard-line, coercive approach toward governance, from her crude battles against unions to her famous claim that "there is no such thing as society,"[6] the motto that encapsulated her government's crackdown on the welfare state. Instead, I will show how Ian McEwan's *The Child in Time* (1987) and Jeanette Winterson's *The Passion* (1987) offer strategies to resist the use of illusory dialogue in maintaining neoliberalism as the consensual ideology that dictates the operations of the state in the contemporary moment. In particular, I want to explore how those strategies might be useful in the wake of the austerity measures implemented by UK prime minister David Cameron (2010–16) in response to the 2008 global economic downturn, which dealt a severe blow to the already weakened welfare state and the future of the countless citizens depending on it.

In doing so, I seek to build a bridge between Thatcher's and Cameron's governments to demonstrate that the latter is a "humane" version (though only in appearance) of the former. As a commentator has asserted, conservative members of parliament under Cameron were "more Thatcherite in outlook than at any other time in the past," whereas Cameron himself could "be understood as a Thatcherite inasmuch as he [was] a free-marketeer who desire[d] less state intervention in the economy and in the lives of the British citizens."[7] In my readings, then, I show how McEwan's and Winterson's novels offer a proleptic critique that reveals the lineage of contemporary neoliberalism and propose ways to confront its assault on citizens' sovereignty and their right to dissent. As Jacques Derrida would argue in his illuminating *Specters of Marx*, what is known as "the 'end of ideologies' and the end of the great emancipatory discourses," the point "where history is finished, there where a certain determined concept of history comes to an end, precisely there the historicity of history begins, there finally it has the chance of heralding itself—of promising itself."[8] I will, thus, consider them historical novels not because they are invested in reflecting on a former time, as we saw in the previous chapter. In situating their plots in times other than their present (McEwan's is set in a quasi-dystopian future and Winterson's in a creatively reconstructed distant past), both narratives "herald" forms of dissent that escape the historical order consensually foreclosed by neoliberalism. In doing so, ultimately, they productively rehearse Derrida's notion of the "historicity of history" and inaugurate new emancipatory horizons that result from the resistance of their protagonists.

More concretely, my argument will aim to critique the affective dimension of Cameron's government's neoliberal mission. In order to do so, I will begin with an exploration of how a series of events forming what was deceptively named a "Listening Exercise" were organized in cities across England so that the privatization of the English branch of the National Health Service (NHS) could be carried out without having to take into account the multiple arguments that were raised against it. As we will see in a moment, the Listening Exercise was in fact an illusory dialogue designed to evoke in the citizens a false sense of attachment to the government by making them believe that they (and their voices) mattered. This arrangement was critical for the manufacturing of the idea that the government was not acting by its own volition but was, instead, collaborating with the people to "modernize" the NHS in an attempt to make the funding cuts that were already planned tolerable.

After addressing the affective qualities of the Listening Exercise against the backdrop of neoliberalism's history and its contemporary totalizing function, I will explore deflection as a second strategy to mount a successful resistance against illusory dialogue. Deflection is an effective counterdialogic response because it works to deviate the self-inflicted dispossession of a minor voice. So that it is not a mere passive response emanating from in the minor voice's refusal to participate, this deviation must be followed by a redrawing of the terms of engagement and the subsequent generation of a new set of conditions that allow that voice to express dissent freely and autonomously. Thus, in my readings of McEwan's and Winterson's novels, I will show how, after becoming entangled in relationships of love and affection that annul their political capacities, their protagonists succeed in articulating alternative personal connections with politically meaningful outcomes. This strategy might have been helpful to confront the illusory dialogue employed by David Cameron's government to legitimize, arguing that all voices in the conversation had been heard, the privatization of the NHS in England.

"There Is No Such Thing as [Big] Society"

Two years after the 2008 global crisis broke out and in the midst of the ensuing economic downturn, a coalition government was formed between Conservatives and Liberal Democrats after Labour prime minister Gordon Brown was defeated in the national elections. With David Cameron at the helm, the government proposed as one of its first wide-ranging policies an austerity plan to rescue Britain's economy from what has been called "the deepest post–World War II recession."[9] In part, the plan was a long-term extension of the state's initial intervention under Brown's premiership, which involved bailouts and other stimulus measures designed to prevent an absolute meltdown of the financial system. Thanks to the state's assistance, the banks and other institutions recovered relatively quickly after the crash. However, the social spending cuts that accompanied this austerity plan were so severe that the consequences—from the closure of public libraries to the exorbitant increase in university tuition fees, and from the deterioration of the health-care system to the weakening of many types of social protection—were immediately apparent across the country. This allowed the government to undertake the task of privatizing many of the services offered by the welfare state, alleging that there was not sufficient public money to fund them. As soon as he became prime minister, Cameron set out to make of the state a major casualty of the crash and not the safety net that the population needed to overcome the crisis.

The privatization of the welfare state was not simply a response to the recession. If the "Thatcher revolution" took advantage of the 1973–75 global recession, causing what Stuart Hall once called an "organic" crisis[10] that justified the systematic weakening of the state's social security responsibilities and the establishment of neoliberalism as the new economic doctrine, Cameron took his cue from Thatcher to pass a series of "much greater"[11] cuts after the 2008 crisis that hamstrung the welfare state and, consequently, prepared its further privatization. Yet this idea was not new; it had been in the Conservatives' agenda for some time. Most notably, a privatization plan is laid out in the misleadingly titled *Direct Democracy*, a book published in 2005 by a think tank composed, among others, of politicians who were later part of Cameron's government (included in that group was Jeremy Hunt, who would oversee the progressive transfer of the English branch of the NHS to private hands as secretary of state for health following the steps of his predecessor Andrew Lansley).[12] The crisis, however, was the perfect framework to put an austerity program in place and "free" the state from its responsibilities toward the essential needs of the citizens.

At a time when both unemployment and the poverty rate soared at an alarming pace, Cameron's government could not simply impose unilaterally a new privatization policy, as Thatcher's had done. As indicated in the 2010 Conservative Manifesto, which delineated the platform on which Cameron would run for prime minister, the state reforms would only be implemented in concert with the citizens, while the cabinet would be assembled in accordance to a long-due devolution of power "from [a] big government that presumes to know best, to the big Society that trusts in the people for ideas and innovation."[13] Galvanizing voters through the deployment of the notion of an inclusive and cooperative "big Society," the Conservatives not only managed to defeat the Labour Party (even though they required a coalition to be able to form a government) but also transmitted the idea that the new government would be grounded in the principles of democratic transparency and collaboration with the citizenry.

Popular dissatisfaction with the government and the new austerity measures, however, quickly grew. While efforts in other parts of the world, such as the Occupy movement, the Spanish Indignados, and the Greek Kínima Aganaktisménon-Politón, were beginning to organize, this immediate rejection of austerity led to demonstrations in the UK. Perhaps the most important of these demonstrations was the March for the Alternative, which took place on March 26, 2011, and gathered between 250,000 and 500,000 citizens in the streets of London. Organized by the Trades Union Congress, Britain's largest federation of unions, the march's program had two distinct objectives: "First we want to give a national voice to all those affected by the cuts. . . . Second we want to show that people reject the argument that there is no alternative."[14] In seeking to coalesce a dissenting popular voice, the message had a clear historical motivation. The claim that there was indeed an alternative way to face the recession unmistakably pointed to the Thatcherite nature of Cameron's privatizations. "There is no alternative" was first employed by Thatcher in 1980 and quickly became one of her rhetorical trademarks to impose her neoliberal brand of governance. At the same time, the objective of the march was to show that, contrary to the government's claims, the citizens had been ignored in the decision-making process behind the harsh economic measures.

In a climate of social and economic unrest, the confrontation between the government and a large portion of the population was becoming untenable. The cabinet was intent on bringing to fruition the austerity measures, yet more and more citizens grew concerned with the dissolution of the welfare state. How could the government, then, maintain its democratic and transparent image while avoiding the proliferation of collective expressions of dissent such as the March for the Alternative? The first step was to establish a consensus that the austerity measures were inevitable lest the country should nose-dive even deeper into the recession, which the prime minister and many of his secretaries stressed throughout the process. This consensus was underpinned by what critics like Mark Fisher have called "capitalist realism," or the claim that capitalism, in this case in its neoliberal variety, is the only realistic economic system and that any alternative is unrealistic, fantastic, or simply impossible.[15] In what can be considered an unoriginal and perhaps out-of-touch replication of Thatcher's motto, Cameron appealed to such realism on several occasions, making typically Thatcherite statements attenuated by expressions of sympathy and concern such as this: "I wish there was another way. I wish there was an easier way. But I tell you: there is no other responsible way."[16] The march's general message, however, showed that this was a debatable notion. In fact, a number of studies have concluded that austerity and privatization are not effective instruments to achieve economic stabilization.[17] The way to bypass the growing dissent, then, was to incorporate it into a larger, mainstream discourse controlled by the government that would deactivate the citizens' power to exert a collective political pressure.

The privatization of NHS England, formally effected by the eventual passing of the Health and Social Care Act 2012, was carried out precisely this way. One of the main pillars of the welfare state ever since the latter was established following World War II, the NHS has been a landmark in the UK's modern history. This is why denationalizing such an essential and iconic institution by sheer imposition would have had an immense cost for the government, which was already struggling to handle popular discontent. Thus, while putting in place attritional strategies such as underfunding and understaffing it to justify the argument that the dysfunctional system must be reformed, Cameron's cabinet deployed an illusory dialogue that, disguised as an exercise in participative democracy, made a political spectacle of the reliance and trust in the people that the *Conservative Manifesto* so emphatically proclaimed.

The reform was, a government's white paper claimed, aimed at "cutting bureaucracy and improving efficiency" via the "liberation" of its management, which would allow health-care provision to "achieve unprecedented efficiency gains, with savings reinvested in front-line services, [and] to meet the current financial challenge and the future costs of demographic and technological change."[18] Behind this reformative agenda, however, was a privatizing plan with a number of disastrous ramifications. Leaving the performance of medical institutions up to market competition would create a divide between hospitals that did financially better and those that did worse (forcing the latter to prioritize financial survival over patient coverage). This was indeed the case with the Hinchingbrooke Hospital in Cambridgeshire, the very first hospital to be administered by a private company (ironically, the hospital was managed by Ali Parsa, who had previously worked for two of the investment banks linked to the 2008 financial crash, Merrill Lynch and Goldman Sachs).[19] Over time, budget cuts also proved to have a crucial negative impact on access to health care, with growing waiting times encouraging those who could afford to do so to undergo operations at private hospitals.[20] Beyond affecting patients, in addition, a wave of job cuts intended "to rescue the NHS from an acute funding crisis" had immediate consequences for the labor force.[21] The operation, ultimately, proved to be deleterious for the national budget, as it was indeed designed to benefit the private sector. In 2015, for instance, the state paid "£301 billion for infrastructure projects with a capital worth of £54.7 billion" through semi-public partnerships known as "private finance initiatives," thus adding a staggering £246.3 billion to the costs that the state would have incurred had those services been provided publicly.[22]

Thus, in the lead-up to the passing of the 2012 privatization act, the government began a campaign of popular participation that, while pretending to give the citizens a role in the management of state affairs, would soon reveal its disciplinary objectives. On April 27, 2011, Deputy Prime Minister Nick Clegg hosted the first Listening Exercise event in London's Chelsea and Westminster Hospital, at which "patients for the first time [would] have their voice heard in the debate" about the imminent privatization plans. In presenting the initiative, Clegg declared: "We haven't won the argument and that's why we've taken the unusual step—and it is an unusual step for governments—to listen. This is not a gimmick or a PR exercise. . . . We have no right to reform [the NHS] if millions of people who use it aren't confident we're making the right changes."[23] The government wanted to acknowledge the general dissatisfaction with its neoliberal policies and, having had its say, it was now the citizens' turn to respond. To this aim, the NHS Future Forum was created as "an independent advisory panel to drive engagement around the listening exercise, listen to people's concerns, report back on what we heard and offer advice . . . on how the Government's modernisation plans for the NHS might be improved."[24] As a third-party arbiter, the NHS Future Forum was put in place as the institutional body in charge of ensuring that an open dialogue would take place.

Since the very day of its inauguration, however, the Listening Exercise was regarded with a great deal of suspicion. Flanked by a host of reporters, an unnamed patient confronted Clegg's statement at the Chelsea and Westminster Hospital, challenging the terms of the proposed dialogue. Reporters covering the event witnessed how she "was quick off the mark in criticising the people in the room who had been chosen to participate," claiming that "the group was 'not a realistic representation' of the patients in west London, but an 'audience of a certain type.'" This denunciation, thus, questioned the credibility of the Listening Exercise and the government's public image the moment it was introduced, particularly since "it was not made clear how the patients in the room were selected."[25] The anonymous patient's protest, most importantly, proved that the dialogue the government proposed was a pretense, and that the selection of "representative" patients was intended to ensure that no disagreement would emerge from the interaction, a concern that was repeatedly expressed throughout the campaign.

What is more, the episode at the Chelsea and Westminster Hospital was not an isolated event but an iteration of a larger scheme. The legitimacy of the entire exercise was smeared by the lack of transparency with which the locations and times of the more than two hundred events were announced. As one critic of the exercise commented, "Apparently if you ask for [a list of the events planned] you are told to contact NHS Future Forum. But it turns out that NHS Future Forum does not take incoming calls."[26] The obscurity with which the events were managed made it in fact more and more difficult to distinguish the Listening Exercise from the "PR exercise" Clegg claimed it was not. More problematic, however, was the fact that an agenda for the events was established beforehand, as the same critic protested: "You can join the conversation. Except that it isn't a conversation so much as a series of outrageously leading questions." Instead of an open debate, the meetings were focused on what the government considered "four key areas"[27] that pertained to the details of the privatization and not, as many citizens demanded, on whether or not it must be carried out in the first place.

In an attempt to dispel the questionable character of the Listening Exercise, a list with locations and times was published, finally providing some tangibility to the tour.[28] Examining the list closely, though, one could find

A 2012 billboard for 38 Degrees' campaign against the privatization of NHS England. Used by permission of 38 Degrees.

a common denominator: all the events were hosted by centers that were part of the National Council for Voluntary Organisations (NCVO), which regulated the entire UK's voluntary and community sector. The events were, therefore, not open to the public but subordinated to the control of the government. As the arrangement and hosting of the events was reserved to member organizations, the NCVO acted as an exclusive network with which the government could forestall criticism against the reforms by selecting the voices that would be listened to. For example, participation at the North East event held on May 9, 2011, in Newcastle was restricted. According to the registration form, "we are targeting this invitation at leaders within the voluntary sector only and at those organisations that have been involved with this process to date."[29] Attendance was similarly controlled at other events, invitations to which employed almost identical language.[30]

The overall development of the Listening Exercise, thus, confirmed that the episode involving the anonymous patient's protest at the Chelsea and Westminster Hospital was not a mere anecdote. The reality of the maneuver was that, in restricting participation during the Listening Exercise events and scripting the discussions beforehand, disagreement was systematically curtailed. Alternative options to communicate with the government such as email, online questionnaires, and written and phone correspondence were offered. Yet after the Listening Exercise concluded, no records were shown that reflected the kinds of responses transmitted through those channels, or even how many people expressed their disapproval of the privatization plan. The aspect that received the most media attention and governmental promotion was the listening tour itself. Even when many voices were not invited to participate and popular dissent was supplanted by the voices of members of the organizations within the NCVO network, the official version was that people had spoken up, the government had listened, and NHS England would be privatized after considering the feedback it had received. In reality, as a photomontage of then secretary of state for health Andrew Lansley dramatizes, the government had managed to go through the consultation without having to listen.

In light of this episode, the notion of the "Big Society" at the center of the *Conservative Manifesto* (a label that ironically echoes quintessentially neoliberal conglomerates such as Big Oil or Big Pharma) was progressively revealed as nothing but a surrogate designation that represented the forced identification of the citizens with a collection of acquiescing voices in agreement with the government. Citizens' disagreement with the process was never acknowledged, an issue that would be dramatically exposed by the fact that a mere month before they became official, a national poll showed that only 18 percent of citizens supported the reforms, while 34 percent

A 2011 newspaper campaign advertisement by 38 Degrees. Reprinted by permission of 38 Degrees.

did not know how they felt about them, and 48 percent opposed them.[31] The government nevertheless maintained its selective strategy in subsequent discussions. For instance, certain professional organizations in the health sector that were known to disagree with the measures were excluded from the "emergency summit" arranged by Cameron to discuss the bill on February 20, 2012. In the words of Conservative MP Simon Burns, these professionals were not invited to the summit because "what they have said . . . is that they oppose the Bill and think it should be dropped."[32] If the government sought to deter dissenting opinions by limiting the attendance to the Listening Exercise events, now it simply refused to listen to those who openly argued against the reforms. The imposition of the predetermined and unilateral consensus was finally carried out. As Cameron put it, "We're not reforming the NHS because it's easy. Let alone popular. We're doing it because it is right and necessary. In fact, it is more than that. It is unavoidable and it is urgent."[33] On March 27, 2012, the Health and Social Care Act 2012 was passed, officially inaugurating the neoliberalization of health care in England.

The privatization of this vital component of the welfare state presents an important parallel between Thatcher's and Cameron's neoliberal governance. Both took advantage of the political and financial landscape of their time to present plans aimed at the elimination of the state's social responsibilities. Yet, whereas in both cases a neoliberal agenda designed to dismantle the welfare state and entrench social precarity was based on the dispossession of dissenting citizens, the deceivingly democratic appearance of the illusory dialogue that the flaunted Listening Exercise actually was renders Cameron's patently more dangerous. Furthermore, the replacement of society by the absolute, all-encompassing "Big Society," which sociologist Richard Sennett has called a form of "economic colonialism,"[34] co-opted the voices of the population at large, dismantling any resistance against the neoliberal government while legitimizing the allegedly inevitable austerity measures. There was no need to negate the existence of society, as Thatcher had done, if it could be replaced by an official, exclusionary version of it couched in a discourse of inclusivity, trust, and cooperation. The deployment of an illusory dialogue, thus, allowed Cameron to add an affective dimension to his neoliberal agenda, betraying a demagogic approach that furthered his predecessor's original agenda without replicating her inflexible and socially hostile mode of governance.

In what follows, I want to examine how literature offers ways to resist the kind of affective appeal that enabled Cameron's imposition of his neoliberal agenda. To do so, I will explore the idea of deflection in my readings of Ian McEwan's *The Child in Time* and Jeanette Winterson's *The*

Passion. The protagonists of both novels, I will suggest, are forced to negotiate their positions in relationships of friendship and love with interlocutors who, while they might have been intended to incarnate the figure of Margaret Thatcher, employ affection in such a disciplinary way that it may be more precise to identify them as predicting fictionalizations of David Cameron. Thus, my analysis will seek to show how both protagonists are successful in their endeavors so long as they reconfigure counterdialogically the terms of that affection. The result will be a reconstitution of their agency that prevents them from becoming victims of the illusory dialogue into which they are beckoned. I will begin by exploring how deflection enables McEwan's protagonist to fight back and activate what has been called the political "radicality of love."[35]

Diverging Affections in Ian McEwan's *The Child in Time*

There is something uncanny about McEwan's *The Child in Time* (1987). The novel was first published in the heyday of Thatcherism, and yet it is in many regards as current as if it had been written in and about the post-2008 era. Set a few years into the future, it features clear dystopian qualities that warn us against the continuation of Thatcher's reactionary agenda beyond her three terms as prime minister. However, if "from the perspective of the twenty-first century, the dystopian elements of the novel are far less pronounced than they were in 1987," this is so "for the simple and sad reason that some of McEwan's projections have become recognizable aspects."[36] Indeed, a number of those aspects suggest that the novel can in fact be read as more than a proleptic rendition of the baleful consequences resulting from the continuation of Thatcherite policy; they make it possible to interpret it also as a diagnosis of the depoliticizing agenda at the core of Cameron's government.

The novel is accurate in many of its predictions, such as the normalization of precarity as evinced by the "licensed beggars" with whom Stephen Lewis—the protagonist—has a few encounters throughout the novel, an increasing social polarization illustrated by those who live in "modernized Victorian terraced houses which they owned" and those who live in "tower blocks and council estates," and the dismantling of state services (schools, for example, are "up for sale to private investors"), all bolstered up by a redefinition of governmental responsibilities "in simpler, purer terms: to keep order, and to defend the State against its enemies."[37] In my opinion, however, the most important point that speaks to the post-2008 neoliberal landscape is the novel's treatment of the politics of affective attachment and its dialogic role in the destruction of citizens' dissent.

The temporal aspect driving such a proleptic critique manifests explicitly in an exploration of time and memory provoked by the disappearance of the protagonist's daughter at a supermarket, an event that remains unresolved throughout the narrative. After Kate goes missing, Stephen's life is radically changed. The plaguing hope that he might find his daughter one day and the strain that her disappearance puts on his marriage lead him to become increasingly introspective, aimless, and dejected while developing an interest in the nature of time and the capacity of humans to comprehend it. This interest is accompanied by rather experimental passages. Among others, Stephen becomes involved in a transtemporal experience in which he seems to witness a moment in his parents' lives when his mother is pregnant with him. Yet this preoccupation with time as triggered by the loss of his daughter also points to a more essential plot line that reveals important political concerns. I want to argue that, as Kate remains painfully and vividly in Stephen's memory, her spectral presence echoes the vestiges of an absent (perhaps even abducted) democratic system in which the involvement of citizens is all but inconsequential. This, of course, can have deleterious consequences if, defeated, citizens choose to forgo—in a dejected manner symbolized by Stephen's reactive introspection—their role in the participative dimensions of democracy. However, unlike the presence of a phantom limb that has been severed and will never grow back, the novel proposes to reconsider how, by renovating and relocating their affective attachments, citizens like Stephen can revert their political disaffection and reactivate their capacity to participate in the democratic process.

Political Disaffection

Stephen's disaffection takes center stage very early in the novel. While walking in the street two years after his daughter inexplicably disappears, he considers whether he should give money to a homeless girl, lamenting that "the art of bad government was to sever the line between public policy and intimate feeling, the instinct for what was right" (8–9). The negative consequence of his otherwise important critique, of course, is that his frustration is directed toward those most affected by the government's neoliberal policies: "These days he left the matter to chance. If he had small change in his pocket he would give it. If not, he gave nothing" (9). Rather than an entirely inconsiderate attitude toward the precarity of the "licensed beggar," Stephen's vacillation is symptomatic of the anomie created by his having to choose between two options that present unsatisfactory results. On the one hand, he can decide to contribute to alleviate the situation of one person, yet this means playing a part in an economy where charity must fill the gap left by a state that fails to provide a social safety net to those in need. On the other hand, he can choose not to give anything, on the grounds that the state should provide for them, an option that comes with the obvious consequence that the girl will not be helped by small but likely crucial spare change that he and other passersby might be able to give her.[38]

Stephen's apathetic attitude toward "a society largely indifferent to the care of its citizens,"[39] however, is mitigated by an unexpected opportunity to participate in a position in service to the public that allows him to overcome the severe depression caused by Kate's disappearance. Due to his friend and publisher Charles Darke's influence and his reputation as a best-selling children's author, Stephen is invited to join the Parmenter Sub-Committee on Reading and Writing. Inscribed in the Official Commission on Childcare, the subcommittee is part of a governmental initiative "to satisfy the disparate ideals of myriad interest groups—the sugar and fast-food lobbies, the garment, toy, formula-milk and firework manufacturers, the charities, the women's organisations, the Pelican Crossing pressure-group people—who pressed in on all sides" and gives Stephen the opportunity to make an impact on the state's future path in child-care policy making (9–10).[40] As he becomes increasingly pessimistic about the likelihood of finding his daughter, Stephen accepts the invitation and becomes involved in the subcommittee, which is charged to deal with matters such as language acquisition, the teaching of reading and writing, and children's literacy.

This turn in Stephen's life, however, is not rendered through a romantic lens. While it revives his faith in the value of citizen participation in matters of national governance, his involvement in the subcommittee is the result of a rather farcical mistake. The book that gave him status as a renowned author, *Lemonade*, was published after the manuscript was sent to the wrong desk as a children's book. This mistake has nonetheless important repercussions. Stephen's fictional rendition of his own "pleasantly dull" childhood (34) becomes, in its recontextualization as a children's book, a disciplinary account that prepares its young readers for "a mode of political infantilism, a refusal to face a world of contingency, loss, otherness and destruction."[41] As his publisher explains, the commercial success of the novel lies in the fact that "you've spoken directly to children. . . . [Y]ou've given them a first, ghostly intimation of their mortality. Reading you, they get wind of the idea that they are finite as children" (33).

Yet the book has a wider reach. In the mind of the editor, Stephen's book is a reminder that childhood is simply a prelude to the depoliticized nature of one's citizenship and that children must understand as soon as possible that they have no say, now and at any other point in the future, about the ways in which their lives are governed: "You put over to them something shocking and sad about grown-ups, about those who have ceased to be children. Something dried-up, powerless, a boredom, a taking for granted. They understand from you that it's all heading towards them" (33). The several million copies that it sells indicate that, while the neoliberal government operates under the directive that there is no alternative for (adult) citizens to conceive of their political agency, *Lemonade* contributes to spreading the message among Britain's children. It is, thus, Stephen's accidental success as propagandist for the neoliberal state that ironically leads him to become involved in the world of institutional politics, giving him a new sense of purpose. He does not simply join the subcommittee in order to distract himself from the dejection that Kate's disappearance brings into his life. Instead, he seems to realize that, unable to do anything about his traumatic loss, he can still do something for the well-being of Britain's children, motivated by a conviction that disagreement can result in positive political action. In fact, the narration highlights on several occasions how, driven by a "spirit of contrariness," Stephen is a politically conscious character who remains very critical of the government (78).

The Limits of Engaged Citizenship

If his involvement seems to give Stephen an outlet for his political dissatisfaction, it quickly reveals itself to be a futile effort. Mirroring the maneuver behind Cameron's Listening Exercise, the government's consultation with selected members of the public is a stratagem to put in place an illusory dialogue that divests the subcommittee (representing the best interest of the citizens) of its capacity to cause change in the cabinet's line of governance. At the end of the novel we learn that, ignoring the activity of all of the subcommittees, the cabinet has secretly been making decisions about the reforms, revealing the inquiries and debates of the entire Official Commission on Childcare as simple simulacra devoid of any consequence. Although this is only exposed as the narrative reaches its conclusion, Stephen seems to suspect early in the process that this may be the case. Talking to his father about the subcommittee, he "shook his head, but he could think of nothing to say" after his father skeptically comments that "you are wasting your time there. This report has already been written in secret and the whole thing's a load of rubbish anyway. . . . It's to make people believe the report when they read it" (88). This suspicion, furthermore, seeps into the narrative on two separate levels as the novel foreshadows the final revelation of the true purpose of the scheme.

First, the Parmenter Sub-Committee's debates are often presented in long, tedious passages that prompt the reader to be dubious of their significance. Stephen's reaction to the meetings is symptomatic, as he is described daydreaming, "dazed from introspection," during many of the sessions (75). When he is urged to contribute to one of the inconsequential debates, moreover, he is confronted with the passivity of the room. Further discouraged by his own lack of interest, he cannot avoid rambling, expressing half-assembled thoughts:

> "Only cynics," Stephen said glaring round the room, "would dispute the desirability of being whole in the way it has been described, or of realizing whatever potential we have. The issue is surely the means."
>
> He paused, hoping for another thought, then began again, unsure of what it was he was going to say. "I'm not a philosopher, but it seems to me . . . that there are some problems to be considered." (78)

Stephen's void speech is followed by a number of partially coherent ideas about reading and writing connected to vague memories of his daughter. Yet he concludes with a much more focused remark that evinces his conviction about the value of critical dialogue, as he states that, by learning to read and write, children can begin to become politically engaged before they turn into full-fledged, engaged citizens: "the written word can be the very means by which the self and the world connect. . . . The written word is a part of the world into which you wish to dissolve the childlike self. Even though it describes the world, it's not something separate from it" (79). In other words, writing can help children grasp why things are the way they are. In appreciating "the written word," they can begin to understand the principles of representation that can render the world intelligible, thus rejecting the notion that there is no possible way to imagine it otherwise—that is, that there is no alternative. Reading has for Stephen equal political weight: "The young child who can read . . . has power, and through that [the child] acquires confidence" (81). This confidence is the vehicle for the budding citizen's self-reliant critical attitude. For Stephen, thus, engaged, politically minded citizens are those who are helped and encouraged to cultivate a capacity to engage in critical dialogue about the circumstances that define the world around them and who have the confidence to try to change them if they deem that necessary.

McEwan's rendition of the debates, in addition, anticipates most powerfully Stephen's challenge to remain, in his already disaffected state, an engaged and participative citizen. Certain commentators have found fault with McEwan for the apparent poor quality of such passages. As a critic has put it, "as fiction it doesn't work. The style, in describing the commission's proceedings, is formal and fatigued: the political debate is sheer caricature, and while it may be that McEwan is sending up the more arid aspects of committee land and the low level of national political engagement, this does not make for an alluring prose style."[42] Yet the stark contrast between other, more imaginative passages (such as Stephen's time-traveling excursions) and the "formal and fatigued" style with which the subcommittee's activities are related seems to be in fact a meaningful choice at the level of craft. Arguably, this "caricature" is not a creative failure but a conscious and critical portrait of institutionalized debate and governmental proceedings. It throws readers into "committee land," making them witnesses of the often insufferable and unproductive activity of the "experts" that inhabit it. Even when the same commentator, unjustly in my opinion, concludes that "*The Child in Time* has still not solved the question of how far 'politics' can go without irritating the reader," he seems to acknowledge the potential of fiction writing as a political tool.[43] For if McEwan indeed irritates his readers, then he will have been successful at connecting them with the reality of the activities carried out by bodies such as the Parmenter Sub-Committee on Reading and Writing. An explicit rendition of the difficulties for institutional debate to be effective, the account exposes one of the main causes of citizen disaffection and prepares the ground for the reader to consider possible alternatives for political action, which will become more urgent when the work of the entire subcommittee is revealed to be a sham.

Stephen's suspicion about the illusory dialogue at play is also mirrored by the epigraphs preceding each of the novel's nine chapters. All are quotations from *The Authorised Childcare Handbook, HMSO*, the manual that lays out the new guidelines secretly written before the Official Commission on Childcare has had the chance to present its conclusions to the cabinet. As Dominic Head has asserted, these quotations "satirize Thatcherite policies, making explicit the fear that a government concerned with promoting individual self-interest and competition probably *is* in the business of infiltrating private consciousness with ideological propaganda" while offering "an ironic contrast with aspects of the narrative development."[44] As I have been arguing, though, the novel offers additional commentary. Not only are the epigraphs illustrative of the Thatcherite ideology that McEwan projects into the future of Britain as a warning call, but as the story becomes updated in the face of the post-2008 landscape, we can also easily identify in them the contemporary neoliberal state's views against dissent and the political autonomy of citizens.

The epigraph to the second chapter, for instance, sets the tone of the state's views on the importance of obedience and discipline: "Make it clear to him that the clock cannot be argued with and that when it is time to leave for school, for Daddy to go to work, for Mummy to attend to her duties, then these changes are as incontestable as the tides" (27). Apart from its heteronormative understanding of the family unit (with the outdated stereotypical figures of the father as breadwinner and the mother as homemaker), the *Handbook*'s directive for the disciplining of children's lives resembles almost to perfection Foucault's notion of "docile bodies": "discipline produces subjected and practised bodies, 'docile' bodies. Discipline increases the forces of the body (in economic terms of utility) and diminishes these same forces (in political terms of obedience)."[45] Subjected from a very early age to a strict, non-negotiable regime of schedules and obligations, children are to be disciplined so that they fulfill their social functions in the future without questioning the consensus that regulates their lives.

Other epigraphs further lay out crucial aspects of this disciplining agenda. Chapter 5's epigraph states that "childhood is not a natural occurrence" but "an invention, a social construct. . . . Above all, childhood is a privilege" (93). This implies that children are unfit protocitizens unable to provide for themselves and, therefore, must be made to understand their role as "productive" members of society at the earliest stage possible. In this indictment of childhood, we also hear echoes of the neoliberal state's paternalistic attitude toward struggling citizens. In comparing children to "a large minority comprising the weakest members of our society," the *Handbook* clearly blames them for their own precarity and denies them the "privilege" of being assisted by the welfare state.[46]

Another instance is the epigraph in chapter 6, which bears the recommendation that a "systematic use of treats and rewards" will help parents instill in their children a sense of respect for authority based on the fact that "incentives, after all, form the basis of our economic structure" (123). Prioritizing personal gain over, for example, the child's understanding of their duty toward the family ("children are at heart selfish," reads the epigraph for chapter 7), the *Handbook* reminds the reader of neoliberalism's discourse of self-enrichment (155). Following this discourse, neoliberal governments justify ruling out the notion that collective responsibility toward the general well-being of the population begins with citizens' commitment to the common good and ends with the state's mission to guarantee it.

At the same time, the epigraphs create a rich contrast in the novel with important aesthetic ramifications. By opening all its chapters with passages from the *Childcare Handbook*, the novel boldly pits the state's preimposed childhood policy against Stephen's involvement in the Parmenter Sub-Committee. On a more fundamental level, this narrative strategy emphasizes the power of fiction writing to counteract the preemptive work of illusory dialogue. The epigraphs operate as a disciplinary framework that restricts, to echo the speech by Stephen that I discussed a moment ago, the novel's efforts to reimagine the world differently. In particular, they loom on the horizon as a constant threat to Stephen's new motivation to make a difference and his ability to express the dissenting views that inform his "contrarian spirit," instilling in the reader the growing suspicion that the protagonist's commitment might be pointless. The more time Stephen spends at the sluggish subcommittee sessions, the more we learn about the state's intention to curtail any form of critical thinking and political action by citizens, starting, as we have seen, as early as possible in their lives. This connection between the novel's fictional world and the narrative scaffolding that McEwan puts in place, thus, forces one to recognize the disaffection with institutional politics that plagues individuals like Stephen as a very real obstacle for citizens to remain committed to the public cause. The work of the epigraphs, finally, is forcefully underscored in retrospect when Stephen is given at the end a copy of the *Handbook* before the subcommittee is finished with its task, to which I will return in a moment.

The idea that Stephen's political disaffection might be justified after all finds its critical point in a meeting he has with the prime minister, who remains genderless and nameless throughout the novel (thus opening up McEwan's critique of heads of government other than Margaret Thatcher). If it is Stephen's friendship with his publisher, Charles Darke, that gets him involved in the subcommittee, it is also this connection with the entrepreneur (who has decided to pursue a career as a politician)[47] that gives him the opportunity to have a discussion with the premier. This encounter with the prime minister, who, in line with the novel's investment in the disciplining of citizens, is referred to as "the nation's parent," presents Stephen with an opportunity to take to task the cabinet's neoliberal agenda (83). In light of the highly inefficient nature of the subcommittee, the ideal scenario of a face-to-face discussion might be the way for him to express his discontent. The question remains, of course, whether expressing his views will have any impact whatsoever on the prime minister. This predicament will be crucial for Stephen because it will prompt him to consider whether and how he will be able to revert his political disaffection.

A Renewed Politics of Affection

In thinking about Stephen's dilemma, it is important to consider the relationship between his potential meeting with the prime minister and the political ramifications of affection that the novel explores. On the one hand, this opportunity comes at a moment in Stephen's life when, while his original disaffection is gradually substituted by more a socially conscious attitude,[48] he is deeply afflicted by the severance of his most important personal relationships (with the exception of his parents, to whom he remains close). His dogged conviction that Kate is alive somewhere is accompanied by moments in which he is troubled by his disconnection from her, which is rendered all the more painful by the lack of closure to her disappearance. As her birthday approaches, for instance, Stephen impulsively buys an inordinate number of toys, from which a pair of walkie-talkies stands out. The walkie-talkies represent Stephen's wish to restore his bond with her dialogically, yet this wish is immediately thwarted by the very mechanical limitations of the device. While he poignantly begins to sing "Happy Birthday" over to the receiver he has left in another room in his apartment, the transmission breaks when he takes "a dozen paces away." Stephen's disheartening conclusion that "this was a machine to encourage proximity" is symbolically reinforced by the message he finds in a piece of paper that has fallen from the package minutes earlier, which announces that "the maximum range of this device . . . is in accordance with Government legislation" (129). This significant moment clearly connects the importance of affective attachment for Stephen in this difficult moment with his hostility toward a government whose plans are centered on dismantling the bond among citizens under the protection of the state. At the same time, it also anticipates the approach that he will soon take to resolve his political disillusionment, as we will see shortly, given that it emphatically and counterintuitively promotes proximity and not distance.

Kate's disappearance also drives a wedge between Stephen and his wife, Julie. The disintegration of their marital relationship manifests as a detachment: "They had no need of comfort from one another, or advice. Their loss had set them on separate paths" (52). Before Julie decides to move to the countryside, their progressive estrangement is punctuated by fleeting moments in which sexual desire brings them together, offering bodily intimacy as a healing agent to the misery that pulls them apart: "All the coolness between them now seemed an elaborate hoax. . . . [H]ome, he was home, enclosed, safe and therefore able to provide, home where he owned and was owned" (64). While this physical comfort provides temporary respite, Kate's spectral presence nonetheless prevents her parents' relationship to be restored: "The lost child was between them. The daughter they did not have was waiting for them outside. . . . They were losing their voices, they were dismayed. The old, careful politeness was re-establishing itself, and they were helpless before it" (65). Echoing his frustrated attempt to connect with Kate using the walkie-talkies, Stephen's disconnection from Julie is represented dialogically, as their voices wane and their capacity to rekindle their personal bond is undermined, once the moment of intimacy is over, by the distance that conversational formalities create.

On the other hand, the prime minister's own affective urges play a crucial role not only because they are the catalyst for a possible meeting with Stephen but also because they will become the very aspect that Stephen can exploit to resist the neutralization of his dissenting views. The prime minister, who is suggested to have been involved in a sexual or romantic relationship with Darke, seeks to reconnect with Darke through Stephen after Darke quits his post in the cabinet for a life in the countryside. As the prime minister acknowledges in confidence, "I want to communicate with Charles, in a personal way, that is. . . . Leadership is isolation. From the moment I am awoken, until late into the night, I am surrounded by civil servants, advisers, and colleagues. The cultivation and expression of feeling is an irrelevance in my profession and I can speak with none of these people in an intimate way" (187). In a clear allusion to Thatcher's stern public image, the prime minister is shown here as a vulnerable individual with affective needs, whose confession that "recently, I have felt almost desperate" stands in stark contrast with the neoliberal agenda aimed at curtailing citizens' solidarity while promoting an individualistic culture that rewards the pursuit of personal gain, as we saw (187).

The prime minister's and Stephen's want for affection, therefore, becomes the commonality that facilitates this unlikely match. If for the former this can be a conduit to establish personal attachments of the kind forbidden by the responsibilities of governance and that the cabinet's agenda seeks to suppress, this can be for the latter a way to make up for his recent losses, which manifests most dramatically in his mistaking a homeless girl for his daughter, a scene that recalls the opening of the novel and is not exempt of its complexities.[49] Yet the power dynamics that dominate this improvised pairing are quickly exposed. First, the prospective meeting takes place literally as a result of the prime minister's interruption of the work of others. The prime minister is suddenly announced to appear during the aforementioned subcommittee meeting and while Stephen is delivering his speech on the political significance of reading and writing for children to develop into critical and autonomous citizens. After he is summoned apart, a few words with the premier in private make Stephen reconsider his contempt for the politician: "For years, Stephen had dealt only scathing or derisive words, imputed only the most cynical intentions, and had declared on a number of occasions feelings of pure hatred." Motivated by his new investment in personal relations, Stephen recognizes now the individual behind the public official: "But the figure standing before him now, unlit by studio lights, unframed by a television set, was neither institution nor legend.... This was a neat, stooped sixty-five-year-old with a collapsing face and filmy stare, a courteous rather than an authoritative presence, disconcertingly vulnerable" (83). This new perception gives Stephen pause, and he agrees to attend a private lunch meeting to be scheduled for a later date.

However, when he is approached about the meeting, Stephen realizes that his opportunity to relay his discontent to the prime minister might mean consenting to a fruitless interaction devoid of any value. In fact, he soon learns that these kinds of meetings are policed in such a way that participants are prevented from openly expressing their own views. As an assistant secretary explains on the phone, "The following topics ... were not expected to be raised since they were covered quite adequately by the Prime Minister in the House and in various speeches and broadcasts: defence, unemployment, religion, the private conduct of any Cabinet Minister or the date of the next general election." A great deal of issues of political import are banished, yet the proposal is still appealing to him: "Stephen had been preparing his excuse.... But as the limitations to the event proliferated, so, perversely, did his interest grow." In line with his contrarian personality, Stephen accepts what is not yet an official invitation but a preliminary attempt to probe his intentions, since "the Prime Minister does not like to be refused" (132). Invitations are, as the assistant warns, sent only to those who are "likely to accept." After Stephen reassures his interlocutor that he will accept in the event he is sent one, the assistant secretary ends the conversation by furtively announcing that "an invitation may or may not be on its way" (133).

Despite the anticipation built around it, Stephen fails to attend the meeting. On the way to the lunch, he desperately runs out of the official car chauffeuring him to chase after another girl he mistakes for Kate. After that, a second meeting is scheduled, which is presented to him as a favor from the prime minister. However, his interest begins to wane while his suspicion that the meeting will be pointless begins to grow again. At the same time, Stephen is more and more attracted to the idea of reconstructing his bond with his wife, which he pursues through gestures like the "affectionate, undemanding postcard" he sends her to tell her that, "if and when she thought the time was right, she should get in touch" (153). Thus, while his initial reluctance to meet the prime minister was motivated by a personal disinclination, his views on the government are now important enough to make him to decide not to attend. When the second meeting is suggested, Stephen responds in the negative: "Ah well ... that's too bad, I don't want another invitation.... In the first place, I'm busy....

In the second, and nothing personal in this, I resent what the Prime Minister's been doing in this country all these years. It's a mess, a disgrace" (154). Stephen's snub suggests a reactivation of his political convictions, which have been kept dormant by his disaffection with the government and the patent ineffectiveness of the subcommittee meetings. Refusal, though, is not an option, as the assistant secretary makes clear by claiming that "the PM absolutely insists on seeing you," to which Stephen responds in irritated acquiescence that "you know where I live." The scene concludes with a farcical touch on the part of the narrator, as the secretary calls Stephen again soon after: "As it happens, we seem to have lost your address" (154).

While his attempt to refuse the prime minister ultimately fails, an opportunity to destabilize the government arises. Stephen receives a proof copy of the *Childcare Handbook* from a civil servant via Harold Morley, another member in the Parmenter Sub-Committee, which proves that the cabinet has been using the consultation as a smoke screen: "Morley's civil servant believed that the intention was to publish a month or two after the Commission had completed its own report, and to claim that the handbook drew from the Commission's work" (162). Hearing this, Stephen wonders why the cabinet would not "trust the Commission to come up with the kind of book they wanted," to which Morley responds: "They couldn't have it both ways . . . even though they tried. They couldn't leave it to the great and good, experts and celebrities gathered for public consumption, to come up with exactly the right book. The grown-ups know best" (162). Stephen then decides to leak the book to the media, seeking to expose and put an end to the illusory dialogue into which the work of the Official Commission on Childcare has been absorbed.

The Birth of a New Democracy

The revelation of the existence of the *Handbook*, which is first unenthusiastically reported "in a single column on the second page of the only newspaper which did not actively support the Government" and then is "moved to the bottom of the front page [containing] tantalising quotations," provokes no initial reaction from the cabinet. Only when the opposition party realizes it can be used against the government does the scandal gain momentum: "Over the weekend a copy of a photocopy made its way to the Leader of the Opposition, and on Monday the newspaper ran a headline which foretold the storm to come and, underneath, generously cited charges from the Opposition headquarters of 'gross and indecent cynicism' and 'a disgusting charade' and 'this vile betrayal of parents, Parliament and principles'" (179). Stephen's move, however, does not result in a public indictment of the government's actions. While it gains visibility, the issue is immediately co-opted and turned into an electoral weapon for the major political parties to challenge each other, and not, as he had intended it, placed at the center of a crisis in the democratic process.

In light of the harm that the unveiling of the *Handbook* could cause to the cabinet's credibility, an "emergency debate" is finally organized, although it is "delayed by a week" (179). This is simply a maneuver by the government to bring to fruition its plan to impose unilaterally the guidelines for future child-care reform it had already designed. In delaying the debate by a week, the cabinet buys time so as to order "two thousand copies of the offending book to be printed and distributed to newspapers and other involved parties" (180). Initially, the government denies knowing about the *Handbook* "until the week before" its public revelation, maintaining that it was the work of a mid-level government clerk (180). This enables the cabinet to proclaim that—having been the victim of "the irresponsible calumnies of its political opponents"—it is on the right side of the scandal. The government, then, encourages the newspapers and "other involved parties" to read the *Handbook*, which deviates the public's attention from the original plan that it would never listen to the recommendations put forth by the Official Commission on Childcare. As a result, the *Handbook* is casually established as the official policy, which the press rushes in consensual unison to celebrate: "masterful and authoritative," reads one newspaper's assessment, whereas the paper that broke the scandal now declares that "with its honest quest for certainties it encapsulates the spirit of the age" (180). Thus, the government succeeds in neutralizing the crisis by making the contents of the book—and not the fact that it was written beforehand to supersede the work of the committee— the central point. A mere "two days before the emergency debate both The Book and the lie faded from discussion," and when the prime minister finally addresses the issue, it is only to deploy a postpolitical rhetoric that dismisses the charges as "childish nonsense" before calling for "a return to commonsense" (180–81).

This is a clear defeat for Stephen. However, he sees a final opportunity to enact his political agency in his eventual meeting with the prime minister, which takes place in his apartment. In order for it to have an effective outcome, though, Stephen must change his approach. Despite his anger and frustration with the way things turn out, he decides not to challenge his interlocutor and opts to enact a deflection. Adopting a very personal tone, the premier finally confesses having developed a strong romantic attachment to Charles Darke (who is revealed at the end to be the coauthor of the *Handbook* with the prime minister) and the reason behind the politician's insistence that they meet: Stephen must put them in touch with each other. At this point, Stephen realizes that his political commitment must materialize differently:

> To be alone with the head of Government was an opportunity to give voice to an interior monologue which had been running for years, to confront the very person responsible, and question, for example, the instinctive siding in all matters with the strong, the exaltation of self-interest, the selling off of schools, the beggars, and so on, but these seemed secondary to what they had been discussing, little more than faded debating points to which there would no doubt be well-rehearsed responses. (190)

Addressed as a confidant, Stephen decides against demanding an explanation for the precarity pervading the country caused by the neoliberal ideology guiding the government's agenda. Only a few ironic comments, which pass unregistered by the premier, punctuate the interaction; yet these are innocuous rhetorical misdemeanors meant to attain self-satisfying amusement rather than a concrete attempt to disrupt the interaction.

The fact that Stephen decides not to debate the prime minister in any serious way is significant. His self-restraint is an important gesture because it avoids a self-inflicted depoliticization. Were he to choose to address the government's destructive policy making and negligence toward its social responsibilities, Stephen would run the risk of turning this meeting with the prime minister into another illusory dialogue that would yield no tangible political outcome. His new approach, however, must be unlike his prior negative responses. His reaction is not simply a passive rebuff that results in the reaffirmation of his political views. In fact, he agrees to put the prime minister and Darke in contact, only to learn minutes later that Darke has died (an event that could partially be read as McEwan's vengeful plot turn to deprive the premier of the chance to satisfy their affective needs). With this deliberate gesture, Stephen initiates a deflection of the forces that caused his political disaffection.

Stephen's refusal to speak his mind amounts to a form of silence that differs greatly from the detrimental silences I explored in the previous chapter and is liberating for two reasons. First, his dissent is protected from being dismissed as departing from the "return to commonsense" with which the government deflated the *Handbook* crisis. The prime minister simply cannot dismantle Stephen's questions by offering meaningless "well-rehearsed responses" or even by letting him give vent to his frustrations with the intention of appeasing him. His silence, in the words of Jean Baudrillard, "is a silence that *refuses to be spoken for in its name*." Baudrillard identifies this kind of resistance in "the masses," whose indeterminacy and unruliness he considers their most important political asset. Their silence, he argues, does not imply their acceptance of the status quo or their passive agreement but rather an absence of discourse that works as "an absolute weapon." Stephen can be said to retreat, as one more citizen, into the silence of the dissenting masses whose political agency *"can no longer be alienated."*[50] This turns Stephen's nonresponse into what could be called a "covert refusal," a rejection that is nevertheless unreadable to the interlocutor with whom one disagrees and is therefore impossible to be challenged or co-opted. Nevertheless, as I have been arguing all along, by itself this refusal would accomplish no productive resistance that generates a new course for political action. That is why it is necessary for Stephen to take a further step.

The other reason his silence is liberating is because it allows him to redirect his affective needs while investing them with a political charge. Stephen's covert refusal is accompanied by the eventual renovation of the love bond between him and Julia, which opens a new horizon at the end of the novel. This renovation is what prevents his decision not to confront the prime minister from being a mere example of passive resistance. After the meeting, he pays a visit to Darke's wife, Thelma, to help her deal with Darke's body. This is followed by a short interval in which he and Thelma mourn Darke's death that symbolizes Stephen's final disconnection from the world of electoral politics and governance. The narrative, then, is brought to its conclusion as Stephen rushes to find Julia. The resolution that McEwan offers is clear: the political disaffection and frustration experienced by citizens like Stephen can be strategically counterbalanced with the restoration of relationships of attachment, and most notably of love, capable of constructing networks of support, solidarity, and collective unity with which to begin building strong resisting fronts. These relationships can become effective alternative forces against affective ruses that seek to obtain the consent of the citizens by falsely making them feel active and useful in the democratic process, as Cameron did in his reworking of Thatcher's divisive and isolating neoliberal policy.

Stephen, thus, reunites with Julie in her countryside house and helps her give birth to a new child, the product of a sexual encounter during a previous visit. This final reconciliation might be read as a conservative resolution that predicts an individualistic retreat caused by the couple's restored parenthood. However, the child could also be understood to suggest "that unhappy circumstances can be altered, that the world (or at any rate British society) can be redeemed, that loss is real but not necessarily permanent."[51] The birth of the child signals an encouraging prospect for Stephen and Julie's otherwise disheartening world. Furthermore, if Kate's disappearance might be understood as a captive democratic culture that bereft citizens are willing but unable to nurture, as I suggested above, this second child might then personify a new political moment born out of the reinforcement of personal attachments among citizens. A new politics shored up by a renovated system of affective networks is possible, the novel's ending suggests, as Stephen and Julia—immersed in a moment of ecstatic, mutual engrossment where they "could only make noises of triumph and wonder, and say each other's names aloud"—are about to find out if the newborn child is a boy or a girl, "in acknowledgement of *the world they were about to rejoin*, and into which they hoped *to take their love*" (220; emphasis added).

The Child in Time, I have tried to show, suggests that the renewal of a democratic spirit lost to apathy might be attained through the redirection of one's affective impulses. While this may seem to be an escapist strategy at first glance, a productive gesture opens up when we consider carefully its outcome. Stephen's reexamination of the importance of intimacy and love, as evinced by his final reunion with Julie, points to the restoration of mutual acknowledgment and care as basic principles that bind the members of a society together. The birth of their child, additionally, suggests the projection of this mutual responsibility into a collaborative effort to care for those who are in need, starting with the youngest members of that society. Together, then, those two moments symbolize the rehabilitation of the solidarity among citizens who, disaffected with their politicians and representative institutions, might choose to strengthen their communal bonds in order to establish a collective position from which to stand against the kind of inconsequential spectacle epitomized by the child-care consultation and the *Handbook* episode.

I want to turn now to Jeanette Winterson's 1987 *The Passion* to consider a different dimension of the relationship between dialogue and the political implications of affection as framed in the context of the relationship between a prime minister and the citizens. If McEwan explores the political substance of affection in his projection of Thatcher's policy making into the future with a critique of an askew sensitivity suggestive of Cameron's approach to governance, Winterson resorts to a historical parable to imagine Thatcher's legacy in the figure of an inheritor. In probing the novel's reflection of a future Thatcherite governance without Thatcher, I will identify this inheritor as Cameron. The result, as we will see, is a different configuration in both the way illusory dialogue can be deployed to establish a depoliticizing affective relationship and the possibility to resist it. Furthermore, whereas deflection is also at the center of the alternative politics that *The Passion* proposes, it appears as a strategy for one of the protagonists to create the conditions for an effective critical dialogue to emerge between her and her interlocutor, and not, as we saw in McEwan's novel, to find a new interlocutor.

Jeanette Winterson's *The Passion*, or Of "Soldiers and Women"

Set during Napoleon's time, *The Passion* revolves around two characters who recount how, while fleeing the French army after its historic 1812 defeat in Russia, they develop a strained relationship that is determined by their disparate expectations about what they mean affectively for each other. Henri, a French kitchen porter working for Napoleon, passionately falls in love with Villanelle as they escape Russia. His attachment to her, however, is not a spontaneous bond as much as a blinding devotion that prompts him to seek to possess her. Villanelle, on the other hand, is a cross-dressing, bisexual Venetian who is sold to the army to work as *vivandière* and prostitute. The main focus of tension in the novel, thus, lies in the fact that, as a denizen of the city of pleasure and debauchery, Villanelle will not return Henri's affection in the ways he desires. This relationship has been the foundation for scores of critics to explore the novel as a denunciation of Thatcher's intolerance toward nontraditional modalities of gender and sexuality, her (neo)imperialist views, and the neoliberal mentality with which her government obdurately negated the existence of a heterogeneous society composed of multiple identities and political collectives in an increasingly diversified Britain. Yet it is also possible to understand Winterson's critique of the British social and political landscape from a different temporal angle. The novel is infused with allegorical and fantastical elements that undermine in original ways the historical foundations of the narrative, thus providing room for other interpretations. Whereas it is easy to construe it as "an imaginative 'mirror' to the actual world of the Thatcher boom years,"[52] Winterson's style provides sufficient historical and narrative flexibility to read *The Passion* also as what could be called a "post-Thatcherite allegory."

To interpret the allegory precisely, if Napoleon stands in as the representation of Thatcher, which critics have frequently argued, then it is crucial to consider the significance of the emperor's campaign and fall in Russia, the event that brings Henri and Villanelle together and the catalyst for the novel's plot. From this point of view, *The Passion* is not about Thatcher's government but about something else. I want to argue that Henri and Villanelle's story is a fictional conceptualization of the continuation of Thatcher's ideology by an inheritor who reinterprets it, in dialogic terms, as an affectionate relationship instead of one of hostility and subjugation. The narrative, therefore, symbolizes proleptically the ways in which Thatcher's successor, David Cameron (represented by Henri), sought to connect with the body politic (for which Villanelle stands in) in what is ultimately a failed love story. This failure is rooted in Villanelle's resistance to Henri's Napoleonic worldview, which is the result of an infatuation with the ruler that heralds in remarkable ways Cameron's veneration of Thatcher, whom he once described with patriotic deference as "a great Briton" and a "titan in British politics" who "saved our country."[53] The novel, moreover, is not about passion (or *the* passion) per se but rather about whether its protagonists can rise above this apolitical kind of desire. For both of them, passion is an intense feeling that cannot sustain a relationship in any equitable or stable way. The novel's central question, then, is whether they manage to reconcile it with an unrestrictive understanding of love as a "becoming-other."[54] To put it differently, the novel asks us to reflect on the possibility of love as a politically charged relationship in which actors can enact their subjectivities without either betraying their sense of individuality and autonomy to their lover's wishes or forcing them to do the same.

This is an adequate interpretation if we consider the affective inflections of Cameron's philosophy of governance as illustrated by Richard Reeves in his study of "Cameronism" in 2008, three years after he was appointed leader of the Conservative Party and two before he was elected prime minister. According to Reeves, Cameron, a politician "hard to paint as a reactionary" who initially outlined his approach to leadership by disavowing his Thatcherite lineage, styled himself as a "compassionate," "modern," "liberal," and "practical" candidate.[55] He expressed his role as future prime minister, furthermore, in the language of love, imbuing his message with notions of caring and mutual responsibility (which were later central to the 2010 *Conservative Manifesto* that served as platform for his election victory). In presenting his project, he stressed the sincerity of his intentions, as a good suitor would, while proclaiming to have an "essentially optimistic view of human nature" and declaring that the success of his leadership was contingent on the reciprocal relationship between the citizens and the state, who must collaborate for the common good.[56] Despite tactically distancing himself from Thatcherism, it was this affectionate discourse that allowed Cameron to deploy a "humane" version of it by adding a dialogic component.

As I want to show now, mirroring the way Cameron refashioned Thatcherism as a collaborative and sympathetic neoliberal doctrine for the twenty-first century, Henri repudiates his original infatuation with Napoleon but replicates it, in reverse, in the context of his newfound love for Villanelle. For Henri, to love means to surrender oneself, and while this is what he once did for the emperor, he demands her now to do the same. Villanelle, for her part, systematically dodges Henri's advances as they travel across Europe and reach Venice, trying to avoid engaging in the illusory dialogue into which their relationship transforms given that Henri's aspirations offer her no space to express her love on her own terms. Only after Henri realizes the unilateral and selfish nature of this arrangement is Villanelle finally able to engage with him in a truly critical dialogue and explain why she will never be able to become his companion. This complicated negotiation develops formally in the confrontation of voices that gives shape to the novel's fragmented textuality.

Two Voices, One Narrative

The task of narrating in *The Passion* falls on both Henri and Villanelle. As a two-voiced account, however, this is not a simple give-and-take, a harmonious collaboration that constructs a cohesive narrative texture, or even a textual mesh composed of contradiction and rebuttal. Instead, portions of the story are conveyed by the two voices, making how and by whom something is told as important as what is and what is not. Events, people, and the central notion of passion operate as common points of contact in which the tensions between the narrators manifest. These tensions, however, develop differently, unraveling as the novel advances. *The Passion*, thus, presents two initial chapters, each narrated by one of the voices, which recount the protagonists' discordant understanding of passion. In the other two chapters that make up the second half of the book, the implicit interaction of the two voices becomes more explicit, turning the text into a more porous narrative plane on which Villanelle's resistance against Henri's advances materialize while their failed love story slowly approaches its conclusion.

Some critics have described this as a dialogic structure in the Bakhtinian sense. The narrative has in fact been discussed as "a kind of dialogue" that reflects a negotiation between the two voices.[57] This characterization, however, overlooks the novel's implicit hierarchy between speakers, which evinces a fractured narrative that leads, as we will see, to disparate fates for the characters. Henri and Villanelle's story is not co-narrated by the protagonists on the metaphorically neutral ground represented by the novel's pages, but is primarily anchored in Henri's relation. He not only opens the novel as the narrator of the first chapter but is also the dominant voice in the novel's second half, channeling the pervasive Napoleonic ideology by which he is enthralled. Villanelle, on the other hand, acts as the agonistic voice countering the narrative foundation that he establishes. While she narrates the second chapter, her voice only appears in intermittent ways in the last two, either reported in Henri's account or temporarily taking it over. The dialogic intricacies of this uneven co-narration, thus, must be treated in two parts. In my analysis of the first two chapters, to which I turn now, I will concentrate on the notion of passion, the point of contention between Henri and Villanelle. In dealing with the second half, I will focus on Villanelle's resistance and her strategies to stave off Henri's love propositions.

The opening chapter, appropriately titled "Emperor," is an account of Henri's infatuation with Napoleon. Narrated in a realistic mode halfway between the memoir and the confession, Henri speaks of his discovery of a new and overwhelming feeling of passion for the emperor, which has the same pervading effect on him as the imperial army has on the European continent. This colors not only Henri's reflections on how joining the army gives him a sense of purpose but also how the whole country, whose people he describes as "lukewarm" (i.e., lacking passion),[58] are equally enthralled by Napoleon and his plans for global conquest. The ruler, however, responds to this passion with a profound disdain for the people of France, much in the same way as Thatcher would show utter contempt for the people of the United Kingdom.

Thus, the novel opens with Henri's description of his opportunity to be in close quarters with the emperor after he is enlisted to work in his kitchen. This physical proximity is nonetheless meaningless. The situations where he could establish a more personal rapport (e.g., waiting on his dinner table or receiving a passing commentary) are reminders of Napoleon's little concern for his subjects. Henri confesses: "He liked me because I am short. I flatter myself. He did not dislike me" (3). The sentiment Napoleon awakens in him, however, quickly turns paradoxical: "He is repulsive and fascinating by turns" (13). Hinging on these two extremes, Henri's devotion develops into an overpowering and subduing sense of security that fuels the kind of affective despotism deployed by Napoleon to secure both the people's loyalty and their consent to his autocratic ruling. For example, talking about his intentions to invade England, which will result in the 1805 defeat at the Battle of Trafalgar, Henri asserts (replicating the ruler's imperialistic bravura) that "all France will be recruited if necessary," of which he has no doubt because "we are in love with him" (8). This sense of being in love, which has nothing to do with the act of loving someone, anticipates the complicated replacement of Henri's passion for Napoleon with a similar sentiment for Villanelle later in the novel: "It was a romance.... [N]ot a contract between equal parties but an explosion of dreams and desires that can find no outlet in everyday life" (13). This kind of infatuation is for Henri as exhilarating as it is overwhelming.

This bond with Napoleon, further, takes on a quasi-religious tone. The words of the local priest to a young Henri before he joins the army explain this precisely: "he'll call you . . . like God called Samuel and you'll go" (17). The priest's comparison of Napoleon to God is an apt allegory to describe the emperor's interpellation of the French and how he gives them a language to speak about the world. As he confesses after giving a short account of the French Revolution and Napoleon's subsequent seizing of power, "these are my words, taught to me by a clever man who was no respecter of persons" (16). Through this acquired Napoleonic discourse, Henri formulates a new worldview that reaches as far as the expanding French empire: "I knew about Egypt because Bonaparte had been there" (17). Even after Napoleon's failed Russian campaign, his interpellative power remains untouched. As he wonders "what made cold and hungry people so sure that another year could only be better," that is, in interrogating the blind devotion of the French for Napoleon, Henri can only respond with a self-abasing conclusion: "What does it matter? Why do I question what I see to be real?" (43). The Napoleonic worldview and the consensual regime it establishes are, in addition, all there is in life for Henri, even in the hardest moments. He encapsulates this sentiment when he acknowledges the emperor's power over his own individuality: "Even when I hated him, he could still make me cry. And not through fear. He was great. Greatness like his is hard to be sensible about" (30). For Henri, thus, passion is an overwhelming abandonment that annuls his sense of autonomy. Mistaking this for love will provoke his struggle to find love elsewhere: "Sequester my heart," he yearns at the end of the chapter before he meets Villanelle; "Wherever love is, I want to be, I will follow it as surely as the land-locked salmon finds the sea" (44). While Napoleon's presence in his life dwindles to the point that he wants to desert the army, Henri's understanding of love as taught by the emperor remains as ardent and all-consuming.

In the second chapter, "Queen of Spades," Villanelle narrates her version of passion, which works in direct opposition to Henri's. Employing a highly subjective tone and incorporating fantastical elements into her account, Villanelle describes how she seeks passion in the unexpected, the unfixed, and the uncertain. Personifying the notions with which Venice is often identified, Villanelle is driven by instinctive desire and a constant motivation to experience pleasure: "It's somewhere between fear and sex. Passion I suppose" (55). Her hesitation to define it is indicative of her inclination toward conjecture as a way of life. Like Henri's, Villanelle's understanding of passion is governed by an overwhelming force that supersedes the individual. Yet this force is freeing instead of restrictive and subduing. It infuses her life with an aleatory spirit that manifests in her attraction to gambling: "Gambling is not a vice, it is an expression of our humanness. . . . You play, you win, you play, you lose. You play" (73). Foreshadowing how it will eventually collide with Henri's, furthermore, the narrative connects Villanelle's understanding of passion with Napoleon's conquest of Venice: "Ever since Bonaparte captured our city of mazes in 1797, we've more or less abandoned ourselves to pleasure" (52). Passion, therefore, enables her and her fellow Venetians to escape fixity. It is, to employ Gilles Deleuze and Félix Guattari's language, a rhizomatic force that ruptures consensus and, instead of engendering chaos, creates new regimes guided by desire as it "moves and produces" spontaneous connections that continue or cease to be according to no fixed law, as a "hallucinatory perception, synesthesia, perverse mutation, or play of images [that] shakes loose, challenging the hegemony of the signifier."[59] In Villanelle's own words, "For us, who travel along the blood vessels, who come to the cities of the interior by chance, there is no preparation. We who were fluent find life is a foreign language. Somewhere between the swamp and the mountains. Somewhere between fear and sex. Somewhere between God and the Devil passion is and the way there is sudden and the way back is worse" (68). Daunting and inexplicable, this rhizomatic attitude is also present in Villanelle's non-essentialist understanding of her selfhood as she constantly travels between the lines of identity.

As a cross-dressing casino croupier, Villanelle participates in a kind of performative masquerade that allows her to tap into the freeing mores of Venice. This leads her to two very different relationships. First, she relates her intense affair over nine nights with the enigmatic Queen of Spades, a well-to-do woman whose merchant husband is temporarily absent from the city. Having met at the casino, they develop a rather platonic relationship ("I can't make love to you. . . . But I can kiss you") that leaves in suspense the consummation of the short-lived affair and gives it a freeing power (67). As Villanelle notes, "I flirt with waiters and gamblers and remember that I enjoy that. . . . Is this freedom delicious because rare? . . . If she were gone for ever these days of mine would not be lit up. Is it because she will return that I take pleasure in being alone?" (73). One day, however, her lover's husband returns and Villanelle is stricken by the realization that they cannot see each other anymore. Later, Villanelle becomes involved with an abusive gambler who supplies goods for Napoleon and takes pleasure in Villanelle's cross-dressing as a boy. Whereas she once turns down his marriage proposal, she accedes in order to forget how the Queen of

Spades, in the most fantastical turn in the novel, literally possesses her heart (this is not because she has stolen it but because, in a fit of passion, Villanelle has given it to her). Thus, she marries the man in exchange of traveling the world with him, "luxury" and "all kinds of fancy goods, provided I go on dressing as a young man in the comfort of our home" (63). Soon after, though, Villanelle regrets her decision and, as the narration reveals in the next chapter, escapes the unnamed European city they are visiting only to be found back in Venice. After losing a gamble with her husband for her freedom, Villanelle is sold to the French army, where she meets Henri.

Henri's and Villanelle's stories of passion frame their fraught relationship in the second half of the novel as they flee the French army, cross Europe from Russia by foot, and reach Venice. This has an important effect on the interaction of their voices because they become at times difficult to distinguish. Yet, whereas the novel features an "alternation of narrative voices," Henri "acts as first-level narrator and Villanelle as second-level narrator."[60] Henri's reflective passages, which obsessively seek to make sense of his passion for Villanelle after painfully relinquishing his attachment to Napoleon, govern the account; Villanelle's voice, in contrast, appears as an insertion that undercuts, sometimes only implicitly, his attempts at making sense (in the manner of Napoleon, i.e., establishing a consensual representation) of their experiences together, a task that becomes increasingly unfeasible as the novel approaches the end.

The tension between the two voices, then, stems not so much from their concurrence as from the political orientation of what they express. In this sense it is possible to argue, as a critic has done, that the repetition of certain lines echoes "uncannily back and forth between Henri's and Villanelle's narratives."[61] They both employ, for instance, "The cities of the interior do not lie on any map," "You play, you win, you play, you lose. You play," and the iconic "I'm telling you stories. Trust me." On the surface these repetitions may seem to show how Henri and Villanelle employ a common vocabulary as a result of the intimacy that grows between them. This interpretation, however, suggests a balanced exchange in which they acquire each other's phrases and mannerisms that collides with the hierarchical structure of the narrative. Instead, if we consider the subversive qualities of such language, we will realize that these repetitions do not suggest interchange but are a sign of Villanelle's intervention in Henri's narrative regime, demonstrating how he slowly internalizes her way of thinking. Having presented accounts illustrating their understanding of passion, the protagonists then proceed narratively to perform, in the second half of the novel, the discord that exists between them, which comes to a head when

Villanelle's deflections of Henri's propositions eventually cause an emancipatory disruption of his most fundamental beliefs.

A Captivating Passion

The third and fourth chapters of the novel ("The Zero Winter" and "The Rock") are concerned with the transformation of a casual spark of passion between Henri and Villanelle into a dispute about whether they will be able to have a love relationship. This dispute, however, quickly degenerates into an illusory dialogue. As the defeat of the French army during Russia's "zero winter" becomes inevitable, Henri decides to desert, triggered by what he sees in retrospect as the emperor's "lie" that "there was no alternative to this war" (83). This implies a rejection of Napoleon's imperial ideology, a gesture that, in recontextualizing the reference to Thatcher's infamous "there is no alternative" dictum, mirrors Cameron's initial repudiation of Thatcher's legacy. Yet, while this is the moment he "started to hate him" (84), Henri does not abandon the ideological precepts taught to him by the emperor. Instead, just as Cameron would adapt the Thatcherite creed in trying to romance the electorate while executing his austerity plan, Henri incorporates them into his effort to woo Villanelle, who decides to leave Russia with him. After they have an erratic sexual relationship that begins during their long journey to Venice, Henri is captivated by Villanelle yet is incapable of loving her without reproducing the principles of defeat and submission defining the love that the French felt for Napoleon.

Villanelle exerts a freeing influence on Henri. The first time they meet, as they discuss whether the Russians have fled or are hiding in the snow, Villanelle says something that strikes him. Snowflakes, she remarks musingly, are "all different. . . . Think of that" (87–88). This sensitive appreciation for the singularity of something as apparently mundane as a snowflake has an instant impact on him: "I did think of that and I fell in love with her" (88). Her genuinely independent outlook complements his new urge to repudiate Napoleon, which he expresses in terms of human fallibility: "I don't want to worship him any more. I want to make my own mistakes" (86). Yet, in replacing Napoleon with Villanelle as his new object of devotion, Henri cannot escape the imperial logic whereby, to become a fully empowered individual, one must make others respond to one's interpellation and subordinate themselves to one's will. Thus, he systematically tries to make Villanelle occupy a subject position that falls within the categories stipulated by the Napoleonic ideology. As he puts it early in the novel, "soldiers and women. That's how the world is. Any other role is temporary. Any other role is a gesture" (45). His views on love, similarly, are modeled after the emperor's military doctrine. The third chapter, for instance, opens with Henri's reflection on Napoleon's imperial ethos: "There's no such thing as a limited victory. Every victory leaves another resentment, another defeated and humiliated people. . . . No one's on your side when you're the conqueror" (79). Not only is victory the only option for the Napoleonic subject, but it must also be total and unconditional. Implicitly equating the object of love with the enemy, then, Henri sets out to conquer Villanelle's heart, a victory that can only be sealed by her eventual surrender.

From the very beginning, Villanelle staunchly resists Henri's propositions. Her self-governing individuality collides directly with the category of "woman" in the "soldiers and women" paradigm. While she is willing to cultivate a relationship based on a mutual affection, her resistance destabilizes Henri's worldview and provokes a rupture that inaugurates the critical dialogue they can finally have to discuss their bond. This critical dialogue, ultimately, will facilitate the emergence of an alternative relationship between them—a new form of love. We can think of Villanelle's resistance as developing along three lines: her identification with the geography of Venice; the subversive nature of her aberrant body; and finally, and more importantly, her deflective response to Henri's love.

The opening of Villanelle's account about her passion in the second chapter is a description of Venice's geography that anticipates the unfixed nature of her individuality: "There is a city surrounded by water with watery alleys that do for streets and roads and silted up back ways that only the rats can cross" (49). Venice's waters signify the destabilization of the spatiality of the polity under Napoleon's colonial siege. Venice is, furthermore, a space that no map can contain: "This the city of mazes. You may set off from the same place to the same place every day and never go by the same route. If you do so, it will be by mistake. Your bloodhound nose will not serve you here. Your course in compass reading will fail you. . . . Although wherever you are going is always in front of you, there is no such thing as straight ahead" (49). For the Venetian, ignorance about one's whereabouts is never a sign of weakness but a reassurance of the futility of trying to find sense in the layout of the city: "Canals hide other canals, alley-ways cross and criss-cross so that you will not know which is which until you have lived here all your life. Even when you have mastered the squares . . . there will still be places you can never find and if you do find them you may never see St Mark's again" (113). Villanelle, thus, identifies herself with Venice by connecting the city's deterritorializing forces that push against the static order of Napoleon's imperial rule to the unpredictability and fluctuation that define her singularity.

Thus, once Henri and Villanelle reach Venice, she declares her identification with the volatility of the city, which she does several times throughout the novel. She tells Henri: "I come from the city of mazes . . . but if you ask me a direction I will tell you straight ahead," even though, as I have just pointed out, "there is no such thing as straight ahead" in Venice according to Villanelle herself (109). Predictably, Henri gets lost in the waterways shortly after arriving: "I got lost from the first. Where Bonaparte goes, straight roads follow, buildings are rationalised, street signs may change to celebrate a battle but they are always clearly marked. . . . Not even Bonaparte could rationalise Venice" (112). Henri's words denote the imperial obsession with discovering, naming, and categorizing that so strongly influences his endeavor to conquer Villanelle's love. In trying to dissuade him from seeking a "rational" explanation, Villanelle tells him that "this is a living city. Things change," to which he responds with incredulity: "Villanelle, cities don't." She then redoubles her point against his reasoning: "Henri, they do" (113). Henri's inability to locate Villanelle's world within the limits of the imperial ideology he has inherited leads him to conclude: "This is a city of madmen" (112). Only irrationality can explain (away) Henri's incomprehension of Venice's labyrinthine geography. In fact, as we will see later, it will be precisely his own madness that allows him to comprehend at the end of the novel that loving Villanelle is the opposite of trying to force her into a predetermined subject position that negates the sense of autonomy on which she thrives.

In step with his imperial indoctrination, then, Henri conflates his puzzlement regarding the city with the second thematization of Villanelle's resistance: her body. Villanelle's cross-dressing and the fact that her body does not correspond to received ideas of womanhood (she describes herself as having "breasts [that] are small, so there's no cleavage to give me away, and I'm tall for a girl, especially a Venetian") are often interpreted as signs of a subversive performance of her gender (56).[62] Yet this is expected of the Venetian casino croupier. As she admits, "It was part of the game, trying to decide which sex was hidden behind tight breeches and extravagant face-paste" (54). It is Villanelle's feet, instead, that represent a much more apt substantiation of her radical singularity. Upon arrival in the "enchanted city," Henri confesses to be "determined . . . to find out more about these boatmen and their boots" (109). In his account, Venetians appear as opposite to the Napoleonic subjects. While the French are described as attached to a territorialism that is stabilized by a staunch nationalism and Napoleon's colonial expansion, "Rumour has it that the inhabitants of this city walk on water. That, more bizarre still, their feet are webbed. Not all feet, but the feet of the boatmen whose trade is hereditary"

(49). What is more, if this marvel of human anatomy is not too radical a challenge for Henri's worldview, Villanelle's webbed feet dissipate any possibility for him to make sense of her. As she announces, "There never was a girl whose feet were webbed in the entire history of the boatmen" (51). As a woman with webbed feet, therefore, Villanelle is not only the object of Henri's incredulous wonder but is presented, too, as an anomaly for the Venetians themselves.

The double discordance of Villanelle's feet is much more than a simple manifestation of the grotesque,[63] which is unsatisfactory to explain the radical valences of Villanelle's resistance. Describing it as grotesque would merely invoke an initial rejection of Villanelle by a consensual regime that regulates what is tolerable and what is not, implying no agency on her part. A better way to assess the political question that her feet present can be addressing them through the lens of Imogen Tyler's idea of the "revolting subject." For Tyler, the revolting subject is the most abject form of personhood under the social order governed by neoliberalism; it not only appears as revolting to others but also revolts against such a debasing appraisal.[64] Understanding Villanelle as a revolting subject, therefore, allows us to see how she decidedly acts ("revolts") against such a rejection, embodying what appears as the unnatural, the anomalous, and even the feigned to the Napoleonic eye. This agency is not exclusive of her webbed feet and manifests in relation to other parts of her physique, too. For instance, when Henri helps her recuperate her heart from the Queen of Spades's home, he is confronted by the irrationality of her body. After she asks him to turn around, Villanelle simply puts her heart back into her chest: "Her heart was beating. *Not possible.* I tell you her heart was beating" (121; emphasis original). However, Henri is not entirely put off. In transferring his unmodified passion for Napoleon to his relationship with Villanelle, he betrays the same contradictory feeling. As I mentioned earlier, Henri once found Napoleon "repulsive and fascinating by turns" (13); similarly, while unable to comprehend Villanelle's singularity, he is also enthralled by it. This will have a profound impact on his worldview, to the point of creating a crisis in the rationality upon which it rests.

Venetian Discord, Consensus Unhinged

Deflection is Villanelle's third and most productive form of resistance against Henri's interpellation. Her new, cautious attitude toward passion is essential for her relationship with Henri to succeed. Her experiences with past lovers in Venice have taught her that passion has a destructive side and, therefore, she decides to curb the desires that drive her to make decisions such as giving her heart away. This is clearly expressed when the

Queen of Spades reappears to propose that they spend one more night together. Turning down the offer, Villanelle gives an account of her new understanding of passion: "If I give in to this passion, my real life, the most solid, the best known, will disappear and I will feed on shadows again like those sad spirits whom Orpheus fled" (146). This fresh outlook leads her to conclude that giving up one's passion "is for the single-minded" (145). Because passion cannot govern her life, Villanelle now turns to love for a less intense and volatile form of affection.

Thus, if she refuses to extend her affair with the Queen of Spades for fear that it will destroy the foundations of her singularity and ruin her autonomy, with Henri she is willing to negotiate the terms of her affection. This affection cannot lead to the romantic relationship he wishes it became but is nonetheless worth cultivating. Through this mode of attachment, Villanelle can contemplate new ways to pursue a different kind of partnership that does not cause her self-effacement. Yet this can only occur if she manages to avoid responding to Henri's proposals for as long as he is incapable of seeing the pitfalls of his understanding of love as passionate abandonment or, to use Alain Badiou's terms, until he conceives it as "experienced, developed and lived from the point of view of difference and not identity."[65] In other words, Henri must understand the encroaching effects of his devotion before she can express her disagreement with it. Deflection, then, provides the necessary time for Villanelle to dispute the constricting and dominative notion of womanhood on which Henri's love is premised.

There are several moments in which this strategy is visibly at play. When Henri agrees to help Villanelle recover her heart, for instance, he does so on the condition that she lets him see her webbed feet. She accepts, though only as long as she can satisfy his request at a later time. In the meantime, Villanelle emphatically avoids answering his questions about her inexplicable anatomy: "She laughed and drew back her hair, and her eyes were bright with two deep furrows between the eyebrows. I thought she was the most beautiful woman I had ever seen" (109). Her charming and nonchalant bodily language matches her digressive response: "'I told you. My father was a boatman. Boatmen do not take off their boots,' and that was all she would say" (109). Villanelle refuses to give him a direct answer. Instead, she buries the peculiarity of her feet in a response that emphasizes tradition and ancestry, two notions with which Henri can easily identify. Another, more important example of Villanelle's deflection occurs when, as Henri prepares to recover her heart, he finally expresses his feelings directly to her: "I love you." Villanelle's only possible response is another evasion: "'You are my brother,' she said and we rowed away" (117). Here

Villanelle resorts to modulating her attachment toward him as fraternal and not carnal love. In so doing, she avoids having to explain the exact terms of their attachment and its future possibilities. Life must continue as it is for now.

In both cases, Villanelle discards engaging in an unproductive argument about the impossibility of their love as he envisages it. Doing so would mean for her to admit that that there is indeed a common ground on which they can discuss—even dispute—the kind of relationship that could emerge from their affection. This is simply not possible given that in Henri's mind Villanelle is still a "woman" in the Napoleonic "soldiers and women" distribution, that is, a subject to be conquered by being made into the object of his passion. In directly engaging with Henri, Villanelle would have to explain in terms that are unrecognizable to him why their love is impossible. This would lead to the kind of deadlock that Roland Barthes describes when two lovers make "a scene," that is, when they "argue according to a set exchange of remarks . . . not to listen to each other, but to submit in common to an egalitarian principle of the distribution of language goods."[66] This is an egalitarian encounter not because it enables the emancipation of its participants but because it equalizes the terms in which they address each other, eliminating their ability to understand and grapple with the object of their discussion differently. A scene, thus, is an "insignificant" interaction in which victory means "having the *last word*." As Barthes further argues, "To speak last, 'to conclude,' is to assign a destiny to everything that has been said, is to master, to possess, to absolve, to bludgeon meaning; in the space of speech, the one who comes last occupies a sovereign position."[67] Given that the ultimate control over language that a scene involves is, as my characterization has shown, everything that Villanelle stands against, it is no surprise to see deflection as her choice to respond to Henri, that is, by neither refusing nor becoming captured by his interpellation.

Villanelle's deflection, though, is not aimed at maintaining a temporary position of power with regard to Henri. Proof of this is her behavior at the end of the novel: she does not abandon him once he has helped her recover her heart. This is because, as is revealed in the final chapter of the novel, "The Rock," the discordance between the protagonists' affection for each other finally reaches a resolution. The chapter offers an account of Henri's incarceration in the prison island of San Servelo, which is known "for the increasing numbers of poor and mad" criminals it contains, after he kills Villanelle's abusive husband, who turns out to be a crude cook working alongside him in Napoleon's kitchen, by carving his heart out (142). While this act of violence might suggest a renovated sense of agency, it is in fact the way Henri acts in facing his punishment that inaugurates his autonomy from the Napoleonic ideology that has so far governed both his subjectivity and his understanding of love as passion. In a later scene, Henri exonerates Villanelle of any complicity in the murder, provoking his elated celebration that "for the first time I realised that I was the powerful one" (138). Yet he declares to Villanelle that he has not killed the man for her sake but "for myself. He made every good thing dirty" (140). This shift, in turn, seems to demonstrate to Villanelle that she can finally express her attachment to him on her own terms. This is anticipated at the very end of the scene involving her husband's murder, which closes with Villanelle walking on Venice's waterways, in pulling their boat away from where her husband's body lies. Henri reminisces: "the only time I've ever seen her feet and they are not what I'd usually call feet" (135). A new relationship emerges.

The murder provokes a cascade of events that lead Henri to recognize how his love for Villanelle cannot be expressed in the imperial language that he learned from Napoleon, a recognition that is paradoxically both enabled and preempted by his becoming insane in the Rock. First, Henri and Villanelle simply enjoy life for a period of six days "cramming our bodies with pleasure" (136), as if revisiting their passions one more time before their lives are changed forever when Henri is apprehended by the law. One may be tempted to call it a honeymoon of sorts, although it is not the celebration of a marriage but of a newly acquired yet temporary freedom. Following that period, Henri is arrested, tried, and sent to the Rock, which strengthens Villanelle's feelings of attachment toward him. She tells her parents, for instance, that she "will take care of Henri," after which he declares that "when I heard those words I slept fully" (136). Perhaps the clearest indication of the intensification of her affection for Henri, however, is the fact that she employs an inclusive "we" to speak about them, which she has refrained from doing until this moment. After Henri is convicted, Villanelle tries to reassure him by telling him, "Courage Henri. We walked from Moscow. We can walk across the water." Correcting her, Henri responds: "You can," to which she replies with a doubling of her bond to him: "We can" (141). Villanelle's husband's murder, then, creates a new space for her to articulate her love for Henri, which can satisfy his expectations only partially. She confesses as much to the reader: "He loves me, I know that, and I love him, but in a brotherly incestuous way. . . . I wonder if things would be different for him if I could return his passion" (146). This, however, does not cause a crisis, as it would have before.

In the prison, Henri undergoes a deep transformation. The most important outcome of his incarceration in the Rock is that he quickly becomes insane. This could be said to elicit two alternative readings: "either the loss of control leads to madness and obsession and Henri is imprisoned within his own desires, or he has taken control of his fantasy and so saved himself from worse events."[68] I consider, however, that those possibilities are in fact the two steps he needs to take in dismantling the illusory dialogue that he has imposed on Villanelle. In losing control of the situation, Henri can finally establish a different kind of agency, one that does not seek to dominate the relationship and can be, therefore, a way of reconstituting his own subjectivity. His solitary confinement in the Rock symbolizes the final reversal of the imperial ideology he has been unable to shed. Initially declared insane by the authorities because of the extreme violence of his actions, Henri becomes truly unhinged and begins to hear voices, most notably that of Napoleon:

> They say the dead don't talk. Silent as the grave they say. It's not true. The dead are talking all the time. On this rock, when the wind is up, I can hear them.
> I can hear Bonaparte; he didn't last long on his rock. (133)

Yet, while Napoleon interpellates Henri from inside the very prison in which he himself was once incarcerated, he does not do so as a master would talk to his subject. Henri depicts Napoleon imploring him now: "When the wind is up, I hear him weeping and he comes to me, his hands still greasy from his last dinner, and he asks me if I love him. His face pleads with me to say I do and I think of those who went into exile with him and one by one took a small boat home" (134). In his account, Henri provides no answer to Napoleon, mirroring the elusive responses he has so far received from Villanelle and, as a consequence, slowly undoing the emperor's grip on his individuality. The world is no longer divided between soldiers and women, and Henri does not have to answer the emperor's calling. In his maddened state, he begins to see Napoleon's own irrationality:

> *Après moi, le deluge.*
> Not really. A few drowned but a few have drowned before.
> He over-estimated himself.
> Odd that a man should come to believe in myths of his own making. . . .
> Now that he's dead, he's becoming a hero again and nobody minds because he can't make the most of it.
> I'm tired of hearing his life-story over and over. He walks in here, small as it is, unannounced and takes up all my room. (151)

Henri's insanity is, therefore, an emancipatory break from the Napoleonic consensual regime that has governed his life until now. While allowing him to articulate fully his liberation from the emperor's grip, this is also a pivotal moment in Henri's rearticulation of his sense of love. If the emperor appears now as a deluded hero who will be remembered for his foolish (though brutal) hubris, Henri's idea of love undergoes a similar change: the passion he once felt for Napoleon and was later redirected to Villanelle amounts to a form of idolatry that negates the conception of one's object of love as an autonomous other.

Henri and Villanelle, thus, can begin to negotiate the terms of their relationship. After ceaselessly fending off his advances, Villanelle finally confronts Henri with a negative that not only preempts her interpellation but also lays out the reasons why they will never be together. When she tells him that she is pregnant, Henri concludes: "Then we can get married." "No," Villanelle responds, and she continues narrating: "I took his hands and tried to explain that I wouldn't marry again and that he couldn't live in Venice and I wouldn't live in France" (148). Their differences no longer impede a truly critical dialogue between them. This negative, however, causes Henri to retreat from the complicated bond that has grown between them. Now in possession of a fortune inherited from her dead husband, Villanelle has the means to get him out of prison and, while this process will take years, she is also set in comforting him with visits and letters, both of which he rejects: "I keep getting letters from Villanelle. I send them back to her unopened and I never reply. . . . I have to send her away because she hurts me too much. . . . There was a time, some years ago I think, when she tried to make me leave this place, though not to be with her. She was asking me to be alone again, just when I felt safe" (151–52). Henri, then, becomes more and more secluded, but not because he has overcome his infatuation. On the contrary, his love for her is even more intense. The difference is that he can now express it in as radical a way as she did to him:

> I am in love with her; not a fantasy or a myth or a creature of my own making.
>
> Her. A person who is not me. I invented Bonaparte as much as he invented himself.
>
> My passion for her, even though she could never return it, showed me the difference between inventing a lover and falling in love.
>
> The one is about you, the other about someone else. (157–58)

Henri realizes that his understanding of passion has made him deploy an illusory dialogue in order to conquer Villanelle, whom he has tried to coerce into playing a specific role as his interlocutor.

Thus, Villanelle's resistance succeeds. The important thing for the novel, however, is not the celebration of Henri's resulting fall. Winterson offers instead a compassionate account of Henri's transformation while giving closure to the story via his self-reclusion, bringing to a logical conclusion the kind of bond that he has attempted to establish with Villanelle. The romantic relationship he has pursued is impossible, yet his love for her becomes liberating. Henri no longer regards his goal to conquer her heart as an obstacle that he must overcome, as an adversary to defeat. Rather, he can take the difference that separates them as the starting point for an interaction that does not assume an eventual interpellative subjectification but thrives on the necessary autonomy of both the lover and the loved one:

> Fools stay for love. I am a fool. I stayed in the army eight years because I loved someone. You'd think that would have been enough. I stayed too because I had nowhere else to go.
> I stay here by choice.
> That means a lot to me. (152)

Henri's choice to remain in confinement, ultimately, is as much the pitiful reflection of his defeat as the assurance of his self-governing singularity. Finally, having faced his ghosts in the isolated environment of the Rock, Henri comprehends the selflessly constructive power of caring for an Other, as he starts a garden in the barren soil of the prison island: "For myself I will plant a cypress tree and it will outlive me. That's what I miss about the fields, the sense of the future as well as the present. That one day what you plant will spring up unexpectedly; a shoot, a tree, just when you were looking the other way, thinking about something else. I like to know that life will outlive me, that's a happiness Bonaparte never understood" (156). Without interfering with his newly articulated love, Henri's new occupation bears clear traces of Villanelle and represents an emancipated and fulfilling attitude about the uncertainty of the future.

The resolution that *The Passion* offers, of course, can hardly stand as a feasible goal if one tries, as I have attempted here, to read Henri's struggle with his Napoleonic indoctrination as a proleptic narrative about David Cameron's genealogical connections with Margaret Thatcher. It seems to me rather unlikely that Cameron would ever undergo the kind of realization that Henri does. And, even if he did, there would be little political gain in what would mostly be a symbolic gesture. Yet the developments that lead to such an outcome are important to contemplate. Villanelle's tenacity, I have tried to show, is worth considering as an example of the type of resistance necessary to fend off the affective pretense of a neoliberal agenda otherwise intended to do away with the state's responsibility toward the welfare of citizens. Villanelle's deflection, thus, could serve as a blueprint for citizens to challenge the heartless realism employed by the government to argue that there is no alternative.

The Specter of Margaret Thatcher

Is postmodernism over? This is a famously difficult question to broach, particularly if we historicize its precursor, modernism, a period purportedly born as a result of a radical break with the past. Perhaps the question must be posed differently. As I have been arguing throughout with regard to the postpolitical, we may be better off thinking about continuities instead of clear-cut periods. Perhaps we must ask how much of the postmodern remains in the contemporary moment, which for lack of a better word I am going to call the present. To answer this question, we may look at the history of neoliberalism, an undoubtedly postmodern phenomenon. In this sense, the genealogy that I have traced here between the forms of governance exercised by Margaret Thatcher and David Cameron demonstrates very clearly that much of what defines the present is decidedly postmodern. In reading two postmodern novels produced in direct response to the Thatcher era against the backdrop of Cameron's post-2008 governance, I have sought to reveal how fiction that originally grappled with the former's neoliberal regime has something important to say about its depoliticizing power in the latter's seemingly benign version of it. In the words of Guy Standing, an important critic of contemporary neoliberalism, I have intended to show how these novels help us "recapture the language of progress" and "revive the future."[69]

Yet the proleptic qualities that I have explored in *The Child in Time* and *The Passion* are not simply the result of a comparative analysis that considers their suitability as descriptive narratives of the present. Their projection to times other than their own—one toward the near future, the other toward a relatively distant past—clearly point to their concern with the historical ramifications of Thatcherism. This is perhaps most evident in McEwan's novel, given that it is set a few years in the future. The potential of *The Passion* as a narrative of the future, despite being set almost two centuries earlier, resides in its preoccupation with the legacy of Napoleon's imperial ideology. Nevertheless, in both novels the specter of Thatcher remains a lasting presence of the futures they invite us to imagine, looming large both in the lives of their protagonists and in our current political conjuncture. This projection toward the future, additionally, is of special importance if we consider the novels' portrayal of the seemingly positive affective qualities with which Cameron enshrouded Thatcher's neoliberalism. Such affective reworking was pivotal in making neoliberalism a consensual doctrine against the principles of the welfare state and the dissent of the citizens, as we saw in my discussion of the Listening Exercise. This is ironic given that Thatcher's administration was in fact characterized by its disregard for the individual and its indifference toward citizens' needs, that is, for not caring about (and definitely not *loving*) them in the framework of a state in which "there is no such thing as society." However, if we think of Cameron's efforts to rebrand Thatcher's doctrine with an electoral program designed "for the people," as the 2010 *Conservative Manifesto* on which he built his platform alleged, reading these novels for their critique of Cameron's "humane" neoliberalism seems more than appropriate.

Thus, I tried to show the regulative power of illusory dialogue when it exploits the kind of personal investment in which affective attachment is rooted. In combating it, the protagonists of McEwan's and Winterson's novels demonstrate the radical political valences of love as a dissensual kind of relationship. Yet the deflection upon which this configuration of love operates is different in each novel. In *The Child in Time*, on the one hand, we saw how Stephen's political urges were intimately connected to the deterioration of his most immediate affective bonds following the disappearance of his daughter and the subsequent disintegration of his marriage. His involvement in the Parmenter Sub-Committee on Reading and Writing seems to fill temporarily this vacuum, though the ineffectiveness of its debates quickly disheartens him. Furthermore, his discovery that the work of the subcommittee and the rest of the Official Commission on Childcare is only an illusory dialogue established by the government to preempt dissent and impose its own policy might justify a return to his original passive resentment. Yet Stephen finds a way to make a meaningful intervention, which does not manifest as a direct confrontation. Instead, he deflects what would certainly become another illusory dialogue with the prime minister while redirecting his affective attachments in order to recuperate the bond that links him to his wife. In doing so, Stephen finds a way to rework his political disaffection. The restoration of the love that binds him and Julia together and the birth of their child, ultimately, suggest a new political agency that hinges on the strengthening of solidarity and mutual care that firmly sustain the social fabric.

In *The Passion*, on the other hand, Villanelle's resistance is successful insofar as it creates a distance, temporal and affective, that protects her from becoming trapped in an illusory dialogue where the autonomous singularity that constitutes her identity is foreclosed and her affection becomes the object to be conquered. Deflection, thus, allows her to turn down Henri's propositions until he reckons with the absolutist nature of the

Napoleonic ideology that he has internalized and has tried to reproduce in wooing her. Fueled by an irresolvable disagreement with Napoleon's imperial worldview as enacted by Henri, Villanelle's endurance challenges the homogenizing power of his attachment and opens up a space for a mode of alterity that Henri finally comprehends as a product of her sovereignty, and not a reflection of his own desires. As a result, Henri stops addressing Villanelle as an embodiment of the "woman" category at the center of the Napoleonic doctrine to identify in her, instead, a singularity that is as fascinating to him as it is the obstacle for the kind of relationship he pursues. Villanelle's resistance, therefore, offers an illustration of the importance of perseverance and patience to counter modes of affection that undermine the political foundations of the subjectivities they interpellate.

The reflections on the politics of affection that both novels offer, to conclude, may also be useful to navigate the kind of politics that have developed in the post-Brexit referendum environment (it is worth noting that one of the rhetorical emblems of the Leave campaign was the impossible promise that £350 million per week would be destined precisely to the overstrained NHS thanks to the cutting of expenses derived from the UK's departure from the European Union). At a moment characterized by the rearrangement of the landscape of electoral politics by new right- and left-wing alignments, McEwan's and Winterson's novels might give us clues about whether dialogue, advertised as an expression of affection for the electorate, is deployed by politicians and institutions to perpetuate the status quo, to make certain fundamental changes that would maintain the depoliticization of citizens all the same, or to lay the foundations for a more equitable politics. The novels, furthermore, can be extremely beneficial as we consider if this juncture will inaugurate a new era in parliamentary governance in the near future, and perhaps leave behind neoliberalism, or, on the contrary, we remain tied to the neoliberal past that Cameron sought to extend into the present, anchored in the dispossession—material as well as political—of the larger part of the electorate.

In next two chapters I want to explore the political intricacies of dialogue in a set of "contemporary" novels, a term I will loosely employ to describe works of fiction produced in the earlier part of the twenty-first century. Apart from the evident temporal qualities that their dates of publication imply, I want to explore how the notion of the contemporary also has geopolitical implications. The contemporary moment, I will suggest, is distinctly global. No matter how localized, regional, or remote, it is difficult to think of contemporary life as exempt from the global substance of issues such as those I investigate in next two chapters, namely, terrorism and environmental destruction. Thus, in the second *contra* of this book I examine the historical entanglements of the United States' response to the 9/11 attacks as a thrust both to the past and the future and the radical effect of remaining anchored in the "here and now." To do so, I will offer a reading of Mohsin Hamid's *The Reluctant Fundamentalist* for its drive to intervene in the historic crisis of representation provoked by the so-called war on terror. In the last chapter I will consider reframing as a third strategy against the work of illusory dialogue. To do so, I will offer an exploration of the visuality, from the point of view of the inhabitants of the global South, of environmental destruction in the context of the Anthropocene—one of the defining narratives of both the present and future of life on the planet—with readings of Indra Sinha's *Animal's People* and Helon Habila's *Oil on Water*.

CHAPTER FOUR

Contra II
Terrorist Counters

> Dissent is quelled, in part, through threatening the speaking subject with an uninhabitable identification. . . . [O]ne fails to speak, or one speaks in throttled ways, in order to sidestep the terrorizing identification that threatens to take hold. This strategy for quelling dissent and limiting the reach of critical debate happens not only through a series of shaming tactics . . . but they work as well by producing what will and will not count as a viable speaking subject and a reasonable opinion within the public domain. . . . Our capacity to feel and to apprehend hangs in the balance. But so, too, does the fate of the reality of certain lives and deaths as well as the ability to think critically and publicly about the effects of war.
>
> —Judith Butler, *Precarious Life*

This is our second stop. As I did in the first *contra*, in this chapter I will tackle the shortcomings of engaging in dialogue as a way for minor voices to resist a depoliticizing consensual order. In my reading of *Waterland* I showed that, while intended to correct the official historical record, Tom Crick's narrative was nonetheless a failure because it established a new exclusionary regime of representation. Here, however, I want to tackle the inadequacy of dialogue from a different angle. I seek to show how, as a consequence of the unassailable nature of certain consensual orders, dialogue is often an insufficient instrument for minor voices to mount an effective resistance. In itself, this is a rather simple argument. Moving beyond it, I want to demonstrate that it is precisely this failure that uncovers the political substance of the dissenting positions that struggle to counter them. While in the first *contra* my argument explored questions regarding the textuality of history-making, furthermore, I situate my thesis in this second one in a very specific and significant moment in recent memory. I will move from the local setting of Swift's postmodern historiographic metafiction to the global arena in order to investigate how Mohsin Hamid's 2007 *The Reluctant Fundamentalist* explores this failure in the context of the September 11, 2001, attacks in New York City.

To be precise, Hamid's novel is not interested in the attacks themselves, which appear only indirectly and without any level of detail. Rather, it provides a wider picture of the geopolitical state of affairs that they reveal by exploring the preceding and succeeding historical processes that have rendered dialogue about international terrorism and the U.S. government's response to it politically inadequate. In fact, the utter violence and horror that they caused were not an interruption of the geopolitical order. As the collective Retort would argue in their urgent effort to provide a context for the attacks and the ensuing U.S. military campaign, 9/11 was not "a world-historical turning point."[1] It must be understood instead, they argued, against the backdrop of a post–World War II mesh of geopolitical tensions, confronted interests, and wars. Nondomestic terrorist activity, moreover, was hardly a new element in U.S. global security, even for New York City and the World Trade Center itself, which had already been attacked in 1993.

The fact that the attacks took place on American soil and had such a symbolic impact on the American imagination, however, provided important ground for 9/11 and its ramifications to have world-changing effects. Most importantly, the attack was employed as a justification for the establishment of a new postpolitical consensus that legitimized the so-called war on terror, which has been a cornerstone of U.S. international military strategy ever since it was inaugurated by George W. Bush's first administration. The idea that terrorism must be eliminated at any cost led to the development of unlawful mechanisms of war, such as the detention of suspects in extralegal camps like those in Guantánamo Bay and Abu Ghraib, preemptive strikes, or the invasions of Afghanistan and Iraq. In the more than a decade and a half that has passed between the attacks and the time of this writing, we have witnessed the intensification of a general state of war that Michael Hardt and Antonio Negri have characterized as a "permanent social relation."[2]

The goal of the war on terror, of course, was not just the defense of the homeland against the perpetrators and those who may strike in the future. More than that, 9/11 warranted the ratification of permanent war as the latest stage in the United States' agenda to establish itself as the world's hegemonic superpower. The ensuing war on terror, thus, redefined the terms in which the United States understands its role as *the* global sovereign nation[3] by provoking the domestication of the sphere of geopolitical relations. By "domestication" I mean two things. On the one hand, I mean that the moment he declared war against terrorism in his televised speech the day of the attacks, George Bush also proclaimed the government's right to make the world an extension of the U.S. homeland, particularly when it came to military authority. As *The 9/11 Commission Report* would conclude, "the American homeland is the planet."[4] On the other hand, I also mean the idea that dissent against the American response to 9/11 has never had a real impact on the status quo that the latter enforced. One only needs to look, for instance, at the name chosen for one of the war on terror's central legislative instruments, the USA Patriot Act, or how those expressing disagreement with it (especially in its early moments) have been accused of being "anti-American" in an attempt to discredit their arguments.[5]

This domesticating effect has also had, naturally, grave dialogic consequences. As Talal Asad maintained shortly after, "there has been scarcely any sustained public *debate* on the significance of the September 11 tragedy for a superpower-dominated world."[6] This is still the case today for both the terrorist attacks and the war on terror. Of course, public analysis and commentary have abounded both nationally and internationally. Yet these have always operated as embedded in the consensus underpinning it, either as efforts to justify the U.S. military agenda or as expressions of opposition to a "realistic" policy and military approach with no proper political influence; the war on terror has remained as destructive as it has been indisputable. Mohsin Hamid broaches precisely this issue in *The Reluctant Fundamentalist*. Adopting an antagonistic approach, Hamid deploys a narrative structure that terrorizes the impossibility of dialogue in and about the post-9/11 world. This terrorization is based on the endeavors of the protagonist and narrator, a young Pakistani man named Changez who struggles to maintain a series of relationships grounded in the present so as to avoid being absorbed by the historical processes that dominate the war-on-terror narrative. Despite such attempts, though, Changez is bound to fail as his story unavoidably succumbs to the representational order that it seeks to confront.

War Exchanges: Mohsin Hamid's *The Reluctant Fundamentalist*

I have titled this *contra* "Terrorist Counters" not because I wish to show how terrorism can break with a consensual apparatus or to justify the use of violence as a political tool. The title, instead, is meant to suggest that Hamid's novel offers an important response to the antinomies of the idea of "counterterrorism," a central component of the war on terror, by upending it. If on the surface counterterrorism is inscribed in the familiar framework of military defense, its practice is often only possible thanks to the implementation of what Giorgio Agamben has famously called a "state of exception." Agamben defines this as the "no-man's land between public law and political fact" that "binds and, at the same time, abandons the living being of the law," and in commenting on the Bush administration's response to 9/11 proper, he further characterizes it as "a situation in which the emergency becomes the rule, and the very distinction between peace and war (and between foreign and civil war) becomes impossible."[7] Unauthorized surveillance, indefinite detention, torture, military operations targeted at civilian populations, and so forth have been instrumental in the war on terror, legitimized by the suspension of the law caused by the implementation of a substitutive, uncontestable directive that authorizes illegal and unethical actions as permissible and necessary to "win" the war.

Thus, I propose to consider *The Reluctant Fundamentalist* as a text that features what I call an "aesthetics of exception," that is, a rogue regime of representation that operates in response to and is authorized precisely by the deployment of a state of exception. I base this argument on the novel's premise. The narrative starts off with the seemingly chance encounter between Changez and an unidentified American man in the district of Old Anarkali, in Lahore. The body of the text, thus, is composed of the conversation between them, which is dominated by Changez's account of his time in New York before and after 9/11. He tells the American about his upper-middle-class upbringing in Lahore, his migration to the United States to study at Princeton, the job he gets afterward at the prestigious New York valuation firm Underwood Samson, his failed relationship with a well-to-do fellow Princeton student named Erica, the terrorist attacks, and the pressures emerging from America's reaction to them, which ultimately make him return to Pakistan, where his new job as a university professor leads him to become an important dissenting voice against the United States' foreign policy.

Yet the narrative does not proceed as a casual exchange. Changez's interlocutor, who is often read to be possibly a CIA agent, seems to him to be "on a *mission*."[8] Changez himself, perhaps suspecting that he is a counterterrorism target, seems to want to tell him about how 9/11 changed the course of his political life for reasons other than simply passing the time. While playing on the ambiguity of the characters' roles, the fact is that the novel arguably acts as a contribution to the debate that Asad protested was absent following the 9/11 attacks. However, it does so by appropriating and subverting what could be considered a dialogic component of the war on terror: the euphemistically termed "enhanced interrogation" of detainees (i.e., the torturing of individuals, including children and the elderly, in many U.S. camps, military bases, and "black sites" around the world so as to obtain counterterrorist intelligence).[9] Thus, while Changez is never detained in the novel, his interaction with the American indeed works as an inverted interrogation session between an official and a counterterrorist operative.

According to Laleh Khalili, the purpose of the interrogation of detainees is to produce "scientific or ethnographic knowledge" that makes suspects "legible to the state" by assigning categories to them ("low level enemy combatant," "high value detainee," "security detainee," etc.) with the purpose of "'understanding' them" and "us[ing] them more functionally and efficiently" to fight insurgencies and terrorism.[10] This means that the production of counterterrorist intelligence is the construction of narratives of a very high order and that, in its capacity as global superpower, the United States acts as the omniscient, unchallengeable narrator. As a senior adviser to George Bush said, "We're an empire now, and when we act, we create our own reality."[11] The narrative that dictates the contours of such a "reality," it must be said, is meant to have no denouement, as the mechanisms to fight terrorism are not intended to put an end to it per se but, rather, to maintain the state of perpetual war that defines the current geopolitical moment. The actors of this narrative, however, are clearly defined by a false dialectical confrontation between protagonists and antagonists. This has been clear, for example, in the forging by the U.S. state and military apparatus (with the help of the complicit media) of a coherent enemy figure that clumsily groups all Muslim, Arab, and Middle Eastern people as potential fundamentalists and/or terrorists, while the U.S. government has fashioned itself as the heroic leader of "the West," fueling racist sentiments and reinforcing negative stereotypes that, shored up by a discourse of "us vs. them," have had harmful consequences in the long term.

The counterterrorist interrogation is, therefore, the ideal trope to subvert the narrative of the war on terror. As a dialogic military tactic, it is one major mechanism for the dominant voice of the United States, channeled by the interrogator, to justify its war-on-terror doctrine on the basis of the "information" revealed by the detainee. The role of the interrogator is, consequently, that of the producer—never a simple obtainer—of key intelligence to construct a suitable "reality" that legitimizes the larger military operation. By putting forward specific questions in high-pressure environments where detainees' physical and mental capacities are under enormous stress, as the innumerable accounts demonstrate,[12] while targeting them in such a way that their answers can be selected, shaped, and arranged according to the preestablished narrative, the counterterrorist interrogation illustrates the insidious ways in which the "reality" of the war on terror is created. Changez's narrative works directly against this very gesture.

Terrorizing Dialogue

Hamid's aesthetics of exception are rooted in a "terroristic" intervention in the face of the domestication of geopolitics by the war on terror. As Jean Baudrillard put it in reflecting on the 9/11 attacks, given that, as the embodiment of global power, the United States had "seiz[ed] all the cards," the "Other" was forced to "change the rules."[13] Similarly, *The Reluctant Fundamentalist* is an exercise that seeks to change the rules of the information-producing counterterrorist interrogation. It is often argued that the political qualities of the novel lie in its exploitation of the uncertainty and paranoia that shroud the interaction between Changez and the unidentified American, especially in readings that center on the possibility that they may be active players as a (potential) terrorist and a CIA agent, respectively. Yet, for reasons that will become clearer at the end of my analysis, I want to argue that what makes it an important political effort, especially from a dialogic point of view, is precisely the certainty with which Hamid controls the exchange in order to expose, from the perspective of the Other, the warped narrative of the war on terror.

The encounter is sometimes mischaracterized as a dramatic monologue, not least by Hamid himself.[14] That is so because, while the reader is privy to every word Changez says, the American has no voice and is only portrayed as reflected in Changez's reactions. This is, in my view, not an adequate way to describe it. The novel is a selective account of a conversation that regulates, in very strict ways, the representation of what is said and what is not. In other words, it is a terrorization of our expectations of dialogue. Even if his interlocutor is mostly quiet, Changez's story cannot be called a monologue (technically it is not one) but a part in an encounter in which the other speaker plays a very small but crucial role as mostly a listener and, on the rare occasions when he says something or reacts through body language, a contributor, even if the conversation is monopolized by Changez. The political significance of his account, in addition, is determined by the fact that its addressee is a suspicious American man who might be an intelligence agent. Changez's ironic tone, the innuendo and suspense generated by his playful way of speaking, and the establishment of a genealogy of his dissenting position against the United States' reaction to 9/11 would simply function very differently (and with varying degrees of success) if the addressee were, for instance, a fellow Pakistani, a relative, a foreigner from another country, or one of his students.

In providing only the protagonist's side of the conversation, thus, Hamid upends the interrogation to which Changez, cast as a (reluctant) fundamentalist, would likely be subjected after being captured. In providing answers to a series of unasked questions about himself and his time in the United States, Changez allows us to gain entry to this world of reversed roles, to another reality in which the future detainee can articulate, with a narrative that is not conditioned by the interrogator's questions, his dissenting position. The novel is, thus, a compelling response to the war-on-terror narrative, that is, in Gayatri Spivak's words, an attempt "to resonate with the other, contemplate the possibility of complicity—wrenching consciousness-raising, which is based on 'knowing things,' however superficially, from its complacency. Response pre-figures change. . . . When we confine our idea of the political to cognitive control alone, it does not just avoid the risk of response, it closes off response altogether. We end up talking to ourselves, or to our clones abroad."[15] The novel is an effort to break that dialogic vicious circle.

Hamid's terrorization of the dialogue between Changez and his interlocutor via its selective representation is characterized by a number of important aspects that convey the narrative's aesthetic and political import. First, as I have already pointed out, Changez does not answer questions but volunteers his story. In doing so, he puts forward a series of details about his life that would be counterproductive to his construction as a terrorist. Changez makes of himself a three-dimensional character and not the stereotype-laden placeholder that the war-on-terror discourse would fashion him to be. Second, and as a result, he is in total control of the narrative. A "mentally ill," "animalized," "numbed to terror," "irrational," or "brainwashed" terrorist[16] would be incapable of constructing a cohesive story imbued with a sense of historical coherence. Thus, by narrating his experiences before and after 9/11, Changez humanizes himself, disavowing the fundamentalist label that his dissent with U.S. policy appears to have earned him. This is emphasized by his extensive use of irony, which is significant because it simultaneously acknowledges the war-on-terror framework into which the encounter is inscribed while allowing him to refuse to play the part of the fundamentalist. For instance, Changez claims that he will do "my *utmost* to avoid eavesdropping on your conversation" when his interlocutor's cell phone rings (30; emphasis original). Later, after noting a "bulge . . . through the lightweight fabric of your suit" in the spot where "undercover security agents . . . tend to favor wearing an armpit holster for their sidearm," he insists that "I did not mean to imply that you were so equipped" (139). Finally, the narrative reverses the epistemological and discursive grasp of the suspect by the counterterrorist interrogation. It not only enforces a silence upon the American interlocutor that reductively constructs him as a passive, voiceless character to be seen exclusively through Changez's account; in addition, Hamid dispossesses him of his singularity by casting him as an "average" American. Indeed, the novel opens with Changez politely and amicably approaching him in spite of evincing the stereotypical post-9/11, Western fear of the Other: "Excuse me, sir, but may I be of assistance? Ah, I see I have alarmed you. Do not be frightened by my beard: I am a lover of America" (1). Changez prompts the encounter instead of being trapped into it.

This inversion of the counterterrorist interrogation is underpinned by a dissensual historical foundation evident in Changez's constant anchoring of the conversation in the present. Hamid achieves this by interposing numerous momentary and seemingly trivial interruptions to his narrator's account. At one point, Changez notices the American surveying their surroundings as he seems to grow inattentive to the conversation: "You appear distracted, sir; those pretty girls from the National College of Arts have clearly recaptured your attention. Or are you watching that man, the one with the beard longer than mine, who has stopped to stand beside them?" (22). Later he points to the food they are about to eat not without a touch of irony: "And with that, sir, the moment has come for us to eat! For your own safety, I would suggest that you avoid this yoghurt and those chopped vegetables. What? No, no, I meant nothing sinister; your stomach might be upset by uncooked foods, that is all. If you insist, I will go so far as to sample each of these plates myself first, to reassure you that there is nothing to fear" (122). While they do add to the increasingly suspenseful tone of the novel, these moments have a more important purpose. They underscore the context of the conversation as it takes place at a café in an old square in Lahore, where the two men drink tea, later enjoy a dinner together, watch people come and go, and see the night fall before Changez walks the American to his hotel.

This emphasis on the immediate circumstances of the conversation works in direct opposition to a deleterious gesture that is, as Edward Said once argued, common to narratives intended to erode the political motivations of the "terrorist" enemy. According to Said, in those narratives one often finds a "wholesale attempt to obliterate history, and indeed temporality itself. For the main thing is to isolate your enemy from time, from causality, from prior action, and thereby to portray him or her as ontologically and gratuitously interested in wreaking havoc for its own sake."[17] Changez's narrative, thus, historicizes the conversation in a present shared by the two men in which the ideological presumptions at the core of the U.S. counterterrorist agenda are called into question. Changez in fact seems to be keenly aware of the effect that this has on their encounter: "Yes, we have acquired a certain familiarity with the recent history of our surroundings, and that—in my humble opinion—allows us to put the present into much better perspective" (45). The political work of Changez's anti-interrogation approach, therefore, resides in its constant return to the here and now, to the contingency of their interaction so that his story, and the dialogic frame in which it is told, can be observed from the perspective of the other realities that the war on terror interdicts.

Yet the radical work done by such an emphasis on contingency is not exclusive to their conversation. The story Changez tells the American, which deals primarily with his ill-fated relationship with Erica and an initial professional success followed by a decision to quit his promising career at Underwood Samson, is underpinned by Changez's similar intention to historicize the present against the temporal pressures regulating the new order dictated by the United States' reaction to 9/11. Thus, the account evidences Changez's struggle to face the tensions afflicting his relationship with these two major aspects of his (American) life, whose symbolic roles in the novel are signaled by yet another dimension of Hamid's aesthetics of exception, namely, the deliberate and ironically unsubtle identification of Erica and Underwood Samson with America/the United States (the latter in the company's acronym). Even though they appear intertwined, I want to address them separately for the sake of clarity, and return, at the end of the chapter, to the story's framing device as it brings about the resolution of Hamid's intervention.

"A Dangerous Nostalgia"

Part of the significance of the 9/11 attacks resided in their momentary ability to mark time as an explosive irruption of the present. For millions of baffled Americans as well as for a government and military caught off guard, the televised dilation of a violent and vertiginous here and now was compounded by an increasing sense of powerlessness and vulnerability as the catastrophe unfolded. Immediately, the war on terror was kick-started by George Bush's address to the nation on the very evening of the attacks, announcing the synchronization of the rest of the world to the perpetual, exceptional present of America's "infinite justice" (as the counterterrorist campaign was named early on), while at home brown-skinned "enemies" like Changez would be the target of a low-intensity, retaliative replication of the fraught here and now to which the terrorists had subjected the nation. For instance, as he travels back to the United States from his first international Underwood Samson assignment in Manila soon after 9/11, Changez is subjected to newly ramped-up immigration measures at the airport. His answer "I live here" is simply not acceptable to the customs officer, who impatiently asks him several times what "the *purpose* of your trip to the United States" is (75; emphasis original). His appearance had, earlier, "elicited looks of concern" around him on the plane to New York, making him "uncomfortable in [his] own face . . . stiff and self-conscious" (74). Later, Changez is the target of a man's xenophobic confrontation in a parking lot that ends with the symptomatically inaccurate and racist "Fucking Arab!" (117). The contingent precarity into which Changez's life is suddenly thrown cannot but engender an existence that is as unpredictable as it is potentially redefined at any given moment.

These moments of intense insecurity and threat exemplify the most immediate reaction to an event that, as Megha Anwer has noted, Hamid otherwise refuses to represent.[18] The 9/11 attacks are included in Changez's story, but only to let the American know how he learns about them from Manila. The attacks in themselves are, as far as their representation is concerned, demoted to a secondary plane; what matters for Hamid is what they trigger. As I have already suggested, the novel is interested in exploring the consensual order underpinning the discourse of the war on terror. In commenting on its significance, Jacques Rancière asserts that "September 11 . . . brought to light the new dominant form of symbolizing the Same and the Other that has been imposed under the conditions of the new world (dis)order. The most distinctive feature of that symbolization is the eclipse of politics; it is the eclipse of an identity that is inclusive of alterity, an identity constituted through polemicizing over the common."[19] In Changez's narrative, this eclipse of politics manifests in his struggle to deploy a radical sense of contingency that grounds him in the present and in contrast with the here and now brought to the fore by attacks. This emphasis on the present, moreover, acts not only against those first moments of immediate existential anxiety but, more importantly, also against the distinct thrusts toward the past and the future with which the United States responded to 9/11, as symbolized in Erica and Underwood Samson.[20]

The American reaction to the attacks was characterized, as many commentators have suggested, by an instant retreat to the past. At the military and governmental levels, the war on terror rested on the resurrection of historical landmarks such as World War II and episodes such as the Cold War, which enabled the discursive renovation of age-old fears and insecurities.[21] Culturally, such a retreat was mirrored by a hypernationalist, romantic nostalgia aimed to allay a wounded national identity. As David Simpson has compellingly shown, this nostalgia "refigured [the] past into patterns open to being made into new and often dangerous forms of sense."[22] In the novel, this is represented in Erica's inability to move on from her relationship with her boyfriend Chris, which was cut short after he died of cancer a year before 9/11 occurs. Erica's mourning is, indeed, deeply nostalgic.

Changez's initial interest in her during a trip to Greece with other Princeton students and his intention to pursue a relationship with her, in turn, place him as the embodiment of an irruption of the here and now into her life. However, while Erica is inclined to reciprocate and indeed agrees to see him a number of times, Changez's presence becomes increasingly intolerable for her. This tension sets the tenor of their relationship and operates as a metaphor for the backlash—ranging from suspicion to xenophobic hatred—of a large portion of the American public against the Other of the war-on-terror narrative, whose presence is both an instigator and a reminder of the negative effects of a sentimental regression to a romantic, mythologized past.

If it is true that Erica's inability to move on from her past life is not provoked by 9/11, neither is the U.S. cultural retreat to a romantic past. From the beginning, Changez remarks that "one got the sense that she existed internally at a degree of remove from those around her" (22) and, alluding to a "crack inside her" (59) that may be read as an inward-looking discourse of exceptionalism at the core of American nationalism already in place before the terrorist attack, wonders how such a strong body could belong "to someone so wounded" (60). After 9/11, however, Erica's retreat to the past (like America's) intensifies, and Changez's intention to connect with her becomes harder to fulfill. On their first meeting since 9/11, Erica confesses to Changez that the attacks have had a regressive effect on her, "kind of like I've been thrown back a year," and admits "feel[ing] haunted" by Chris (80). Changez's longing for an elusive Erica, thus, leads him to seek to live with her in a sensuous present underpinned by their physical intimacy, which he hopes will release her from "a current that pulled her within herself" (86). He is, in his own words, determined to "serve as her anchor," which he realizes he can do by making himself noticeable, almost "touching her . . . and then . . . wait[ing] for her to become aware of my physical presence," as he does at a party (86–87). Later, as their relationship hobbles on and they try to have sex for the first time, Erica is emphatically absent: "She did not respond; she did not resist; she merely acceded as I undressed her" (89). Changez then suggests that she talk to him about Chris, and suddenly a "liveliness entered her eyes; they ceased to be turned inward" (91). They grow relaxed and talk before falling asleep, connected in the present via the link afforded by a most delicate form of physical contact, "shoulder to shoulder, with our knuckles touching at our sides" (92). This attention to the present is nevertheless too tenuous to keep their relationship grounded.

As some time passes before they see each other again, Erica becomes increasingly detached. The next time they meet, Changez finds a "diminished

Erica" who is even more withdrawn, "a pale, nervous creature who could almost have been a stranger" (102). This state is, moreover, the result of a "bad patch" that she compares to "the first time, after Chris died," thus symbolizing the deterioration of a nationalist sentiment that, while initially palliative, seems to pose now difficulties for Americans' reckoning with the first stages of the war on terror (103). Changez's insistent efforts to anchor her by way of physical contact, symptomatically, become harder to maintain: "I considered giving her an embrace but decided against it; she seemed too brittle to be touched" (103). Later, at Changez's apartment, Erica says she cannot see him anymore, which she explains is her way to protect him from her as much as herself from him. Desperate to "hold on to her—indeed . . . to hold on to *us*," Changez tells Erica again to pretend he is Chris, and they "made love with a physical intimacy that Erica and I had never enjoyed" (104–5; emphasis original). While they are momentarily connected in the present once more, Changez's willingness to accommodate Erica's past proves only to be an inadequate way to help her avoid the self-consuming consequences of her slipping back toward an irrecoverable, glorified former life.

Compounded by the weakening of her health, Erica's condition intensifies and she continues to withdraw from social life, including and especially Changez. On a visit to her parents' apartment, Changez realizes the extent of her constant abstraction. He describes their meeting in her bedroom by explaining how she was having a conversation with Chris, not with him, "a conversation occurring on some plane that I could not reach" (112–13). Erica, he concludes, "was disappearing into a powerful *nostalgia*, one from which only she could choose whether or not to return" (113; emphasis original). This comment bears clear implications with regard to the American reaction to 9/11. Immediately following the scene, Changez draws a parallel between Erica and the United States: "America, too, was increasingly giving itself over to a dangerous nostalgia at that time" (115). Spurred by the revival of a self-image dominated by the "retro" look of "flags and uniforms," with "generals addressing cameras in war rooms and newspaper headlines featuring such words as *duty* and *honor*," the country has succumbed to a "determination to look *back*" (115; emphasis original). Which moment in the past the United States wants to return to remains uncertain: "a time of unquestioned dominance? of safety? of moral certainty?" One thing that is clear to Changez, though, is that, as with Erica, the new, backward-looking present seems not to have room for "someone like me" (115).

After a period apart, Changez tries to reestablish contact with Erica. When he learns that she has been committed to an institution, he decides to pay her a visit. Before he can see her, however, a nurse tells him that her state of introspective nostalgia is so acute that Chris, with whom "she was in love," was for Erica "alive enough," and "in her mind she was experiencing things that were stronger and more meaningful than the things she could experience with the rest of us" (133). In other words, Erica's link with the here and now is at its most tenuous. In response, Changez protests that one cannot live in the past: "Eventually she will have to leave here.... Perhaps she will want to be with me then" (133). Yet his anchoring presence is precisely what makes him "the one who upsets her the most," as the nurse tells him, "because you are most real, and you make her lose her balance" (133). Here Hamid renders most apparent the symbolism of Changez's futile attempt to root his relationship with Erica in the present as the failing relationship of a stunned America with its post-9/11 Other. Finally, Changez is allowed to see Erica, and as they wander around the institution's grounds he tries one last time to convince her to live sensuously in the present, to "be lustful" and "come back to New York with me" (135). When his plea passes unregistered, Hamid has Changez entertain with acid irony "the wild notion of abducting her and taking her away in my rental car," a rather farcical scenario that he dismisses right away, against the grain of the crazed and desperate terrorist cliché, with a rational and principled response: "the absurdity—and disrespect to her—of such an act was immediately obvious to me, and did nothing of the sort" (135). Discarding the abduction, he runs out of options.

Changez's endeavors to connect with Erica are finally thwarted by the indefinite suspension caused by her disappearance. On his return from an assignment in Chile, Changez wants to pay her a last visit, but the same nurse he once talked to tells him that she has wandered off into the woods and only her clothes have been found by the Hudson River. Changez assumes that she has committed suicide, but even though "she'd been saying goodbye to everyone," the nurse points out, "technically she's a missing person" (163). This open-ended suspension is Changez's final motivation to leave the United States for Pakistan and the basis for a kind of "progressive and politically radical"[23] form of mourning that rests on his urge to thrive, if only in his imagination, on the contingency of their fraught relationship. Changez recounts how he has pictured his life if Erica was in Lahore with him in a series of mundane episodes such as "breakfast[ing] with my parents" or "go[ing] out for an inexpensive but delicious dinner in the open air" (172–73). He even confesses to have entertained the idea that she might still be alive, which keeps him diligently looking for traces of her in the *Princeton Alumni Weekly*, "with particular attention to the class notes and obituaries sections," drawing "hope and sorrow in equal measure from each of her episodic absences" (174–75). Changez continues to email Erica "until her account became inactive," to then limit himself "to a single letter each year, sent on the anniversary of her disappearance, but it was always returned to me" (175). Ultimately, though, his mourning is a process necessarily anchored in the present, as he explains at the end of his account of it: "Not, of course, that I actually *believe* I am having a relationship . . . with Erica at this moment, or that she will one day appear. . . . But I am still young and see no need to marry another, and for now I am content to wait" (176; emphasis original). The present becomes Changez's only refuge. Yet this is not only in contrast with Erica's retreat to the past.

The Shape of the Future

A parallel temporal pressure towards the future assails Changez's focus on the contingency of the present. After he graduates from Princeton, Changez begins to work for the valuation company Underwood Samson, whose hubristic forward-looking ethos greatly attracts him. As he admits in describing his first international assignment in Manila, "I felt enormously powerful . . . knowing my team was shaping the future" (66). Like Erica's regressive condition, this thrust toward the future is not triggered by 9/11 proper. Instead, it figures as an important aspect of the new geopolitical order that is exposed to Changez via his progressive reckoning with the American response to the attacks. Militarily, the United States sought to (re)claim its hegemony in part via the invasion and ensuing wars in Afghanistan and Iraq, which were legitimated by a (largely manufactured) fear of an uncertain future marked by further attacks. Yet, while these aspects appear in the novel, Hamid seeks to explore in more detail how the invasive work of global capital operates as a mirror image of the military securitization of the future. As Leerom Medovoi has suggested, "Changez's overt presentation of American imperialism as an endlessly expansionist project . . . belies a more complex analysis hinted at by the novel in which empires are inextricable from the territorial logics of capital accumulation."[24] This is in keeping with history. George Bush, for instance, made no attempt to conceal this connection in a speech that he gave on the first anniversary of the 9/11 attacks tellingly titled "Securing Freedom's Triumph." In it, Bush expressed hopes for "a better future based on democracy and the free market," pledged to work "with the entire global trading community to build a world that trades in freedom and therefore grows in prosperity," and declared the United States the leader in the global effort to spread "democracy, development, free markets and free trade" around the world.[25]

Immediately, Changez understands the company's orientation toward the future as a way to fulfill his own version of the American dream. Having worked hard first to be accepted into Princeton, holding several jobs to pay for his schooling, and then not only making it through the company's famously competitive selection process but becoming the top junior employee, Changez sees his job as both a reward and the prospect of a successful, accomplished life. He recalls, for instance, leaving his job interview with the feeling that Underwood Samson "had the potential to transform my life . . . making my concerns about money and status things of the distant past" (14). Later, while at the company's annual summer party at his boss Jim's glamorous beach house, Jim, who acts as a mentor and role model for Changez, casually tells him: "I remember my first Underwood Samson summer party. Barbecue going, music playing. . . . I figured I wouldn't mind having a place out in the Hamptons myself one day." Acknowledging how Jim has anticipated his dreams of future comfort and luxury, Changez remarks: "I smiled; Jim made one feel he could hear one's thoughts" (43–44). The appeal of a bright future, however, soon dwindles in the face of the exploitation that sustains it.

At first, Changez seems to approach the company's future-shaping mission rather casually. As he says regarding an early assignment in New Jersey, "our client was unconcerned with the potential for future growth. No, our mandate was to determine how much fat could be cut" (95). To fulfill this mandate seems to be very a simple task: "Call centers could be outsourced; truck rolls could be reduced; purchasing could be consolidated. . . . The potential for headcount reduction was substantial" (95). Yet the fashioning of the global economy's future through ruthless financial intervention begins to reveal itself to Changez as what Saskia Sassen has called the brutal and predatory forms of "expulsion" that characterize the current moment.[26] Shaping the future becomes a kind of violence, which Hamid compares to terroristic fundamentalism when his protagonist tells himself to "focus on the fundamentals," the company's motto, to overcome his initial doubts about the ethics of the job (98). After a succession of moments that focus his attention onto a global here and now, Changez becomes aware of the destructive outcome of forcing the future into the shape of the dollar sign and, consequently, his own complicity with it.

As we saw, Changez's response to Erica's dangerous nostalgia is to emphasize a sensuous sense of self-actualization that connects her to him in the present. Here he resorts to observing his surroundings—especially the things and people that his new professional status has allowed him to ignore—so as to try to understand his position in the context of a planetary present dominated by the ferocious capitalist hegemony of the global

North (spearheaded by the United States) over the global South. The first such observation occurs during his assignment in Manila. One day, while stopped in heavy traffic, Changez looks out the window of the limousine in which he and his colleagues travel and encounters the gaze of a Filipino driver: "There was an undisguised hostility in his expression; I had no idea why. We had not met before . . . and in a few minutes we would probably never see one another again. But his dislike was so obvious, so intimate, that it got under my skin. I stared back at him, getting angry myself . . . and I maintained eye contact until he was obliged by the movement of the car in front to return his attention to the road" (66–67). This hostility gives Changez pause: "I remained preoccupied with this matter far longer than I should have, pursuing several possibilities that all assumed—as their unconscious starting point—that he and I shared a sort of Third World sensibility" (67). Significantly, the ephemeral transnational connection he experiences in the here-and-now standstill of traffic is also the catalyst of a disconnection. As one of his colleagues in the limousine asks him a question, Changez contemplates his "fair hair and light eyes and, most of all, his oblivious immersion in the minutiae of our work" and concludes: "you are so *foreign*" (67; emphasis original). Even the physical immediacy forced by the limousine's confined space is unable to provoke Changez's identification with his coworker.

Upon return from Manila shortly after 9/11, the clash between Changez's new global South, transnational sensitivity, and his participation in a financial system designed to perpetuate the exploitation of those with whom he feels connected now is exacerbated. Symptomatically, his job does not allow him to dwell on the implications of his responsibilities in shaping the future: "I found it difficult to sleep at night. Fortunately, however, the intensity of our assignment did not permit me to indulge in further bouts of insomnia" (68). Critical reflection—the ultimate manifestation of being intellectually in the present—is annulled by Underwood Samson's relentless demands of his full attention. Yet, growing concerned with the tensions between Pakistan and India and the bombing of Afghanistan ("Pakistan's neighbor, our friend, and a fellow Muslim nation") by the United States, Changez decides to spend the winter holiday in Lahore to recuperate his connection with the contingent global realities that his commitment to his job has made him neglect (100). Reflecting on the way he observes his surroundings, including his family home, Changez realizes that he has been looking at the world through "the eyes of a foreigner, and not just any foreigner, but that particular type of entitled and unsympathetic American who so annoyed me when I encountered him in the classrooms and workplaces of your country's elite" (124). This realization is followed by pledges to help his family financially and a sense of despair toward the general state of insecurity dominating the post-9/11 moment, which reinforce his reconnection with a planetary present experienced from the point of view of the global South. As a token of this reconnection and a reassertion of his identity, he decides to grow a beard that, in yet another ironic gesture by Hamid targeted at dismantling the discourse of the war on terror, makes him look not like a terrorist but "like a mouse" (128). The beard, nevertheless, is provocative enough to elicit hostile, knee-jerk reactions in New York, such as "verbal abuse by complete strangers" in the subway and "whispers and stares" at Underwood Samson, demonstrating how radical yet taxing his focus on the contingency of the here and now already is (130).

This new sensitivity toward the global South finally reaches a point of no return. After he is told by Jim that the best way to cope with whatever is worrying him "is to get yourself busy" (i.e., to forget about the present and to concentrate on shaping the future), Changez is sent to Valparaíso, Chile, for his next and last assignment (137). From the very beginning, he is incapable of fulfilling his tasks under the supervision of a senior Underwood Samson officer. Instead, he spends his time online trying to learn more about the growing tensions between Pakistan and India and seeking to understand why the United States does not support his country as an ally, while developing an interest in the Chilean city. Valparaíso "was itself a distraction: the city was powerfully atmospheric; a sense of melancholy," which he identifies with Lahore on the grounds of a common history of past prosperity, "pervaded its boulevards and hillsides" (143–44). Changez then begins to neglect his job more deliberately to his superior's increasing anger by letting himself be absorbed by Valparaíso, its history, and its architecture, thus enacting a strong resistance to the processes of capitalist destruction with which he has been complicit via a newfound desire to idle, muse, and be in touch with the world immediately around him. His conclusion proves the importance of such moments for the formation of his political position toward the war on terror and its geopolitical implications: "Now I saw that in this constant striving to realize a financial future, no thought was given to the critical personal and political issues that affect one's emotional present. In other words, my blinders were coming off" (145). The future can no longer take precedence over the present.

Changez's urgent sense of critical reflection is stoked by his conversations with Juan-Bautista, the contemplative and observant chief of the company he is sent to appraise and with whom he feels a strong affinity. During a conversation over lunch, Juan-Bautista gently but sincerely confronts Changez for his contribution to secure the United States' economic supremacy through his job at Underwood Samson. After asking Changez if "it trouble[s] you . . . to make your living by disrupting the lives of others," he compares him to the Ottoman janissaries, "Christian boys . . . captured . . . and trained to be soldiers in a Muslim army" to "erase their own civilizations" (151). This comparison does not only reveal his responsibility in furthering the hegemony of the American empire; crucially, it also prefigures Changez's new antagonism against the world of global finance, "a primary means by which the American empire exercised its power" (156), and drives him to relinquish the caste of "officers of the empire" of which he was once a member after he declares he will not complete his assignment in Chile (152). Changez then returns to New York to face the consequences of his revolt, not without a great deal of trepidation toward the idea of having put an end to his American dream. This decision, however, is instantly liberating. As he leaves the Underwood Samson headquarters, he observes the streets of Manhattan in a fresh way, "with an ex-janissary's gaze" that allows him to register the state of securitization, the hypermilitarization of public space, and the strict, hierarchical class structures that define the empire supposedly fighting international terrorism to protect the future of freedom and democracy (157).

Changez's determination to ground himself in the contingency of the present, thus, embodies a radical temporality that negates the totalization of history with which the United States reacted to 9/11. If, as Niklas Luhmann once argued, "Anything is contingent that is neither necessary nor impossible,"[27] Changez's story about his time in New York is an important dimension of Hamid's aesthetics of exception. This is so not because he fulfills the role of an irrational perpetrator of violence seeking to wreak havoc and destabilize peace, threatening the national unity and economic prosperity of the United States, as the war-on-terror narrative would have it. On the contrary, his story promotes an alternative worldview anchored in a dissensual present that clashes directly with Erica's dangerous nostalgia and Underwood Samson's future-shaping securitization of all things according to their financial value. As he finishes his account, however, this radical temporality will bring to bear the failure of Changez's antagonism in the conclusion of the (terrorized) dialogue he maintains with his American interlocutor.

Redacting the Narrative

Changez's story gradually reaches the moment of its telling. After deciding to return to Pakistan, he becomes convinced that "America had to be stopped" (168). His contribution to this effort, which "was not much and I fear it may well fail your expectations," is to turn into a strong public voice of dissent against the war on terror and its deathly repercussions for his country (169). This new commitment is illustrated by two key aspects of his new life in Lahore. On the one hand, at his new job as a university professor, Changez incorporates a critical component to his courses in finance, ironically employing what he has learned in the American elite academic institutions and corporate world to critique the U.S. global hegemony. On the other, he becomes active in demonstrations in which people "of all possible affiliations," including "communists, capitalists, feminists [and] religious literalists," participate, becoming a prominent leader in the student movement (179).

Changez's militancy, however, is hampered by complications ranging from the violent activity of some members of the movement, who he admits "are no better than common thugs," to "official warnings" from his university, which nonetheless does not suspend him given the popularity of his courses (180). These complications, further, take on distinctly global attributes when the consensual apparatus of the war on terror catches up with him. Drawn by his growing notoriety, the international media are ready to tokenize him as a Middle Eastern antagonist with no name, history, or acceptable political views to be demonized for his position against the United States. As his outspoken dissenting stance intensifies and he insists that his intentions are pacific and democratic, the movement is instantly labeled as "anti-American" by "the foreign press" (179). Far from retreating by fear of retaliation, though, Changez pushes on. His address to the "international television news networks" about the fact that "no country inflicts death so readily upon the inhabitants of other countries, frightens so many people so far away, as America" is incorporated into the news-cycle spectacle, "replayed for days" and excerpted "in the occasional war-on-terror montage" (182). While this has obvious counterproductive consequences, he confesses he "was possibly trying to attract attention to myself," hoping that "if Erica was watching—which rationally, I knew, she almost certainly was not—she might have seen me and been moved *to correspond*" (182; emphasis added). Changez's willingness to expose himself to the manipulation of the media so as to call for his beloved (Am) Erica to mobilize against the war on terror is nevertheless followed by his acceptance that his dissent has likely marked him as a counterterror target: "I must meet my fate when it confronts me, and in the meantime I must conduct myself without panic" (183). Calmly, Changez embraces the inevitability of the preestablished, spurious role of the fundamentalist that the Western counterterrorist narrative coerces him to play.

Thus, having finished their dinner, Changez and the American walk through the dark alleys of Lahore to the latter's hotel. It is at this point that the novel reaches its conclusion as the conversation is suddenly invaded by a sense of suspicion and paranoia, which is farcically reflected in Changez's account. The American, who has "ceased to listen to my chatter," is alarmed by the sight of several men who "are now rather close, and yes, the expression on the face of that one—what a coincidence; it is our waiter; he has offered me a nod of recognition—is rather grim" (183). Reacting to Changez's ironic hint that he might be after all conspiring with the waiter to kill him, he cannot but act out the role that he has been assigned by the war-on-terror narrative, which dictates that the men's suspicious behavior is enough grounds to consider Changez and the other men potential terrorists. The American appears now as a panicked enemy of the Pakistanis, who seem to be closing in on him. As Changez nonchalantly intends to say goodbye, the American reaches into his pocket and retrieves something with the "glint of metal," which the narrator hopes comes "from the holder of your business cards" (184). Nothing more is reported, and the novel closes without resolution.

On the face of it, this uncertainty seems to give the narrative a satisfactory ending given that Changez's story is from the beginning extremely unreliable, not least because of its one-sided rendition of the long conversation between the two characters. Therefore, nothing can be gleaned out about what really happens in the final scene. In addition, a simple textual analysis would lead us to the same conclusion. Does the American have a gun? Does he kill Changez? Or is he going to give Changez his card? On the other hand, is Changez colluding with the waiter to kill his interlocutor? Or is he as innocent as he has made himself out to be through his account? We simply do not know. Strictly speaking, the ending is, as one critic has put it, "a classic cliff-hanger."[28] Yet I want to argue, to conclude, that Hamid's exceptional aesthetics necessitate that we consider it through the lens of the state of exception that has governed the war on terror. This would lead us to consider an alternative reading of the ending that falls outside of the options that the novel seems to offer: either Changez is killed by the American, who is after all a CIA agent, or he is not. This choice, which is arguably foreshadowed by Changez's prior admission that he will patiently await his fate, is nonetheless equivocal. Regardless of the outcome of his conversation with the American, I want to suggest, Changez would eventually be killed or at least indefinitely detained for his political views and his intention to articulate an effective antagonist discourse countering the U.S. geopolitical campaign against international terrorism. In other words, his narrative is destined to be irrevocably superseded by the larger, all-encompassing narrative of the war on terror.[29]

Of course, this information is nowhere to be found in the novel, but a great deal of other, crucial information, such as Changez's interlocutor's voice, is not included either. *The Reluctant Fundamentalist* operates, one may say, as one of the most characteristic textual modes of the war on terror, the redacted document, which has arguably regained a prominent position in the public imagination and has become, as a result, somewhat of an emblem of the post-9/11 moment. A redacted document is, by definition, a text that is modified (often through the blacking out of words and passages) so that key information that would otherwise be incriminatory or dangerous to disclose is unreadable. In the redacted text, thus, specific events and people are kept from being identified in the secondary story lines making up the war-on-terror narrative. Yet the information is not strictly speaking left out; rather, it remains in it, only impossible to interpret within the explicit parameters of that particular text. Details of a military operation, for instance, may not be legible in a redacted report. However, in putting the operation within the larger context of what we do know about the war on terror (largely thanks to the efforts of journalists and nongovernmental organizations to bring transparency and accountability to the U.S. counterterror agenda), not knowing who or what is involved in a specific operation does not preclude us from knowing that, breaking the codes of international law, many U.S. military operations have systematically targeted civilian populations or that the detention of individuals at Guantánamo Bay continues unchallenged to this day.[30] The details are omitted, but the story is there.

Thus, maintaining that the novel's ending is too uncertain (i.e., that crucial details are missing) for one to decide what happens to Changez is to entertain the idea that there is a fair and ethical side to the totalizing counterterror apparatus, one that does not lead to the killing of Changez, or at the very least his arrest, because of his political views. Yet the war-on-terror narrative has shown us time and time again that an individual of his profile, a vocal, antiwar Muslim activist with an avowed intention to challenge the U.S. geopolitical agenda, will be captured by the counterterrorist apparatus, his hypervisibility as a "fundamentalist" amplified by the complicit Western media. It is simply not possible to think of an alternative ending. Who detains him or kills him, whether the American or someone else, is irrelevant. This is why I propose such a reading of the end. As Changez says at an earlier moment in reflecting on his newly acquired sensitivity for the global here and now, "try as we might, we cannot reconstitute ourselves as the autonomous beings we previously imagined ourselves to be. Something of us is now outside, and something of the outside is now within us" (174). No matter how terrorized, the dialogue that the novel invokes is unavoidably subjected to the grip of the counterterror narrative.

Changez's attempt to explain his antagonistic position in dialogue is, therefore, bound to fail. The possibility to think that he will not be killed is nothing other than a postpolitical fantasy against the historical backdrop of the war on terror. This is not an excessive reading, but the interpretive act of following to its logical conclusion the consensual order that allows the United States, in its role as exceptional state, to exert its global hegemony by whatever means necessary. Yet the failure of this dialogue is productive insofar as it exposes the geopolitical regime that Changez seeks to counter. His caution to the panicked American in the last stages of the novel that "you should not imagine that we Pakistanis are all potential terrorists, just as we should not imagine that you Americans are all undercover assassins" becomes, ironically, both powerfully valid and obsolete (183). The terrorist, either self-described as such or appointed as the official enemy of the United States, must and will be eliminated.

As I have shown here, *The Reluctant Fundamentalist* rehearses the unavoidable failure that results from an attempt to dispute the global narrative of the war on terror as a major component of the U.S. agenda to exert its geopolitical hegemony at a planetary level. In the next and final chapter, I want to explore how narrative fiction can effect a counterdialogic intervention in order to take control of another kind of global narrative. I will read Indra Sinha's *Animal's People* and Helon Habila's *Oil on Water* for their ability to challenge the narrative of the Anthropocene, which describes the new epoch into which the planet has been ushered due to the impact of human activity on its geological, chemical, and biological cycles. A crucial aspect of such a narrative, as we will see, is that while it is being currently established by a rather democratic coming together of voices, the Anthropocene nevertheless has the potential to generate a consensual order that diminishes the political agency of the most vulnerable inhabitants of the Earth, and particularly those in the global South. I will, thus, address one last strategy, reframing, to articulate an effective resistance against the illusory dialogue that the construction of the Anthropocene narrative runs the risk of becoming. To do so, I will focus on how Sinha's and Habila's novels provide important reflections on the visuality of environmental destruction and how, in offering alternative representations, they contribute to envisaging a more egalitarian future on the planet.

CHAPTER FIVE

Reframing

Visualizing Environmental Violence
in the Anthropocene

> There is some reason to suspect, therefore, that the knowledge and discourse of the Anthropocene may itself form part, perhaps unknowingly, of a hegemonic system for representing the world as a totality to be governed. . . . It is rather a matter of opening up the official narrative of the Anthropocene to discussion, so as to enable closer reflection on the particularities of our representations of the world. So that other voices *from* and *for* the Earth can be heard, coming from other cultures and other social groups.
>
> —Christophe Bonneuil and Jean-Baptiste Fressoz,
> *The Shock of the Anthropocene*

> The images of art are operations that produce a discrepancy, a dissemblance. Words describe what the eye might see or express what it will never see; they deliberately clarify or obscure an idea. Visible forms yield a meaning to be construed or subtract it. . . . This means two things. In the first place, the images of art are, as such, dissemblances. Secondly, the image is not exclusive to the visible. There is visibility that does not amount to an image; there are images which consist wholly in words.
>
> —Jacques Rancière, *The Future of the Image*

In this final chapter, I wish to address the presence of illusory dialogue in the current construction of the idea of the Anthropocene. A relatively new term, *Anthropocene* was popularized at the turn of the twenty-first century to describe the new geological epoch resulting from the deep and irreversible alteration of the Earth's chemical, physical, and biological processes by human activity.[1] The Anthropocene was initially conceived as a discourse intended to open new lines of inquiry and reflection to understand the long history of human-caused ecological shifts at the planetary level and the resulting new relationships between humans and the environment. However, I want to explore here how it runs the risk of becoming a consensual notion with serious depoliticizing implications. As a narrative by (certain) humans about (all) humans, the Anthropocene rests on a supreme and unexamined "we" that is politically detrimental with regard to the differing sovereignties, responsibilities, and vulnerabilities of the *anthropos* that it encompasses. Such a narrative must, therefore, be reframed so that it critically attends to these differences and accounts for the impact of human activity on the Earth accurately and fairly.

My argument will focus on how two works of fiction from the global South, Indra Sinha's *Animal's People* (2007) and Helon Habila's *Oil on Water* (2010), destabilize with politically productive outcomes the representational order that governs the narrative of the Anthropocene. Through the analysis of these novels, I will seek to reveal how the critical presentation of specific iterations of environmental violence can become a crucial dissenting intervention that lays bare the potential postpolitical implications of such a holistic narrative. The novels deal with two very different events—a massive gas leak in a pesticide factory in Bhopal, India, and the devastation caused in the Niger Delta, Nigeria, by the oil-extraction industry. Yet both grapple with the visuality of environmental violence and emphasize the ways in which portrayals of those events originating from the global North ultimately cause a certain depoliticization. In response to this, the novels employ specific aesthetic strategies targeted to the reaffirmation of the right of the peoples of the global South to represent the disasters by which their lives are directly affected and, in doing so, participate in the composition of the Anthropocene narrative from their point of view.

As I continue to explore ways in which minor voices can articulate radical counterdialogic strategies that allow them to retain their political agency, I will concentrate on how both novels critically reflect on the role of journalism in representing such violence. The production, circulation, and consumption of journalistic material is the most widespread manner in which environmental catastrophes are registered. As we will see, however, this is not a simple question of whether they are visible or not. In fact, the Bhopal leak and the oil industry's ruination of the Niger Delta are among the world's best-known (and, therefore, visible) ecological disasters. What the novels explore, instead, is how they are visible and whether their visibility is regulated by specific consensual orders of visuality. In other words, they illustrate how minor voices deploy modes of "countervisuality"[2] that can contribute to the general narrative of the Anthropocene without participating in an illusory dialogue that subordinates their environmentalism to certain representational regimes. Whereas I have so far discussed illusory dialogue in purely linguistic terms, I will consider here images (as translated into textual matter) for both their vulnerability to be co-opted for disciplinary purposes as well as their capacity to act as resisting tools in the narratives I will examine below.

In focusing on the fictional treatment of two ongoing catastrophes, furthermore, I seek to understand better how minor voices can represent ecological disaster against the grain of the spectacular tonalities of the most prominent discourses of the Anthropocene. This is important not only because those catastrophes appear as forms of "slow violence"[3] that are lost in most registers of the Anthropocene. More significantly, this is also crucial because, given the fundamentally spectacular dimensions of illusory dialogue, they gesture toward the possibility of an emancipatory planetary coalition of environmentalist minor voices. Taken individually, the destruction in Sinha's and Habila's narratives provides us with examples of the ravaging of the global South by the impulses of the industrial and technological modernity enforced by the global North. Considered as instantiations of a larger framework, however, they become segments of a planetary story whose grammar redraws the ethical and agential distributions of the individuals and collectives in the subject and object positions. As Jean-Luc Nancy has recently put it, "Catastrophes are not all of the same gravity, but they all connect with the totality of interdependences that make up general equivalence."[4] In this light, the Anthropocene can be rethought to operate as the differential base for the interconnection of catastrophes, modulating the (hi)story of human life on Earth with specific accounts of their social, economic, and historical specificity. In their equivalence as catastrophes, the ecological events at the center of the narratives I have chosen to analyze are not simple exceptions, accidents in the normal state of affairs or even inevitable consequences of global industrial processes of production and exploitation, but part and parcel of the destructive activity described in the narrative of the Anthropocene.

Countervisualities of the Anthropocene

Now that it is still a relatively new term, the Anthropocene can easily be critiqued and expanded, as some environmental critics have already begun to do. Rob Nixon, for example, has cautioned that the Anthropocene as signifier of our geological epoch presents an important pitfall with regard to the human agency that it presupposes. He asks: "What is lost and gained by adopting the Anthropocene's grand species perspective on the human? Does this epic vantage point risk suppressing—historically and in the present—unequal human impacts, unequal human agency, and unequal human vulnerabilities?"[5] In response to this question, Nixon argues that the Anthropocene must be accounted for at two distinct yet complementary narrative levels: one comprehensive, which involves the human species as a whole, and the other fractured, concerned with human political and social history. It is with the capacities of narratives at this second level that I am particularly concerned here.

Two crucial questions immediately arise about how narratives operating at this fractured level can articulate a dissenting position vis-à-vis the Anthropocene. First, the Anthropocene was originally a scientific account that emerged in the global North. Since then it has gained enormous currency and has become prominent in a variety of contexts, from the international media to a large number of academic disciplines, while also turning into an important anchor for those working to promote the necessary policy- and law-making decisions to tackle the environmental challenges of our era. Yet how can it accommodate voices that neither come from the scientific community nor have influence on policy-making circles, voices that do not belong to the globally recognized nodes of academic activity or cannot reach audiences via media conglomerates and networks?

A second, related question emerges. Climate change is the main notion with which the Anthropocene is identified, leading the agendas of activists who try both to raise awareness about its consequences and to propose tangible ways to begin mitigating its effects. Yet this is not the only manifestation of the disastrous effects of the Anthropocene. The systematic destruction of the biosphere, the mass extinction of species, increasingly stronger and more deathly epidemics, the ruination of ecosystems, the disastrous contamination of major water reserves, and the growing impoverishment of air quality, among others, are also crucial events that describe our new ecological epoch. These, at the same time, affect certain global regions and populations more profoundly than others. How, then, can other aspects of the Anthropocene that are equally responsible for shaping the current ecological crisis be visualized in ways that can motivate an adequate intervention in the activities causing them?

One way to begin is by moving beyond planetary cycles, phenomena, and trends to offer alternative explorations that allow us to imagine the Anthropocene otherwise. If it is to be conceived of as a collective narrative coalescing a global multiplicity of voices, the Anthropocene must not operate as an illusory dialogue in which the participation of minor voices is welcomed insofar as they abide by a set of preordained representational conditions. Moreover, their descriptions of the forms of ecological destruction that assail them cannot be subordinated to a planetary consensus that connects all humans through a totalizing narrative, as if they were placed on an equalizing imaginary plane. As Christophe Bonneuil and Jean-Baptiste Fressoz have compellingly asserted, "the Anthropocene is political inasmuch as it requires arbitrating between various conflicting human forcings on the planet, between the footprints of different human groups (classes, nations), between different technological and industrial options, or between different ways of life and consumption."[6] Sinha's and Habila's novels, I want to argue, intervene in the general narrative of the Anthropocene by reframing it, that is, by revisualizing it in concrete and situated ways.

My appraisal of the Anthropocene through the lens of these novels is preceded by a series of rich and important debates that have appeared across the spectrum of social and humanist critique in recent years. Some critics have even questioned the very suitability of the term, proposing alternative denominations that describe the epochal change, such as the Oliganthropocene, the Anthrobscene, the Capitalocene, or the Chthulucene.[7] In continuing to outline the agonistic form of political resistance with which this book is concerned, however, I will engage with the Anthropocene narrative instead of substituting it with another to explore how minor voices can reclaim the category of the *anthropos* and root their counterdialogic political agency in it. Despite some of the universalizing claims he has made in the past, I will follow Dipesh Chakrabarty, who argues that "the human" must be conceived "on multiple scales and registers" given that "there is no corresponding 'humanity' that in its oneness can act as a political agent."[8] Thus, I will consider the Anthropocene as both the new epoch that the planetary destruction caused by the activities of certain humans has ushered in, as it is commonly defined, as well as the different forms of environmental resistance of certain other humans facing such destruction.[9] Rather than the fundamental consensus that humans have modified the Earth's geological structures and processes, therefore, the unexamined "we" that the Anthropocene might presume can be reformulated as the dissensual core of the ethical and political implications of the anthropogenic planetary events that have already changed the lives of millions.

As a consequence, the imbalances in the degrees to which the Anthropocene poses a threat to populations around the world, the erosion of environmental sovereignties and responsibilities at a planetary level, and the urgent need for a renovated democratic platform that tackles these global challenges immediately reveal themselves as critical questions for the current postpolitical moment. Yet these questions have been approached rather unevenly inscribed in such a frame of analysis. Some of the most important theorists have addressed humans' relationship with the environment but, generally speaking, not with the goal of making it the main objective of their writing. Michael Hardt and Antonio Negri, for example, defend the idea of "an ecology of the common—an ecology focused equally on nature and society, on humans and the nonhuman world in a dynamic of interdependence, care, and mutual transformation."[10] Others remain more skeptical. Alain Badiou, for instance, questions the increasing attention paid to the environment in recent times while acknowledging that "ecology solely concerns me inasmuch as it can be proven that it is an intrinsic dimension of the politics of the emancipation of humanity," for which he nonetheless sees "no proof."[11] Slavoj Žižek, for his part, considers "the universal problem (of the survival of the species)" to be subordinate to the history of capitalism, arguing that "one can solve [it] only by first resolving the particular deadlock of the capitalist mode of production."[12] Other critics, although often in the social sciences, have approached the questions related to the environment from a postpolitical perspective more directly, with Erik Swyngedouw as the most important figure.[13] A fully focused humanistic engagement, then, can still shed important light on this matter.

Thus, as I have already advanced, while deemphasizing climate change in favor of other human-caused destructive events occurring at smaller scales and expanding the theoretical purview of environmental postpolitical critique, I seek to explore the capacity for narrative fiction to offer, in a translational gesture, important reflections on the visual aspects of life in the Anthropocene from the point of view of the global South. While the novels I have selected help us imagine the specificities and scales of certain manifestations of environmental destruction, it is also important to note that they incorporate questions of sovereignty, agency, and self-representation. What these novels tackle, therefore, is the visuality—and not merely visibility—of that destruction.

Questions of visuality and alternative representations of the Anthropocene are not uncommon in ecocritical work, especially by literary and cultural theorists.[14] My own exploration of the visual politics of the Anthropocene is based on the figurative spatial relationship between Sinha's and Habila's narrators and their implied audiences. In a dialogue, the relationship between interlocutors could be said to be expressed as a horizontal arrangement. At the same time, my critique of illusory dialogue implies a vertical distribution between a higher, dominant position and a lower, minor one. An agonistic intervention of illusory dialogue, therefore, seeks to return the interaction to a horizontal plane. As we have seen throughout this book, this gesture is not intended to erase the power imbalances that undermine the political agency of minor voices but rather to acknowledge them as the basis of their strategies to counter the illusory dialogue concealing them. Thus, I will characterize the novels' reframing of the narrative of the Anthropocene as manifestations of a dissensual "view from across."[15]

Instead of rejecting it, the novels repurpose this spatialized visual relationship between subject and object, between capturer and captured, in order to articulate their counterdialogic interventions. As we will see, it is important that their protagonists are the voices responsible for depicting the specific ecological disasters they are concerned with; it legitimizes those stories as first-person accounts that challenge the consensus underpinning the unexamined "we" of the Anthropocene. In carrying the weight of the narration, they can contribute to making one of the most important global narratives of our time fairer and more nuanced. In other words, they do not simply break up the divide between a world that remains unseen and the official realm of the visible. They incorporate—to modify Ursula K. Heise's argument—their sense of place into the general (common) sense of planet[16] in order to challenge the totalizing order that it might otherwise enforce.

The novels' engagement with the world of journalism and the media is equally important for the dissenting character of their undertakings. In placing it at the center of their stories, Sinha and Habila ask us to ponder the importance of the politics, technologies, and cultures of representation that determine the scope and limitations of the Anthropocene, offering reflections, to cite T. J. Demos, "not centered solely on the 'politics of aesthetics' of the image, but also on the wider channels of image circulation, the institutions of containment, and the . . . assemblages that frame and in part determine the visual culture of environmentalism."[17] Thus, in focusing their accounts on the temporal and geographical immediacy of the catastrophes, both narrators act as "Anthropocene correspondents" who shorten the distance from which their audiences apprehend them. The aesthetic contribution of their accounts, to follow Jacques Rancière, hinges on their capacity to reconfigure, "in accordance with new procedures," the relationship between "words and forms, the sayable and the visible, the visible and the invisible," so that "the stable relations" at the core of the narrative of the Anthropocene can be disrupted and, consequently, new modes of visuality can be created that reflect the historical and ecological specificities of the violence that they portray.[18]

Instead of presenting a general problem to then proceed with close readings of the novels, as I have done so far, I will pair each novel with an example that illustrates the major point I intend to show.

Directing the Gaze in Indra Sinha's *Animal's People*

The year 2014 marked the thirtieth anniversary of the massive gas leak in Bhopal, in central India, that gave the city its unfortunate prominence in the global environmental imagination. On the night of December 2, 1984, a leak in the Union Carbide India pesticide factory killed between 15,000 and 30,000 people (1,700 to 10,000 of whom died instantly) and left over 500,000 affected by disproportionate cancer rates, congenital diseases, as well as birth defects and many other illnesses.[19] While the disaster was reported by the press worldwide, the occasion of its thirtieth anniversary led to a similar international response. Virtually all of the major newspapers published stories about the disaster's long-term impact, many accompanied by harrowing images taken by photographer Alex Masi in 2009. Images of the site, the shantytown where the factory was located (and remains, defunct, to this day), and its peoples illustrated the story of a disaster that still has to be given legal and historical closure.[20]

One of those photographs, however, drastically contrasted the visual archive of the catastrophe and attracted the attention of public and media commentators. The picture of a young girl named Poonam Jatev was not an image of destruction or pain, unlike most photographic reporting of the city; it was an image of optimism. In it, Poonam's poverty is rendered apparent, not only by her modest, gray dress but also by the context of the moment: the muddy road, a tarp-covered shack beyond her, an overturned table in the background, an improvised fence. Yet the young girl appears crouching on the road, face up with her eyes closed, visibly pleased by the light rain falling on her, which is soaking her dress, her hair, and everything around her. Capturing a fleeting moment of relief, perhaps even escape, the photograph subverted the Bhopal imagery by celebrating her rather than condemning her suffering; it offered an alternative, rather hopeful view. The positivity of the photograph, which was widely circulated, was additionally underscored by external factors that gave it even more prominent visibility, such as the Photographers Giving Back Award it won, a $5,000 prize presented to the subject of the winner's work; the charity that the photographer started to fund Poonam and her siblings' schooling; and the blog he started in order to record Poonam's story.[21] However, despite appealing to an equalizing view from across that arguably prevented spectators from adopting a condescending or pitiful stance toward the victims of the gas leak, there are aspects of Poonam's photograph that seem to have serious depoliticizing effects.

The Subject of Photography

If several photographs were published on the thirtieth anniversary, the fact that Poonam's gained iconic status raises a number of questions regarding the visuality of the Bhopal tragedy and its victims. The most important issue is one that has been at the core of the practice of photography ever since its invention. Simply put, the relationship between photographer and subject seems to be far from collaborative. Poonam appears not to contribute actively in the making of the image; in fact, a number of details indicate this is the case. While her eyes are closed and her body and head face away from the camera, she seems immersed in her own thoughts, suggesting ignorance of the photographer's presence. The photograph, furthermore, casts her as a figure of virtuous redemption that collides with the realities of Bhopal and its unresolved predicament. For instance, the impact of the gas leak on her health—if there is any—is not visible. This is not to argue for a spectacular representation of her afflictions; many injuries caused by the gas leak are indeed internal and the catastrophe has victimized Bhopal's people in many ways other than illness and physical suffering too, such as the trauma caused by the death and pain of others or the despair caused by an uncertain, hopeless future. I mean to point out, instead, how the iconicity of this image seems to be fueled by the fact that it deemphasizes the severe impact of the leak on humans' lives. Poonam's innocent pose facing the sky, moreover, evokes discourses of piety and sainthood that might motivate, especially among Western audiences, the Orientalizing gesture of reimagining her as a "spiritual" individual. Poonam's symbolic cleansing by the rain, additionally, contributes to this aura of positivity and piety, which is at odds with Bhopal's prospects of ecological, political, and social reparation.[22]

Equally important is the fact that the depoliticizing implications of Poonam's photograph's iconicity were amplified by the way it was covered by the media. Poonam herself, her relationship with the catastrophe, and the link between the accident and the industrial and capitalist enterprises that caused it are relegated to a secondary plane. This is crystallized in one of several *New York Times* pieces on the photograph, "A Child's Life Changes and a Story Begins." Its title already reveals how the young girl and the Bhopal victims—for whom she is proxy—are not worthy of having a story prior to the photographer's arrival. It only begins, and has life-changing repercussions, once her picture is taken. Poonam's role is that of a passive placeholder. The headline also makes apparent that what is worth taking notice of is the photographer's experience, not what it means to live in a place so severely damaged by an environmental disaster of such magnitude. Gaining the unchallengeable authority to tell Poonam's story the moment he points his camera at her (a power that is extended as he curates the narrative of her life in his blog, which allows readers to "easily follow her story"), the photographer becomes the spokesperson for Poonam and her family.[23] This is also how the account itself proceeds.

After providing some general context about the photograph, the text makes a point about how "it changed her life. And that was only the beginning." What follows is, indeed, an account of how Poonam's life was altered, but only as far as it related to the photographer's achievements: "Since 2009, Mr. Masi has traveled a number of times to Oriya Basti, the colony in Bhopal where Poonam lives. It is not your typical photographer-subject relationship. And frankly, he isn't concerned." The photographer is increasingly the focus of the story. Poonam and her family only appear in secondhand descriptions of the developments in their lives since the photograph appeared: "They are, Mr. Masi said, 'very happy at the moment.'" Of Poonam, we know that she is now an "aspiring teacher" who has "just started her third year of school," wears "one of the frocks paid for with the award money," and "looks older, but the youthful spirit that came through the original photograph—her face lifted to the sky, head tipped back to taste the rain—is still there." In other words, she is a recipient of Western charity whose plight makes for a riveting story: "This is a very special story I have in my hands," the photographer concludes.

As a result, the journalistic piece creates a politically suspect narrative based on two extremely problematic relationships. First, the photographer is placed at the center of the action. He becomes "the point of origin of the discussion of photography," imposing an "illegitimate sovereignty" on "the event of photography" and everything to which it is related.[24] This has important implications. If the visual aspects of the photograph literally capture Poonam's agency, the account reinforces that capture by uncritically drawing attention to the photographer's power to make choices and plans for her, no matter how well intentioned they may be (we are told, for instance, about a "deal" between him and Poonam's father that "she and her siblings . . . must finish their schooling before they marry").

Second, the narrative confirms what even a cursory analysis of the image such as mine above reveals, namely, that the photograph cannot simply be considered a dialogic visual collaboration between the photographer and his subject. The reality is that Poonam's photograph is the conduit of an illusory dialogue between its subject, who is attributed a form of expression insomuch as it fulfills a predetermined message, and its spectators. The newspaper story illuminates this fact by constructing an explanation that determines her role in the "meaning" of the photograph. Poonam is cast as the protagonist of a scene of piety and redemption that responds to the expectations of an audience that is either already familiar with (and, therefore, no longer interested in) harsher images of the disaster or is not willing to be confronted by them. In any case, her image is turned into an aesthetic commodity mobilized in response to an already saturated and capricious attention economy. Further proof of this point is the use of the photograph as the cover of a nonfiction book about life in the slum of

Annawadi, in Mumbai—a city 480 miles (770 kilometers) away from Bhopal—that bears no connection with the gas leak.[25] Ultimately, this is not to suggest that we dismiss Masi's larger body of work (which includes multiple other portraits of Bhopal locals' suffering)[26] but to lay bare how the abjection of the victims of the reckless industrialism and environmental neglect at the core of the narrative of the Anthropocene is visualized.

Indra Sinha's 2007 *Animal's People* makes an important intervention in this mesh of visual and narrative relations. Moving beyond the claim that the novel renders visible the violence of the Bhopal disaster, I want to examine below the efforts of its narrator, Animal, to preempt the appropriation of the tragedy through its visual representation. Animal pursues this goal by constructing a counternarrative that works against consensual visual-narrative entanglements such as the one governing Poonam's photograph. In doing so, Animal revitalizes the emancipatory principle at the core of what Ariella Azoulay calls "the civil contract of photography," the set of relationships between the photographer, the photographed, the spectator, the moment captured, the technology of capture, and the dissemination of the image that constitute a photograph. This civil contract, Azoulay argues, is held when a photograph is not interpreted as "an exercise in aesthetic appreciation" but rather as the active acknowledgment of how "the subject of the photograph is a person who has suffered some form of injury," thus "anchor[ing] spectatorship in civic duty toward the photographed persons who haven't stopped being 'there.'"[27] *Animal's People* demonstrates how narrative fiction can reframe the visual relationships at play in countless representations of ecological suffering such as Poonam's photograph and the discourses constructed around it. The novel, I will argue, proposes a new visual politics of environmental violence that intervenes not only in the ways something or someone is registered optically but, more importantly, in the relationships created by narratives that sanction the act of seeing.

Taped Reflections: Animal's Story

Animal's People concerns the life of a young man who cannot stand upright due to spinal injuries caused by a gas leak that took place in the city of Khaufpur, a fictionalized version of Bhopal, a few days after his birth. Told in the first person by Animal himself, the story recounts the impact of the environmental catastrophe on everyday life from the point of view of one of the most abject populations on Earth. In the transcription of the tapes he accepts to record, which an editor's note informs us have been translated from Hindi and French into English, Animal's story offers an account of what life is like for those suffering the consequences of the leak, the rationale behind his refusal to consider himself a human being, and the possibility for him to undergo corrective spinal surgery. At the same time, Animal recounts his involvement with a group of local activists seeking to bring justice for the disaster's victims, spearheaded by Zafar (a sometimes sanctimonious but judicious pacifist leader) and Nisha (an outspoken and fierce student with whom Animal falls in love). Yet the narrative is also concerned with the illusory dialogue that an account like his risks entering. As he proceeds, Animal engages with two related modes of visuality, one that operates externally and one internally, that connect him and his audience in a way that does not eliminate the political charge of his outlook. I will address the first one now, which bears a number of connections with the visuality of Poonam's photograph as I have just discussed it, to return to the other mode of visuality in the following section.

Approached by a journalist who offers him money in exchange for his story, Animal first rejects the proposition, arguing that the journalist is "like all the others, come to suck our stories from us, so strangers in far off countries can marvel there's so much pain in the world."[28] Animal refuses to enact a role previously assigned to him as a victim whose story must conform to specific narrative conventions and satisfy certain expectations: "You have turned us Khaufpuris into storytellers, but always of the same story. . . . You were hoping the gibberish sounds coming from my mouth were the horrible stories you'd come to hear. Well, fuck that. No way was I going to tell those stories" (5). Animal's first response is an unnegotiable stance that stems from his rejection of the image that the Western world, especially through global disaster reporting, has made of Khaufpur and its people. This critique is emphasized by a remark about the ramifications of narrative capture and dissemination with which Animal expresses his suspicion about the publishing business: "This jarnalis already has a plan for his book. It is already agreed. . . . How can foreigners at the world's other end, who've never set foot in Khaufpur, decide what's to be said about this place?" (9). Yet, after temporarily discarding the tape machine that the journalist has left behind, Animal changes his mind and begins recording, transforming his initial refusal into an opportunity to articulate an agonistic response with radical potential.

Even though the story is translated, mediated, and printed as a book, a process that arguably erodes his command over it, Animal's narrative authority stems from the control that the recording machine gives him. This control is complemented by two other aspects. One is the way in which he will tell his story. As he defiantly puts it, "If you want my story, you'll have to put up with how I tell it" (2). Animal's diction is irreverent and often abrasive; the tone of his account is jocular, salacious, and riddled with profanity; and the veracity of certain moments is subordinated to the indisputable yet necessary plot developments facilitated by his capacity to hear people's thoughts or talk with inert beings such as embalmed fetuses, whose damaged bodies demonstrate the scope of the disaster's toll on human life. The other aspect of the narrative that bestows Animal with representational control, and one that is crucial for my discussion, is his emphasis on the visual registers that he refuses to ratify with yet another dramatic story of pain and suffering.

This emphasis on the visuality of the disaster is illustrated by Animal's association of words and images, an important dimension in the novel's reflection about how visual representations of Khaufpur's plight are embedded in complex structures of agency, visibility, and value: "What I say becomes a picture and the eyes settle on it like flies" (13). These eyes are, he reveals later, Animal's interlocutors, the audience for whom he produces his account. Animal's direct identification of his audience is prompted by the journalist's exhortation that the whole world must know his story. In the words of the cunning Chunaram, a local who deals with the journalist as Animal's de facto agent, "He will write what you say in his book. Thousands will read it. Maybe you will become famous. Look at him, see his eyes. He says thousands of other people are looking through his eyes" (7). Animal's suspicion, though, never dissipates: "I think of this awful idea. Your eyes full of eyes. Thousands staring at me through the holes in your head. Their curiosity feels like acid on my skin" (7). Despite his reservations, however, he is fully aware that this may be an opportunity to address the consensual visuality that governs the registers of the disaster. As he says in the opening, "The world of humans is meant to be viewed from eye level. Your eyes" (2). Thus, Animal takes this narrative-visual relationship with his audience to its most intimate expression, addressing them directly: "So from this moment I am no longer speaking to my friend the Kakadu Jarnalis [i.e., Australian journalist], name's Phuoc, I am talking to the eyes that are reading these words." He tellingly concludes: "Now I am talking to you" (12). Dubbing his intended audience "Eyes," he describes to them his view of the world, a dissensual view from across that finds its horizon not at eye level but, as the four-legged narrator insists, at "crotch" level: "Whole nother world it's, below the waist" (2).

Thus, Animal offers a response to the kind of visuality that emanates from Poonam's photograph. The two figures could not be further apart. Poonam is angelical, graciously quiet, and inspiring; Animal is vulgar, unpredictable, and "feel[s] raw disgust" by his own image (1–2). Whereas she embodies the hopeful aspirations of a planetary liberal humanism that demands environmental justice for all, he refuses to be human in an embodied critique of the consensual impositions of what being human must look like to which he is subjected. To echo Judith Butler, Animal "embod[ies] the 'inhuman' by offering a critique of the will, of assertion, and of resolve as prerequisites of the human." His inhumanity, therefore, "is not the opposite of the human but an essential means by which" he "become[s] human in and through the destitution" of his "humanness."[29] Whereas Poonam is a mystified figure at the center of the picture, furthermore, Animal is not one but many; he hears voices in his head and incarnates what has been called a kind of "transpersonality, an ability to experience the objective existence of the entire environment of Khaufpur as a network composed of related subjects."[30] On the surface, his aggregative voice grasps our attention and commands us with belligerent originality; below the surface, a host of voices—including a constant disparate cacophony in his own head—confound the normal distribution of storytelling, disturbing the operations of narrative representation.

Yet Animal voluntarily submits himself to the kind of depoliticizing arrangement I identified in my analysis of Poonam's photograph. The fact that he does this by his own volition, though, is what separates him from her. The narrative frame of his story renders implicit and palatable to the reader the explicit power imbalance between the gaze and its object. Like Poonam, Animal plays a role in a preestablished narrative of suffering and victimization, even if it is to be humorously deconstructed. He is a "unique but not exceptional . . . synecdoche for the spectrum of mutations to which Khaufpuris have been subjected over time."[31] It is true that he exerts a discursive agency that is entirely negated for Poonam, but his voice is also subject to the predetermined categorizations of the narrative order with which he must comply. Animal is alive to this: "I am a small person not even human, what difference will my story make? You told me that sometimes the stories of small people in this world can achieve big things, this is the way you buggers always talk. . . . On that night it was poison, now it's words that are choking us" (3). Further, the journalist's exhortation that he tell his true story contributes to Animal's iconicity as the representative figure of the tragedy. Animal is, in the parlance of the publishing business, a "fascinating character" with a "compelling voice," a question of which, the framing of the story as a book to be published in the West shows, both Sinha and Animal are clearly aware. What is the reason, then, behind Animal's addressing his audience as he would "a friend" (14), as the journalist encourages him, as an equal interlocutor in a dialogue that is so clearly determined by the power positions of the reader/seer and the narrator/seen?

Animal's urge to tell his story emerges from his need to understand certain recent events in his life in what becomes an important defense of narrative as a vehicle for self-reflection and the careful pondering of politically complex questions: "I'm not talking to this tape for truth or fifty rupees or Chunaram's fucking kebabs. I have a choice to make, let's say it's between heaven and hell, my problem is knowing which is which" (11). At its core, this problem concerns Animal's decision whether to undergo surgery to correct his back, an option that is presented to him later in the novel. Animal, thus, produces his story not for his readers but in spite of them. His account is not intended to create a connection with readers, for them to identify with Animal, or for him "to tell a story that will make the 'Eyes' see from his perspective."[32] If this were the case, Animal's story would simply enable the reader to partake in what Susan Sontag calls the "quintessential modern experience" of "being a spectator of calamities taking place in another country."[33] This spectatorship would only fulfill a voyeuristic desire to see what the world must look like if one's back were so inhumanly twisted.

Animal does not only expose himself to the depoliticizing act of becoming a representative of the catastrophe[34] in order to sort out his predicament. Aware of the fact that agreeing to tell his story is to engage in an illusory dialogue with Eyes, he also deploys the supposedly equitable horizontal arrangement that governs his engagement with his audience in order to deactivate their power over his visual agency. This is crucial in the more important portions where he meditates about whether to live as an animalized human or as a humanized animal. For Animal, the question is not whether the victims of the Khaufpur disaster are visible or not. In fact, visibility in itself seems to be a rather unproductive notion: To whom are Animal and his people visible? What exactly happens once they are recognized as victims of the gas leak by the readers of a book? Are representatives of Union Carbide likely to read this story? The question, instead, is how to counteract narratives "that eliminate from" the images that represent them "anything that might exceed the simple superfluous illustration of their meaning" and that "tell us what [those images] show and what we should make of them."[35] Animal, in other words, strategically accedes to fulfill the expectations of his readers as a four-legged image of the impact of the Khaufpur disaster in order to perform another form of visuality: an internal set of visual relations that surpass the relationship between him and Eyes.

A clue to this gesture lies in an early reflection on the power that his body has on certain audiences and his awareness of how he can exploit it. At the end of his introduction to his daily life in Khaufpur, Animal speaks of how his friend Faqri shows him that the front, and not the back of restaurants, is where he should be begging for food. One day "I began parading up and down in view of the clientele, nothing puts a person off their food more than a starving Animal watching every mouthful. . . . [I]f you act powerless, you are powerless, the way to get what you want is to demand it" (19). What allows him to survive is precisely making a spectacle of his body, a sight too compelling to ignore. Animal adopts the same approach in his account, where he directs his audience's gaze in order to mount a nonreductive narrative of himself and Khaufpur. As he says, "people see the outside, but it's inside where the real things happen, no one looks in there, maybe they don't dare" (11). This "inside" is the second mode of visuality in Animal's story and the novel's intervention in the regime of visualization governing the Anthropocene and its attendant violence.

Khaufpur's Internal Visuality

This second kind of visuality concerns the internal relationships that constitute the plot of the novel. In this mode of visuality, Eyes are not participants but mere observers.[36] In producing a rather salacious scene, for instance, Animal reminds them of their powerlessness over what they can and cannot see: "Eyes, I don't know if you are a man or a woman. I'm thinking the things I am telling are not suited to a woman's ears, but if a person leaves things unsaid so as to avoid looking bad, it's a lie" (79). His claim to the truth and his (apparent) concern about his audience's expectations toward narrative convention show Animal's preoccupation with his legitimacy as recognized by Eyes. This, however, is also a reminder that, without his mediation, they would have no access to that truth. To put it differently, whereas Animal is willing to spectacularize himself in his address to Eyes, he does not relinquish his narrative power over the events that drive the plot and, by extension, the visual relationships that sustain such events. These relationships are rooted in the triangulation between Animal's dissenting ontology, the activist movement, and Elli Barber, the American doctor who arrives in Khaufpur to establish a free clinic to help reduce the long-term impact of the gas leak.

The chief point on which Animal's narrative rests is his insistence to be seen as an animal. Even though his story certainly invites readers to rethink their assumptions about what it is to be human, as most commentators of the novel argue, it is his continuous disputes with other people in Khaufpur that propel his long mediation about his condition. For Animal, to live on four legs is to live like a beast. In order to have a modicum of agency in a world that insists on dehumanizing him, then, he takes his animality literally and expects others in Khaufpur to accept his dissensual understanding of it as a marker of his inhuman existence. Initially, this remains unchallenged. Nisha, the first person he meets from the activist group, seems to find no fault with it: "From the first she took me exactly as I was. When she called me Jaanvar, Animal, it was a name, nothing more. She never seemed to notice I was crippled, nor pretend I wasn't" (22). With others, this is more difficult. Zafar, for instance, disputes Animal's self-determination on the basis of his name. True to the principle of championing the self-regard of the dispossessed, Zafar tells him that "you should not allow yourself to be called Animal. You are a human being, entitled to dignity and respect" (23). In a later scene, Farouq, another member of the group, is less subtle: "You look a lot like a human being to me.... You pretend to be an animal so you can escape the responsibility of being human" (209). The argument between Animal and his fellow slum-dwellers, then, is about whether one should defend one's humanity despite its outward manifestation or, on the contrary, whether one should stop deceiving oneself and embrace one's lack of humanity on the basis of that very manifestation, as Animal argues.

If this constant dispute over his (visual) recognition as an animal is productive, it is so because his "sense of absolute difference from humans has gradations built into it."[37] For example, Animal's ontological certainty is shaken in the climactic scene in which the Khaufpuris finally rise up to protest the government's corruption and the efforts of the company operating the factory (or the Kampani, as the locals call it) to stall the legal process that will determine its responsibility toward and subsequent compensations to the victims of the disaster. As he remembers while being abused by the police during the riot that finally causes the movement to be able to negotiate with the local government: "I don't know what is being beaten here. If they kill me what will die?" (313). Here Animal hesitates to identify himself as a nonhuman animal, as he has all along. This reflection, therefore, may be read to imply that the government's outrageous attitude toward the catastrophe and, more immediately, the physical pain of being brutalized connect him to other protesters who are subjected to the same violence. Even if momentarily, his sense of belonging to the citywide upheaval outstrips Animal's repudiation of his humanness, because it shows him that he is no different than his fellow Khaufpuris in the face of the government and the Kampani's disregard for their suffering.

The dissensual ontology at the fault line between Animal's humanness and his animality plays an essential role in his involvement in the movement to bring justice to Khaufpur. His inability to stand upright makes him, in Zafar's words, "especially abled" to contribute to its activities (23). Animal's condition, furthermore, has important scopic advantages as he is appointed by Zafar to "jamispond" (a vernacularized version of "James Bond," meaning "to spy") for the group. His crooked back and his going on four legs allow him to conceal himself, easily climb up trees to have a better view of things, and move through people's legs in a crowd without being seen. As a result, Animal has the power to see what others in Khaufpur cannot, a fact that will be crucial when Elli Barber arrives from the United States to start her clinic. From the outset, Elli is suspected by the environmental group—especially by Zafar—of working for the Kampani to collect data so that the latter can argue that the health impact of the gas leak is smaller than it has been advertised and, consequently, that the Kampani's liabilities are lesser than initially posited. To put it in optic terms, the group's main objective is to prevent the Kampani from creating a false image of the disaster and its victims, and Animal is particularly skilled to help the group anticipate the Kampani's moves.[38] Animal's jamisponding, however, is not significant because it reveals whether Elli works for the Kampani (she does not); instead, it is a narrative vehicle for Sinha to show the complications that emerge from the visual entanglements that bring Animal, the grassroots movement, and Elli together.

As an American doctor, thus, Elli is suspected the moment her arrival is announced. Immediately, Zafar commissions Nisha to find information about Elli on the "internest," but she fails to produce a single piece about her: "Doctor doing an important job in a hospital. . . . You would expect the internest to have that kind of information" (96). In a clear reference to the kind of external visibility that I discussed earlier, however, she finds information about Khaufpur, including an image featuring "the tiny figure of" Abdul Saliq, a well-known beggar, "with his hand out" (97). This makes Animal's jamisponding all the more important for the group even though, from the beginning, "my instinct says Zafar is wrong. [Elli] does not fit my idea of a Kampani person and I'm not the only one who thinks this" (69). While Zafar instructs that no one visits her clinic until they find out who she is, Pandit Somraj, Nisha's father and a famous singer suffering from lung injuries caused by the leak, argues that, besides having no proof about Elli's culpability, Khaufpuris are not in a position to refuse help, no matter where it comes from. Nevertheless, even though it is disclosed later that Zafar is wrong, his suspicions on the basis of what things look like cannot be easily dismissed. They confirm Khaufpuris' vulnerability and highlight the difficult choices they have to make about charitable initiatives from the same part of the world that gave them the Kampani.

Elli's struggle to connect with the Khaufpuris is, first and foremost, due to complications at the visual level. Her first impression reveals the Western and medical lens through which she sees Khaufpur. Elli inveighs: "Look at this filth, litter and plastic all over, open drains stinking right outside the houses. Flies. Every bit of waste ground is used as a latrine. I've seen people defecating on the railway lines" (105). Yet, where the rest of the Khaufpuris stay away from her, Animal confronts Elli's views and the position from which she produces them as a Western doctor. Her concerned complaints are met by Animal's disarmingly crass humor, which is more than an attempt to deflate her agitation, as when he tells her that "there's a lot to be said for communal shitting. For a start the camaraderie. Jokes and insults. A chance to discuss things. It's about the only opportunity you get to unload a piece of your mind" (184). Animal's goal is for Elli to shift the way she sees Khaufpur. However, this shift must indeed be reciprocal. When Somraj—whom she has mistakenly taken as the voice behind the local boycott of her clinic—tries to explain to her why people will not go to her clinic, arguing that "Amrikans don't have a good reputation in this town," Elli immediately protests against being viewed as a stereotypical representation of the United States and the West: "I won't have that dumped on me" (158). After a drawn-out and rocky process of mutual reappraisal, Elli's understanding of Khaufpur in Khaufpur's terms and Khaufpuris' trust in Elli progressively bring them together. Her proactive efforts not to impose her own views on the town will be key, such as a visit accompanied by Animal to ill Khaufpuris in their homes so she can "see for yourself" their suffering (171).

This reciprocity also applies to Animal. If he helps Elli adjust her gaze to the realities of post-catastrophe Khaufpur, she will similarly have an impact on how he sees life in Khaufpur. First, their relationship is based on the new future that Elli opens up for Animal. As Elli's first and only patient for a long time, Animal is shown a new way to see himself as other than an animal, as she offers to study his case and consider whether surgery could be performed to correct his spine. Animal describes this new horizon in rather vivid language as something "unbelievable . . . which I cannot speak about, hardly dare to admit to myself. . . . [T]his terrifying thought struck like a hurricane, surged up my spine like electricity, changed everything, the wild, stupid, unforgivable hope that she might cure me" (141). Elli's power to change Animal's worldview is also manifest in one of the rare moments in which he reevaluates his point of view. When Elli says that Paradise Alley, a muddy road in Animal's neighborhood, the Nutcracker, looks "like it was flung up by an earthquake," he reacts in a surprising manner. Instead of rejecting her comment as a self-entitled Westerner's judgmental observation, Animal puts in perspective what he has always seen as Khaufpur's version of Paris's Champs-Élysées: "Suddenly I'm seeing as she does. Paradise Alley is a wreckage of baked earth mounds and piles of planks on which hang gunny sacks, plastic sheets, dried palm leaves.... Truly I see how poor and disgusting are our lives" (106). Elli's impact on Animal's gaze is nevertheless far from overbearing. Her comparison of the state of Paradise Alley to an earthquake's aftermath shows Animal how to look differently at the city, not how his way of looking at it is necessarily wrong.

Predictably, Animal's jamisponding duties complicate his relationship with Elli. In one of his first missions, Animal, from the top of a tree, accidentally sees Elli naked in her home. This moment exemplifies a self-destructive kind of power that Animal's gaze grants him. Driven by his ravenous sexual desire, he is incapable of looking away. This voyeuristic moment, which he replicates while spying on Nisha to see if she is having sexual relations with Zafar, would seem to give him "some sort of power over her," as he claims, based on his gaze's intrusion upon the vulnerability of Elli's naked body (94). Yet this is not the case. The power of the gaze is inexistent unless it is acknowledged as such outside of itself, and Animal is, throughout the novel, incapable of telling anyone about what he has seen. His compassion, decency, and generosity toward others, which are first almost inexistent but increase as the events develop, is one reason he does not; on a more self-interested level, though, Animal knows that he would harm himself more than he would her if he mentioned having seen her naked, because it would ruin his chance to stop having to live halfway between a human and an animal life. His attitude toward this voyeuristic, self-destructive empowerment foreshadows the dilemma of having to report on Elli's activities when the Kampani lawyers are in the town to attend a secret meeting that, Khaufpuris infer, will predetermine the outcome of the imminent hearing about the next stage in the inquiry on the Kampani's responsibilities for the disaster.

In hiding by the pool of the luxurious hotel where the lawyers are staying, Animal overhears Elli talking intimately with one of them. Immediately, Animal becomes assailed by the disappointing suspicion that, after all, Elli has been working for the Kampani. Disobeying his duties to report on what he sees, Animal struggles to share this information with the rest of the group, which is engrossed in the hunger strike Zafar and Farouq have started in protest of the secret talks. He knows that acting on what he thinks he has seen and heard will not only endanger the hunger strikers' lives (Elli has offered to medically attend to them while they fast in the dangerous heat preceding the monsoon rains) but will also put an end to the new life that she has enabled him to see for himself. The self-destructive power conceded by his gaze, thus, has now an added disarming influence over Animal: "I cannot look at her, who must at this moment be play-acting, for how else could she so badly betray us?" (281). After long and agonizing deliberation, Animal finally confesses to Zafar, who responds that he already knows and that Animal should "try to see that she . . . is okay" (304).

Despite Elli's alleged secret cooperation with Kampani, it is finally announced that no deal has been reached between the government and the lawyers, which means that the prosecution will proceed. Yet celebrations are interrupted by the rumor that Zafar and Farouq have died as a consequence of their hunger strike, which leads to a riot that starts in front of the chief minister's house. As we learn later, though, this is a mere strategic deployment of a certain visual narrative to motivate Khaufpuris to rise up. Zafar understands the power of disseminating his own image as martyr, which not only mobilizes the locals but also gives him power to negotiate with the chief minister, who fears the riot might get out of hand and might have repercussions on his public image. For his part, Animal finds Elli and, mustering the courage to confront her, angrily tells her that he knows about her work for the Kampani. Without losing her composure, Elli discloses to Animal that it was all a strategy to derail the secret talks, while complaining that she has been judged, once again, only upon appearances: "You saw me, and immediately you assumed the worst?" (317). Elli then reveals to Animal how, in playing with the line that divides the visible and the invisible, she managed to reach the lawyer with whom he saw her at the hotel pool by wearing a black burqa that disguised her. The lawyer, Elli tells Animal, is her ex-husband and one of the reasons she has decided to come to Khaufpur to set up the clinic. In exchange for delaying the meeting, Elli promises to return to the United States, implying that she would reconsider their relationship. Yet Elli's plans are different. Animal learns later that the meeting is ultimately aborted thanks to Elli alone, who, still disguised by the burqa, enters the meeting room and empties the contents of a stink bomb in the air-conditioner, making all the attendees (whose "eyes began to sting" [360]) flee the room in a panic, thinking that they are breathing "the same gas that leaked that night" (361). Outside, tipped-off members of the press "waiting with their cameras" duly capture the inculpating image verifying the existence of the meeting and, in yet another turn involving the power of appearances and of the gaze, "once the secret was out, the deal was dead" (361).

The triangulation between the environmental group's suspicions, Animal's talent for jamisponding, and Elli's difficulties to overcome a preestablished image of herself even when she stops the legal process from being derailed demonstrates Sinha's intention to show a complex set of internal visual relations that escape Animal's initial scopic capture by Eyes. The language of images, the novel seems to suggest, is not just crucial to the ways we understand catastrophes at a global level; it is also, and very importantly, at the core of political struggles at the local level rarely registered by the media. Even when journalists work to capture them, as in the case of Poonam's photograph, those struggles run the risk of becoming co-opted and simplified for spectacular purposes. The work of narratives like Animal's is, therefore, critical for preventing such gestures. There is one more aspect of the internal visuality of Khaufpur's environmental battle that, in concluding Animal's account, connects these internal relations with the external visuality that sustains the illusory dialogue he is willing to enter in order to examine the events that lead to the Khaufpuris' partial victory.

Signs of the Anthropocene

Animal's story concludes with two dramatic and, in some ways, complementary moments that represent the novel's reflection on the Anthropocene as framed by environmental disasters of the magnitude of Bhopal's gas leak. These two episodes illuminate Animal's final decision not to undergo surgery. Yet they also reveal a warning about how the challenges of living in the Anthropocene cannot be interpreted according to a consensual sense of planetarity but on a differential understanding of how those challenges affect people around the world with varying intensities. That warning is, of course, rooted in Animal's dissensual visuality of the Khaufpur catastrophe, and it involves an apocalyptic rendition of the final popular revolt against the government and a hallucinatory adventure in the forest during which he has a revelatory experience about his humanity.

After hearing Elli's side of the story, Animal runs to find Ma Franci, the French nun who became his de facto adoptive mother after his family was killed by the leak. Animal senses that the destructive force of the riot following the news of Zafar's and Farouq's purported deaths will spread through the city, and he leaves to make sure she is safe. When he finally meets her in their derelict home inside the Kampani's factory, Ma Franci lugubriously announces that the "Apokalis" (the Apocalypse) has finally come. For Ma Franci, the Apokalis is the catastrophic end of times that turned Khaufpur into a toxic hell on earth and is now returning with a vengeance. It is telling that she is not surprised when she learns about the 9/11 attacks, which she interprets as the Apokalis too, only happening in another part of the world. In response to Animal's incredulity toward the images of the attacks he has seen in the news in Chunaram's chai house, Ma Franci says that they are real because God "began the job right here in Khaufpur, now others are getting a taste" (62). In connecting the terrorist attacks with Khaufpur's catastrophe, Ma Franci tellingly emphasizes their commonality as extreme forms of human-caused violence with the potential of destroying life on Earth as we know it. In that sense, 9/11 signals the advent of the Anthropocene. Additionally, just as with the attacks on New York City, the human agency in such destruction is not distributed equally, and therefore it requires a reading of the Anthropocene that does not inculpate all humans evenly, as Animal urges his readers at the very end of the novel.

At this point, Animal's narration of the Apokalis is subordinated to his crazed point of view. Given that the Apokalis will forever change life in Khaufpur, Animal becomes assailed by a deep despair and tries to commit suicide by swallowing the remaining pills he has been secretly administering Zafar to lower his libido and thus boycott his relationship with Nisha. Harassed by the constant cacophony of voices in his head, he runs to Elli's clinic to find a jar containing a rowdy two-headed fetus with whom he has quarreled in the past during his visits to Elli's office. The Khā-in-the-jar, as Animal refers to him, is a reminder of what happened "that night" and the variety of ways in which the catastrophe affected human life. As he rebukes Animal in their first conversation, "Your back is twisted . . . but at least you are alive. Me, I'm still fucking waiting to be born" (58). In a later scene, the Khā-in-the-jar tells Animal that he and the other jarred unborn babies are now on the board of directors of the Kampani in order to "undo everything the Kampani does" (237). Reasoning in rather Anthropocenic terms, then, he argues in his final conversation with Animal that "everyone on this earth has in their body a share of the Kampani's poisons. But . . . [w]e unborn paid the highest price. Never mind dying, we never even got a fucking shot at life." He concludes: "Release us . . . and then Animal, you may rest your troubled mind" (237). Thus, the opportunity comes. In a hallucinatory state caused by the pills, Animal returns to the factory with the jar to burn the fetus and put an end to his suffering but, anticlimactically, he drops the jar while climbing the factory wall and smashes it. As he later tries to give his two-headed friend closure by burning him, Animal causes a fire in the factory that wreaks havoc in Khaufpur's slums.

This fire makes a reality of the apocalyptic signs that Ma Franci has already identified in the riots, collapsing the environmental catastrophe and the Khaufpuris' political movement into one event. The fumes caused by the remaining chemicals that were released in the first catastrophe may cause a second catastrophe, and the fire sends the city into a panic. As Ma Franci puts it, "Animal, the angels are here, thousands and thousands of them, they've come to make an end of this sinning, sorrowful world, tonight it will go up in flames, it will burn and shrivel into ashes and become dust" (328). The destructive force of this event could be read from

Ma Franci's end-of-the-world point of view as the destruction of the consensual understanding that Khaufpuris' life on this planet can only be a life of suffering. This is clear in the connections she draws between the original disaster, the suffering of successive generations of Khaufpuris, and the future of life in the Anthropocene: "On this night the dead are going to come up out of the earth, like big mushrooms their skulls will push up out of the soil. . . . [A]nd all their bones will join together and they will walk again. Tonight, mark my words, this city will be full of the dead" (329). Uncannily, Ma Franci's prophecy echoes certain premodern discourses of madness (undoubtedly a form of dissensual thinking)[39] that presage the rising of those bearing the brunt of the Anthropocene against the capitalist activities that have brought life in the global South to its current state.

This mobilization of the Apocalypse as a politicized scenario, however, is contrasted by Animal's final decision not to undergo surgery. Having lost consciousness, Animal finds himself being taken to a hospital on a truck the morning after, though he jumps off and runs into a forest. In this forest, a sort of rude awakening awaits him as, still under the influence of the drugs, he is aggressively confronted by its trees and animals. The forest first appears as an arid landscape in which life seems simply impossible. A tree shows no mercy when he asks for water: "Lie here, die here, we are no friends of yours, soon will have no need for your bones" (344). Later, when he becomes hungry, he is confronted by a lizard that tells him he is not an animal because he cannot fend for himself: "You are human, if you were an animal you would have eaten me" (346). The importance of these encounters for Animal's understanding of his animality, which wavers at the forest creatures' indifference, is emphasized by moments in which his humanity resurfaces. In despair, his most compassionate and sensitive side finds expression in fond memories of his parents, first, and then his people. Now unable to find the line that divides his humanity and his animality, Animal expresses what will be eventually the solution to his dilemma: "I am a small burning, freezing creature, naked and alone in a vast world, in a wilderness where is neither food nor water and not a single friendly soul. But I'll not be bullied. If this self of mine doesn't belong in this world, I'll be my own world, I'll be a world complete in myself" (350). The solution to his existential doubts lies in a dignified acknowledgment of his uniqueness, which Zafar and the other members of the group celebrate as they rescue him, telling him about the riots and how Ma Franci and an old local couple died trying to help people leave the blazing factory.

Thus, as the novel draws to a close, Animal considers his experience in the forest and finally decides to turn down the surgery. In addition, in his first real act of selflessness, he decides that the large amount of money already raised for his operation should be used to pay for the freedom of Anjali, a prostitute whom he knew during his childhood and who never discounted him as a human on four legs. Animal reflects: "Is life so bad? If I'm an upright human, I would be one of millions, not even a healthy one at that. Stay four-foot, I'm the one and only Animal" (366). Animal's dissenting account of the visuality of Khaufpur's struggle, therefore, comes to fruition and his agonistic engagement with his Western audience concludes. If he began his account accepting his role as a "representative" of the catastrophe, he finishes it by affirming the dignity of his precarious situation as a singular case of the destruction caused by the Kampani who nevertheless does not need to be legitimized by his spectators. With no other option but to accept living in the Anthropocene (or, in its local version, the Kampanicene), Animal abandons his ontological battle with the *anthropos* by turning down the surgery. This gesture is, emphatically, a political one precisely because it liberates him from the consensual distribution of victim and perpetrator that conceals relationships such as his triangulation with Elli and Khaufpur's movement and, therefore, renders environmental destruction events such as the Bhopal catastrophe in oversimplified terms.

Still, Animal acknowledges at the very end of his account the difficulties for Khaufpuris to escape this consensual regime. The "hearing's again been postponed, the Kampani's still trying to find ways to avoid appearing," while "there is still sickness all over Khaufpur" and "the factory is still there, blackened by fire" (365). Animal, though, concludes his narrative by making an appeal to his readers: "Eyes, I'm done. Khuda hafez. Go well. Remember me. All things pass, but the poor remain. We are the people of the Apokalis. Tomorrow there will be more of us" (366). In closing, he entreats us to remember that, as the increasingly harder conditions of the new, global environmental era affect more and more people (beginning, of course, with the poorest), a sense of communal belonging must prevail if we truly want to call this the age of the *anthropos*. His narrative, thus, invokes what Rancière calls a sense of "being together apart," which is the result of a dissensual expression that creates a sense of aesthetic community by establishing a relationship of tension between two groups, in this case Animal's Western audience and the victims of the Khaufpur/Bhopal disaster.[40] For Rancière, this aesthetic community is projected into a common future: "The paradoxical relationship between the 'apart' and the 'together' is also a paradoxical relationship between the present and the future. The artwork is the people to come and it is a monument to its expectation, a monument to its absence."[41] Animal's narrative enables the same kind of link. In projecting its ending into the future, it mobilizes its audience to question the type of relationships of capture to which images of Khaufpur and its people are subjected while underscoring the importance of visuality for understanding, in alternative ways, similar catastrophes lying ahead.

With my reading of Sinha's novel, I have explored one way in which reframing the visuality of environmental disaster can operate as a counterdialogic strategy to combat the illusory dialogue that the narrative of the Anthropocene might become if it is intended to represent a collective yet undifferentiated human "we." Images of the Anthropocene, the novel clearly shows, are not objects to be simply consumed from the distance (as in the case of Poonam's photograph) but elements of signification and capture that result in intimate communicative and visual relationships. Neither are images from across, that is, established on a horizontal level of correspondence, devoid of power imbalances. In directing his narrator's account to an eyeing audience, Sinha provides a complex reflection of the visuality of environmental catastrophe that intervenes in those relationships by upending certain expectations about them. I want to consider now a different counterdialogic intervention of the visuality of the Anthropocene from across with an analysis of Helon Habila's 2010 novel *Oil on Water*, which approaches the function of journalism in reporting on ecological disasters from a different point of view. Unlike Sinha's novel, which is concerned with the depoliticizing mediation of its protagonist's account, Habila's explores how narrative representation can bring to the center the peripheral aspects of the damaged ecosystem in which the story takes place.

Chasing the Story: Helon Habila's *Oil on Water*

Oil on Water focuses on the irruption of the oil-extraction industry in the Niger Delta, exploring the ecological destruction it has caused, the resulting extreme ruination of human and nonhuman life, and the ongoing conflict between the military (which acts to protect the interests of the industry following the dictates of the government), rebel militias, and a group of inhabitants fighting to subsist in the devastated Delta. Like *Animal's People*, though, Habila's novel is also a reflection of the visual codes governing the representation of ecological catastrophe. Far from being an unfamiliar sight, the Delta has become an emblem of environmental violence. Depictions of hellish landscapes composed of oil-drenched mangroves and pipeline webs crowned by gas flares have circulated around the globe for some time now. The novel, I want to argue here, demonstrates how important it is to render this kind of violence visible in new ways, focusing on obscured aspects and neglected dynamics, throwing light onto the connections of such ecological disasters and the complicit parties (governments, companies, consumers) that perpetuate them. What happens when a catastrophic event like this has already reached a certain degree of visibility? What if the visual representations already in circulation present images that occlude the political questions underlying it?[42] This is precisely what concerns *Oil on Water*. The novel interrogates in counterdialogic terms the visuality of the destruction caused by this dimension of the Anthropocene by demonstrating how important it is to render this kind of violence visible in alternative, dissensual ways.

One scene powerfully illustrates this idea. In it, Rufus, a young Port Harcourt journalist and the novel's protagonist and narrator, discusses the oil question with James Floode, a British oil engineer whose wife, Isabel, has been kidnapped by the militia. Rufus has returned from a short trip into the Delta with other journalists to find out whether Isabel is alive. Unable to ascertain this, he is nonetheless approached by Floode, who ignores the embassy's advice and authorizes him to begin negotiating with the kidnappers. Before that happens, however, their conversation veers toward the general state of affairs in the Delta.

In the background, a TV displays images from a BBC broadcast of "picketing youths holding placards in front of an oil-company building in Port Harcourt," which are "accompanied by a long, rote-like voice-over about poverty in Nigeria, and how corruption sustained that poverty, and how oil was the main source of revenue, and how because the country was so corrupt, only a few had access to that wealth."[43] In response, Floode condescendingly tells Rufus that "you people could easily become the Japan of Africa, the USA of Africa, but the corruption is incredible," and adds a complaint: "Our pipelines are vandalized daily, losing us millions . . . and millions for the country as well. The people don't understand what they do to themselves" (103). Trying to show where he is wrong, Rufus replies that "they do understand," and tells him the story of how his home village, Junction, "went up in smoke" due to an accident caused by local oil smugglers (we learn later it is, in fact, his father who accidentally provoked the fire) (103). Rufus continues: "But I don't blame them for wanting to get some benefit out of the pipelines that have brought nothing but suffering to their lives, leaking into the rivers and wells, killing the fish and poisoning the farmlands. And all they are told by the companies and the government is that the pipelines are there for their own good" (103). Rufus then confronts Floode more directly: "And you think the people are corrupt? No, they are just hungry, and tired" (104). Rufus's retort, however, does not produce the outcome he intends. Floode replies by simply admitting knowledge of that part of the narrative: "Hmmm, well, I've read about it before. A tragedy. But it does illustrate my point" (104). Underlying this acknowledgment is Floode's power to dismiss Rufus's argument in order to avoid explaining his and his company's complicity in such instability. Yet Rufus counters immediately in the negative, asserting that "actually, it illustrates my point," implying that it is precisely Floode's claim about how this is part of the acceptable state of affairs that justifies the local population's acts (104). Floode then nonchalantly cuts the discussion short, trying to restore a cordial tone: "Ha ha! You argue well, I must give you that" (104).

This scene illustrates one of the most important problems concerning the ongoing political and ecological crisis provoked by oil-drilling activities in the Delta. It does not just show the deterioration caused by the oil industry to the point that one of the few ways for the inhabitants to exert any political agency is by boycotting and attacking its infrastructures, or that those inhabitants are, on certain occasions, forced to further endanger their lives in order to survive. Neither does it just encapsulate the workings of what is often called the "resource curse," which ultimately provokes the diminution of sovereignty and the "militarization of both commerce and development,"[44] as represented in the novel by the clash between the army and the militias. The problem this scene represents most clearly is that an all-too-visible form of violence is otherwise seen as one of the many parts in a consensual regime of visuality that determines the ongoing ecological disaster as a mere contingency. Rufus's discussion with Floode is, surely, an illusory dialogue framed by the failure of the media, present in the scene via the BBC program playing in the background, to offer something other than a "full picture" narrative that is as reluctant to shine a light onto the veritable causes of the instability in the region as it is complicit with dismissive discourses like Floode's.

Indeed, stances like Floode's and the detached media narratives that justify it seem to be the main driving force for Rufus to begin constructing a dissensual narrative of the Delta that seeks to generate different responses from the public. To do so, Rufus must find a balance between his role as Floode's envoy and what he perceives are his responsibilities as a journalist so as not to fall into a larger illusory dialogue in which his voice would become neutralized, absorbed by the representational vicious circle that constitutes the consensual visuality of the catastrophe as an acceptable and unavoidable component of the global oil economy. He achieves this by doubling up on the scopic possibilities of his mission to find Isabel Floode. While he plays the neutral role reserved to journalists as a messenger in her kidnapping by obtaining firsthand proof that she is alive (i.e., ascertaining it with his own eyes), Rufus also acts as a witness to the ecological destruction of the Delta.[45] Yet this is not an easy undertaking given the saturation of the visual registers of the catastrophe. As with many other episodes of environmental violence, constructing effective representations that can have a meaningful impact on their audiences is restricted to very few modes. As Sontag has asked in another context, "How else to make a dent when there is incessant exposure to images, and overexposure to a handful of images seen again and again?"[46] This is a crucial aesthetico-political goal of the novel. With Rufus's first-person account, Habila manages to render the environmental violence on the Delta and its biosphere glaringly visible by forcing the reader into a new visual relationship with what is already visible. This is more than a matter of redoubling the presence of those images or making readers look again; it is about staging a strict engagement with the view from across. We can see the visual equivalent of Habila's narrative endeavors in the work of documentarian Lars Johansson on the Niger Delta disaster, to which I briefly turn now to then revisit a number of key passages from the novel that substantiate in complex ways this idea.

Glaring

Lars Johansson's *Poison Fire: Gas and Oil Abuse in Nigeria* (2008) is a powerful documentary that is intended, as one environmentalist who appears in it says, "for the whole world" to see the damage caused by oil extraction in the Delta.[47] Its scope is wide-ranging. It features interviews with locals, who explain the ecological, personal, and socioeconomic harm caused by the oil industry, but also a semi-improvised interview between the CEO of Royal Dutch Shell, one of the first companies to begin operations in the Delta in the 1950s, and two environmentalists from the Delta, who only get a promise that the damages caused by the firm will be evaluated at the next shareholders' meeting and are politely thanked for coming. Yet I want to focus on a small but very significant detail in the film. Early on, the documentary introduces some of the inhabitants of the Delta, who articulate the utterly devastating ways in which the activity of Shell and other oil companies have interrupted their lives. A local woman named Tina Esegi, for instance, indignantly talks about how, in destroying the ecology of the Delta, the oil industry is also destroying the livelihood of its people: "We have nowhere to live," she says to the camera. Minutes later, a community activist, Jonah Gbemre, gives us undeniable proof of the damage caused by gas flares (bursts of flame resulting from the burning of unwanted gas in the oil deposits exploited that emit large amounts of polluting agents and have major negative health effects). As he also looks into the camera, Gbemre compellingly shows the impact of these gas discharges on his eyes.

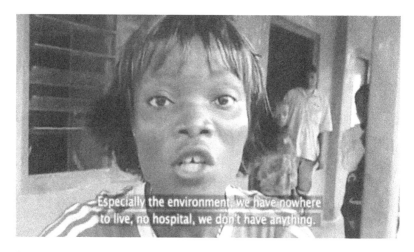

Still from *Poison Fire*. Reprinted by permission of director Lars Johansson.

What makes these images so powerful is the fact that the people on the screen address their situation directly to the audience. They interpellate us by showing us their plights. One could even say that they, indeed, glare at us. The intensity with which they do so is undeniable because of what it expresses, of course, but also because it demands that we look back at them. They provoke a relationship that "enables the spectator to exceed the limits of professional discourse and to regard the image, not as source and end in itself, but first and foremost as a platform that bears the traces of others, and thus as a junction that articulates between such traces and the spectator who sees them."[48] These images entreat us; they force us to look back at them, to acknowledge them in a dialogic manner that does not conceal their political urgency. In other words, they avoid becoming caught in an illusory dialogue with the audience by means of their capacity to address us directly. While the camera shortens the distance between us and them, the visual effect that it creates in making it appear as if they are looking at us causes us to become their interlocutors. Thus, as we witness the accounts of individuals like Tina Esegi and Jonah Gbemre, we are confronted not only with questions about who they are or what their stories might be but also how it is possible that their lives have been ruined in such a way and why they continue to be so. Yet we cannot ask them those questions. We cannot direct their narrative; we can only look and listen. We are part of a narrative that accounts for a very specific way of living in the Anthropocene: not the Anthropocene of an absolute and undifferentiated human species provoking spectacular geological shifts and alterations

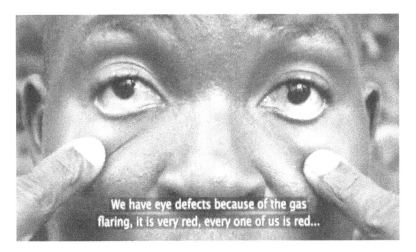

Still from *Poison Fire*. Reprinted by permission of director Lars Johansson.

in the Earth's chemical composition, but the Anthropocene of the victims of savage capitalism and globalization; of the neglectful destruction of people's living means and the poverty that it causes; of the irreversible degradation of ecosystems and the resulting deterioration of the bodies that inhabit them.

The kind of bold engagement provoked by these and many other individuals in *Poison Fire* glaring at the camera can also be found in Habila's novel, and not only by the people Rufus encounters in the Delta. Things, landscapes, vegetation, gas flares, dead matter, and so forth appear glaringly to us. I am not suggesting that the novel attributes them a voice or a capacity to look back at us. As visual theorist W. J. T. Mitchell puts it, "We need to reckon with not just the meaning of images but their silence, their reticence, their wildness and nonsensical obduracy."[49] It is the persistence of the images of people, objects, and places, of a deeply damaged ecosystem, much of which remains silent, that makes them most compelling. And that persistence is underscored in Habila's novel because it is not explained away by the narrator but, rather, constantly recorded and unavoidably present. Like the individuals in Johansson's documentary, they stare at us. Thus, I want to employ "glaring" as a trope to describe the visibility of the ravages caused by oil extraction, which is much more than the background to Isabel's kidnapping, the novel's main plot. This glaring, I want to argue, offers a way of seeing otherwise the current situation in the Delta by means of a quiet rendition that nevertheless does not turn it into a spectacle. Habila's refusal to present striking and impressive images, then, might be understood as an effort to visualize this profoundly damaged environment as glaringly evident without diminishing its gravity.

Thus, Rufus's account does not evoke extraordinariness, pity, or a form of sublime that elevates the reader into a state of aesthetic engagement,[50] but a kind of compelling relationality. The images we encounter are outrageous not because they are terribly dreadful but because they are part of the normal state of affairs. In certain contexts, shock can be effective to describe the most wretched aspects of the violence at the core of the Anthropocene, but representations that emphasize their mundaneness are also necessary to offset a reversed normalization of environmental destruction via its rendition through spectacular images. Before I offer some examples of how Habila does that, I want to explore the representational crisis that the novel sees in contemporary journalism and the kind of realistic representation that, in trying to make up for that crisis, can make the environmental destruction of the Delta glaringly visible.

Narrative and the Crisis of Reportage

One of the most notable characteristics of *Oil on Water* is its avoidance to employ the narrative mode that Arundhati Roy has called in a different context "crisis reportage." Roy describes this kind of reportage as follows: "Crisis reportage in the twenty-first century has evolved into an independent discipline—almost a science. The money, the technology and the orchestrated mass hysteria that goes into crisis reporting have a curious effect. It isolates the crisis, unmoors it from the particularities of the history, the geography, and the culture that produced it. . . . We have entered the era of crisis as a consumer item, crisis as spectacle, as theater."[51] Roy's critique says something important about the ways in which environmental disasters in the Anthropocene are largely reported. The harsh competition between media corporations to gain audiences' already divided attention, the manufactured need for constant real-time reporting, newsflashes, and last-minute updates, and the current conflation of information and entertainment are causing media reporting to be increasingly unable to depict environmental disaster in registers other than the spectacular. This register, as Roy points out, separates devastating events from their immediate contexts, delocalizing them by inscribing them in narrative and visual vacuums whose life span is determined by their capacity to remain newsworthy.

Oil on Water provides a critique of crisis reportage, revealing it as the mode of representation that legitimizes an illusory dialogue between the ecologically dispossessed in the Delta, on the one hand, and a public thirsty for shocking renditions of the destruction that affects them, on the other. This does not mean, however, that a different kind of reportage can easily take its place that depicts ecological violence, its perpetrators, and its victims without reducing them to placeholders at the service of sensationalism or the business of selling newspapers. For Habila, the solution lies in generating a response that upends the expectations of the audience while renovating their interest in the destruction caused by the oil industry beyond dramatic explosions, violent spills, and ravaging fires. The novel, thus, suggests as alternative the restorative work of careful narrative craft that engages in slow, nuanced, and situated ways with the material it portrays. The blueprint for this mode of representation is encapsulated in the conversations between Rufus—the unseasoned and avid reporter—and his hero Zaq—a former star journalist whose career is now on its last legs—as they travel across the Delta with other reporters in search of Isabel Floode.

After opening with a partial retelling of the accident in his hometown, which heralds the novel's intention to capture what crisis reportage cannot or will not, Rufus turns to one of several conversations with Zaq. The first one, though, is crucial because it pertains to both their task in the Delta and the very mission of journalists, who, according to the experienced reporter, should not be driven by the sense of accomplishment provoked by having their stories published but by creating an effect on their audience. In trying to dissuade Rufus from following the clues and finding the people involved in the kidnapping, as a "good" journalist would, Zaq advises: "Forget the woman and her kidnappers for a moment. What we really seek is not them. . . . Remember, the story is not the final goal." What he must strive for instead is "the meaning of the story" (5). Musing about the possibility of gaining professional accolades and building a career, however, Rufus confesses to the reader his excitement at maybe being on the trail of the "perfect story," which makes him feel "a stirring of some hunger inside me . . . a conviction that, almost, I was meant to be here" (8). Initially ignoring Zaq's advice, Rufus is motivated by his hunger to pursue the full story of Isabel's kidnapping, yet this will also be the motor for the novel gradually to expand its focus in order to show the glaring ecological violence that surrounds it.

The novel continues to provide clues about the importance of narrative craft in other conversations between the two men. Recalling a visit to his journalism school to deliver the graduation lecture, Rufus tells of Zaq's advice on the importance of the headline to three selected students, including him, invited to the dinner following the event. The headline, Zaq insists, must show the writer's narrative creativity; it has to be "witty, truthful, intriguing, compelling and with some literary appeal," although, he confesses romantically, this is an impossible task, because "the perfect headline is never thought up; it's given to you. An inspiration. A revelation," and it "always comes to you after you've already published your story" (22). This may well be the case of a story Zaq wrote about a kidnapping similar to Isabel's whose headline read, "Gangsters or Freedom Fighters?" (31). The unsubtle binary dilemma on which it is premised, arguably neither particularly inspirational nor revelatory, however, may be read as the precedent against which Rufus must write a gripping and urgent story, especially given Zaq's disenchantment with the profession and his death at the end of the novel, which leaves the responsibility to write about the Delta in Rufus's hands.

This responsibility, furthermore, requires the personal commitment of the journalist. In a later scene, Rufus remembers the lesson he learned from Zaq's lecture: "the best stories are the ones we write with tears in our eyes, the ones whose stings we feel personally" (134). The foggy memory of the accident in his village and Isabel's kidnapping, thus, become now part of a larger story, one that is the result of a violent economy in which the inhabitants of the Delta are trapped. As a journalist, then, Rufus begins to sense that his duty is to give a voice to the "communities [that] had borne the brunt of the oil wars, caught between the militants and the military," especially because "the only way they could avoid being crushed out of existence was to pretend to be deaf and dumb and blind" (37). In other words, his writing must account for the ways in which life in the Delta is not reported, and it must, ultimately, serve every journalist's duty to witness. As he claims while a group of militia is punished by the military in his presence, "my job was to observe, and to write about it later. To be a witness for posterity" (60), a sentiment that he attributes to Zaq's influence: "In that lecture you talked about journalists being conservationists . . . that we scribble for posterity" and that "maybe once in a lifetime, comes a transcendental moment, a great story only the true journalist can do justice to—" Rufus's sentence trails without ending. Ultimately, Zaq's point during the lecture was that one must "know a great story when it comes, and to be ready for it, with the words and the talent and the daring to go after it" (79). Otherwise, the reporter's job is doomed to fail.

Rufus and Zaq's reflections on the principles of journalism, however, are pitted against the backdrop of an industry that is enfeebled at best and pointless at worst. The days of rigorous, socially conscious journalism are over. Zaq's own career is on the wane due to government pressures as much as the cannibalizing tendencies of a business thriving on people's desire for spectacle. As a former colleague of Zaq's tells Rufus back in Port Harcourt, he became a national hero for a serialized story that humanized the plight of five Lagos prostitutes, titled "Five Women," which caused such a reaction from the public ("people cried as they read the intimate stories of these girls") that "the politicians were compelled to act" (121). Later, he was admired for becoming involved in the "pro-democracy movement" during the last stages of Sani Abacha's dictatorship, writing "fiery, fearless anti-military pieces that even our editor was hesitant to publish" (122). Yet "at a certain point he stopped being the man behind the news and became the news," as he spent a year in prison in the UK at the end of a trip to London after cocaine was found in his luggage, later suspected to belong to his fiancée (122–23). The end of Zaq's career is more than a negative landmark for Rufus, who laments the present state of journalism: "A generation of papers, his generation, had died out, its place taken by another generation, my generation. Broader, glossier, racier, cockier" (89). At a global level, the BBC program playing in the background during Rufus and James Floode's argument is a clear example of this kind of journalism. From a detached distance, the segment merely reproduces stories that offer no substantial analysis while contributing to the normalization of a status quo governed by the environmental and social crisis in which all the parties involved are seen as unavoidable participants. Writing from the Delta, thus, Rufus's urge is to produce a well-crafted, complex, and transformative story.

However, Rufus encounters several obstacles in trying to do his job. While his writing and photographing skills earn him a coveted spot on the paper *The Reporter*, his success depends on the moody and autocratic management of its owner, who "controlled every aspect of the paper" and runs its newsroom by fueling constant rivalry among writers and editors, who fight for his attention (97–98). While initially intrigued by Isabel's kidnapping, the owner is clearly more interested in selling papers than in untangling the complicated issue, and pressures Rufus for "a good interview" with James Floode even though the latter has said he would give none "till after everything is over" (99). Later, when Rufus decides to stay in the Delta to pursue the story, he is told by another journalist that he has lost his job. He reflects on his boss's fickleness: "How quickly things change. It seemed like only yesterday I was seated at the Chairman's right hand, being toasted by the staff, and now I had no job" (171). Driven by a dedication that supersedes the practice of journalism for the sake of making a profit, then, Rufus must continue his mission without the industry's support.

As he travels the Delta, Rufus's journalistic mission will be subjected to other pressures from individuals in positions of power in the oil wars. The major heading the military operation that Rufus and Zaq accidentally run into, for instance, tells him that the militants are responsible for the crisis: "they call themselves freedom fighters, but they are rebels, terrorists, kidnappers. Do you keep up with the news? Ah, yes, you write the news" (156). Implying that there is only one true version of the current conflict, the overbearing major threatens Rufus's life on several occasions if he does not follow the official narrative. His response to Rufus's insistence to interview prisoners is telling: "Insist? Did you say insist? . . . There's a war going on! People are being shot. In Port Harcourt oil companies are being bombed, police stations are being overrun, the world oil price is shooting through the roof. You insist! I can shoot you right now and throw you into the swamp and that's it. Now get out" (64). On the other hand, the leader of the militia group that has intercepted Isabel from her initial kidnappers urges Rufus at the end of the novel to "write the truth" about their cause, arguing that "we are different" from "the barbarians the government propagandists say we are" (232). While the implication is that their responsibility for the violence occasioned on the Delta is an unavoidable political necessity, the militiaman nevertheless warns him to "be careful, whatever you write" because "I am watching you" (232).

How can Rufus, then, write about the environmental catastrophe caused by the oil industry in the Delta and its attendant violence, about "every detail, every petrol trickle, every howl of pain" (63) that he witnesses during his time there, while neither rehearsing the decontextualizing, spectacular moves typical of crisis reportage nor giving in to the pressures of some of his interlocutors? How can his reporting become disentangled from the consensus that the state, the military authorities, the militia, the oil companies, and the journalistic industry itself have an interest in maintaining so that a critical portrayal of the consequences of the violence inflicted by both oil pipe and gun can bring about the kind of reaction that Zaq's "Five Women" piece once did? Rufus's solution is to infuse his work as a journalist with a specific mode of realism.

Stereoscopic Realism

Contrary to what one might expect of a narrative seeking to give a different type of visibility to the deterioration of life in the Niger Delta, Rufus's account does not seek to disentangle the intricate mesh of events that he witnesses. As a critic has put it, "Habila's novel does not so much ask us to contemplate the ruining of the Niger delta's natural environment per se as it encourages our reflection on the new conditions of life in a sickening environment that the extraction of petroleum has created."[52] Thus, Rufus's self-appointed task is to register the abysmal state of the Delta in a new way that allows the reader to pause and look again. This requires that, as Zaq entreats Rufus, we forget Isabel's kidnapping to pay attention to something else. While the plot is carried forward by Rufus's eagerness to break the story and a sense of anticipation that is not satisfied until the end ("Events were always a step ahead of us"), the novel is not simply a journalistic report governed by the quest to find Isabel and her captors, which he nonetheless eventually does (29). It incorporates passages in which the narrator deploys what I call a "stereoscopic realism," a descriptive mode that emphasizes the narrator's attentive perception of his dilapidated milieu as one that, as the stereoscopic photographic device does, provides as sense of depth based on the relationships between foreground and background.

The novel is more concerned with the state of things than with how they became the way they are.[53] As a fictional work of narrative reportage, it draws attention to the Delta as a severely damaged ecosystem. Yet Rufus's chronicle does not merely seek to bring the peripheral aspects of Isabel's capture to the foreground in trying to "color" the story. Instead, it unspectacularly and systematically records every person and thing that Rufus comes across in order to critique the normalization of the environmental violence they sustain. Thus, the stereoscopic realism that he deploys bears certain connections with the visuality of the artistic genre of the picturesque and the role of found objects in it. The picturesque is a genre that, in "reframing . . . the found object . . . raise[s] things up, elevate[s] them from their abject, supine condition and put[s] them on display without forgetting where they came from."[54] Rufus's narrative is similarly preoccupied with the mundane, although the way he reframes the Delta's landscape and its inhabitants (human and nonhuman alike) may be better labeled antipicturesque. It is the found objects of his narrative that carry, to recall Zaq's advice to Rufus in the opening of the novel, the meaning of the story. And, through his depiction of those objects, Rufus can appeal to an unelevated "ethics of the spectator" that refuses to take for granted a "stable meaning" of what is seen and recuperates the spectator's "responsibility toward what is visible."[55]

It is telling that the first site Rufus records after his conversation with Zaq about the importance of the story is a small village where we can only see the aftermath of the oil wars and the violent interruption of the extraction of crude. The village, abandoned by its inhabitants due to "too much fighting," as a local tells him, "looked as if a deadly epidemic has swept through it" (8). At the center, "abandoned oil-drilling paraphernalia were strewn around" whereas "some appeared to be sprouting out widening cracks in the concrete alongside thick clumps of grass" (8–9). In the houses next to the platform, Rufus witnesses the traces of a community forced out by oil: "a chicken pen with about ten chickens inside, all dead and decomposing, the maggots trafficking beneath the feathers," while "cooking pots stood open and empty" and "water pots [sat] filled with water on whose surface mosquito larvae thickly flourished" (9). After leaving, Rufus, Zaq, and their guide enter "a dense mangrove swamp" where "the water underneath us had turned foul and sulfurous" and "the atmosphere grew heavy with the suspended stench of dead matter" (9). Soon, oil appears, pervasive, blended with the rest of the war-torn landscape. Rufus sees "dead birds draped over tree branches, outstretched wings black and slick with oil; dead fish bobbed white-bellied between tree roots" (10). The next village "was almost a replica of the last: the same squat dwellings, the same ripe and flagrant stench, the barrenness, the oil slick and the same indefinable sadness in the air," where "the patch of grass growing by the water was suffocated by a film of oil" (10).

Rufus's description is powerful and poetic. It does not offer images of the common spillages associated with drilling, or of burst pipes or explosions. While Rufus will experience firsthand the confrontation between the army and the militias, no vivid re-creation of oil flowing, bursting, trickling, or sliding is provided here or in the descriptions of any of the other villages he visits. Instead, this scene registers the calm desolation of a "toxic present" that, as Rufus's attention to the rotting and festering of organic matter emphasizes, slowly permeates life in the Delta, inching forward just as the oil that spreads over the land- and waterscapes. Habila's objective, therefore, is not to provide a reconstructive, comprehensive account of the resource curse, with its communities disrupted by European oilmen drawing abusive contracts with the Delta inhabitants, drilling, and laying down pipes under the protection of the state and threatened to be trapped between the crossfire of the army and the guerrillas. Instead, the point is to draw attention to the realities of what life is like for those in the periphery of the main plot. To extend the analogy in Habila's title, the novel also seeks to show us the water on top of which the unearthed oil now sits. That is why the first thing Rufus does at the first village is "taking pictures, hoping to meet perhaps one accidental straggler, one survivor, one voice to interview" (9). These encounters will produce the kind of depth that his story requires, focusing as much on the background as on the foreground.

Even though, in point of fact, most of his interactions take place from a distance, Rufus runs across a large number of people. Apart from members of the army and the militias, he has the opportunity to spend time with the members of the Irikefe community, whose island is taken over by the militants and is the place where Isabel is held hostage. Perhaps more powerful, however, are his accidental and often brief encounters with unnamed inhabitants of the Delta. Like the individuals in Johansson's *Poison*

Fire, a number of locals—who are frequently depicted as scared, impoverished, and exhausted—appear looking directly at him, engaging his gaze in silence. Some of them are tolerant of his presence, like the group of old women in a village who "stared into the camera lens silently, their tired, lined faces neither acknowledging nor forbidding my action," while younger women and children amusingly pose for him (28), or the members of a family hiding away from the fighting, whom he accidentally meets while escaping the military camp where he has been detained and whose "expressions told me they felt more pity for me than fear" (188). Others are less welcoming, such as the women and children in a village who "stared out at us inquisitively, but . . . quickly closed their doors or turned to some task when we waved or called out to them" (11–12), or the victims of an attack by the militia, who "would look up and stare at me and I'd look back at them, my face full of questions, but I got only silent head shakes" (172). A great deal is communicated by means of a simple stare, a glancing recognition, or a look of suspicion.

In Rufus's stereoscopic rendition of the Delta, thus, human and nonhuman life merge as parts of a collapsing ecosystem. Before all journalists but Zaq and Rufus flee the area after being held up by the militants, Rufus establishes this relationship while making a point about the spectacularization of the conflict. While the other journalists hover over a corpse "in an excited huddle, cameras flashing," Rufus describes it as a "body in a torn blue shirt. It was half covered by bamboo leaves so that the torn stomach was only partially visible" (77). Additional graphic details follow, yet Rufus strives to put into context what he sees: "The face was squeezed in a grimace of pain . . . he must have seen the gun raised and pointed at him just before the bullet ripped into him. . . . There was a trail of blood that started from the body and disappeared into the grass, indicating how he must have dragged himself after being hit" (77). Rufus does not gather disposable images of war soon to be replaced by equally gruesome images from a different site; rather, he records them as proof of the ramifications of oil's violent irruption. In trying to reconstruct the attack, he contextualizes the oil wars not from the point of view of either the army or the militia but from the point of view of each and every innocent victim he comes across, whose relationship with the landscape is evoked by the material continuity between their dead bodies and the soil where they lie.

The irruption of oil in the Delta's ecosystem is forcefully illustrated in Rufus's descriptions of the mechanics of petroleum extraction as well. As they arrive at one island, he describes what he thinks at first is a village: "It looked like a setting for a sci-fi movie: the meager landscape was covered in pipelines flying in all directions, sprouting from the evil-smelling, oil-fecund earth. The pipes crisscrossed and interconnected endlessly all over the eerie field. We walked inland, ducking under or hopping over the giant pipes, our shoes and trousers turning black with oil" (38). Not a village but an oil station, it nonetheless appears as the settlement of an exploitative alien presence (exactly what the Western oil companies are in the Delta) that separates humans from the land they struggle to inhabit. Moreover, the mesh of pipes looks distinctly unearthly not simply because of its foreignness to the beholder but because it is a place in which the development of human and certain nonhuman forms of life is now simply impossible.

Yet the most dramatic trope to visualize oil's occupation of the Delta is the gas flare. Gas flares punctuate the landscape and are conspicuous in many scenes, especially those taking place at night. In one, Rufus writes about how "not far away in the swamps," while one could hear the "bullfrogs bellowing, we could see the glow of gas flares like distant malfunctioning stars" (65). Virtually the only visible things in the dark nights of the Delta, gas flares double as a metaphor for oil money's substitution of the substantial and robust development that the region desperately needs, further obscuring the scarcity, poor health, and lack of resources that plague its inhabitants. Rufus relays a secondhand account by a rural doctor about the power of oil money in the extremely poor village where he used to practice. One day "oil was discovered": "They got their orange fire. . . . Night and day it burned" and "everything was illuminated. That light soon became the village square" and, not long afterward, a "night market developed around that glow" and even "village meetings . . . now took place at night under the orange fire" (152). After a while, though, all forms of life start to suffer severely from the polluting effects of the constant flow of gas. When people begin to die, the doctor decides to run some tests and discovers dangerous levels of toxins in the drinking water. Extremely concerned, he sends the results to the government, only to receive a disheartening response: "They thanked me and dumped the results in some filing cabinet." In a further attempt to give visibility to this urgent problem, he sends them to "NGOs and international organizations, which published them and urged the government to do something about the flares, but nothing happened" (153). If on the fields the flares are visible landmarks literally pinpointing the pervasive presence of oil on the landscape, they could also be read as a metaphor for the dazzling power of the oil industry to make the locals, the government, and the public at large become blind to the deleterious consequences of its practices.

Despite Rufus's intention to collect such images of the Delta, his attention is nevertheless divided. Finding Isabel is still his priority, as his inability to contain the anticipation of following Zaq's steps shows: "I had a draft of my story in my head, and trapped for posterity in my point-and-shoot Sony digital camera were images of the gutted bodies half hidden in the bushes, the thatchless, burned-down huts, the bullet-broken palm trees, and the spectacular fire throwing up a cloud of smoke over the tall trees" (85). His thirst for "the perfect story" becomes an obstacle for his commitment to witness the poor state of the Delta. Rufus eventually finds Isabel on the run, free from her captors (or, rather, stumbles upon her as yet another found object in his journey), after some locals tell him about how "a white woman was there three days ago, wanting a boat to go to Port Harcourt" (191). Instead of offering a satisfactory resolution to the plot, this confirms Zaq's point that what is important is not the story, but its meaning. Still thinking that "I was being handed a major scoop" (200), Rufus has the chance to interview Salomon (the Floodes' driver), who becomes embroiled in what is first a mediocre attempt to kidnap her before a militia group leader known as the Professor takes over, and is later found dead under unclear circumstances. Rufus also has the chance to interview Isabel, but he eventually realizes that the point of his story is not that he has found her. First, his task is now pointless: "Your husband . . . sent us to see if you were alive and well . . . but now that you are free . . ." (197). Second, the way Isabel responds to his questions symbolically suggests the true meaning of his mission. Instead of looking at him, Isabel deviates her gaze to "the little slit through which a line of light came into the tent" where she is hiding from the Professor: "I wondered what she was staring at outside, or if she was expecting something or someone to come charging in" (197). This is, of course, the natural reaction of a person unsure of whether she is still in danger. Yet her looking outward also forces us not to divert our gaze from what is really important: the Niger Delta's catastrophe.

The end of the novel redoubles the impossibility for the story to reach its closure. Getting ready to leave Irikefe, which is now free from the Professor's grip and is in the process of repairing the damage caused by the oil wars, Rufus broods at the top of a hill, from where he oversees the landscape: "Far away on the horizon the flares were still sending up smoke into the air, and for a moment I imagined, somewhere on the river, a refinery up in flames, sabotaged by the Professor and his men. . . . I imagined huge cliffs of smoke and giant escarpments of orange fire rising into the atmosphere, and thousands of gallons of oil floating on the water, the weight of the oil tight like a hangman's noose around the neck of whatever life-form lay underneath" (238). In imagining the Professor's likely and disastrous next move in the perpetually deadlocked oil war, while predicting that for Isabel "this would all be nothing but a memory, an anecdote for the dinner table," Rufus confirms his conviction that his job is to register over and again the glaring images of a desolate Delta (239). In finishing his story looking down from the hill before he begins his return to Port Harcourt, Rufus acts as a surrogate for his readers, who are entreated to look at the Delta's damaged environment one more time before turning their attention to something else.

A Blurry Picture

I want to make a final point about the shortcomings that some critics have noted in the narrative structure of *Oil on Water*. Jennifer Wenzel, for instance, has argued that the novel suffers from an exceedingly convoluted temporal organization governed by numerous flashbacks and the jumbled arrangement of its chronology, as well as an ambivalence "about militancy as a response to petroleum extraction" and its "harm to communities and ecosystems."[56] Wenzel is right. Given Habila's aim to reorient Rufus's initial hunger to produce the perfect story about Isabel's kidnapping, the protagonist can only offer a collection of loosely connected moments that ultimately lead to no definite conclusion. Yet, Wenzel continues, "The novel's most compelling writing is its vivid and varied descriptions of hastily abandoned villages, eerie drilling installations, and land- and waterscapes choked by oil. . . . Unlike the militants and the soldiers, the land and water seem to speak directly, in their own voice, without quotation marks."[57] The novel's unclear temporal arrangement and its weak political alignments are clear limitations if we seek to find a well-defined argument about the conflict caused by the discovery of oil underpinning the narrative. However, we can also read them as elements that contribute to Habila's attempt to renew the visibility of the glaring environmental damage of the Niger Delta while revealing how oil remains "hidden in plain sight."[58]

The novel's narrative attributes force one to confront the damage caused by the oil industry and the oil wars as it appears before us in a disorderly but also unspectacular manner. Through my analysis of Rufus's stereoscopic realism, I have sought to show how this is provoked by the collection of images that are peripheral to the kidnapping plot but, the novel's ending suggests, are ultimately the more important aspect of the reporter's narrative goal. The environmental destruction, the violence between the militias and the army, and the entrenchment of local poverty and insecurity caused by the irruption of multinational corporations in the local economy are all, like the mesh of pipes that Rufus encounters on one of the first islands, entangled in the processes of life and death in the Delta. Habila's novel, thus, carries out what has been called "the difficult task of bringing together the violence that has been repeatedly deployed to secure arrangements for the production of oil and the forms of spectacle and representation that seem somehow an equally indispensable aspect of the undemocratic politics of oil."[59] The task of the writer, it seems to suggest, is to remain alert and observant, to register the consequences of this catastrophe.

In looking at *Oil on Water* as a self-contained narrative, perhaps what we are left with is a blurry picture of the state of the Delta and the depoliticizing presence of oil. Yet this is not so much a desensitizing normalization of the destruction the novel records as the accentuation of its obvious but no less critical outcome. The more we struggle to put the pieces together in a narrative that actively dismantles a teleological understanding of plot, the more we hang onto the pieces themselves. If relationships between the actors involved become more and more blurred, the damage done becomes clearer and clearer. Similarly, the novel's allegedly unclear commitments could be interpreted to imply that it is ultimately less concerned with presenting a case for or against the militias (or the army, or the government, or the international companies exploiting the oil reserves, or the charity work of certain characters in the novel, etc.). Perhaps that is not what we should ask of *Oil on Water*. Perhaps we should pay attention to its reflection on the difficulty of taking a side when the possibilities of motivating a resolution to the oil problem are curbed by the consensual view that this is the normal state of affairs in the region, a view that is rendered especially difficult to modify given the distance from which the public stays informed about this problem through the newspapers, in this case, but also the rest of the media more generally speaking. Subscribing to this reading would mean, ultimately, to locate the political commitment of *Oil on Water* in the articulation of a countervisuality of the disaster.

Yet *Oil on Water* does not attempt to provide a "full picture" of the environmental and political consequences of oil extraction in the Niger Delta either. Instead, it intervenes in the comprehensive scope of the Anthropocene narrative by exposing how, as aggressive a human activity as it is, oil extraction must be accounted for not only from the distance at which international diplomacy, global capitalism, and planetary preservation operate, but also by constructing narratives that expose their impact at the local level. One of the most important outcomes of Habila's stereoscopic realism, in my view, is that it refuses to offer the kind of spectacularly emblematic images that Rufus imagines would accompany his scoop. As John Berger would say in a different context, those images are "discontinuous with all other moments" of the catastrophe, limiting the reader/spectator's reaction to isolated shocking images instead of what I called earlier the toxic present in which they are inscribed, therefore rendering the catastrophe they depict "effectively depoliticized."[60] Habila's narrative strategy, to conclude, provides us with a mode of representation that is as forceful as it is subtle. With its unclear trajectory and its attention to the found objects that Rufus comes across, the novel provides us with a counterdialogic view from across that interrogates the difficulties of giving visibility to a problem that is, in many ways, already visible.

Anthropocenic Prospects

As ecological crises increasingly become primarily global threats, the narrative of the Anthropocene will be crucial to formulate effective and egalitarian ways to live on the Earth. It has the potential of bringing together the voices of activists, experts, artists, and policy makers to express in concrete ways the magnitude of the environmental impact of human activity on a planetary scale. The cohering of voices under the auspices of one single narrative will be, furthermore, key for the consolidation of what is still an inchoate agenda under initiatives—such as the UNESCO-sponsored "How to Think the Anthropocene" conference held in Paris in 2015—that determine the decisions humans will need to make in order to face both current and upcoming ecological challenges. Yet, in order to promote an equitable environmental planetary politics to sustain such an agenda, the dialogic engagement of those voices must avoid becoming an illusory dialogue that keeps minor voices in the periphery while trying to make a meaningful contribution to the construction of that narrative. Instead, this dialogic arrangement must be propelled by certain productive tensions that prevent the establishment of an unchallengeable consensus about what the Anthropocene means exactly. In fact, several debates are already trying to shed light, from different disciplinary points of view, on the nature of this new geological era. What is the principal motor of the Anthropocene, the "Great Acceleration" caused by the post–World War II capitalist boom or the Industrial Revolution? Do we locate its origins in the early modern era, as Europe systematized its imperial project by means of genocide and mass ecological destruction, or in the discovery of fossil fuels a few thousand years ago? Do we take the collapse of the climate as its principal manifestation, or do we consider a wider range of phenomena to define it, such as the depletion of resources, the acidification of the oceans, or the proliferation of mass extinction events? These are questions that are best considered in conjunction with and not in opposition to each other.

Sinha's and Habila's novels offer important counterdialogic engagements that challenge, agonistically, what the narrative of the Anthropocene represents and how humans may organize themselves around it. As individual events, the catastrophes that they fictionalize are no doubt incapable of having an undeniable long-term impact on the planet's biological, geological, and chemical cycles comparable to climate change or other large-scale phenomena. However, they do prompt us to reconsider the agential and causal assumptions underpinning the narrative by reenvisioning how human activity's destructive environmental impact is understood. They articulate how the absolute terms in which the ruination of the planet's ecology is measured must not be the only way to delineate the contours of the Anthropocene. The environmental characteristics of the world that the Anthropocene conjures up may not be forever altered by the Khaufpur gas leak or the oil industry's irruption in the Niger Delta, but the worlds of the inhabitants of those locales certainly are. Reading them as parts of a constellation that includes countless other local catastrophes caused by an exploitative global economy governed by a select few actors in the global North with the complicit participation of local bodies of governance and their branches of law enforcement, we can see how these novels challenge a postpolitical human agency that might be installed at the core of the Anthropocene according to which a single, inscrutable *anthropos* is the central figure of the consensus underpinning the narrative.

Yet their concern is not limited to showing how those minor events demonstrate that the *anthropos* causing the environmental damage and the *anthropos* suffering it are not the same. How this showing occurs is equally crucial. The novels deploy a reframing strategy with which they articulate a dissenting view (quite literally) of environmental violence. In refashioning the visuality of such violence, I have tried to show, they preempt their narratives from being framed in an illusory dialogue that co-opts their efforts to render environmental catastrophe visible. The result is a countervisuality of the Anthropocene that reveals how, as Sean Cubitt has recently argued, "only a politics rebuilt on aesthetic principles, that is, by remaking communications, offers the possibility of changing the conduct of relations between human beings and nature, and between both of them and the technologies that so profoundly and multifariously mediate between them."[61] Shifting the frame of what is shown, therefore, is an important way to redraw the politics of environmental violence, making visible what the regulative aspects of the Anthropocene narrative might otherwise obscure.

It is no coincidence, then, that both novels are concerned with the role of journalism in depicting environmental violence. Journalistic mediation is perhaps the most important way in which we learn about it, especially when it takes place in faraway locales with which most people cannot have direct contact. In *Animal's People*, thus, we saw a countervisual intervention in Animal's quasi-erasure of the mediator between him and his audience, the journalist who initially comes to Khaufpur to interview him. While he remains the ultimate arbitrator of Animal's words as translator, transcriber, and editor (and this should never be disregarded as a simple anecdotal aspect of the text), the journalist is pushed to the side of the narrative. In doing so, Animal liberates his story—and therefore his visibility—from the journalist's questions and produces an account of the internal visuality governing his relationships with Elli and the local activist movement, which would otherwise be likely cast under a reductive and depoliticizing light of the kind we saw in the case of Poonam's photograph. As a result, Animal takes control of the representation of life in Khaufpur, which is underscored by his highly suggestive insistence to show it at waist level from his four-legged position. This narrative arrangement prevents Animal and his people from becoming the objects of what Animal suspects will be the journalist's superficial and spectacular rendition. Significantly calling his interlocutors Eyes, therefore, he repurposes the eagerness of certain Western readers to consume images of catastrophe by forcing them to look at the individuals, things, and events that they cannot or wish not to see.

Oil on Water approaches the question of journalism differently. Instead of sidestepping the journalist with an alternative narrator, Habila proposes a representational intervention by creating a journalist who becomes aware that the most important point of his story are the peripheral aspects that contextualize it. The Niger Delta and its inhabitants are, in Rufus's account, depicted through a stereoscopic realism intended to bring to the center what is seen only through the corner of one's eye. This does not mean that his objective is exclusively to record the ruinous state of the Delta's ecology, as his eagerness to pursue the scoop of Isabel's kidnapping is nonetheless, and despite its jumbled chronology, what brings the story forward. Ironically—and, one could argue, evidencing the competitive race for spectacular scoops and images that the practice of journalism has become—Rufus has to find Isabel in order to understand that, while he may be able to construct a riveting story, composing a narrative of the oil wars would put the ecological devastation that oil's irruption has caused, literally and figuratively speaking, in the background. The countervisual work of his narrative, thus, becomes evident in retrospect, as his rendition is not a step-by-step account of his journey to find Isabel but rather a highly reflective story that underscores everything else that he finds along the way. If *Oil on Water* seems to lack a clear assertion about which side it takes in the conflict it portrays, this apparent lack of commitment is not apolitical. As I explained, the blurry picture that one may ultimately see is an effective way to express how trying to fit the Delta's ecological disaster into a narrative of culprits and saviors would demote it to a simple contextualizing frame, and not, as Rufus seeks to show it, the plight of its inhabitants.

Animal's People and *Oil on Water*, finally, tell us something important about the contemporary occasion. One of the most successful aspects of both novels is that they reflect on mundane notions that are generally absent in most investigative reportage on catastrophic events, challenging the instant gratification and profit of highly spectacular renditions of environmental disaster to which the journalistic media tend to gravitate. Their focus on the mundane, moreover, hints at a different understanding of time that has important political value within the frame of the Anthropocene. If only indirectly, the novels suggest that we must understand the ecologically untenable present they depict as connected to a future that does not bode any better. This is not to cast Bhopal and the Niger Delta communities as exemplary of what the future might hold for the rest of the planet. The point is, rather, to extend the urgent claim that "we must act now" to the collective planetary efforts that are necessary to begin correcting the attitudes and practices that have led to the ecological destruction that those communities endure. In their attempts to reframe the issue, thus, the novels invite readers to become active agents in a committed but justly qualified "we" at the center of the narrative of the Anthropocene.

EPILOGUE

Arguing On

We reach the end of our exploration of the power of fiction to prompt a critical reassessment of the workings of dialogue. In arguing that we must resist dialogue, I have made a case for what would be, at least initially, inarguable. The very act of arguing, for one thing, is intrinsically a dialogic act. Additionally, I have not proposed to do away with dialogue altogether, but to rethink some of our main assumptions about it and consider the instances where it does not enable the kinds of democratic, discursive collaboration with which we instinctively associate it. Arguing the inarguable, thus, has allowed me to produce a critique of dialogue against its grain to discern ways in which it can be, despite our deepest convictions, a depoliticizing linguistic instrument. In the preceding chapters, I have tried to show not only how dialogue can be weaponized as an illusion that, simulating a critical engagement, will not produce a politically meaningful outcome, but also how it can result in the perpetuation of the disenfranchisement of certain minor actors even when employed to rectify an injustice. My objective has been to defend the idea that we indeed need to challenge effectively certain deployments of dialogue while safeguarding the appropriate conditions for dialogic interactions to take place that can lead to political change.

I have sought to show here how, now perhaps more than ever, we must defend and protect dialogue. Yet, instead of employing it to reinforce the consensus that dictates the permissible and impermissible behaviors in a community, we need to be able to practice it as a means to transform disagreement into tangible forms of dissent. We need critical confrontation and dispute in our lives. As I have tried to demonstrate, though, an ethical commitment must remain at the core of any interaction to be considered properly political. Otherwise it risks becoming a meaningless kind of negotiation at best and, at worst, a simple ruse employed by the administrators of dialogue—the voices commanding it—to evacuate it of its radical potential. Dialogue cannot be taken for granted; this is precisely what enables the erosion of its emancipatory valences. We must remain vigilant and, instead of celebrating it as a sign of a robust democratic culture, work constantly to ensure that it indeed acts to safeguard democracy. If we want life in common to be equitable and just, we must come up with creative ways to resist the constant depoliticization carried out by post-political disciplining orders seeking to neutralize dissent. In other words, we need to argue on.

This is particularly important with respect to the work of illusory dialogue. While my task here is finished, the argument is in no way over. I have organized my study around a number of important themes that contribute to defining the main contours of modernity and providing crucial clues to understand the current moment. However, those are only some manifestations of a wide range of issues where we can identify the insidious operation of illusory dialogue. One could turn to questions of gender and sexuality I have not considered here in order to investigate the power hierarchies that are maintained, for instance, in debates about the articulation of political agendas by LGBTQ individuals and collectives, the production and perpetuation of toxic masculinities, or the constitution of sovereignties anchored in the struggle for reproductive rights. A similar point can be made, in ways I have not, about the role of illusory dialogue in maintaining the disenfranchisement of individuals and collectives along racial lines in a variety of debates, from the connections between racism and social inequality to the systematic criminalization of race as well as the racialization of crime. This is not to overlook the important victories against the dominant voices that have historically turned gender and race into instruments to maintain normative identities in power. This is, rather, to argue that we should not lose sight of the positions from which those dominant voices may be willing to engage in certain debates, and whether the solutions reached as a result are based on the recognition and advancement of the rights of the minor voices challenging them, instead of being small concessions that do not interfere with the maintenance of the status quo.

Phenomena belonging to the realm of traditional electoral politics are also worth exploring. The recent rise of populism in response to a widespread disillusionment toward the institutions of representation also warrants that we further investigate the deployment of illusory dialogue. When populist discourses have been produced in order to "shake up" the processes and principles of governance, illusory dialogue can play a crucial role in justifying certain deceitful platforms to motivate the articulation of a politics for the people. There is much work to be done on this front. If populism is based on the idea that there must indeed be a dialogue between the electorate and their representatives, that the latter are listening to the former, as they often claim, further study of the ramifications of illusory dialogue must tackle the disconnection between the original populist claim and the actual policies that those platforms promote. We are also witnessing the emergence of independence movements that are based on the configuration of nationalist identities seeking to reenergize their agency as minor voices. Because it is in their interest to articulate their agendas within the framework of democracy, their political demands have to be expressed in dialogic relationships with the nations from which they seek to separate themselves. Careful scrutiny of their discourses of self-determination, thus, can ascertain whether it is an illusory dialogue that governs the distribution of sovereignties they seek to challenge. If those movements are successful, moreover, the constitution of new dominant voices stemming from the autonomy they have achieved must also be explored for possible replications of the orders of governance to which they originally objected.

To mention one last but crucial example of the many other dimensions in which illusory dialogue can have an important influence, we need to consider the ways in which internet-based forms of communication have a clear dialogic component. In particular, the relatively recent social media boom has given rise to new discursive modes that cannot be left unexplored. It is important to acknowledge the positive aspects of this phenomenon, from the construction of political networks that allow for the mutual recognition of minor voices to the fashioning of coalitions with enough clout to bring about change in certain aspects of public life. Yet several negative aspects threaten to distort our understanding of dialogue as a political notion. Among many others, one might choose to pay close attention to the ways in which the actual encounter of confronted positions is occluded by the ossification of discursive communities and what are often referred to as "echo chambers," the erroneous assumption that the pervasive presence of the technologies of the internet neatly corresponds to the democratization of public discourse, or the slow and subtle erosion of certain political agencies caused by the substitution of engagement in debates for the work of activism. The idea of illusory dialogue, thus, may be productive to understand how certain online discursive practices not simply contribute but are designed to perpetuate the depoliticization of civic debate.

Apart from analyzing other modulations, it is also necessary to configure further strategies for minor voices to counter illusory dialogue beyond the three that I have proposed here. Illusory dialogue is as pervasive as it is intrusive, and it must be theorized in as many scenarios as one can find it operating. What other forms of agonistic resistance can minor voices put into practice that are sufficiently resilient to sustain an engagement with illusory dialogue in order to dismantle its regulatory powers? Equally important is the fact that these new strategies need to be the product of an imaginative agenda that takes on the challenge of producing responses that work in excess of the disciplinary mechanisms of illusory dialogue. What types of intervention can this resistance attain to prevent the ways in which it underpins, shapes, controls, and orients the regulatory precepts of consensus?

There are also other central notions to the functioning of illusory dialogue that I have not been able to approach here and nonetheless deserve critical attention. The central argument of this book is rooted in a discussion of the dangers of a depoliticizing form of listening that amounts to no political change. An effective way to dismantle such an act of listening, I have sought to reveal, is based on specific discursive actions that force the interaction to generate a different outcome from the one it was designed to produce. Yet this kind of listening can take many shapes, which I have collapsed into one for the sake of streamlining my argument. First, the listening that dominant voices do to placate and ultimately ignore the demands of minor voices can materialize in many different ways. We can ask ourselves, then, what the varieties and shapes of this void form of listening are and what specific purposes they serve as they seek to neutralize minor voices' political agency. At the same time, and considered from the opposite angle, there are other kinds of listening that can be said to work toward the renovation of the political substance of dialogue. If critical dialogue is a cohesive instrument, this is so because it implies the expression of an idea by one interlocutor as much as its reception by another. Thus, if my study of impasse, deflection, and reframing has sought to formulate radical responses against illusory dialogue, can we then speak of radical ways of listening? If so, how can such ways of listening manifest, and what kinds of relationships can they generate?

Silence, likewise, is a complex matter that is worth considering carefully. I have treated it here as a discursive element, as what is not said that acts as coterminous with what is said. Yet there is in the silences of those who refuse to speak up or are prevented from doing so much more than I have been able to excavate. Silence implies a presence that must be recognized in the specificity of the politics that motivates it as well as the oppression that gives rise to it. What discursive modalities, if any, can we identify in silence understood as absence of speech? What happens when silence is met with further silence? Or, to push this idea even further, would it be possible to think of silence as outside of the realm of discourse? If so, what ontological categories can silence be attached to that are not constituted linguistically?

At a larger level, other registers of the general idea of dialogue must also be probed. As I argued in the introduction, illusory dialogue is only one of many possible notions necessary to begin reevaluating our understanding of dialogue. Defenses of the notion of dialogue are often accompanied by the rather unsophisticated claim that all ideas can always be approached from two confronted perspectives. In principle, this posture promotes an understanding of democracy that ensures that no one single point of view prevails over others. However, taken as a general rule instead of a political guarantee, it tends to prescribe the two possible positions one can take about an issue by virtue of their relationship with each other. This is the case in a number of contexts, from bipartisan parliamentary activity (which puts in place a rigid dialectic framework in which policy decisions are determined by the opposition between parties) to a popular subgenre of media spectacle such as TV pundit commentary (whose goal to exploit conflict for superficial purposes is powerfully symbolized by the split-screen editing technique). Such superficial polarization has important consequences. It contributes to the oversimplification of political matters in discussions governed by warped binaries that erase their complexity while ruling out some of the possible solutions beforehand. This polarization, in addition, is closely connected with the increasingly prevalent notion that—no matter how askew—one's opinions are as valid as anyone else's and is, consequently, the main justification behind obtuse systems of false equivalence that populate much public discourse.

With all of these questions in mind, I would like to end by reemphasizing the importance of the literary imagination in our political lives. I have made an argument for the novel as a particularly adequate genre that lends itself to understanding the workings of illusory dialogue as well as the negative ramifications of practicing certain dialogically responsive politics. However, other genres also have the potential to reveal how one can think of literature as intrinsically political, and further study of these will only widen our possibilities of response. This kind of task could begin by acknowledging that both direct oppression and postpolitical ruses aimed at undermining our political capacities do not have access to the solitary act of reading, thus making it a radical exercise in itself. In practicing here a way of reading dangerously, furthermore, I have sought to involve intimately the work of the critic and that of the reader to try and uncover the theoretical fabric that emerges from certain works of prose fiction. Yet, if my approach to the politics of literature positions the figure of the citizen-reader at the center of its practice, it cannot be successful without the often-invisible support of those who encourage, teach, and show us how to do so. The emancipatory move that reading dangerously presupposes, then, is forcibly a communal one as well. Understanding dialogue more precisely, as has been my goal here, is only the first step to a much more complex social process that involves critical thinking, the possibility to engage in slow and nuanced reflection, and the availability of discourses and spaces for critical debate to emerge.

ACKNOWLEDGMENTS

A number of people have been involved in bringing this book to its present form. I would like to express my deepest gratitude to Robert Marzec, who has been an inspiring mentor and friend, and who was instrumental as I began to work out the intricacies of my argument when the project was still in its early stages. Thank you to Alfred López, Joe Palmer, Peggy Rowe, Jennifer Wenzel, Grant Farred, and Katarzyna Marciniak, who provided generous support, insightful comments, and invaluable advice about how to make this book what it is now.

At the University of North Carolina at Charlotte I have found a group of extremely supportive colleagues who always show interest in my work and have been encouraging while I was working through the more difficult parts of this book. In particular, I thank Alan Rauch, Lara Vetter, Mark West, Kent Brintnall, Kirk Melnikoff, Katie Hogan, Tony Jackson, Chris Davis, Matt Rowney, and Ton Pujol.

I want to acknowledge my friends, too, especially those who helped me develop the initial idea that there was a problem with dialogue worth exploring and have been there when I needed them. There are many, but I cannot fail to mention Marc Dziak, Megha Anwer, Steve Gooch, Brent Prater, Carmen Jiménez, Matt Varner, Anida Hadžić, Seirin Nagano, Aaron Houck, and Emre Koyuncu. Thank you for the music, the discussions, the movies, the trips, and the invaluable time we have spent together doing nothing.

I would like to express my most sincere thanks to all of the individuals involved in the production of this book at the University of Minnesota Press, and in particular to Doug Armato and Gabe Levin for having been the most accommodating and pleasant people I could ever have worked with, always ready to find solutions and facilitate my work. I am indebted, too, to the readers of the manuscript, who provided extremely perceptive comments and suggestions that made many of the arguments here much more effective than they originally were.

I am grateful to the University of North Carolina at Charlotte for the financial support it provided me as well as a reassignment of duties awarded by its College of Liberal Arts and Sciences, which allowed me to concentrate on working toward the completion of this book. I thank Dean Nancy Gutierrez for making that possible.

The support of my family from the distance has been vital in ways I cannot express. My parents, Julio and Loly, who became adults under an authoritarian regime, imbued in us the urge to think otherwise, just as they tried to do under the heel of a dictator. I hope some of that spirit is apparent in these pages. From the Vila de Gràcia, Sánchez barked enthusiastically, and Anna cheered incessantly, always willing to offer a heartening word. And I owe a particular debt, personal and intellectual, to my brother Julio, a tremendous scholar with an admirable commitment to social justice and the betterment of people's lives, my teacher, and my friend.

Finally, I thank my more immediate family for being there at all times, good and not so. To Pepette, I thank you for letting me enter your life. You have enriched mine in unimaginable ways and have taught me to communicate—and even argue—differently, despite the barriers that your being a cat and my being a human might have posed. Thank you, lastly, to Allison. You have been an inspiration for years, and the support you have given me is much more than I will ever be able to return. Your unfailing encouragement is there every time I think a project is going nowhere or has no real consequence; this book would never have existed without you. You teach me, every day, to be compassionate, patient, and resilient. Thank you for the walks, the conversations, the poetry, and the love through all these years. And for the laughs.

NOTES

Prologue

1. Francis Fukuyama, "The End of History?" *The National Interest* 16 (1989): 4. For an extension of this argument, see Fukuyama, *The End of History and the Last Man* (New York: Free Press, 1992).

2. For an important volume that explores the boundaries of postpolitics, see Japhy Wilson and Erik Swyngedouw, eds., *The Post-Political and Its Discontents: Spaces of Depoliticisation, Spectres of Radical Politics* (Edinburgh: Edinburgh University Press, 2014).

3. Antonio Gramsci, *Selections from the Prison Notebooks of Antonio Gramsci*, trans. Quintin Hoare and Geoffrey Nowell Smith (New York: International Publishers, 1971), 12.

4. See Gramsci's theorization of what he calls "philosophy of praxis," a mode of critique that "becomes actual and lives historically (that is socially and no longer just in the brains of individuals)." Gramsci, *Selections from the Prison Notebooks*, 369.

5. Jacques Rancière, *Dissensus: On Politics and Aesthetics*, trans. Steven Corcoran (London: Bloomsbury, 2010), 69.

6. The work of Jacques Rancière is the best example of this. See "The Politics of Literature," *SubStance* 33, no. 1 (2004): 10–24. For analyses of specific works, see *The Politics of Literature*, trans. Julie Rose (Cambridge: Polity, 2001), and *The Lost Thread: The Democracy of Modern Fiction*, trans. Steven Corcoran (London: Bloomsbury, 2017).

7. Slavoj Žižek, *The Year of Dreaming Dangerously* (London: Verso, 2012), 127.

8. See, e.g., Jodi Dean's commentary on the notion of postpolitics at large, which, according to her, "not only overlooks the reality of politics on the ground, but it cedes in advance key terrains of activism and struggle." Dean, *Democracy and Other Neoliberal Fantasies: Communicative Capitalism and Left Politics* (Durham: Duke University Press, 2009), 12.

9. Slavoj Žižek, *The Ticklish Subject: The Absent Centre of Political Ontology* (London: Verso, 2008), 236.

10. See, e.g., Mark Edmundson, *Why Read?* (London: Bloomsbury, 2005); Rita Felski, *Uses of Literature* (Malden: Blackwell, 2008); Blakey Vermeule, *Why Do We Care about Literary Characters?* (Baltimore: Johns Hopkins University Press, 2010); Cristina Vischer Bruns, *Why Literature? The Value of Literary Reading and What It Means for Teaching* (London: Continuum, 2011); or Peter Boxall, *The Value of the Novel* (Cambridge: Cambridge University Press, 2015).

11. Alain Badiou, *The Rebirth of History: Times of Riots and Uprisings*, trans. Gregory Elliott (London: Verso, 2012), 56; emphasis original.

12. Rancière, *Dissensus*, 155.

Introduction

1. Kōichirō Matsuura, "Round Table: Dialogue among Civilizations," *UNESCO,* September 5, 2000, http://unesdoc.unesco.org/ark:/48223/pf0000123890.

2. Samuel P. Huntington, *The Clash of Civilizations and the Remaking of World Order* (New York: Touchstone, 1997), 28.

3. "Government Statement on Preparations for Brexit," *Merrion Street, Irish Government News Service,* October 4, 2016, http://merrionstreet.ie/en/News-Room/News/Government_Statement_on_Preparations_for_Brexit.html.

4. Steven Gordon, Ben Roberts, and Jarè Struwig, "Slow Walk to Freedom: Attitudes towards Race Relations," *Human Sciences Research Council Review* 10, no. 3 (2012): 6.

5. Film Forward was conceived as "a touring program designed to enhance greater cultural understanding, collaboration and dialogue around the globe by engaging audiences through the exhibition of films and conversations with filmmakers." "Program Overview," *Sundance Film Forward,* n.d., http://www2.sundance.org/filmforward/about.

6. Sondre Bratland and Javed Bashir, *Dialogue* (Oslo: Kirkelig Kulturverksted, 2006).

7. *The New Museum,* n.d., http://www.newmuseum.org/exhibitions/view/talking-back-the-audience-in-dialogue.

8. Jean-François Lyotard, *The Postmodern Condition: A Report on Knowledge*, trans. Geoff Bennington and Brian Massumi (Minneapolis: University of Minnesota Press, 1984), 16.

9. Niccolò Machiavelli, *The Portable Machiavelli*, trans. Peter Bondanella and Mark Musa (London: Penguin, 1979), 391.

10. This is, as Dmitri Nikulin has shown, a paradoxical phenomenon given that dialogue is not a manifestation of the dialectic but its very origin. Nikulin builds several bridges between Plato and a host of modern thinkers, from Descartes to Hegel to Gadamer, in order to describe the genetic relationship between dialogue,

a singular oral event, and dialectic, a written (and therefore asynchronic) philosophical approach. Nikulin, *Dialectic and Dialogue* (Stanford: Stanford University Press, 2010).

11. Key works by these thinkers are Edmund Husserl, *Cartesian Meditations: An Introduction to Phenomenology*, trans. Dorin Cairns (London: Kluwer Academic, 1977); Emmanuel Levinas, *Totality and Infinity: An Essay on Exteriority*, trans. Alphonso Lingis (Pittsburgh: Duquesne University Press, 1969); Jürgen Habermas, *The Structural Transformation of the Public Sphere: An Inquiry into a Category of Bourgeois Society*, trans. Thomas Burger and Frederick Lawrence (Cambridge: MIT Press, 1989); Hans-Georg Gadamer, *Truth and Method*, trans. Joel Weinsheimer and Donald G. Marshall (London: Bloomsbury, 2004) and *Dialogue and Dialectic: Eight Hermeneutical Studies on Plato*, trans. P. Christopher Smith (New Haven: Yale University Press, 1980); Martin Buber, *I and Thou*, trans. Ronald Gregor Smith (London: Bloomsbury, 2004); and Paulo Freire, *Pedagogy of the Oppressed*, trans. Myra Bergman Ramos (London: Continuum, 1993).

12. Peter Womack, *Dialogue* (London: Routledge, 2011), 6.

13. Ken Hirschkop, *Mikhail Bakhtin: An Aesthetic for Democracy* (Oxford: Oxford University Press, 1999), 4; emphasis original.

14. Mikhail M. Bakhtin, *Problems of Dostoevsky's Poetics*, trans. Caryl Emerson (Minneapolis: University of Minnesota Press, 1984), 6, emphasis original; hereafter cited in the text as *PDP*.

15. See *PDP*, 122–80.

16. Mikhail M. Bakhtin, *Rabelais and His World*, trans. Hélène Iswolsky (Bloomington: Indiana University Press, 1984), 58.

17. Mikhail M. Bakhtin, *The Dialogic Imagination: Four Essays*, trans. Caryl Emerson (Austin: University of Texas Press, 1982), 271; hereafter cited in the text as *DI*.

18. In "Epic and the Novel," Bakhtin describes how the epic is the perfect textual embodiment of a unitary language that operates monologically as a narrative based on an ahistorical "absolute past." This narrative, Bakhtin maintains, is both embedded in and constitutive of a "national tradition" that is governed by "an absolute epic distance [that] separates the epic world from contemporary reality, that is, from the time in which the singer (the author and his audience) lives" (*DI* 13). It is against this distance that Bakhtin highlights the radical valences of the novel and the latter's power to dismantle the ossification of a nation's past and the homogenization of its political present.

19. Timothy Brennan has commented on this phenomenon by centering on the reception and accommodation of Bakhtin in American culture, maintaining that the radical power of Bakhtin's work is lost to those who regard it as "an abstract democratic sublime where dialogue is considered a rejection of polemical confrontation." Brennan, *Wars of Position: The Cultural Politics of Left and Right* (New York: Columbia University Press, 2006), 2.

20. Raymond Williams, *The Politics of Modernism: Against the New Conformists* (London: Verso, 1989), 181–82.

21. Alain Badiou, *Metapolitics*, trans. Jason Barker (London: Verso, 2005), 18; emphasis original.

22. As Michael Gardiner has argued, "Bakhtin is never entirely clear on precisely why and how [the] decentering and subversion of official discourse occurred when it did, although he seems to suggest that this is inevitable when a given society opens itself up to multiplicity of linguistic and artistic influences." Gardiner, *The Dialogics of Critique: M. M. Bakhtin and the Theory of Ideology* (London: Routledge, 1992), 35.

23. Christopher Falzon, *Foucault and Social Dialogue* (London: Routledge, 1998), 45.

24. Michel Foucault, *The History of Sexuality, Vol. 1: An Introduction*, trans. Robert Hurley (New York: Vintage, 1990), 101.

25. Daphna Erdinast-Vulcan, *Between Philosophy and Literature: Bakhtin and the Question of the Subject* (Stanford: Stanford University Press, 2013), 14.

26. In contrast, Bakhtin maintains that "dialogue . . . is not the threshold to action, it is the action itself. It is not a means for revealing, for bringing to the surface the already-made character of a person; no, in dialogue a person not only shows himself outwardly, but *he becomes for the first time that which he is* . . . not only for others but for himself as well" (*DI* 252; emphasis added).

27. Caryl Emerson, *The First Hundred Years of Mikhail Bakhtin* (Princeton: Princeton University Press, 1997), 155.

28. As Aaron Fogel once argued, "in practice not all dialogue is free, natural, spontaneous, informal, or lively. On the contrary, it may be true that most real dialogue is variously constrained and forced." Fogel, *Coercion to Speak: Conrad's Poetics of Dialogue* (Cambridge: Harvard University Press, 1985), 16.

29. Arundhati Roy, *Power Politics* (Cambridge: South End Press, 2001), 33.

30. Etymologically speaking, "dialogue" does not mean the encounter of two people, as it is sometimes understood. The prefix "dia-" means "through" or "by means of," whereas "logos" denotes, among other things, "words," "speaking," "language use," etc. I will, however, concentrate on the confrontation of two sides for a methodological reason. Since I am interested in exploring the nature of political confrontation and its materialization through disagreement, even though my thematization of certain theoretical and rhetorical aspects of (illusory) dialogue implicate the efforts of collectivities, I will limit my discussion to its minimum expression as articulated in such a dialectical fashion.

31. This is, e.g., the view of David Bohm, who maintains that the "object of a dialogue is not to analyze things, or to win an argument, or to exchange opinions. Rather, it is to suspend your opinions and to look at the opinions—to listen to everybody's opinions, to suspend them, and to see what all that means" (26). Bohm also discounts the political value of dialogue by claiming that "conviction and persuasion are not called for in a dialogue" because "if something is right, you

don't need to be persuaded" (27); that, with regard to the "kind of government" a society wants, "if some people don't agree, then we have political struggle" and when disagreement "goes further, it breaks down into civil war" (28); that a "defensive attitude" gets in the way of intelligence because "intelligence requires that you don't defend an assumption" (34); and that in dialogue "the important point is not the answer . . . but rather the softening up, the opening up of the mind, and looking at all the opinions" (46). All these views, of course, run drastically against my argument. Bohm, *On Dialogue* (London: Routledge, 1996).

32. Ali Riza Taşkale, for example, names four (ressentiment, fear, cynicism, and spite) in his exploration of how the administrators of consensus address the population so that it "can be rendered governable and manageable." Taşkale, *Post-Politics in Context* (London: Routledge, 2016), 11.

33. As Jacques Rancière has argued, recognition can indeed contribute to the perpetuation of disempowerment. Rancière asks: "How far does the concept that makes recognition the object of a struggle depart from . . . the identification of preexisting entities and the idea of a response to a demand?" The struggle for recognition, he asserts, usually manifests as a "demand by a subject already constituted to be recognized in his or her identity," thus limiting the political power of those seeking to change the conditions that determine their disenfranchisement. Rancière, "Critical Questions on the Theory of Recognition," in *Recognition or Disagreement: A Critical Encounter on the Politics of Freedom, Equality, and Identity*, ed. Katia Genel and Jean-Philippe Deranty (New York: Columbia University Press, 2016), 85, 90.

34. For Debord, the spectacle is "the existing order's uninterrupted discourse about itself, its laudatory monologue," operating as "the self-portrait of power in the epoch of its totalitarian management of the conditions of existence" (24) and determining "the diplomatic representation of hierarchic society to itself, where all other expression is banned" (23). As a representational regime, the spectacle is "nothing but an official language of generalized separation" (3), "which escapes the activity of men, [and] escapes reconsideration and correction by their work. It is the opposite of dialogue" (18). Emancipation from the grasp of spectacle, Debord asserts in the final sentence of his book, is possible "only where individuals are 'directly linked to universal history'; only where dialogue arms itself to make its own conditions victorious" (221). Debord, *Society of the Spectacle*, trans. Fredy Perlman et al. (Detroit: Black and Red, 1983).

35. Habermas's goal is to theorize political relations in positive terms. Yet the shortcomings of his theory are indeed useful to describe the functioning of illusory dialogue. Jürgen Habermas, *On the Pragmatics of Social Interaction: Preliminary Studies in the Theory of Communicative Action*, trans. Barbara Fultner (Cambridge: MIT Press, 2001), 97.

36. Chantal Mouffe, *The Democratic Paradox* (London: Verso, 2000), 104.

37. Slavoj Žižek, *First as Tragedy, Then as Farce* (London: Verso, 2009), 109.

38. Jacques Rancière, *Disagreement: Politics and Philosophy*, trans. Julie Rose (Minneapolis: University of Minnesota Press, 1999), 29.

39. Michael Hardt and Antonio Negri, *Empire* (Cambridge: Harvard University Press, 2000), 202.

40. Rancière, *Disagreement*, xi–xii.

41. Michel Foucault, "The Subject and Power," in *Power: Essential Works of Foucault, 1954–1984,* vol. 3, trans. Robert Hurley (New York: The New York Press, 2000), 342. Chantal Mouffe has also focused on agonism, positing it as an intervention that engages the opponent as an adversary, not an enemy, which makes a given consensus "susceptible of being redefined." Mouffe, *On the Political* (London: Routledge, 2006), 33. For a more recent exploration, see Mouffe, *Agonistics: Thinking the World Politically* (London: Verso, 2013).

42. Rancière, *Disagreement*, 11–12.

43. Rancière, *Disagreement*, 39, 116.

44. I am echoing here the process that is, following Alain Badiou, necessary to protect the notion of ethics from the grip of consensus, according to which an "immanent break" stems from the formulation of an "event" ("a new way of being and acting") and is the result of the "fidelity" of an individual to the "truth" that constitutes it, i.e., to the necessary conditions and discursive realities that enable a challenge to "consensual ethics." Badiou, *Ethics: An Essay on the Understanding of Evil*, trans. Pater Hallward (London: Verso, 2001), 40–44.

45. Rancière, *Disagreement*, 40; emphasis original.

46. "Jeanette Winterson Discusses the Role of Books and Faith in Her Life," *PEN America,* August 27, 2015, http://pen.org/podcast/jeanette-winterson-discusses-the-role-of-books-and-faith-in-her-life.

47. Ernesto Laclau and Chantal Mouffe, *Hegemony and Socialist Strategy: Towards a Radical Democratic Politics* (London: Verso, 1985), 159–60.

48. While this is largely animated by the power of the soundbite-driven media culture, I do not mean this as an attack on the internet or electronic texts, or as a romantic lamentation about the predigital era. In fact, my general points about time, politics, and critical thought relation to reading novels are not exclusive to traditional printed books. Instead, this is a recognition that, as David Mikics claims, "Engulfed in a never-ending flood of text"—as well as other forms of "content" available on a whole array of media platforms, I would add—"we barely have time to stop and reflect." Mikics, *Slow Reading in a Hurried Age* (Cambridge: Harvard University Press, 2013), 8.

49. Edward W. Said, "Opponents, Audiences, Constituencies, and Community," in *Reflections on Exile and Other Essays* (Cambridge: Harvard University Press, 2000), 141.

50. Amir Eshel, *Futurity: Contemporary Literature and the Quest for the Past* (Chicago: University of Chicago Press, 2013), 5.

51. I am evoking here the phrase famously coined by Bill Ashcroft, Gareth Griffiths, and Helen Tiffin to describe this decentering gesture as a key aspect of

postcolonial writing. Ashcroft, Griffiths, and Tiffin, *The Empire Writes Back: Theory and Practice in Post-Colonial Literatures* (London: Routledge, 1989).

52. Susie O'Brien and Imre Szeman, "Introduction: The Globalization of Fiction/The Fiction of Globalization," *South Atlantic Quarterly* 100, no. 3 (2001): 604, 610. See also John Marx, who has argued that Anglophone literature "names a particular kind of object embedded in one institution or another" while "readers are used to fiction linking language to population, specifying how a way of speaking equates a way of seeing the world." Marx, *Geopolitics and the Anglophone Novel, 1890–2011* (Cambridge: Cambridge University Press, 2012), 11–12.

53. Pheng Cheah, *What Is a World? On Postcolonial Literature as World Literature* (Durham: Duke University Press, 2016), 6. World literature, Cheah argues later, must be understood "as literature that is *of* the world, something that can play a fundamental role and be a force in the ongoing cartography and creation of the world instead of a body of timeless aesthetic objects" (42; emphasis original).

54. Salman Rushdie once famously used this term to describe "the folly of trying to contain writers inside passports." Rushdie, "Commonwealth Literature Does Not Exist," in *Imaginary Homelands: Essays and Criticism, 1981–1991* (London: Penguin, 1981), 67.

55. Pascale Casanova, *The World Republic of Letters*, trans. M. B. Debevoise (Cambridge: Harvard University Press, 2004), 3–4.

56. Casanova, *The World Republic of Letters,* 11.

57. Casanova, *The World Republic of Letters,* 4–5.

58. Emily Apter, *Against World Literature: On the Politics of Untranslatability* (London: Verso, 2013), 16. I am aware of the ways in which my taxonomic choices of language (English) and period (the modern, broadly construed between the early twentieth century and the present) collide with Apter's general point about world literature and untranslatability. Yet our arguments are connected by an urge to deglobalize the politics of world literature in the spirit of Gayatri Chakravorty Spivak's notion of "planetarity." For a discussion of this notion, see Spivak, *Death of a Discipline* (New York: Columbia University Press, 2003), 71–102.

1. Impasse

1. Kwame Nkrumah, *Neo-Colonialism: The Last Stage of Imperialism* (London: Panaf Books, 1965).

2. This is one of the main points of contention of critics of the term *postcolonial* and what it entails for what they consider to be the unfinished history of colonialism. For some of the most important and now classic critiques, see Ella Shohat, "Notes on the 'Post-Colonial,'" *Social Text,* no. 31/32 (1992): 99–113; Anne McClintock, "The Angel of Progress: Pitfalls of the Term 'Post-Colonialism,'" *Social Text,* no. 31/32 (1994): 84–98; and Arif Dirlik, "The Postcolonial Aura: Third World Criticism in the Age of Global Capitalism," *Critical Inquiry* 20, no. 2 (1994): 328–56.

3. As Ania Loomba concludes, this collaborative paradigm was already employed in the colonial period. Loomba points out that "hegemony is achieved not by force or coercion alone, but also by creating subjects who 'willingly' submit to being ruled," and "even the most repressive [imperial] rule involved some give-and-take." Loomba, *Colonialism/Postcolonialism* (London: Routledge, 2005), 30, 32.

4. Chantal Mouffe, *On the Political* (London: Routledge, 2005), 90.

5. This is the case in Michael Hardt and Antonio Negri's *Empire* (Cambridge: Harvard University Press, 2000). For an important critique that questions the suggestion that imperialism is a thing of the past and the absence of the "colonized of *today*" (338) in Hardt and Negri's book, see Timothy Brennan, "The Empire's New Clothes," *Critical Inquiry* 29, no. 2 (2003): 337–67; emphasis original.

6. See, for instance, Revathi Krishnaswamy and John C. Hawley, eds., *The Postcolonial and the Global* (Minneapolis: University of Minnesota Press, 2008); Janet Wilson, Cristina Șandru, and Sarah Lawson Welsh, eds., *Re-Routing the Postcolonial: New Directions for the New Millennium* (London: Routledge, 2010); and Chantal Zabus, ed., *The Future of Postcolonial Studies* (London: Routledge, 2015).

7. Pheng Cheah, *What Is a World? On Postcolonial Literature as World Literature* (Durham: Duke University Press, 2016), 3.

8. I am, of course, echoing here Kwame Anthony Appiah's "Is the Post- in Postmodernism the Post- in Postcolonial?" *Critical Inquiry* 17, no. 2 (1991): 336–57.

9. Benita Parry, *Postcolonial Studies: A Materialist Critique* (London: Routledge, 2004), 12.

10. Neil Lazarus, *The Postcolonial Unconscious* (Cambridge: Cambridge University Press, 2011), 21. More recently, critical responses to Vivek Chibber's contentious reassessment of subaltern studies have revitalized the importance of materialism. See Chibber, *Postcolonial Theory and the Specter of Capital* (London: Verso, 2013). For some important retorts, see Massimiliano Tomba, "Marx's Temporal Bridges and Other Pathways," *Historical Materialism* 23, no. 4 (2015): 75–91; Neil Lazarus, "Vivek Chibber and the Spectre of Postcolonial Theory," *Race & Class* 57, no. 3 (2016): 88–106; and Benita Parry, "The Constraints of Chibber's Criticism: A Review of *Postcolonial Theory and the Specter of Capital* by Vivek Chibber," *Historical Materialism* 25, no. 1 (2017): 185–206.

11. As Jean-François Lyotard defines it, a differend is "a case of conflict, between (at least) two parties, that cannot be equitably resolved for lack of a rule of judgment applicable to both arguments," the regulation of which "is done in the idiom of one of the parties while the wrong suffered by the other is not signified in that idiom." Lyotard, *The Differend: Phrases in Dispute,* trans. Georges Van Den Abbeele (Minneapolis: University of Minnesota Press, 1988), xi, 9.

12. Simon Gikandi, "Preface: Modernism in the World," *Modernism/modernity* 13, no. 3 (2006): 421.

13. Fredric Jameson, "Modernism and Imperialism," in Terry Eagleton, Fredric Jameson, and Edward W. Said, *Nationalism, Colonialism, and Literature* (Minneapolis: University of Minnesota Press, 1990): 43–66; and Edward W. Said, *Culture and Imperialism* (New York: Vintage, 1993).

14. Mao and Walkowitz account for this turn in part by highlighting its renovated interest in "engag[ing] with postcolonial theory and concern[ing] itself with the interrelation of cultural, political, and economic transactions," while placing in the foreground questions of citizenship and the agency of individuals as "embedded in political situations that they may in some way affect." Douglas Mao and Rebecca L. Walkowitz, "The New Modernist Studies," *PMLA* 123, no. 3 (2008): 739, 745.

15. For some of the most important accounts, see Jessica Berman, *Modernist Fiction: Cosmopolitanism and the Politics of Community* (Cambridge: Cambridge University Press, 2001) and, more recently, *Modernist Commitments: Ethics, Politics, and Transnational Modernism* (New York: Columbia University Press, 2012); Rebecca L. Walkowitz, *Cosmopolitan Style: Modernism beyond the Nation* (New York: Columbia University Press, 2007); Janet Lyon, "Cosmopolitanism and Modernism," in *The Oxford Handbook of Global Modernisms,* ed. Mark Wollaeger and Matt Eatough (Oxford: Oxford University Press, 2012), 387–412; and Peter J. Kalliney, *Modernism in a Global Context* (London: Bloomsbury, 2016).

16. Susan Stanford Friedman has offered an approach to modernity that situates it at different points over several millennia, whereas David James and Urmila Seshagiri have considered the afterlives of modernism they find in contemporary fiction. See Friedman, *Planetary Modernisms: Provocations on Modernity across Time* (New York: Columbia University Press, 2015); James and Seshagiri, "Metamodernism: Narratives of Continuity and Revolution," *PMLA* 129, no. 1 (2014): 87–100; and James, *Modernist Futures: Innovation and Inheritance in the Contemporary Novel* (Cambridge: Cambridge University Press, 2012).

17. Friedman, *Planetary Modernisms*, 79.

18. Edward W. Said, *Orientalism* (New York: Vintage, 1979), 3; hereafter cited in the text.

19. This appears in a portion of the speech Said does not quote but to which he nonetheless alludes. Arthur James Balfour, "Balfour on the Imperial Idea: June 1910," in A. P. Thornton, *The Imperial Idea and Its Enemies* (New York: St. Martin's Press, 1985), 360.

20. Balfour, "Balfour on the Imperial Idea," 361; emphasis mine.

21. Raymond F. Betts, *Decolonization* (London: Routledge, 1998), 33.

22. Macmillan advocates in it for a rather progressive economic agenda, yet he justifies it on a premise that seems to be a precursor of contemporary postpolitical discourse. Early in the book he argues for an ideology-free form of state management by stating that both "right" and "left" "reveal a tendency, common to most controversies, to distort the arguments which they wish to refute and to discredit the authors of the new [economic] theories by attributing to them views which they

do not hold." Macmillan, *The Middle Way: A Study of the Problem of Economic and Social Progress in a Free and Democratic Society* (London: Macmillan, 1938), 10.

23. Martin Thomas, Bob Moore, and L. J. Butler, *Crises of Empire: Decolonization and Europe's Imperial States* (London: Bloomsbury, 2015), 84.

24. Harold Macmillan, "Harold Macmillan: 'Winds of Change,' 1960," in *The Cold War: A History in Documents and Eyewitness Accounts*, ed. Jussi M. Hanhimäki and Odd Arne Westad (Oxford: Oxford University Press, 2003), 356; hereafter cited in the text. (The speech's original title was "Wind of Change." At some point, however, it was misquoted as "Winds of Change," an alternate version that has caught on and is sometimes used to refer to the address.)

25. Wm. Roger Louis and R. Robinson, "The Imperialism of Decolonization," *Journal of Imperial and Commonwealth History* 22, no. 3 (1994): 485.

26. Louis and Robinson, "The Imperialism of Decolonization," 494–95.

27. Frantz Fanon, *The Wretched of the Earth*, trans. Richard Philcox (New York: Grove Press, 2004), 27.

28. Louis and Robinson, "The Imperialism of Decolonization," 495.

29. Dipesh Chakrabarty, "The Legacies of Bandung: Decolonization and the Politics of Culture," in *Making a World after Empire: The Bandung Moment and Its Political Afterlives*, ed. Christopher J. Lee (Athens: Ohio University Press, 2010), 47.

30. Kwame Anthony Appiah, *Cosmopolitanism: Ethics in a World of Strangers* (New York: Norton, 2006), xix.

31. Jenny Sharpe remains an excellent account of Forster's fictional treatment of these historical events, and particularly of the questions that the novel's ambiguous rape subplot opens up. Sharpe, *Allegories of Empire: The Figure of Woman in the Colonial Text* (Minneapolis: University of Minnesota Press, 1993), 113–36.

32. Said, *Culture and Imperialism*, 75.

33. Sara Suleri, *The Rhetoric of English India* (Chicago: University of Chicago Press, 1992), 132.

34. Originally the epigraph to his 1910 novel *Howards End*, "only connect" has been taken to represent the prevalent liberal humanist spirit in Forster's writing. E. M. Forster, *Howards End* (New York: Vintage, 2000).

35. E. M. Forster, *A Passage to India* (London: Penguin, 2005), 5; hereafter cited in the text.

36. Mary Louise Pratt, *Imperial Eyes: Travel Writing and Transculturation* (London: Routledge, 1992), 202.

37. As Jenny Sharpe has pointed out, Forster's "privileging of speech-agency can . . . cause us to overlook the roles of less vocal actors" in the novel, particularly the inhabitants of the lower part of the city. Sharpe, *Allegories of Empire*, 131.

38. Peter Morey has commented in this regard that "Forster errs in making the Muslim Aziz his central Indian character because of the ambiguous relationship between the Muslim community and the British." Morey, "Postcolonial Forster,"

in *The Cambridge Companion to E. M. Forster,* ed. David Bradshaw (Cambridge: Cambridge University Press, 2007), 256. However, I would argue that this ambiguity seems to be less a mistake than Forster's way to illustrate how difficult it is for British and Indians to establish a genuine personal relationship.

39. Kalliney, *Modernism in a Global Context,* 59.

40. An early indication of how Fielding's individualism matches Aziz's wish to become autonomous as an Indian is his reaction to being summoned by Major Callendar, his superior at the hospital, which interrupts his soiree with Mahmoud Ali and Hamidullah. As he prepares to leave, Aziz addresses the criticism to which he might be subjected for not abiding by European etiquette rules: "If my teeth are to be cleaned, I don't go at all. I am an Indian, it is an Indian habit to take pan" (13).

41. Parry, *Postcolonial Studies,* 170.

42. R. Radhakrishnan, "Why Compare?" in *Comparison: Theories, Approaches, Uses,* ed. Rita Felski and Susan Stanford Friedman (Baltimore: Johns Hopkins University Press, 2013), 30.

43. Fanon, *The Wretched of the Earth,* 168.

44. Partha Chatterjee, *The Nation and Its Fragments: Colonial and Postcolonial Histories* (Princeton: Princeton University Press, 1993), 5; emphasis original.

45. W. J. T. Mitchell, "Imperial Landscape," in *Landscape and Power,* ed. W. J. T. Mitchell (Chicago: University of Chicago Press, 2002), 5.

46. E. M. Forster, "Appendix III. Forster's Programme Note to Santha Rama Rau's Dramatized Version," in Forster, *A Passage to India,* 327.

47. Although the decolonization of the West Indies would take place decades later, important anticolonial nationalist and labor movements that paved the way to independence were already in place by the time Rhys began working on the novel in 1911. For an account of such movements, see Richard Hart, *From Occupation to Independence: A History of the Peoples of the English-Speaking Caribbean Region* (London: Pluto, 1998), 110–34.

48. Jean Rhys, *Voyage in the Dark* (New York: Norton, 1982), 23; hereafter cited in the text.

49. Paul Gilroy, *Postcolonial Melancholia* (New York: Columbia University Press, 2005), 42; emphasis original.

50. Urmila Seshagiri, "Modernist Ashes, Postcolonial Phoenix: Jean Rhys and the Evolution of the English Novel in the Twentieth Century," *Modernism/modernity* 13, no. 3 (2006): 491.

51. The island remains unnamed in the novel but is identified by its geographical coordinates: "Lying between 15° 10' and 15° 40' N. and 61° 14' and 61° 30' W." (17).

52. Jessica Berman, for instance, speaks of a "new hybrid location" that emerges from the "bifurcati[on] [of] the novel's landscape." Berman, *Modernist Commitments,* 82.

53. Homi K. Bhabha, *The Location of Culture* (London: Routledge, 2004), 160.

54. There is a certain convergence between Bhabha's hybridity and Bakhtin's dialogism. For Bakhtin, the novelistic genre has "potential" to conceive "new worldviews" by setting "two points of view . . . against each other dialogically," resulting in what he calls both "deliberate" and "unintentional hybridization." Mikhail M. Bakhtin, *The Dialogic Imagination: Four Essays*, trans. Caryl Emerson (Austin: University of Texas Press, 1982), 360.

55. Edward W. Said, "Secular Criticism," in *The World, the Text, and the Critic* (Cambridge: Harvard University Press, 1983), 1–30.

56. Carol Dell'Amico, *Colonialism and the Modernist Moment in the Early Novels of Jean Rhys* (London: Routledge, 2005), 52.

57. Anna Snaith, *Modernist Voyages: Colonial Women Writers in London, 1890–1945* (Cambridge: Cambridge University Press, 2014), 134.

58. Jed Esty, *Unseasonable Youth: Modernism, Colonialism, and the Fiction of Development* (Oxford: Oxford University Press, 2011), 166.

59. Peter J. Kalliney, *Commonwealth of Letters: British Literary Culture and the Emergence of Postcolonial Aesthetics* (Oxford: Oxford University Press, 2013), 230.

60. Hardt and Negri, *Empire*, 128.

61. Ross Chambers, "The Unexamined," *Minnesota Review* 47 (1996): 141–56.

62. Judith Butler, *Gender Trouble: Feminism and the Subversion of Identity* (London: Routledge, 1990), 32.

63. On one of her first London outings in search for good clothes, for instance, Anna expresses her discomfort at the judgmental "Miss Cohens," the two women in charge of a shop who "were sisters because their noses were the same and their eyes—opaque and shining—and their insolence that was only a mask" (27).

64. See, for instance, Snaith, *Modernist Voyages*, 149–50.

65. Frantz Fanon, *Black Skin, White Masks*, trans. Richard Philcox (New York: Grove Press, 2008), 1.

66. See Coral Ann Howells, "Jean Rhys (1890–1979)," in *The Gender of Modernism: A Critical Anthology,* ed. Bonnie Kime Scott (Bloomington: Indiana University Press, 1990), 377–89.

67. Sara Ahmed, *Willful Subjects* (Durham: Duke University Press, 2014), 137.

68. For Slaughter, this kind of bildungsroman "cosign[s] the ideal of the egalitarian imaginary (e.g. democratic citizenship and equal opportunity) while exposing the disparities and paradoxes that emerge when that ideal is practiced in specific institutions and social relations." Slaughter, *Human Rights Inc.: The World Novel, Narrative Form, and International Law* (New York: Fordham University Press, 2007), 28.

69. Mouffe, *On the Political*, 106.

70. Gayatri Chakravorty Spivak, *Outside in the Teaching Machine* (London: Routledge, 1993), 60.

2. Contra I

1. See Gayatri Chakravorty Spivak, "Can the Subaltern Speak?" in *Marxism and the Interpretation of Culture,* ed. Cary Nelson and Lawrence Grossberg (Chicago: University of Illinois Press, 1988), 280–91.

2. Hayden White is a prominent figure whose work has sought to illuminate this very issue. See, e.g., his *Metahistory: The Historical Imagination in Nineteenth-Century Europe* (Baltimore: Johns Hopkins University Press, 1973).

3. Jean-François Lyotard, *The Postmodern Condition: A Report on Knowledge*, trans. Geoff Bennington and Brian Massumi (Minneapolis: University of Minnesota Press, 1984), xxiv.

4. Lyotard, *The Postmodern Condition*, 60.

5. Ernesto Laclau, *Emancipation(s)* (London: Verso, 1996), 90.

6. Graham Swift, *Waterland* (New York: Vintage, 1992), 16–17; hereafter cited in the text.

7. Hutcheon first coined this term in *A Poetics of Postmodernism: History, Theory, Fiction* (London: Routledge, 1988).

8. Hutcheon argues that Swift "raise[s] the issue of narrative emplotment and its relation to both fictionality and historiography at the same time as he begins his problematization of the notion of historical knowledge." Linda Hutcheon, *The Politics of Postmodernism* (London: Routledge, 1989), 53.

9. Hutcheon, *The Politics of Postmodernism*, 51.

10. Hutcheon, *The Politics of Postmodernism*, 51.

11. The often-playful dialectical sparring between Crick and Price, however, never constitutes a critical dialogue but serves, instead, as a reminder of Crick's intention to fend off any challenge to his story.

12. Edward W. Said, *Culture and Imperialism* (New York: Vintage, 1994), 273.

13. Hutcheon, *The Politics of Postmodernism*, 66.

14. George Landow, "History, His Story, and Stories in Graham Swift's *Waterland*," *Studies in the Literary Imagination* 23 (1990): 197.

15. Daniel Lea, *Graham Swift* (Manchester: Manchester University Press, 2005), 96.

16. I will use the term *his-story*, which I borrow from Michael Robinson, in order to emphasize an inherent mark of power that emerges from the possessive "his" and its resulting impact on the agency of those who do not participate in the making of the account. In addition, the term's obvious resemblance to the word *history* reflects the fact that, while presented as a story, it is meant to replace the official narrative. Robinson, "History and His-Story," *Scandinavian Studies* 62, no. 1 (1990): 53–66.

17. See Robert K. Irish for an account on the relationship of necessity between the novel and its audience or, in Irish's words, "how Graham Swift's *Waterland* desires me, maneuvers or positions me, and as it does so how it is constituted in and constitutes my subjectivity." Irish, "'Let Me Tell You': About Desire and Narrativity in Graham Swift's *Waterland*," *Modern Fiction Studies* 44, no. 4 (1998): 917.

18. Evelyn Cobley, "Graham Swift's *Waterland* and the Ideology of Efficiency," *Critique: Studies in Contemporary Fiction* 55, no. 3 (2014): 280.

19. Katrina M. Powell, "Mary Metcalf's Attempt at Reclamation: Maternal Representation in Graham Swift's *Waterland*," *Women's Studies* 32, no. 1 (2003): 60.

20. Eric Berlatsky, "'The Swamps of Myth . . . and Empirical Fishing Lines': Historiography, Narrativity, and the 'Here and Now' in Graham Swift's *Waterland*," *Journal of Narrative Theory* 36, no. 2 (2006): 265.

21. Pamela Cooper, "Imperial Topographies: The Spaces of History in *Waterland*," *Modern Fiction Studies* 42, no. 2 (1996): 378.

22. I am echoing here the work of Philippe Lejeune, who devotes a chapter titled "The Autobiography of Those Who Do Not Write" in his *On Autobiography* to discuss those who willingly participate in the writing of someone else's autobiography, those who do not have the means to narrate their own lives or are uninterested in doing so, and those whose lives are incorporated—sometimes forcibly so—in the autobiographies of writers who appeal to a sense of collective belonging to justify their assimilative representation. Henry and Dick fall within the last category. Lejeune, *On Autobiography*, trans. Katherine Leary (Minneapolis: University of Minnesota Press, 1985), 185–215.

23. Cooper, "Imperial Topographies," 381.

24. Giorgio Agamben, *Homo Sacer: Sovereign Power and Bare Life*, trans. Daniel Heller-Roazen (Stanford: Stanford University Press, 1998), 8; hereafter cited in the text.

25. Lea, *Graham Swift*, 73.

26. Powell, "Mary Metcalf's Attempt at Reclamation," 67.

27. Balachandra Rajan, *Under Western Eyes: India from Milton to Macaulay* (Durham: Duke University Press, 1999), 23.

28. Maurice Blanchot, *The Infinite Conversation*, trans. Susan Hanson (Minneapolis: University of Minnesota Press, 1993), 76.

29. Michel Foucault, *The History of Sexuality, Vol. 1: An Introduction*, trans. Robert Hurley (New York: Vintage, 1990), 27.

30. Gayatri Chakravorty Spivak, "Questions of Multi-Culturalism," in *The Postcolonial Critic: Interviews, Strategies, Dialogues*, ed. Sarah Harasym (London: Routledge, 1990), 63.

3. Deflection

1. Fredric Jameson, *Postmodernism, or the Cultural Logic of Late Capitalism* (Durham: Duke University Press, 1991), xviii, 185.

2. Michel Foucault, *The Birth of Biopolitics: Lectures at the Collège de France, 1978–1979*, trans. Graham Burchell (New York: Picador, 2008); Wendy Brown, *Undoing the Demos: Neoliberalism's Stealth Revolution* (New York: Zone Books, 2015); Pierre Bourdieu, *Acts of Resistance: Against the Tyranny of the Market*, trans. Richard Nice (New York: The New Press, 1998); and David Harvey, *A Brief History of Neoliberalism* (Oxford: Oxford University Press, 2005).

3. Colin Crouch argues that the rise of neoliberalism is one important factor in the constitution of the current "post-democratic" moment. Crouch, *Post-Democracy* (Cambridge: Polity, 2004). A related consequence is the translation of this phenomenon into citizens' "hatred of democracy," which "gives the strongest minority," among whom neoliberals must be counted, "the power to govern without trouble." Jacques Rancière, *Hatred of Democracy*, trans. Steve Corcoran (London: Verso, 2006), 76.

4. Foucault, *The Birth of Biopolitics*, 186.

5. Thatcher incited a great deal of literary responses. Dominic Head, e.g., deems Thatcher's governance an important sociohistorical landmark in the development of the modern and contemporary British novel, qualifying the years she was prime minister as a "period of renaissance in English fiction." Head, *The Cambridge Introduction to Modern British Fiction: 1950–2000* (Cambridge: Cambridge University Press, 2002), 45.

6. The passage from which this assertion has been adapted is worth quoting at length: "Too many children and people have been given to understand 'I have a problem, it is the Government's job to cope with it!' or 'I have a problem, I will go and get a grant to cope with it!' 'I am homeless, the Government must house me!' and so they are casting their problems on society and who is society? There is no such thing! There are individual men and women and there are families and no government can do anything except through people and people look to themselves first." Thatcher, "Interview for *Woman's Own*," *Margaret Thatcher Foundation*, n.d., http://www.margaretthatcher.org/document/106689.

7. Matt Beech, "Cameron and Conservative Ideology," in *The Conservatives under Cameron: Built to Last?* ed. Simon Lee and Matt Beech (Basingstoke: Palgrave, 2009), 24.

8. Jacques Derrida, *Specters of Marx: The State of the Debt, the Work of Mourning, and the New International*, trans. Peggy Kamuf (London: Routledge, 1994), 106, 93.

9. Steve Schifferes, "'Deeper' Recession Ahead Says IMF," *BBC*, April 22, 2009, http://news.bbc.co.uk/2/hi/business/8011907.stm.

10. Stuart Hall, "The Great Moving Right Show," *Marxism Today* 23, no. 1 (1979): 15. See also Harvey, *A Brief History of Neoliberalism*, 5–63.

11. John Gray, "Margaret Thatcher's Austerity Programme Was Far Less of a Gamble Than George Osborne's Cuts," *The Guardian*, October 22, 2010, http://www.theguardian.com/commentisfree/2010/oct/22/margaret-thatcher-george-osborne-cuts.

12. The document is worth examining for the authors' strained efforts to subscribe to Thatcher's privatization policies while claiming that they are not simply "arguing for reheated Thatcherism." Douglas Carswell et al., *Direct Democracy: An Agenda for a New Model Party* (London: Impress Print Services, 2005), 35.

13. *The Conservative Manifesto 2010: Invitation to Join the Government of Britain,* viii, *Conservatives,* http://www.conservatives.com/~/media/Files/Manifesto 2010.

14. "Why We're Marching," *March for the Alternative,* n.d., http://marchforthealternative.org.uk/why-were-marching.

15. Mark Fisher, *Capitalist Realism: Is There No Alternative?* (Winchester: Zero, 2009).

16. Nicholas Watt, "David Cameron Makes Leaner State a Permanent Goal," *The Guardian,* November 13, 2013, http://www.theguardian.com/politics/2013/nov/11/david-cameron-policy-shift-leaner-efficient-state.

17. Even the International Monetary Fund, one of the principal global bodies shoring up the precepts of neoliberalism, began to doubt the idea that these might be effective ways to face the crisis and its aftermath eight years after the recession started. See Jonathan D. Ostry, Prakash Loungani, and Davide Furceri, "Neoliberalism: Oversold?" *Finance & Development: A Quarterly Publication of the International Monetary Fund* 53, no. 2 (2016): 38–41.

18. "Equity and Excellence: Liberating the NHS," *Department of Health,* July 10, 2010, 5, http://www.gov.uk/government/uploads/system/uploads/attachment_data/file/213823/dh_117794.pdf.

19. In November 2011, Circle Health assumed control of the hospital. Exactly a year later, the company reportedly admitted that it was "already feeling a strain on resources due to its aggressive business strategy" and that "the firm's ambition to further expand into the NHS 'could affect its ability to provide a consistent level of service to its patients.'" Daniel Boffey, "Care May Suffer, Admits Private Company Taking Over NHS Hospital," *The Guardian,* November 12, 2011, http://www.theguardian.com/politics/2011/nov/12/care-private-company-nhs-hospital.

20. Denis Campbell, "NHS Waiting Times 'Driving People to Turn to Private Treatment,'" *The Guardian,* September 11, 2017, http://www.theguardian.com/society/2017/sep/11/nhs-waiting-times-driving-people-to-private-treatment.

21. Denis Campbell, "Hospitals Told to Cut Staff Amid Spiralling NHS Cash Crisis," *The Guardian,* January 29, 2016, http://www.theguardian.com/society/2016/jan/29/hospitals-told-cut-staff-nhs-cash-crisis.

22. Youssef El-Gingihy, *How to Dismantle the NHS in 10 Easy Steps* (Winchester: Zero, 2015), 10.

23. Randeep Ramesh and Rowenna Davis, "NHS Reform Live Blog—Is the Government Listening?" *The Guardian,* April 27, 2011, http://www.theguardian.com/uk/2011/apr/27/nhs-reform-live-blog-mental-health.

24. "The NHS Future Forum: Summary Report on Proposed Changes to the NHS," *Department of Health and Social Care,* June 13, 2011, http://www.gov.uk/

government/publications/nhs-future-forum-recommendations-to-government-on-nhs-modernisation.

25. Ramesh and Davis, "NHS Reform Live Blog."

26. Paul Taylor, "Read Their Lips," *London Review of Books,* May 5, 2011, http://www.lrb.co.uk/blog/2011/05/05/paul-taylor/read-their-lips.

27. As listed on the government's website, the events would tackle "the role of choice and competition for improving quality," "how to ensure public accountability and patient involvement in the new system," "how new arrangements for education and training can support the modernisation process," and "how advice from across a range of healthcare professions can improve patient care." "Government Launches NHS 'Listening Exercise,'" *Deputy Prime Minister's Office,* April 11, 2011, http://www.gov.uk/government/news/government-launches-nhs-listening-exercise.

28. "Regional Voices," *Regional Voices,* April 21, 2011, http://www.regional-voices.net/2011/04/nhs-future-forum-listening-events-programme-hosted-by-regional-voices. At the time of writing this link seems to be broken, but it is included in other websites that publicized the official list of events. See, e.g., "NHS Future Forum 'Listening Events,'" *Carers Hub Lambeth,* n.d., http://carershub.org.uk/news/nhs-future-forum-listening-events.

29. "Listening Event 9th of May," *NHS Future Forum Listening Event for Voluntary Sector Leaders,* n.d., http://www.surveymonkey.com/s/listeningeventNEregisterinterest.

30. The invitation for the Leicester event held on May 18, 2011, e.g., read: "Attendance to this event is by invitation only to network members, however, to ensure we can gather as many voices as possible from the sector." *Health and Social Care Bill Listening Event,* n.d., http://www.eventbrite.co.uk/e/health-and-social-care-bill-listening-event-tickets-1598558331.

31. "YouGov/Sunday Times Survey Results 9th–10th February 2012," *YouGov,* February 12, 2012, http://cdn.yougov.com/cumulus_uploads/document/ly9ei68uye/YG-Archives-Pol-ST-results-10-120212.pdf.

32. "NHS 'Too Precious to Be Political Football,'" *BBC,* February 20, 2012, http://news.bbc.co.uk/today/hi/today/newsid_9697000/9697832.stm.

33. Toby Helm, "David Cameron Pledges to Continue Radical Programme Despite Losing Aide," *The Guardian,* March 3, 2012, http://www.theguardian.com/politics/2012/mar/03/david-cameron-radical-programme-aide.

34. Richard Sennett, *Together: The Rituals, Pleasures and Politics of Cooperation* (New Haven: Yale University Press, 2012), 252.

35. See Srećko Horvat, *The Radicality of Love* (Cambridge: Polity, 2016).

36. Dominic Head, *Ian McEwan* (Manchester: Manchester University Press, 2008), 85.

37. Ian McEwan, *The Child in Time* (London: Vintage, 1997), 15, 28; hereafter cited in the text.

38. David Harvey explores this issue at a larger scale when he discusses the neoliberal state's reliance on the work of nongovernmental organizations to make up for its deliberate deficiencies in welfare coverage. Harvey, *A Brief History of Neoliberalism*, 175–82.

39. Peter Childs, "'Fascinating Violation': Ian McEwan's Children," in *British Fiction of the 1990s*, ed. Nick Bentley (London: Routledge, 2005), 127.

40. It is worth noting the reverberations between the Official Commission on Childcare and Thatcher's crackdown on the Child Benefit program. With the alleged objective of making the Child Benefit program fairer, the government handed its management over to the market, which severely weakened its effectiveness. As a chronicler of its privatization would put it, "even as Child Benefit survived frontal assaults . . . low-visibility efforts to let inflation and economic growth curb its role were quite successful. As with many other programs, even a maintenance of real benefits meant a shrinking role in an expanding economy. The government, moreover, acted on a number of occasions to uprate Child Benefit in line with price increases only partially, or to freeze it entirely," causing "benefits [to be] frozen in 1988, 1989, and 1990." Paul Pierson, *Dismantling the Welfare State? Reagan, Thatcher, and the Politics of Retrenchment* (Cambridge: Cambridge University Press, 1994), 108–109.

41. Claire Colebrook, "The Innocent as Anti-Oedipal Critique of Cultural Pornography," in *Ian McEwan: Contemporary Critical Perspectives*, ed. Sebastian Groes (London: Continuum, 2009), 54–55.

42. D. J. Taylor, *A Vain Conceit: British Fiction in the 1980s* (London: Bloomsbury, 1989), 59.

43. Taylor, *A Vain Conceit*, 59.

44. Head, *Ian McEwan*, 84; emphasis original.

45. Michel Foucault, *Discipline and Punish: The Birth of the Prison*, trans. Alan Sheridan (New York: Vintage, 1995), 138.

46. Wendy Brown discusses this doctrine in terms of neoliberalism's appeal to rationality: "neoliberalism normatively constructs and interpellates individuals as entrepreneurial actors in every sphere of life. It figures individuals as rational, calculating creatures whose moral autonomy is measured by their capacity for 'self-care'—the ability to provide for their own needs and service their own ambitions." Thus, Brown adds, "a 'mismanaged life,' the neoliberal appellation for failure to navigate impediments to prosperity, becomes a new mode of depoliticizing social and economic powers and at the same time reduces political citizenship to an unprecedented degree of passivity and political complacency." Brown, *Edgework: Critical Essays on Knowledge and Politics* (Princeton: Princeton University Press, 2005), 42–43.

47. Darke's interest in this new career is characteristically postpolitical. This becomes clear when he tries to decide the platform from which he should run for office: "which party should he join? . . . Darke had no convictions, only managerial skill and great ambition. . . . [H]e could argue for . . . the support of the weak [or]

for the advancement of the strong." After a stint in the cabinet, Darke becomes one of the prime minister's favorite junior ministers despite the premier's initial distrust due to "his past connection with books" (37).

48. After narrowly avoiding being hit by a lorry while driving in the countryside, e.g., he resents his prejudiced privilege while acknowledging that "he had become the sort who casts about for a policeman at the sight of the scruffy poor. He was on the other side now" (102). Signaling a change in outlook provoked by this event, Stephen wonders if he has "started to think that the things he owned were really . . . inalienably his" (103).

49. After he realizes the girl is not his daughter, Stephen takes off his coat and places it over her. However, this act of charity is received with derision. Whereas the girl's eyes "continued to stare" in the distance (perhaps suggesting that the cold has already killed her), a man sitting next to her ridicules Stephen's act by implying a salacious intention behind this moment: "Oi, oi. Fancy that, do ya? She's not interested" (193).

50. Jean Baudrillard, *In the Shadow of the Silent Majorities*, trans. John Johnston, Paul Patton and Stuart Kendall (Los Angeles: Semiotext(e), 2007), 49; emphasis original.

51. David Malcolm, *Understanding Ian McEwan* (Columbia: University of South Carolina Press, 2002), 109. Similarly, Thomas Docherty has argued that this birth functions as a "counter" to the "structure of the capitalism of which the novel's content is critical." Docherty, *Confessions: The Philosophy of Transparency* (London: Bloomsbury, 2012), 87.

52. Peter Childs, *Contemporary Novelists: British Fiction since 1970* (Basingstoke: Palgrave, 2004), 256.

53. These are Cameron's words in reaction to her death in 2013. Amy Willis, "Margaret Thatcher: Queen Expresses Her Sadness as Tributes Paid," *The Telegraph*, April 8, 2013, http://www.telegraph.co.uk/news/politics/margaret-thatcher/9978854/Margaret-Thatcher-Queen-expresses-her-sadness-as-tributes-paid.html.

54. Jacques Rancière, "Critical Questions on the Theory of Recognition," in *Recognition or Disagreement: A Critical Encounter on the Politics of Freedom, Equality, and Identity*, ed. Katia Genel and Jean-Philippe Deranty (New York: Columbia University Press, 2016), 89.

55. Richard Reeves, "This Is David Cameron," *Public Policy Research*, June–August 2008, 63–64.

56. Reeves, "This Is David Cameron," 64–65.

57. Judith Seaboyer, "Second Death in Venice: Romanticism and the Compulsion to Repeat in Jeanette Winterson's *The Passion*," *Contemporary Literature* 38, no. 3 (1997): 493.

58. Jeanette Winterson, *The Passion* (New York: Grove Press, 1987), 5; hereafter cited in the text.

59. Gilles Deleuze and Félix Guattari, *A Thousand Plateaus: Capitalism and Schizophrenia*, trans. Brian Massumi (Minneapolis: University of Minnesota Press, 1987), 14, 15.

60. Susana Onega, *Jeanette Winterson* (Manchester: Manchester University Press, 2006), 57.

61. Seaboyer, "Second Death in Venice," 494.

62. Laura L. Doan, "Jeanette Winterson's Sexing the Postmodern," in *The Lesbian Postmodern*, ed. Laura L. Doan (New York: Columbia University Press, 1994), 149.

63. See, e.g., Paulina Palmer, "*The Passion*: Storytelling, Fantasy, Desire," in *"I'm Telling You Stories": Jeanette Winterson and the Politics of Reading*, ed. Helena Grice and Tim Woods (Amsterdam: Rodopi, 1998), 111.

64. Imogen Tyler, *Revolting Subjects: Social Abjection and Resistance in Neoliberal Britain* (London: Zed Books, 2013), 5.

65. Alain Badiou with Nicholas Truong, *In Praise of Love*, trans. Peter Bush (New York: The New Press, 2012), 22–23.

66. Roland Barthes, *A Lover's Discourse: Fragments*, trans. Richard Howard (New York: Farrar, Straus and Giroux, 1978), 204.

67. Barthes, *A Lover's Discourse*, 207; emphasis original.

68. Christy L. Burns, "Fantastic Language: Jeanette Winterson's Recovery of the Postmodern Word," *Contemporary Literature* 37, no. 2 (1996): 290.

69. Guy Standing, *A Precariat Charter: From Denizens to Citizens* (London: Bloomsbury, 2014), 386–88.

4. Contra II

1. Retort (Iain A. Boal, T. J. Clark, Joseph Matthews, and Michael Watts), *Afflicted Powers: Capital and Spectacle in a New Age of War* (London: Verso, 2006), 24.

2. Michael Hardt and Antonio Negri, *Multitude: War and Democracy in the Age of Empire* (London: Penguin, 2004), 12.

3. I am following here Judith Butler's discussion of the sovereignty of the United States as exceeding the disciplinary work of governmentality. Butler, *Precarious Life: The Powers of Mourning and Violence* (London: Verso, 2004), 52–67.

4. *The 9/11 Commission Report: Final Report of the National Commission on Terrorist Attacks upon the United States* (New York: Norton, 2004), 362.

5. Arundhati Roy has called the characterization of antiwar dissent as anti-American "not just racist" but also "a failure of the imagination." Roy, "Come September," in *War Talk* (Cambridge: South End Press, 2003). "USA Patriot Act" is an acronym that stands for the Uniting and Strengthening of America to Provide Appropriate Tools Required to Intercept and Obstruct Terrorism Act of 2001.

6. Talal Asad, *Formations of the Secular: Christianity, Islam, Modernity* (Stanford: Stanford University Press, 2003), 7; emphasis original.

7. Giorgio Agamben, *State of Exception*, trans. Kevin Attell (Chicago: University of Chicago Press, 2005), 3, 22.

8. Mohsin Hamid, *The Reluctant Fundamentalist* (Boston: Mariner, 2008), 1, emphasis original; hereafter cited in the text.

9. While the existence of such practices was corroborated and condemned by a special U.S. Senate Intelligence Committee report in 2014, given the secrecy with which detention and interrogation procedures are still kept, it is not possible to ascertain that they are no longer employed. For a journalistic account, see Tara McKelvey, *Monstering: Inside America's Policy of Secret Interrogations and Torture in the Terror War* (New York: Carroll and Graf, 2007).

10. Laleh Khalili, *Time in the Shadows: Confinement in Counterinsurgencies* (Stanford: Stanford University Press, 2013), 57.

11. This statement is often attributed to Karl Rove. Ron Suskind, "Faith, Certainty and the Presidency of George W. Bush," *New York Times Magazine,* October 17, 2004, http://www.nytimes.com/2004/10/17/magazine/faith-certainty-and-the-presidency-of-george-w-bush.html.

12. Reports with new findings about the methods employed during interrogation sessions continue to be produced as of this writing. See, e.g., Larry Siems, "Inside the CIA Black Site Torture Room," *The Guardian,* October 17, 2017, http://www.theguardian.com/us-news/ng-interactive/2017/oct/09/cia-torture-black-site-enhanced-interrogation.

13. Jean Baudrillard, *The Spirit of Terrorism*, trans. Chris Turner (London: Verso, 2002), 9.

14. Mohsin Hamid, *Discontent and Its Civilizations: Dispatches from Lahore, New York, and London* (New York: Riverhead, 2015), 93. Margaret-Anne Hutton has proposed, alternatively, to label it an "implied dialogue," but I think this is not a satisfactory descriptor, because it conflates the interaction between the interlocutors with its representation. Hutton, "The Janus and the Janissary: Reading into Camus's *La Chute* and Hamid's *The Reluctant Fundamentalist*," *Comparative Literature* 68, no. 1 (2016): 60.

15. Gayatri Chakravorty Spivak, "Terror: A Speech after 9-11," *boundary 2* 31, no. 2 (2004): 87.

16. Critiques of such characterizations come from, respectively, Butler, *Precarious Life*, 72, 78; Spivak, "Terror," 92; Terry Eagleton, *Holy Terror* (Oxford: Oxford University Press, 2005), 116–17; and Arjun Appadurai, *Fear of Small Numbers: An Essay on the Geography of Anger* (Durham: Duke University Press, 2006), 78.

17. Edward W. Said, "The Essential Terrorist," in *Blaming the Victims: Spurious Scholarship and the Palestinian Question,* ed. Edward W. Said and Christopher Hitchens (London: Verso, 1988), 154.

18. The absence of the attacks in the novel, Anwer argues, radically undermines their spectacular veneer as a "cataclysmic, all-determining event." Megha Anwer, "Resisting the Event: Aesthetics of the Non-Event in the Contemporary South Asian Novel," *Ariel: A Review of International English Literature* 45, no. 4 (2014): 1.

19. Jacques Rancière, "September 11 and Afterwards: A Rupture in the Symbolic Order?" in *Dissensus: On Politics and Aesthetics*, trans. Steven Corcoran (London: Bloomsbury, 2010), 104.

20. Anna Hartnell has connected the projections of these two actors into the past and the future, but her goal is to explore the vestiges of European colonialism that they reveal. Hartnell, "Moving through America: Race, Place and Resistance in Mohsin Hamid's *The Reluctant Fundamentalist*," *Journal of Postcolonial Writing* 46, nos. 3–4 (2010): 341–45.

21. See Richard Jackson, *Writing the War on Terrorism: Language, Politics and Counter-Terrorism* (Manchester: Manchester University Press, 2005), 40–47.

22. David Simpson, *9/11: The Culture of Commemoration* (Chicago: University of Chicago Press, 2006), 13.

23. Anwer, "Resisting the Event," 22.

24. Leerom Medovoi, "'Terminal Crisis?': From the Worlding of American Literature to World-System Literature," *American Literary History* 23, no. 3 (2011): 651.

25. George W. Bush, "Securing Freedom's Triumph," *New York Times*, September 11, 2002, http://www.nytimes.com/2002/09/11/opinion/securing-freedom-s-triumph.html.

26. Saskia Sassen, *Expulsions: Brutality and Complexity in the Global Economy* (Cambridge: Harvard University Press, 2014).

27. Niklas Luhmann, *Observations on Modernity*, trans. William Whobrey (Stanford: Stanford University Press, 1998), 45.

28. Margaret Scanlan, "Migrating from Terror: The Postcolonial Novel after September 11," *Journal of Postcolonial Writing* 46, nos. 3–4 (2010): 276.

29. As Derek Gregory has argued, "the war on terror is an attempt to establish a new global narrative in which the power to narrate is vested in a particular constellation of power and knowledge within the United States of America." Gregory, *The Colonial Present* (Malden: Blackwell, 2004), 16.

30. A Brown University study estimates that, as of this writing, "480,000 people have died due to direct war violence" and "many times more have died indirectly in these wars, due to malnutrition, damaged infrastructure, and environmental degradation," with "244,000 civilians . . . killed in direct violence by all parties to these conflicts." At the same time, "the United States government [has] detained well over 100,000 people for various periods in conjunction with the War on Terror in the years since 9/11." "Costs of War," *Watson Institute for International and Public Affairs*, n.d., http://watson.brown.edu/costsofwar.

5. Reframing

1. The term was coined by biologist Eugene F. Stoermer in the 1980s and has been popularized more recently by Paul J. Crutzen. See Paul J. Crutzen and Eugene F. Stoermer, "The 'Anthropocene,'" *Global Change Newsletter* 41 (2000): 17–18.

2. I borrow this term from Nicholas Mirzoeff, who employs it to describe the radical politics that emanate from the "attempt to reconfigure visuality as a whole," which upends the consensual authority enabled by the techniques, instruments, and power relations that sustain visuality, and allows the disenfranchised to claim their "right to look." Mirzoeff, *The Right to Look: A Counterhistory of Visuality* (Durham: Duke University Press, 2011), 24.

3. Rob Nixon's productive term is helpful to identify "violence that occurs gradually and out of sight, a violence of delayed destruction that is dispersed across time and space, an attritional violence that is typically not viewed as violence at all." Nixon, *Slow Violence and the Environmentalism of the Poor* (Cambridge: Harvard University Press, 2011), 2.

4. Jean-Luc Nancy, *After Fukushima: The Equivalence of Catastrophes*, trans. Charlotte Mandell (New York: Fordham University Press, 2015), 6.

5. Rob Nixon, "The Anthropocene: Promise and Pitfalls of an Epochal Idea," *Edge Effects*, November 6, 2014, http://edgeeffects.net/anthropocene-promise-and-pitfalls.

6. Christophe Bonneuil and Jean-Baptiste Fressoz, *The Shock of the Anthropocene: The Earth, History and Us*, trans. David Fernbach (London: Verso, 2015), 26.

7. See, respectively, Erik Swyngedouw, "Anthropocenic Promises: The End of Nature, Climate Change and the Process of Post-Politicization," Lecture at the Center for International Studies and Research (CERI), Paris (2014), cited in François Gemenne, "The Anthropocene and Its Victims," in *The Anthropocene and the Global Environmental Crisis: Rethinking Modernity in a New Epoch*, ed. Clive Hamilton, François Gemenne, and Christophe Bonneuil (London: Routledge, 2015), 168–74; Jussi Parikka, *The Anthrobscene* (Minneapolis: University of Minnesota Press, 2014); Jason W. Moore, *Capitalism in the Web of Life: Ecology and the Accumulation of Capital* (London: Verso, 2015); and Donna J. Haraway, *Staying with the Trouble: Making Kin in the Chthulucene* (Durham: Duke University Press, 2016).

8. Dipesh Chakrabarty, "Postcolonial Studies and the Challenge of Climate Change," *New Literary History* 43, no. 1 (2012): 1, 14. Chakrabarty remains an important but contentious figure in debates about the Anthropocene. This is in part due to his embracing, in earlier work, the mythologized "we" that I am disputing here, with claims that humans must think of themselves as a species and with calls for a universal history of humans. See Chakrabarty, "The Climate of History: Four Theses," *Critical Inquiry* 35, no. 2 (2009): 197–222.

9. I am echoing here one of the major questions in David Harvey's important *Justice, Nature, and the Geography of Difference*. In the book, Harvey is concerned with the difficult and often elusive connection between particularity and what he calls a general "theory" of environmental justice, that is, the construction of critical discourses that address the problems that affect individuals and communities both in the short and long term. Harvey, *Justice, Nature, and the Geography of Difference* (Malden: Blackwell, 1996), 9–15.

10. Michael Hardt and Antonio Negri, *Commonwealth* (Cambridge: Harvard University Press, 2009), 171. See also Michael Hardt, "Two Faces of Apocalypse: Letter from Copenhagen," *Polygraph* 22 (2010): 265–74.

11. Oliver Feltham, *Alain Badiou: Live Theory* (London: Continuum, 2008), 139.

12. Slavoj Žižek, *Living in the End Times* (London: Verso, 2010), 334.

13. See, e.g., Erik Swyngedouw, "Depoliticized Environments: The End of Nature, Climate Change and the Post-Political Condition," *Royal Institute of Philosophy Supplement* 69 (2011): 253–74.

14. Rob Nixon's notion of slow violence has been groundbreaking, yet several other critics have recently offered reflections from a variety of perspectives. See Robert P. Marzec, *Militarizing the Environment: Climate Change and the Security State* (Minneapolis: University of Minnesota Press, 2015); Stacy Alaimo, *Exposed: Environmental Politics and Pleasures in Posthuman Times* (Minneapolis: University of Minnesota Press, 2016); Ursula K. Heise, *Imagining Extinction: The Cultural Meanings of Endangered Species* (Chicago: University of Chicago Press, 2016); and Elizabeth DeLoughrey, "Submarine Futures of the Anthropocene," *Comparative Literature* 69, no. 1 (2017): 32–44.

15. In his exploration of the production of images that can only be registered from above, Robert Marzec has discussed how certain environmentalist movements seeking to counter their visual capture from high altitudes have strategically deployed operations such as the "view from above" to mount meaningful forms of resistance. Marzec, *Militarizing the Environment*, 62. My concept, thus, would work as complementary to this kind of intervention.

16. The original passage reads as follows: "In a context of rapid increasing connections around the globe, what is crucial for ecological awareness and environmental ethics is arguably not so much a sense of place as a sense of planet—a sense of how political, economic, technological, social, cultural, and ecological networks shape daily routines." Ursula K. Heise, *Sense of Place and Sense of Planet: The Environmental Imagination of the Global* (Oxford: Oxford University Press, 2008), 55.

17. T. J. Demos, *Decolonizing Nature: Contemporary Art and the Politics of Ecology* (Berlin: Sternberg Press, 2016), 11.

18. Jacques Rancière, *The Future of the Image*, trans. Gregory Elliott (London: Verso, 2007), 12–13.

19. "Basic Facts & Figures, Numbers of Dead and Injured, Bhopal Disaster," *The Bhopal Medical Appeal*, n.d., http://bhopal.org/basic-facts-figures-numbers-of-dead-and-injured-bhopal-disaster.

20. Even though Union Carbide's responsibility is becoming clearer over the years, several, often contradictory hypotheses point to a number of actors, from the workers operating the plant to the company. This inconclusiveness is largely due to the fact that a lawsuit involving Union Carbide (Union Carbide India's parent company, based in the United States), the U.S. and Indian governments,

Bhopal's local authorities, and representatives of the victims has not taken place. The adjudication of responsibilities remains uncompleted, since Warren Anderson (CEO of Union Carbide at the time), eight other Union Carbide officials, and two affiliates ignored a 1987 summons issued by the Indian government to return to India to be tried on homicide charges. Anderson, in addition, died in 2014 without ever facing prosecution.

21. "A Better Tomorrow: Poonam's Tale of Hope in Bhopal," *Facebook*, n.d., http://www.facebook.com/poonam.jatev.

22. Commentators often point out that, had it rained the night of the leak, the impact would have been much less disastrous. The disaster has also had important ramifications for Bhopal's water resources. One of the most important long-term repercussions is the contamination of its groundwater, which the poorest inhabitants have had no choice but to continue using at their own peril. To compound this problem, droughts have caused in recent years what is already considered a water crisis in the region.

23. Kerri Macdonald, "A Child's Life Changes and a Story Begins," *New York Times*, August 9, 2012, http://lens.blogs.nytimes.com/2012/08/09/three-years-later-the-storys-just-beginning.

24. Ariella Azoulay, *Civil Imagination: A Political Ontology of Photography*, trans. Louise Bethlehem (London: Verso, 2012), 23–24.

25. Katherine Boo, *Behind the Beautiful Forevers: Life, Death, and Hope in a Mumbai Undercity* (New York: Random House, 2012). I thank Alan Rauch for drawing my attention to this detail.

26. See Alex Masi, *Bhopal: Second Disaster* (New York: FotoEvidence, 2013).

27. Ariella Azoulay, *The Civil Contract of Photography*, trans. Rela Mazali and Ruvik Danieli (London: Zone Books, 2008), 14, 16.

28. Indra Sinha, *Animal's People* (New York: Simon & Schuster, 2007), 5; hereafter cited in the text.

29. Judith Butler, *Giving an Account of Oneself* (New York: Fordham University Press, 2005), 106.

30. Pablo Mukherjee, "'Tomorrow There Will Be More of Us': Toxic Postcoloniality in *Animal's People*," in *Postcolonial Ecologies: Literatures of the Environment*, ed. Elizabeth DeLoughrey and George B. Handley (Oxford: Oxford University Press, 2011), 226.

31. Nixon, *Slow Violence*, 57.

32. Andrew Malhsted, "Animal's Eyes: Spectacular Invisibility and the Terms of Recognition in Indra Sinha's *Animal's People*," *Mosaic* 46, no. 3 (2013): 68. Adele Holoch, who offers a reading of the novel partly based on Bakhtinian theory, reaches a similar conclusion as she argues that the novel brings Khaufpuris and Animal's audience together as "beings who share desires, share the experiences of suffering, [and] share participation in the fluid processes of change and becoming." Holoch, "Profanity and the Grotesque in Indra Sinha's *Animal's People*," *Interventions* 18, no. 1 (2016): 133.

33. Susan Sontag, *Regarding the Pain of Others* (New York: Picador, 2003), 18.

34. As Ariella Azoulay explains, "in many archives, photographs are filed under categories including 'refugees,' 'torture,' or 'expulsion' in a way that turns the photograph into a representation of phenomena or situations," thus annulling "the excess and lack that were inscribed in the photograph, subordinating it to one, supposedly factual, point of view." Azoulay, *Civil Imagination*, 223.

35. Jacques Rancière, *The Emancipated Spectator*, trans. Gregory Elliott (London: Verso, 2009), 96.

36. Jennifer Rickel contends that readers cannot be considered mere witnesses, as the collaborative relationship between a "testifier" (Animal) and his "witness" (Eyes) is upended in the novel because it does not aim to resolve a trauma but to expose its political problems. Rickel, "'The Poor Remain': A Posthumanist Rethinking of Literary Humanitarianism in Indra Sinha's *Animal's People*," *Ariel: A Review of International English Literature* 43, no. 1 (2012): 87–108.

37. Mukherjee, "'Tomorrow There Will Be More of Us,'" 224.

38. A similar concern regarding the group's image motivates Zafar to urge its members always to act peacefully, not only because breaking the law will put them at the same level as the criminal Kampani, but also because it would enable the Kampani's "armies of lobbyists, PR agencies, [and] hired editorialists" to build a smear campaign that labels them as "extremists": "from there it's a short step to 'these Khaufpuris are terrorists'" (282).

39. In *Madness and Civilization*, Michel Foucault describes one common apocalyptic narrative in the fifteenth century that differs from iterations in the previous century and has clear ecological connotations: "Apocalyptic dreams are not new." Yet, Foucault adds, "the delicately fantastic iconography of the fourteenth century . . . gives way to a vision of the world where all wisdom is annihilated. This is the witches' Sabbath of nature: *mountains melt and become plains, the earth vomits up the dead and bones tumble out of tombs; the stars fall, the earth catches fire. All life withers and comes to death.*" Foucault, *Madness and Civilization: A History of Insanity in the Age of Reason*, trans. Richard Howard (New York: Vintage, 1988), 23; emphasis added.

40. Rancière, *The Emancipated Spectator*, 58.

41. Rancière, *The Emancipated Spectator*, 59.

42. Consider, for instance, how the photograph of Macon Hawkins, an American hostage surrounded by heavily armed members of the Movement for the Emancipation of the Niger Delta (MEND), became an iconic yet extremely reductive representation of the politics of the Delta's ecological disaster in 2006. For a discussion, see Philip Aghoghovwia, "Nigeria," in *Fueling Culture: 101 Words for Energy and Environment*, ed. Imre Szeman, Jennifer Wenzel, and Patricia Yaeger (New York: Fordham University Press, 2017), 238–41.

43. Helon Habila, *Oil on Water* (New York: Norton, 2010), 102–3; hereafter cited in the text.

44. Nixon, *Slow Violence*, 4.

45. See Byron Caminero-Santangelo, "Witnessing the Nature of Violence: Resource Extraction and Political Ecologies in the Contemporary African Novel," in *Global Ecologies and the Environmental Humanities: Postcolonial Approaches*, ed. Elizabeth DeLoughrey, Jill Didur, and Anthony Carrigan (London: Routledge, 2015), 226–41.

46. Sontag, *Regarding the Pain of Others*, 23.

47. *Poison Fire: Gas and Oil Abuse in Nigeria* (dir. Lars Johansson, 2008), July 15, 2008, http://www.youtube.com/watch?v=bq2TBOHWFRc.

48. Azoulay, *Civil Imagination*, 118.

49. W. J. T. Mitchell, *What Do Pictures Want? The Lives and Loves of Images* (Chicago: University of Chicago Press, 2005), 10.

50. For an argument about the shortcomings of "toxic sublimity" as a spectacular mode for representing wastelands visually, see Jill Gatlin, "Toxic Sublimity and the Crisis of Human Perception: Rethinking Aesthetic, Documentary, and Political Appeals in Contemporary Wasteland Photography," *ISLE: Interdisciplinary Studies in Literature and Environment* 22, no. 4 (2015): 717–41.

51. Arundhati Roy, *An Ordinary Person's Guide to Empire* (Cambridge: South End Press, 2004), 6–7.

52. Leerom Medovoi, "Remediation as Pharmikon," *Comparative Literature* 66, no. 1 (2014): 23.

53. As Caminero-Santangelo has suggested, it "has few references to the history of how foreign national governments, oil companies, the Nigerian petrostate, and resistance movements have shaped that crisis." Caminero-Santangelo, "Witnessing the Nature of Violence," 234.

54. Mitchell, *What Do Pictures Want?* 120.

55. Azoulay, *The Civil Contract of Photography*, 130.

56. Jennifer Wenzel, "Behind the Headlines," *American Book Review* 33, no. 3 (2012): 14.

57. Wenzel, "Behind the Headlines," 14.

58. Sheena Wilson, Adam Carlson, and Imre Szeman, "Introduction: On Petrocultures," in *Petrocultures: Oil, Politics, Culture*, ed. Sheena Wilson, Adam Carlson, and Imre Szeman (Montreal: McGill-Queen's University Press, 2017), 5.

59. Timothy Mitchell, *Carbon Democracy: Political Power in the Age of Oil* (London: Verso, 2011), 2.

60. John Berger, *About Looking* (New York: Vintage, 1991), 43–44.

61. Sean Cubitt, *Finite Media: Environmental Implications of Digital Technologies* (Durham: Duke University Press, 2017), 151.

INDEX

abortion: as interruption of a consensual order, 71–73
Abu Ghraib, 150
aesthetics, xii, xiv, 3, 8, 24, 28; of exception, 152, 154, 157, 166, 168
affiliation, 34; as constituted against colonial precepts, 60, 66, 73, 75; incongruous, 63, 60–65, 68–69, 71, 75. *See also* filiation
Agamben, Giorgio, xi, 89–90, 151–52
agency, viii, 14, 21; non-consensual, xii, 221–22; as undermined by illusory dialogue, 5, 15, 19. *See also* voice
Age of Dialogue, the, 4, 14, 17, 21
agonism: as opposed to antagonism, 22, 36, 232n41. *See also* counterdialogic politics
Ahmed, Sara, 72
Alaimo, Stacy, 250n14
Amritsar massacre, 43
Anderson, Warren, 250n20
Anglophone literature, x, 5, 24–30; disciplinary complexities of, 27–29; as expansive descriptor, 27–28; as non-totalizing, 29; postcolonial literature and, 27; as world literature, 28

animality: as dissensual gesture, 186–87
Animal's People (Sinha), 29, 172, 173, 175–76, 177–96, 214–15, 215–16
antagonism, 33, 151, 153, 166, 167, 168, 170; agonism as alternative to, 22, 36, 76. *See also* counterdialogic politics
Anthropocene, the, 29, 171; alternatives to, 175; manifestations other than climate change of, 174, 176; as narrative currently being constructed, 171, 174–75, 181; as part of human history, 171, 173, 174, 249n8; as totalizing narrative, 174–75, 177; visuality of, 173–77. *See also* climate change; environmental disasters
Appiah, Kwame Anthony, 234n8
Apter, Emily, 29, 233n58
Arab Spring, xii
Asad, Talal, 151, 152
Ashcroft, Bill, 232n51
attention economy, the, 180. *See also* media, the
austerity, 101, 103–4, 134; as ineffective measure for economic stabilization, 105; movements against, xii,

104; presented as inevitable, 110. *See also* welfare state, the
authority, 15, 20–21, 95, 117, 197; consensual narrative, 7, 44–46, 82, 84, 87–91, 96–97, 249n2; dissensual narrative, 179, 182; imperial, 37–38, 47, 50, 61, 85, 134–36; the war on terror and, 151, 152. *See also* meaning-making
autobiography, 81, 87–88, 240n22
autonomy: as detached politics, 49–50; as emancipatory condition, 23, 24, 35–36, 43, 50, 56, 59, 102, 116, 120, 128, 138, 140, 143, 237n40; as legitimation to impose a consensus, 15, 221; as political impossibility, 169; as political problem, 79; as threatened by a consensual apparatus, 131, 136, 142, 145, 244n46. *See also* singularity
Azoulay, Ariella, 181, 252n34

Baartman, Saartjie, 68
Badiou, Alain, xiii, 11, 138, 176, 232n44
Bakhtin, Mikhail M., 6–14, 15, 24, 34, 60, 129, 251n32; canonical status of, 6, 10–11; on the carnivalesque, 7; dialogism, 6–14; on the grotesque, 7; heteroglossia, 6, 8–9, 14; hybridity for, 238n54; on laughter, 7, 8; monoglossia, 9, 10, 12, 14; need to move beyond, 9–14; on the novel, 6–7, 8, 238n54; on the Other, 9; polyphony, 6, 7; shortcomings of dialogism, 6–7, 10–14; on singularity, 7, 8–9, 13, 14; uncritical acceptance of, 229n19; versatility of dialogism, 9, 10; on voice, 9, 10
Balfour, Arthur, 36, 37–39, 42
Bandung Conference, 39
Barthes, Roland, 139

Baudrillard, Jean, 124–25, 154
BBC, 187, 198, 205. *See also* journalism; media, the
belonging, viii, 62, 174, 187, 194, 195, 240n22
Berger, John, 213
Berman, Jessica, 235n15, 237n52
Beveridge, William, 39. *See also* welfare state, the
Bhabha, Homi K., 61, 238n54
Bhopal environmental disaster, 171–81, 181–96, 250n20
Big Oil, 108
Big Pharma, 108
Big Society (UK), 103–4, 108–10
bildungsroman, the, 60, 73, 238n68
Blanchot, Maurice, 94
body, the: Bakhtin on, 8; as connected with the present, 157–62; as conquerable, 136, 138–40; disciplining of, 117; as dissensually revolting, 135–37; impact of environmental violence on, 185–89, 193, 209; language of, 154; and sexual assault, 43, 50, 52, 66; spectacularization of pain, 182–83, 186; spectacularization of the female, 68, 71–72
Bohm, David, 230n31
Bonneuil, Christophe, 171, 175
Bourdieu, Pierre, 100
Brennan, Timothy, 229n19, 234n5
Brexit, 3, 146
Brown, Gordon, 102–3
Brown, Wendy, 99, 100, 244n46
Buber, Martin, 6
Bush, George W., 150, 153–52, 157, 162. *See also* war on terror, the
Butler, Judith, 69, 149, 184, 246n3

cacophony, 51, 52, 184, 193
Cameron, David, 99, 102, 103, 111, 114, 126, 146; as heir to Margaret Thatcher, 101, 103–5, 110, 125,

126, 128, 134, 143, 144–45. *See also* neoliberalism
Caminero-Santangelo, Byron, 253n45, 253n53
capitalism, 40–41, 81, 84–85, 176, 179, 245n51; the environment and, 176, 179, 194, 201, 213–14; global, 163–64, 165, 167, 194, 201, 213, 214; neoliberalism and, 99–100, 104
carnivalesque, the, 6–7, 71
Casanova, Pascale, 28
catastrophe. *See* environmental disasters
Chakrabarty, Dipesh, 42, 175, 249n8
Chambers, Ross, 67
charity, 113, 178, 213, 245n49; as mechanism to compensate for the neoliberal abolition of social security, 112–13; Western, 180, 188. *See also* nongovernmental organizations
Chatterjee, Partha, 57
Cheah, Pheng, 28, 33, 233n53
childbirth: as anomalous disruption of lineage, 88–89, 93; as continuation of a consensual order, 72, 145; as symbolic of the emergence of a new politics, 122–27, 245n51. *See also* abortion
child care, 112–18, 122–23, 244n40. *See also* welfare state, the
Child in Time, The (McEwan), 29, 101, 102, 111–27, 144–45, 145, 146
citizenship, 32, 223; as collective political designator, 103–5, 108, 112, 120; as political responsibility, 114–18, 125–26; the state's interested appeal to, 100–101, 102, 106, 125, 145, 244n46; the state's intrusion in the politics of, 108

civil war, 2, 33, 152, 230n31
"clash of civilizations, the," (Huntington), 2
Clausewitz, Carl von, 17
climate change, 3, 249n8; as one of many manifestations of the Anthropocene, 174, 176, 214, 215; talks, 18. *See also* Anthropocene, the; environmental disasters
close reading, 25; as civic and political act, 26; as vehicle to rethink dialogue, xiv–xv. *See also* fiction; literature
coercion, ix, x, 23; postpolitics and, 17. *See also* collaboration; illusory dialogue
Cold War, x, 39, 42, 99, 158
collaboration: consensual narrative orders concealed as, 82–87, 129; depoliticizing order of consensus disguised as, ix; illusory dialogue as, 15, 19; imposition of neoliberalism shrouded as a form of, 102, 104, 110, 128; as key notion in democracy, viii, 2, 3, 10, 219; maintenance of imperial relations through, 32, 43, 234n3; as necessary in the construction of the Anthropocene narrative, 171–77; as necessary for an egalitarian understanding of history, 95–97; photography as a relationship of, 179, 180; postpolitics and, xiii; reactivation of politics via, 4, 126, 220. *See also* coercion; participation
colonialism. *See* imperialism
common ground: reversed replication of, 45–46
common sense: consensus and, ix; as dominant governing logic, ix, x–xi, 18. *See also* rationality
communism, 40–41, 167

community: activism, 199; Bakhtin on, 8–10; and communication as a problem, 11; consensus at the core of the, viii–ix; ecology and, 176; emancipatory politics and the, 22–23, 195; illusory dialogue and, 15–16; the international, 1, 2, 39–40, 42; the internet and, 221; the scientific, 174; voluntary work and the, 108

consensus: the Anthropocene and, 172, 174–75, 177; as collective agreement, viii–ix; as common ground, 16; common sense and, ix; cosmopolitan, 34, 36, 43; as deterrent of dissent, xiii, xiv; global, xii; historical discourse as, 80–81, 87, 97; neoliberalism and, 100–101, 104–5, 110; postcolonial, 32, 34, 41, 42; as regulated by illusory dialogue, 15–21; as regulatory principle, viii–ix, x, xiii, xiv, 1, 22; as resolution, 9, 15, 16, 18; as unchallengeable, 20; the war on terror and, 149–51, 158, 167. *See also* dissensus; realism

consent, ix, 18, 97, 121, 125, 130; manufacture of, 19. *See also* consensus

contemporary, the. *See* present, the

cosmopolitanism: colonialism and, 52; consensual, 33–36, 43; critically reconsidered, 33; detached, 49–50, 53–59; dissensual, 35, 43, 62; failure to maintain critical dialogue of, 53, 54–59; friendship and, 46–50, 54–59; liberal, 48, 49; as negation of the political, 32; postcolonial, 32; secular, 49; theistic, 48, 52–53

counterdialogic politics: as alternative to refusal, 22; the novel and, 23, 24–27, 30, 221–23; as procedure to counter illusory dialogue, 22, 32. *See also* dissent

counterterrorism, 151–57, 168, 169. *See also* September 11, 2001 attacks; terrorist

countervisuality, 172–77, 213, 215, 249n2. *See also* visuality

crisis reportage, 202–3, 206

Crouch, Colin, 241n3

Crutzen, Paul J., 248n1

Cubitt, Sean, 215

cultural studies, 3–4, 10

Dean, Jodi, 227n8

death, xiii, 8; caused by environmental disaster, 178, 187, 193, 194, 197, 204, 210; at the center of the Anthropocene, 174, 252n39; as closure, 72; employed as spectacle to activate a political movement, 191, 192; forestalling of closure by, 94–95; as symbolic trigger of an insular nostalgia, 158, 160; as unacknowledged certainty, 168–70, 245n49; violent, 43, 81, 83–86, 91–94, 204, 248n30. *See also* suicide

debate: as depoliticizing spectacle, 110, 114–16, 123; as public political exercise, 149, 150, 152. *See also* dialogue; illusory dialogue

Debord, Guy, 18, 231n34. *See also* spectacle

decolonization, 1, 27, 31–35, 37–42, 74; dialogue and, 42. *See also* imperialism

Deleuze, Gilles, 132

DeLoughrey, Elizabeth, 250n14

democracy, 23, 219–20, 221, 223; absence of, 74, 112, 213; the Anthropocene and, 175–76; consensus and, viii; dialogue and, 10, 11, 229n19; illusory dialogue and,

15; imperial relations and, 38, 39, 74; need to protect, ix, xiii, xv, 220; neoliberal assault on, 29, 97, 104, 110; participatory democracy, xi, 3, 15, 105, 112; problem of, 241n3; revitalization of, 122–27; the war on terror and, 166, 167; western variety of, vii, 7, 99, 162. *See also* collaboration; consensus; dissent

Demos, T. J., 177

Derrida, Jacques, 101–2

Descartes, René, 228n10

detachment: as instrument to alienate politically, 89–91, 178–81; as means to undo the work of consensus, 140–44; privileged, 52, 53–59; traumatic, 52–53, 158–62

detention: indefinite, 150, 152, 169, 247n9. *See also* counterterrorism; imprisonment

dialectics, 5, 33, 35–36, 61, 66, 153, 223, 228n10, 230n30, 239n11

Dialogic Imagination, The (Bakhtin), 8–9, 10, 12, 229n18, 230n26

dialogue: as act of dispossession, xiv; as attempt to correct the historical record, 80–82, 84; as attempt to counter the narrative of the war on terror, 150–53, 154–57; as bridge for global relations, 1–2, 3; capacity to redraw power relations of, 16; as collaboration, 1, 3; as consensual instrument, ix–x, xiii, 5; context in, 11, 12, 13–14; critical, 20; cross-cultural, 42, 46–50; and democracy, 10, 11; depoliticization of, x, 5, 6; and dialectics, 228n10; diplomacy and, 2; failure to right a wrong of, 95–97, 166–70; as form of communication between citizens and the state, 3, 220–21; history of the idea of, 5–6; individuality as shaped by, 13; inevitable power imbalance in, 16; the internet and, 4, 221; narration as an apparent, 129–34; as never neutral, 15; paradoxical nature of, ix–x; participation and, 10–13; positive aspects of, 4; and postcolonial studies, 34; as postpolitical problem, x, xv, 5; power relations in, 12, 15, 18; radical power of, 12, 14; as rhetorical trope, 5; role of the media in, 223, 232n48; silence and, 12; spectacularization of, 18; subjectivity in, 17, 23; ubiquity of, 2–4; uncritical understandings of, 4, 11, 12, 14, 18, 203n31; understood as democratic instrument, ix, 1; universality of, 1, 5; as vehicle for mutual understanding, 3–4, 9, 13; voice and, 4, 13, 16–20. *See also* Age of Dialogue, the; Bakhtin, Mikhail M.; illusory dialogue; postpolitics; silence

difference, 2, 8, 11. *See also* foreignness; Other, the

dignity, xiii, 100, 187, 195

Dirlik, Arif, 233n2

disability: as reason for the prevalence of a consensual order, 90, 91. *See also* irrationality

disaffection, 29, 115–16, 118, 119, 124; love as antidote to political, 124–26. *See also* detachment; love

disagreement, x, 4, 11; characterized as politically unproductive, 230n31; as dialectical operation, 230n30; as discursive action, 19; dissent and, 10, 14, 19, 22, 219; need to reactivate the political power of, 21–23; uncritical understanding of, 11, 17; vulnerability of, 14, 17, 18, 23. *See also* dissent; illusory dialogue; resistance; voice

Disagreement: Politics and Philosophy (Rancière), 21–23
dissensus, x, xiii; and literary critique, xiv; literature and, 24–25. *See also* Rancière, Jacques
dissent, vii, xii, 10; destruction of, 19; disagreement and, 22; as political endeavor, 14. *See also* consensus; disagreement; illusory dialogue; preemption; resistance; voice
Docherty, Thomas, 245n51
dominant voices, 4, 15–17, 18, 19, 20, 20–23; consequences of minor voices' transformation into, 80; dependence on minor voices of, 19, 22. *See also* authority; illusory dialogue; meaning-making; voice

ecocriticism, xi, 176
"end of history, the," (Fukuyama), vii
environmental disasters, xi, xiii, 3, 33, 172–74; commodification of, 178–81; journalistic coverage of, 178–81, 182, 202–3; and spectacle, 192, 200, 202, 213, 216; as unspectacular events, 201, 207, 212; visuality of, 183, 185, 188, 198. *See also* Anthropocene, the; Bhopal environmental disaster; climate change; Niger Delta environmental ruination
epistemology, 4, 5; contestation and, 80; counterterrorism and, 155–56; imperial, 45, 50; violence and, 31. *See also* meaning-making
ethics, viii, 14, 28, 83, 219, 232n44; the Anthropocene and, 173, 175; and capitalism, 163; detached, 49, 53; spectatorship and, 207; the war on terror and, 152, 169
exclusion, 1, 10, 18–19, 23, 60, 89–95, 110. *See also* expulsion

expulsion, 33, 163, 252n34. *See also* exclusion

Fanon, Frantz, 31, 42, 54, 71
fiction: counterdialogic qualities of, 25; emancipatory power of, vii, xi, xiv, 5. *See also* literature; metafiction; narrative; novel, the
filiation, 62, 65–66, 67, 69, 72. *See also* affiliation
Fisher, Mark, 104
foreignness: 57, 62, 70, 132, 164, 182, 210. *See also* migration; Other, the
Forster, E. M., 29, 32, 33, 34, 36, 43–59, 74, 75, 76
Foucault, Michel, 12, 79, 94–95, 100, 117, 252n39
free speech, xiii, 4, 15, 149. *See also* agency; voice
Freire, Paulo, 6
Fressoz, Jean-Baptiste, 171, 175
friendship: political impossibility of, 53, 54–59; as potential platform for cross-cultural dialogue, 44, 46–50; as precarious manifestation of solidarity, 68, 70, 113, 183, 184, 193. *See also* love
Fukuyama, Francis, vii
full picture, the: as totalizing visualization, 198, 213. *See also* representation; visual capture
future, the, 1; political foreclosure in, 15, 19–20; politics of, xii, xv, 20, 26–27. *See also* history; preemption; present, the

Gadamer, Hans-Georg, 6
Gardiner, Michael, 230n22
gas flares, 196, 199, 201; as visualization of the ecological ruination caused by oil extraction, 210–12
gaze, the, 59, 70; narrative effort to challenge the, 179–92;

self-destructive power of, 190–91. *See also* visibility; visuality
genealogy: as mode of history-writing, 82–87. *See also* historiography
gender, xii, 220; normativity as disciplinary, 60, 66–70, 85, 117, 134–35, 220; and race, 66–70; as site of political dispute, 66, 132, 135–39, 146
geopolitics, 28, 31, 150–51, 154, 162, 165, 168, 169–70
Gilroy, Paul, 60
glaring: as visual intervention, 199–206, 212
globalization, 1, 27, 32–33, 201
global North, the, 163–64, 172, 173, 174, 215. *See also* West, the
global South, the, xi, 164–65, 172, 173, 176, 194. *See also* Third World, the
global studies, 32–33
Goldman Sachs, 105
Gramsci, Antonio, ix, x, 227n4. *See also* consensus
grand narratives, 80–81; historical, 83–85, 90, 96–97
grassroots activism, vii, x, 3, 188. *See also* agency; politics
Gregory, Derek, 248n29
Griffiths, Gareth, 232n51
grotesque, the, 8, 137
Guantánamo Bay, 150, 169
Guattari, Félix, 132

Habermas, Jürgen, 6, 18, 231n35
Habila, Helon, 29, 172, 173, 175, 176–77, 196–214, 214–15, 216–17
Hall, Stuart, 103
Hamid, Mohsin, 29, 149–70
Hardt, Michael, xi, 22, 66, 150, 175–76, 234n5, 250n10
Harvey, David, 100, 241n10, 244n38, 249n9

Head, Dominic, 116, 241n5
health care. *See* National Health Service
Hegel, G. W. F., 228n10
hegemony, ix, x, 1, 18, 21, 22, 26; of the Anthropocene narrative, 171; of Britain in the postcolonial era, 35, 36, 39; of the global North, 163–64; imperial, 31, 234n3; neoliberal, 100; of postpolitics, xiii, 5, 19, 30, 43; representational, 44–46, 131–32, 171; resulting from an emancipatory act, 80; of the United States in the present, 150, 162, 166, 167, 170. *See also* authority; common sense; consensus
Heise, Ursula K., 177, 250n14, 250n16
historiography, 76, 81, 83, 84, 96–97, 239n8. *See also* metafiction
history, xi, xii, xiv, 1–2, 13, 16, 26, 29; Anthropocenic, 172–75, 214–17, 249n8; as common across the global South, 164–65; contestation of official, 79–83; dissensual grounding of the self in, 155–57; epic understanding of, 41, 166, 173; exclusionary, 96–97; no longer driven by ideology, vii; vindication against claims about the end of ideology of, 101–2. *See also* grand narratives; historiography
humanism: liberal, 44, 53, 183, 236n34. *See also* liberalism
Huntington, Samuel, 2
Husserl, Edmund, 6
Hutcheon, Linda, 81, 239n7, 239n8
hybridity, 33, 60, 237n52; Bakhtin and, 238n54; as consensual notion, 61, 65. *See also* third space, the
hypernationalism, 33, 47, 158. *See also* nationalism

ideology, vii; attempted elimination of, viii, 235n22; and history-writing, 81–82; imperial, 37–38, 43–46, 49–50, 51, 58, 61, 66; as impossible to eliminate, xiii; as learned worldview, 134, 136, 140–41, 144–46; neoliberal, 100–101, 127; Orientalist, 43, 63, 179; of the war on terror, 156

illusory dialogue, 4–5, 9, 14, 15–20; as alternative to coercion, 4; between citizens and the state, 102, 105, 110–11, 114, 116–18, 122–26; conclusion of an, 19; as constitutive relationship, 17, 20; construction of the Anthropocene narrative as, 171–77, 180–81, 185, 196, 198–203; as a continuation of coercion by other means, 17; definition of, 15; deployed to extend imperial relations after decolonization, 39–43; emergence of, 6; employed for the privatization of social security services, 102, 106–10, 114; as instrument to foreclose alternatives, 19; necessary endurance to challenge, 23; neutral veneer of, 18, 23; in the postcolonial era, 32, 36, 37; productive operation of, 20; reciprocity of, 19; rhetorical strategies in, 17; rules of engagement in, 15; as self-disciplining apparatus, 17; status quo maintained by, 17; strategies against, 5; subjectivity and, 17, 22–23. *See also* consensus; counterdialogic politics; dissent; silence; voice

imagination, xiv, 8, 68, 150, 169, 170, 176, 177; as neither conjectural nor fantastical, 28; literary, xiii, 23, 25–27; political, xii, 24–26, 28, 80, 115, 174–75, 222, 223, 238n68, 246n5; postpolitics' grip on the, xiv. *See also* literature; reading dangerously

imperialism, 1, 27–28, 31–43, 54–56, 58, 60–61, 73–76, 94, 162, 214, 234n5; international coalition against, 39; and modernism, 34; movements against, 31, 37. *See also* neocolonialism

imprisonment, 139–43, 205. *See also* detention

inclusion, x, 3, 10; as form of exclusion, 17, 19, 87–91. *See also* collaboration; participation

independence movements, 32, 38–39, 44, 47, 56–58, 221; Britain's response to anti-colonial, 40–43

Indignados, 104

individualism, 50, 53, 120, 237n40

individuality: as determined by a dialogue, 13. *See also* singularity; subjectivity

infantilization: as depoliticizing strategy, 116–18

information, xiii; conflation of entertainment and, 202; implied, 169; as source of power, 153, 154, 188; untimely, 190. *See also* internet, the; meaning-making; media, the

insanity: as designator deployed to safeguard consensus, 85, 94, 155, 161; as destabilization of consensus, 52–53, 136, 140–42, 184, 193. *See also* irrationality; rationality

International Monetary Fund, 242n17

internet, the, 4, 188, 232n48; dialogue and, 4, 221. *See also* media, the

interpellation: consensual predetermination of interlocutors via, 20, 25, 131, 137, 139, 141–43; as method to establish solidarity, 199–201

interrogation: as counterterrorist mechanism to produce information, 154–55, 247n9, 247n12;

"enhanced," 152; narrative reversal of, 156–57. *See also* meaning-making; war on terror, the
introspection: as reflection of political disillusionment, 112, 115; as symbolic of national insularity, 161
invisibility, 10, 85, 90, 100, 177, 191. *See also* representation; visuality
irrationality: attacks on dissent as, 93, 155, 166; crisis of consensus as, 141–42; explanation of dissent as, 136, 137. *See also* insanity; rationality

Jameson, Fredric, 34, 100
Johansson, Lars, 199–201, 208
journalism: as complicit with consensual governance, 122–23, 160, 167, 206; dissensual work of, 169, 197–98, 203–4, 209, 247n9; precarious state of, 205; spectacular, 178–81, 182–84; and visibility of environmental disaster, 178, 215–16. *See also* media, the

Kalliney, Peter, 49, 66, 235n15
Khalili, Laleh, 153
Kínima Aganaktisménon-Politón, 104
knowledge. *See* meaning-making

Laclau, Ernesto, 80
landscape, the: as imperial artistic genre, 58. *See also* representation; visuality
language: of the body, 154; as coercive instrument, 90, 95, 229n18, 231n34; as emancipatory instrument, 24; as ideological vehicle, 131, 140; of images, 191; postpolitical grip on, xiii, 23; power to employ, 90, 94; as site for political contestation, 25, 27, 113, 132, 133, 139, 144, 230n30. *See also* Bakhtin, Mikhail M.; cacophony; ideology; silence; voice
laughter: emancipatory power of, 72; political valences of, 7, 138
Lazarus, Neil, 33, 234n10
Lejeune, Philippe, 240n22. *See also* autobiography
Levinas, Emmanuel, 5
liberalism, 10, 44, 47–49, 53, 54, 128, 183, 236n34; Western, vii, 48
listening: as form of dispossession, 14, 17, 19, 21. *See also* Listening Exercise
Listening Exercise, 102, 106–10, 114, 145. *See also* Cameron, David; National Health Service
literary critique, 4, 7, 27–28; political, xiii; political questions and, xii–xiii; postpolitics and, xi–xv. *See also* reading dangerously
literary theory, xi, 11; interdisciplinary approach to, xiv; and political theory, xi–xii
literature: and politics, xii, 24, 26; and postpolitics, xi; radical power of, xi, xiii–xiv, 23, 24–30; study of, xi, 27; uses of, xiii. *See also* Anglophone literature; literary critique
Loomba, Ania, 31, 234n3
love: as expression of nationalist devotion, 130–31, 134; as form of dispossession, 131, 134–35, 138–42; fraternal as opposed to carnal, 139–40; as humanizing, 120; political impossibility of, 138–40; as radical politics, 111, 125–26, 128, 135, 138, 142–45; as symbol of political solidarity, 125, 126; as vehicle to impose a neoliberal consensus, 110–11, 127–29, 134. *See also* friendship
Lyon, Janet, 235n15
Lyotard, Jean-François, 4, 80, 234n11

Machiavelli, Niccolò, 1, 4
Macmillan, Harold, 36, 39–43, 74; as precursor of postpolitics, 39, 235n22
management: as method of governance, vii, 32, 100, 231n32, 235n22. *See also* postpolitics
Mao, Douglas, 34, 235n14
March for the Alternative (UK), 104–5
Marx, John, 233n52
Marzec, Robert P., 250n14, 250n15
Masi, Alex, 178, 180, 181
masquerade: as gender performance, 132; as racial performance, 71–72
Matsuura, Kōichirō, 1, 5
McClintock, Anne, 233n2
McEwan, Ian, 29, 101, 102, 111–27, 144–45, 145, 146
meaning-making, xiii, xiv; and dialogue, 4; historiography and, 81, 95–97, 239n16; ideological replication as, 134–37; images and, 171, 177–81, 201; imperialism and, 37, 44–46; literature and, 24; narrative and, 81–82, 181–86, 203, 207, 211; neoliberalism and, 103–5; the war on terror and, 153, 156–57. *See also* authority; epistemology; representation
media, the: in the Age of Dialogue, 4, 221, 223; as complicit with governmental spectacular politics, 122–23; environmental violence and, 172, 178–81, 205; as participant in the war on terror, 167, 169. *See also* internet, the; journalism
Merrill Lynch, 105
metafiction: historiographic, 81
middle ground, the: as consensual distribution, 19, 36

middle way, the, viii, 39
Middle Way: A Study of the Problem of Economic and Social Progress in a Free and Democratic Society, The (Macmillan), 39, 235n22
migration, 27, 99; contemporary, 152, 157; crises, 33; as planetary problem, 2, 3; within the British Empire, 48–50, 59, 60–61, 63, 65–68. *See also* hybridity
minorities, 10, 15–16, 27, 117; literatures of, 27. *See also* minor voices
minor voices, 4, 15–17, 18, 219, 220, 221–22; capacity to challenge illusory dialogue of, 20–23; compulsory complicity of, 19; dependence of dominant voices on, 19, 22. *See also* voice
Mirzoeff, Nicholas, 249n2
misrecognition: colonial, 29, 63, 66–70, 73. *See also* recognition
Mitchell, W. J. T., 201
modernism: and colonialism, 34; facing its own representational crisis, 44; historical boundaries of, 35, 235n16; and planetarity, 36; postcolonial, 35–36, 235n14; postpolitical connections of, 35; proleptic qualities of, 73–76
modernist studies, 34
monologue, 154; interior, 124; the spectacle as, 231n34
Morey, Peter, 236n38
Mouffe, Chantal, vii, 1, 232n41. *See also* agonism; hegemony
multiculturalism, xiii, 33, 43
mutuality: based on solidarity, 52, 126, 189; as cover-up for consensus, xiii, 19, 43, 128; operation of dialogue as, 9, 13; political relationships as, 57, 59, 135, 145, 176, 221. *See also* collaboration; recognition

Nancy, Jean-Luc, 173
Napoleon, 87, 127–28, 129–31, 132–44, 146. *See also* Thatcher, Margaret
narrative, xii; as apparently dialogic endeavor, 129–34; disruption of expectations, 82–83, 92–95, 154–57, 182–83, 206–13, 216; as form of emancipatory agency, 131–34, 152–57, 181–86, 199, 206–12; manifesting epistemological limitations, 50–52, 55, 58, 82, 92–95, 134–35, 139, 166–70, 178–81; as power to establish a hegemonic consensus, 7, 44–46, 82, 84, 86, 96–97, 249n2. *See also* representation; silence
National Health Service (NHS), 102–10. *See also* austerity; privatization of social services; welfare state, the
nationalism: as emancipatory gesture against imperialism, 38–39, 54; insular, 158–60. *See also* hypernationalism; independence movements
NCVO (National Council for Voluntary Organisations), 108
Negri, Antonio, xi, 22, 66, 150, 175–76, 234n5
neocolonialism, 27, 32, 76. *See also* imperialism
neoliberalism, 29; characterized as unchallengeable economic doctrine, 102–5; as global hegemonic regime, 100, 162–64; as main theme in postpolitics, x–xi
Niger Delta environmental ruination, 196–214, 216, 217, 252n42
Nikulin, Dmitri, 228n10
9/11. *See* September 11, 2001 attacks
9/11 Commission Report: Final Report of the National Commission on Terrorist Attacks upon the United States, The, 151

Nixon, Rob, 173–74, 249n3, 250n14
Nkrumah, Kwame, 32
nongovernmental organizations (NGOs), 3, 169; neoliberalism's reliance on, 244n38. *See also* charity
novel, the: as counterdialogic genre, 23, 24–27, 30, 223; as opposed to other discursive modes, 25, 232n48. *See also* fiction; imagination; literature

O'Brien, Suzie, 27–28
Occupy movement, xii
oil extraction, 172, 196–97, 199, 201, 206, 209, 212, 213
Oil on Water (Habila), 29, 172, 173, 175, 176–77, 196–214, 214–15, 216–17
oil wars, 204, 205, 207, 209, 211, 212, 216
ontology, 156, 187, 195, 223; dissensual, 35, 60, 74–75, 186, 187; negation of one's, 10; negative, 66. *See also* subjectivity
opinion, x, 8, 11, 149, 223, 230n31
Orientalism (Said), 37–38
Other, the, 6, 220; the Anthropocene and, 171, 175, 179; Bakhtin on, 8, 9; colonialism and, 48–49, 53, 58; historical invisibility and, 80, 82, 85, 97; illusory dialogue and, 17; love and, 128, 131, 135–44; the United States and, 154, 156, 158, 159, 161. *See also* difference; foreignness

Parry, Benita, 31, 33, 51, 234n10
participation, vii, viii, x, xi, 3; in the construction of the Anthropocene narrative, 172, 174, 205, 215; dialogue understood as form of, 10–13, 14; illusory dialogue as

depoliticized, 16–17, 19–20, 22; and imperial relations, 39, 42–44, 47, 53, 56, 59, 74; neoliberal governance and, 100, 102, 105–8, 112–15, 121, 132, 139. *See also* collaboration

Passage to India, A (Forster), 29, 32, 33, 34, 36, 43–59, 74, 75, 76

Passion, The (Winterson), 29, 101, 102, 127–44, 144–45, 146

pensée unique, ix, xiv. *See also* consensus; realism

photography: depoliticizing use of, 178–81, 252n42; as relationship of capture, 176–77, 178, 180–81, 195–96; relationship of narrative with, 181, 183–84, 206–12. *See also* countervisuality; visuality

picturesque, the: as form of visual capture, 207. *See also* landscape, the; visuality

planetarity, 36, 73, 192, 233n58. *See also* geopolitics

Plato, 228n10

plurality, 3, 7, 11

Poison Fire (Johansson), 199–201, 208

policing, 7, 10, 21, 23, 121. *See also* dissent; silence

policy making, vii, 223; counterterrorism and, 151, 155, 174; environmental degradation and, 214; neoliberal, 100, 103, 111–13, 118, 123–26, 145

political disillusionment, 29, 112–27, 145, 220. *See also* disaffection

political philosophy, xiv, 227n4

politics: activism, xi, 3, 18; as break, xiii; consensual operation of, vii, xi, xiii, 21; definition of vii; electoral, vii, 29; end of, viii, xiii; and literature, xii; literature as site to practice, 24; participation in, vii, 23; regeneration of, xii, xiii, 14, 22–23; as self-empowerment, 23. *See also* counterdialogic politics; dissent

Politics of Postmodernism, The (Hutcheon), 81

populism, 220–21

postcolonialism: consensus and, 32, 34, 41–43, 60–61, 72; cosmopolitanism and, 33, 58–59; imperial relations in the era of, 36–43; postpolitics and, 33; radical politics and, 44

postcolonial studies, xi, 32–33, 37, 234n6, 232n51; dialogue and, 34

postdemocracy, 241n3

postmodernism, x, 79–80, 81, 82, 83, 149, 234n8; connections to the present, 101, 144–46; neoliberalism and, 100, 101

postpolitics: the Anthropocene and, 171–72, 175–76; as beneficial for the few, viii; as contingent on consensus, viii; decolonization and, 31–35; definition of, vii–viii; as dominant mode of governance, viii, xiii; elimination of dissent in, xiii; expansion beyond neoliberalism of, x–xi; as geopolitical regime, 34–35, 150–51; historical projections into the present of, 73–77, 144–47, 214–17; historiography and, 96–97; and literature, vii, x–xv, xiii, xiv; negative registers of, 17, 231n32; neoliberalism and, 99–100; neutral appearance of, viii; origins of, x; and postcolonialism, 33; precursor of, 235n22; productive gestures of, xiii, 17; role of dialogue in, ix–xi; theory of, vii; as totalizing regime, xiii; the war on terror and, 150–51. *See also* consensus; dissent; illusory dialogue poverty, 2, 33, 245n48; compounded by environmental degradation, 190, 195, 197, 201, 210, 212; as consequence of the decline of colonialism, 63; exacerbated by neoliberalism, 111, 112, 114, 245n49; in the post-2008 moment, 103. *See also* precarity

power, xii, 1; relations and illusory dialogue, 15–19, 22–23, 222; relations in dialogue, 12–13, 15; self-destructive, 190–91; void kind of, 21

pragmatism: as method of governance, viii, ix, 38, 39

Pratt, Mary Louise, 45

precarity, xiii, 110–12, 117, 124, 195. *See also* poverty

preemption, xiii, 14, 38, 91, 96, 181; as a result of an illusory dialogue, 19–20, 35, 67, 98, 118, 145; war as a means of, 150. *See also* future, the

present, the, x, xiii, 26; as anchor against a nostalgic past, 157–62; as anchor against a totalized future, 162–66; as fixed historical circumstance, 156–57; irruption of history in, 82–83, 94; projection of the postpolitical into, 73–77, 144–47, 214–17; toxic, 208, 213. *See also* history

prison. *See* detention; imprisonment

privatization of social services, 102–3, 104, 105–10, 242n12, 244n40. *See also* austerity; National Health Service

Problems of Dostoevsky's Poetics (Bakhtin), 7, 10, 13–14, 229n15

public life, viii–ix, xiii, 4, 7, 21, 221, 223; impact of neoliberalism on, 100, 102–11, 113, 118; precarity of dissent in, 149. *See also* politics

Rabelais and His World (Bakhtin), 7–8

race, xii, 34, 49; affiliation on the basis of, 53, 59; gender and, 66–70; misrecognition on the basis of, 29, 63, 66–70, 73; tensions, 3, 220. *See also* racism; whiteness

racism, 33, 220; colonialism and, 68, 70, 72; environmental disaster in the global South and, 179; the war on terror and, 153, 158, 246n5. *See also* misrecognition; whiteness

Radhakrishnan, R., 51

Rajan, Balachandra, 94

Rancière, Jacques, vii, x–xi, xi, xiv, 21–23, 158, 171, 177, 195, 227n6, 231n33, 241n3. *See also* dissensus; politics; visuality

rationality: as exclusionary operation, 18–19; as imperial logic, 45, 136–37; neoliberalism's appeal to, 244n46; as response against misidentification, 161, 166. *See also* common sense; consensus; irrationality; meaning-making

reading dangerously, xii–xv, 24, 223–24. *See also* imagination

realism: as justification for the ineluctability of neoliberalism, 104–5, 144; as justification for the ineluctability of the war on terror, 151; political underpinnings of literary, 35, 81, 206; as replacement for political principles, viii. *See also* consensus; rationality; stereoscopic realism

recognition, xiv, 17; depoliticizing operation of, 17, 231n33; dissensual consequences of, 140, 186–87. *See also* misrecognition

redaction, 169

refusal: characterized as inadmissible by a dominant voice, 94, 121, 122;

as contingently necessary, 22, 24, 47–48, 54–56, 73, 93, 138, 155, 182–84, 222; covert, 124–25; exertion of consensual power through, 20, 92, 110; as insufficient political strategy, 19, 21–23, 102, 139, 188

Reluctant Fundamentalist, The (Hamid), 29, 149–70

representation, xii, 26, 27, 33, 58; assault of postpolitics on, xiii; hegemonic, 44, 132, 171; impossibility of, 50; limits of narrative, 50–52, 55, 58, 82, 92–95, 134–35, 139, 166–70; nothingness as legitimate form of, 50–51; parliamentary, 3, 33; as regulated by illusory dialogue, 23; selective, 106–10, 154–55. See also narrative; self-representation; visuality

resilience, 23, 59, 60, 146, 71–73, 75, 143, 222, 226

resistance, xii–xiii, 10, 14; language of, xiii, 16, 24, 26; need for a new vocabulary of, 14; reactivation of, 21–23. See also counterdialogic politics; dissent

resource curse, 198, 208. See also environmental disasters

Retort (collective), 150

Rhys, Jean, 29, 32, 33, 34, 36, 59–73, 74, 75, 76

Roy, Arundhati, 14, 202, 246n5

Royal Dutch Shell, 199

Rushdie, Salman, 233n54

Said, Edward W., 10–11, 26, 34, 37–38, 44, 62, 82, 156, 235n19

Sassen, Saskia, 163

"Secular Criticism" (Said), 62

self-representation, x, 17, 18, 25, 63–66, 136, 176, 181–82

Sennett, Richard, 110

September 11, 2001 attacks, 29, 150–53, 154–66, 169, 192–93, 247n18. See also war on terror, the

Seshagiri, Urmila, 235n16

Shohat, Ella, 233n2

silence, xiv, 79, 222–23; as conduit to enact an alternative political intervention, 91–95, 97, 124–25; as dissensual textual strategy, 155–56; as form of evasion, 70; of images, 201; imposed, 80, 81–82, 85, 178–81; as inherent to dialogue, 12; as justification of narrative authority, 87–90; manifestation of distrust via, 208–9; as a result of trauma 52–53, 88–89; selective, 92–94. See also voice

Simpson, David, 158

singularity: appreciation of, 134; as form of autonomy, 7–9, 13, 135–38, 143, 145–46, 156, 195. See also individuality; subjectivity

Sinha, Indra, 29, 172, 173, 175–76, 177–96, 214–15, 215–16

Slaughter, Joseph R., 73, 238n68

social media, 4, 221. See also internet, the

social security. See welfare state, the

Society of the Spectacle (Debord), 18, 231n34

solidarity, 3, 120, 125–26, 145, 164

sovereignty: as embodiment of consensual power, 72, 90, 139, 180, 246n3; as form of emancipatory autonomy, xii, 36, 67, 100, 101, 175, 198, 220, 221; national, 16, 32, 41

spectacle, 4; dialogue as, 18; environmental destruction as, 173, 200–202, 213, 217; female body as, 68, 71–72; illusory dialogue as, 18; media, 167, 204, 209, 216, 223; public relations as, 106–7, 252n38; as radical strategy, 186

Specters of Marx: The State of the Debt, the Work of Mourning, and the New International (Derrida), 101

spiritualism: as commonality for a dialogic relationship, 45, 48; as obstacle for a dialogic relationship, 52–53; Orientalist undertones of, 179

Spivak, Gayatri Chakravorty, 76, 79, 95, 155, 233n58

Standing, Guy, 144

stereoscopic realism, 206–13, 216. *See also* countervisuality; visual capture; visuality

Stoermer, Eugene F., 248n1

storytelling: as agonistic dispute, 129–34; as corrective, 81–84, 88–89; as depoliticizing, 182

subjectivity, xii; as already constituted in recognition, 17, 231n33; dialogue and, 12–13; dissensual formation of, 92–95, 131–33, 135–42, 154–57, 167, 182–85; as historical absence, 85, 91, 93–95; illusory dialogue and, 17, 22–23; as imposed by an external consensual order, 45–48, 56–58, 60–73, 87–91, 134–37, 152–53, 167, 169, 178–81, 181–83; as new political formulation, 23, 24. *See also* ontology

Suez crisis, 38, 39

suicide: as disruption of consensus, 82, 92–95; resulting from the pressures of a consensual order, 161–62, 193. *See also* death

Swift, Graham, 29, 79–98, 149

Swyngedouw, Erik, 176, 227n2, 250n13

Szeman, Imre, 27–28, 252n42

teleology, 87, 213

temporality, 14; the novel's internal, 25–26. *See also* future, the; history; present, the

terrorism. *See* September 11, 2001 attacks

terrorist: constructions of the, 153, 155–57, 161, 165, 168, 205. *See also* September 11, 2001 attacks; war on terror, the

Thatcher, Margaret, 29, 99, 100–105, 110, 111, 116, 118, 120, 125, 144–45; Napoleon as, 127–29, 130, 134, 143; as predecessor of David Cameron, 99, 101, 103–4, 110–11, 111, 116, 125–29, 134, 143, 144–45; "there is no alternative," 104–5, 134; "there is no such thing as society," 101, 110, 145, 241n6

third space, the: as consensual notion, 61

third way, the, viii

Third World, the, 39, 164. *See also* global South, the

38 Degrees, 107, 109

Tiffin, Helen, 232n51

tolerance, xiii, 3, 17, 137; as spectacle, 4

Trades Union Congress, 104

trauma, 69, 72, 75, 88–89, 93, 95, 114, 179, 252n36

2008 financial crisis, xii, 101–3, 105, 111, 116

2010 *Conservative Manifesto,* 103, 105, 108, 128, 145

Tyler, Imogen, 137

uncertainty: dissensual charge of, 131–32; ontological precarity resulting from, 162, 165–66, 168–70; as openness to an emancipatory politics to come, 26, 143

UNESCO, 1, 214. *See also* United Nations

Union Carbide, 178, 185, 250n20

United Nations, 1–2, 3, 26, 38

Venice: as colonized space, 132; as dissensual space, 131, 135–36
visibility: as disenfranchising, x, 21, 123, 169, 185, 197–99; dissensual work of, 171, 191, 206–10, 212–14; as first political step, x, xiv, 16, 178, 181; historical, 90–91; as multidimensional, 14; as reenfranchising, 196, 199–202, 215–16; regulation of, 21, 172, 177, 183. *See also* representation; visual capture; visuality
visual capture, 44–46, 59, 177–78, 180–82, 191, 196, 199–202, 207–9, 210–14. *See also* countervisuality; photography; visuality
visuality, 170–78, 182–83, 185–86, 195–96, 207, 213, 216, 249n2. *See also* countervisuality; photography; representation; visibility
visual studies, xiv
voice: Bakhtin on, 4–14; dialogue and, 13; illusory dialogue and the policing of, 4, 16–20; politics and, vii, 6; privileging of, 37, 82; resistance against illusory dialogue and, 22–25; as vehicle to reclaim autonomy, 182–83. *See also* silence
Voyage in the Dark (Jean Rhys), 29, 32, 33, 34, 36, 59–73, 74, 75, 76

Walkowitz, Rebecca L., 34, 235n14, 235n15
war on terror, the: as consensus, 149, 150–51, 158, 168, 170; as geopolitical order, 150, 153, 154, 162, 165, 168–70; domesticating effect of, 150–51, 154; as perpetual, 150, 153, 157. *See also* September 11, 2001 attacks; terrorist
water: impact of environmental violence on, 174, 197, 207–8, 210, 211, 251n22; as symbol of consensus, 82–87; as symbol of dissensus, 135–36, 140; as symbol of healing, 180
Waterland (Swift), 29, 79–98, 149
wealth, xiii, 197
welfare state, the, 39, 103, 105; characterized as privilege, 117; dismantling of, 101, 110, 244n38. *See also* child care; National Health Service
Wenzel, Jennifer, 212, 252n42
West, the: charity from, 180; democracy and, vii, 99; imperialism and, 32–33, 37, 39–42, 75; the media in, 179, 182, 184, 195, 216; the war on terror and, 153, 156, 167, 169. *See also* global North, the
White, Hayden, 239n2
whiteness, 60–62; as assimilative form of recognition, 64–73; as unexamined notion, 67
Williams, Raymond, 10–11
"Wind of Change" (Macmillan), 40–43, 74, 236n24
Winterson, Jeanette, 29, 101, 102, 127–44, 144–45, 145–46; on the political power of literature, 24
world literature, 28–29, 233n58. *See also* Anglophone literature
World War I, 1, 38, 88
World War II, 1, 38, 39, 56, 103, 105, 150, 158, 214

Yaeger, Patricia, 252n42
Year of Dialogue among Civilizations, 1–2, 26
Year of Dreaming Dangerously, The (Žižek), xii

Žižek, Slavoj, vii, xii, 1, 19, 176

JUAN MENESES is assistant professor of English at the University of North Carolina at Charlotte.

CPSIA information can be obtained
at www.ICGtesting.com
Printed in the USA
BVHW042321120120
569127BV00007B/31/P